2ND EDITION

AQA A2
Economics

Ray Powell

PHILIP ALLAN FOR
HODDER
EDUCATION
AN HACHETTE UK COMPANY

Philip Allan, an imprint of Hodder Education, an Hachette UK company, Market Place, Deddington, Oxfordshire OX15 0SE

Orders
Bookpoint Ltd, 130 Milton Park, Abingdon, Oxfordshire OX14 4SB
tel: 01235 827720
fax: 01235 400454
e-mail: uk.orders@bookpoint.co.uk

Lines are open 9.00 a.m.–5.00 p.m., Monday to Saturday, with a 24-hour message answering service. You can also order through the Philip Allan website: www.philipallan.co.uk

Impression number	5	4	3	2	1
Year		2018	2017	2016	2015	2014

The publishers would like to thank the following for permission to reproduce photographs: **Cover** fkdkondmi/Fotolia; **p. 6** Allstar Picture Library/Alamy; **p. 9** axway/Fotolia; **p. 18** M&S Library; **p. 20** BP; **p. 32** Rolls-Royce plc 2012; **p. 37** Microsoft; **p. 57** Microsoft; **p. 71** TopFoto; **p. 83** Allstar Picture Library/Alamy; **p. 103** BT; **p. 106** TopFoto; **p. 130** Claudio Divizia/Fotolia; **p. 143** Jenny Thompson/Fotolia; **p. 150** David Warren/Alamy; **p. 169** Minerva Studio/Fotolia; **p. 179** Image Works; **p. 181** TopFoto; **p. 204** Ingram; **p. 211** Blend Images/Alamy; **p. 217** TopFoto; **p. 221** Tesco; **p. 235** pjdespa/Fotolia; **p. 241** Ingram; **p. 253** Amazon; **p. 267** TopFoto; **p. 271** Photodisc; **p. 272** TopFoto; **p. 283** TopFoto; **p. 290** Tori Jayne/Fotolia; **p. 310** Ingram; **p. 325** The Coca-Cola Co.; **p. 336** Pictorman/Alamy; **p. 346** Ikon/Cadmium; **p. 363** Eccolo/Fotolia; **p. 366** Bernhard Classen/Alamy

Data drawn from the National Statistics website www.statistics.gov.uk contains public sector information licensed under the Open Government Licence v1.0.

Typeset by Integra Software Services Pvt., Pondicherry, India.
Printed in Dubai.

Hachette UK's policy is to use papers that are natural, renewable and recyclable products and made from wood grown in sustainable forests. The logging and manufacturing processes are expected to conform to the environmental regulations of the country of origin.

P2273

Contents

Foreword

Welcome back to economics and your second year of A-level study. At the start of my *AQA AS Economics* textbook I stated that my most important objective is to help you achieve the highest possible examination grades.

However, I have a second objective, namely to turn you into a good economist. In an important sense, my two objectives come together at A2. To achieve the highest A* grade for the overall A-level (AS + A2), you have to be a good economist. The A* grade requires a mark of 90% at A2, together with a mark of 80% for the whole AS and A2 course. In future years, top-rated universities such as Cambridge, Oxford, the London School of Economics, Bristol and Warwick are likely to require A* grades rather than the basic A grade that was the highest on offer before 2010.

Of course, most students end up earning grades that fall some way short of A*. My books are meant for *all* AQA economics students, and aim to help you to gain high rather than low grades in all your economics exams. To help you to get the most out of your studies, I have included **extension material** in most of the chapters of the book. This goes beyond the immediate demands of the A-level specification, introducing you to new theories and to developments of existing theories. There are also many **case studies** in the book. These enable you to link theory to up-to-date events taking place in the UK and the international economy.

Synopticity

I have tried to present A2 economics as a coherent whole, building on what you learnt at AS. Wherever possible, I have avoided unnecessary repetition of material you learnt a year ago at AS. However, do remember that the A2 exam papers are synoptic. To prepare for the synoptic nature of the questions, make sure you note the **'What you should already know'** section at the beginning of each chapter (apart from Chapter 1).

Synopticity means that questions in an A2 examination paper require reference to knowledge and economic theory from one or more of the other AS or A2 units. Synopticity may be vertical, horizontal or diagonal. A Unit 3 examination question is vertically synoptic when it tests knowledge learnt in Unit 1. Two examples of such subjects are supply and demand and elasticity. Likewise, a Unit 4 examination question testing knowledge learnt in Unit 2 is vertically synoptic. Examples include national income, the multiplier and *AD/AS* analysis.

Horizontal synopticity requires the application of a macroeconomic concept or theory from Unit 4 to a microeconomics question in the Unit 3 examination (or vice versa). For example, a question on poverty (in Unit 3) could test knowledge of how fiscal policy (a Unit 4 topic) may reduce poverty. Diagonal synopticity requires the use of Unit 2 macroeconomic terms and concepts to answer a microeconomics Unit 3 question, or the use of microeconomics knowledge from Unit 1 to answer a Unit 4 question.

Moving up

Much of the subject matter of Unit 3, Business economics and the distribution of income, differs significantly from the content of Unit 1, Markets and market failure. As the Unit 1 title indicates, AS microeconomics focuses on how a competitive market functions, and on the various causes of market failure. By contrast, A2 microeconomics concentrates much more on businesses and how they behave. Of course, supply and demand and the market mechanism do figure in A2 microeconomics, but in the context of labour markets rather than the product or goods markets covered in Unit 1. The coverage of market failure in Unit 3 encompasses but develops further all that you learnt about this topic at AS.

Unit 4, The national and international economy, is rather different. Many of the Unit 2 National economy topics you studied a year ago at AS are equally as important at A2. These topics include macroeconomic policy objectives such as economic growth, full employment and control of inflation, together with the main types of macroeconomic policy, monetary policy, fiscal policy and supply-side policy. Most important of all is the aggregate demand/aggregate supply (*AD/AS*) macroeconomic model. This is the key theoretical model in both AS and A2 macroeconomics. You don't need to learn much more about the *AD/AS* model at A2, over and above what you learnt at AS. The main difference is that A2 exam questions, particularly essay questions, require a greater depth of analysis, together with more sophisticated evaluation of the issues posed by the question.

Both the Unit 2 and Unit 4 specifications focus on the national economy. The main add-on in Unit 4 is the international economy. This develops your understanding of the balance of payments and exchange rates that you first encountered at AS, but adds on important international topics such as trade theory and globalisation.

Background knowledge

The AQA economics specification requires candidates to 'acquire a good knowledge of trends and developments in the economy which have taken place during the past 10 years and also have an awareness of earlier events where this helps to give recent developments a longer term perspective'. With this in mind, I firmly believe that students benefit from a basic knowledge of economic history and of different schools of economic thought, such as Keynesianism and monetarism. Where I think it helps, I have adopted a historical approach, particularly in the explanation of macroeconomic topics such as theories of inflation and unemployment, and in the way monetary policy, fiscal policy and supply-side economics have developed over the years.

Using this book

Special features
The text contains several special features designed to aid your understanding of the concepts and examination techniques required by AQA:
- **Learning outcomes:** a list of the intended learning outcomes is given at the beginning of each chapter. These are closely linked to the specification.

- **What you should already know:** these notes will remind you of the material you learnt at AS to help you prepare for the synoptic nature of the exam questions.
- **Key terms:** the key terms boxes provide definitions of important economic terms or concepts relevant to the topics in the chapter and mentioned in the AQA A2 specification. A list of the key terms is also provided at the end of each unit.
- **Exam tips:** these explain how the chapter content is relevant to the A2 examinations. In some instances, these highlight the presence of useful background information in the text, designed to increase your depth of knowledge and understanding. Full marks for a question can be earned without this background information, but it supports your knowledge.
- **Case studies:** the case studies come with follow-up questions which will help you to analyse, evaluate and improve your exam answers.
- **Synoptic links:** these give examples of subjects where you can apply knowledge and economic theory from one or more of the other AS and A2 units.
- **Summaries:** these appear at the end of each chapter and will help you to focus your revision.

Exam-style questions

At the end of each chapter, apart from Chapter 1, there are four **exam-style questions**. Two of the questions, carrying 15 marks in each case, are in the style of the first part of an essay question. The third and fourth questions, carrying 25 marks, resemble the final parts of a context data-response question or an essay question.

The Unit 1 and Unit 2 exams at AS did not include essay questions, so at the beginning of the A2 course, you may not be used to writing extended essays over 45 minutes. Essay writing requires practice, particularly in the higher-level skills of economic analysis and evaluation, which account for 44% of the total marks at A2 (as against 40% at AS).

A2 data-response questions also differ from those you encountered at AS. At A2 they are context questions, which relate to the impact on the UK economy of events taking place in the European Union (the EU context) or the wider international economy (the global context).

Online resources

Extra resources to help you revise are available online at www.hodderplus.co.uk/philipallan. These include PowerPoints with advice on exam technique, and additional extension material to help you develop your A2 skills and gain the highest possible grades.

It now remains for you to use this book to become an even better economist than you were at the end of the AS course, and to pass your A2 exams with flying colours. I wish you every success.

Ray Powell

Introduction

In the foreword of my *AQA AS Economics* textbook I stated that two of my main objectives in writing the book were for you to do well in the exams and for you to become a good economist. I want students to be capable of reading newspapers fruitfully to find out more about how economies work, and of conversing intelligently with both economists and non-economists about economic issues and government policies. This objective underlies all the chapters in this book, but as the title indicates, especially this chapter.

LEARNING OUTCOMES

This chapter will:
- remind you of the nature and importance of economic models
- advise on understanding and interpreting economic statistics
- explain why it is important to draw graphs accurately
- question whether government statistics are always accurate
- discuss the interpretation and use of economic policy and performance indicators

Understanding and applying economic models

The AQA specification for A2 states that: 'Candidates should be able to recognise both the value and limitations of **economic models** as a means of explaining and evaluating the conduct and performance of firms in the real world. They should be able to evaluate economic models in written, numerical and graphical forms.'

KEY TERM

economic model: a small-scale replica of real-world phenomena.

Model-building is one of the most important analytical techniques used by economists. Much of the economic theory you learnt last year at AS and will continue to learn this year centres around the use of economic models. At a microeconomic level, economic models are used to try to explain the economic behaviour of the individuals and firms that make up the economy. Last year, you learnt about the **supply and demand model** of a particular market in the economy, such as the market for strawberries or the market for automobiles. This year, a large part of your microeconomic studies will focus on the **theory of the firm** in the context of **business economics**. You will also re-visit the supply and demand model, but in the context of the **labour market**.

Economic models are also at the centre of macroeconomic theory. The two main macroeconomic models you learnt last year were the **circular flow model** and the **aggregate demand/aggregate supply (*AD/AS*) model**. The *AD/AS* model is just as important at A2 as it is at AS. You won't need to learn much more about the model itself this year than you learnt last year. However, A2 exam questions are more demanding than AS questions, so your main task will be to apply what you already know in greater depth and breadth than was the case last year.

CASE STUDY 1.1

The Phillips machine: a Heath Robinson economic model

Heath Robinson was a cartoonist and illustrator, who became famous for his drawings of eccentric machines. The label 'Heath Robinson' is now used to describe any quirky, complex and implausible machine or contraption. The **Phillips machine** has been described as 'a Heath Robinson device at its finest'.

A wonderful thing is a Phillips machine
In the Meade Room in the Dept of Applied Economics of Cambridge University stands a Phillips machine, a device so cunning and ingenious that it can predict the running

of the national economy to within 4% accuracy. And all by means of pipes and buckets, trickling with pink-coloured water, powered by a pump scavenged from the landing gear of a Lancaster bomber. It is a hydraulic computer, invented by Bill Phillips.

Allan McRobie at CUED said 'The machine is absolutely brilliant. We all know that engineers should have a knowledge of economics, but Phillips made an enormous contribution and showed that economists could learn much from engineering.'

Source: Issue 12 of *Enginuity*, 2003. The full article can be seen at: www-g.eng.cam.ac.uk/enginuity

Later in the A2 course, in Chapter 17 and in the context of inflation and unemployment, you will learn about an important part of macroeconomic theory called the **Phillips curve**. The curve is named after Professor Bill Phillips, a New Zealand engineer who became an economist, and later professor of statistics at the London School of Economics. Nine years before 1958 when Phillips published a paper which introduced the famous Phillips curve, he designed and built the **Phillips machine**. This machine, which is described in Case Study 1.1, is an example of a macroeconomic model, albeit a rather unusual one. Complex modern economic models, such as the **Treasury model** used by the government to forecast changes in the UK economy, are driven by computers. However, the Phillips machine, which pre-dated most of the developments in computer technology, was essentially a contraption of buckets and pipes around which pink fluid flowed, depicting the **circular flow of income** or money around the economy.

The essentials of an economic model

A model is a small-scale replica of real-world phenomena, often incorporating a number of simplifications. An economic model simplifies the real world in such a way that the essential features of an economic relationship or set of relationships are explained using diagrams, words and often algebra. Models are used by economists, first to understand and explain the working of the economy and second, to predict what might happen in the future. The ultimate purpose of model-building is to derive predictions about economic behaviour, such as the prediction of demand theory that demand will increase when price falls.

The main economic models you studied at AS are listed in the top half of Table 1.1. In a similar way, the bottom half of the table lists models not in the AS course, but which feature strongly in the A2 course. Note that rather more new models are included in A2 microeconomics, than are in A2 macroeconomics. This does not mean there is less to learn when studying Unit 4; rather it means that much of A2 macroeconomics simply develops with greater depth the circular flow and *AD/AS* models you came across at AS.

Table 1.1 Economic models at AS and at A2

AS models	
Micro	**Macro**
Supply and demand model	Circular flow model
	Aggregate demand/aggregate supply model
A2 models	
Micro	**Macro**
Theory of the firm:	■ Aggregate demand/aggregate supply model
■ Perfect competition model	■ Phillips curve model
■ Monopoly model	■ International trade model
■ Oligopoly model	
■ Game theory models	
Labour market models:	
■ Monopsony model	

Specification advice on the use of economic statistics

For AS candidates, the specification advises: 'Candidates should be familiar with the various types of statistical and other data which are commonly used by economists. For example, they should be able to interpret data presented in the form of index numbers.' Obviously, this advice is just as relevant at A2. However, the A2 specification goes on to add: 'Candidates should be able to interpret different types of economic data, such as the Human Development Index, and use them to compare the living standards of the residents of different countries. They should be able to discuss the limitations of using such data to arrive at conclusions.' And in the context of inflation, the advice is: 'Candidates should have an understanding of how index numbers are calculated and used to measure changes in the price level.' Although a detailed technical knowledge is not expected of indices such as the retail prices index (RPI) and consumer prices index (CPI), candidates should have an awareness of the underlying features: for example, the Living Costs and Food Survey (LCF), the concept of the 'average family', the basket of goods and services, and weighting.

Interpreting economic statistics

Unlike university economics, A-level economics makes few mathematical demands on its students. The main skills you will have to develop in the context of economic data are **identification of relationships, description, comparison** and **explanation.**

The demands on your skills at A2 are no different from those you applied when answering AS questions last year. So in this sense, you don't have to become an *even better economist* at A2 in order to score more marks in your handling of economic data. Also, at the beginning of your A2 course, you should be familiar with economic data presented in index numbers, for example the retail prices index (RPI) and the consumer prices index (CPI), together with the two main measures of unemployment, the claimant count and the Labour Force Survey (LFS) measure. Likewise, your AS studies should have provided you with an understanding of the difference between data presented in real and nominal (or money) forms.

If you have forgotten some or all of the above, you will be well advised to buy, or get your school to buy, the A2 Student Unit Guides for AQA economics, also published by Philip Allan Updates, in which I explain, and give plenty of examples of, the statistical data that are likely to be in the Unit 3 and Unit 4 data-response questions.

Using government statistics

Government statistics, often drawn from the **Office for National Statistics (ONS)**, are used in most A2 (and AS) data-response questions. The ONS provides up-to-date information on a range of macroeconomic variables, including output, economic growth, employment, unemployment, wages, prices, the inflation rate and trade figures. Until quite recently, it was generally agreed that, over the years, there had been a general improvement in the quality of information about the economy available to policy-makers. In recent years, however, a number of worries have emerged about the accuracy of ONS statistics. Mervyn King, the previous governor of the Bank of England, has hinted that the effectiveness of monetary policy has been adversely affected by possible inaccuracy in the unemployment and population figures. In July 2004, the headline of a news story in the *Independent* was 'Government statisticians lose 60,000 people in latest ONS gaffe'. Concern has also been expressed about an alleged creeping privatisation of the production of official statistics. There has been a considerable increase in the extent to which data analyses paid for by public funds have been outsourced to private companies whose analyses are available only to those who pay. At the same time, cutbacks at the ONS led to a loss of over 700 full-time jobs between 2004 and March 2008.

CASE STUDY 1.2

Lies, damned lies and statistics

Official statistics are data, 'produced by government for government', which have always been subject to political interference. Many official statistics are used selectively to support public policies and the positions of those in power.

This can especially be seen with unemployment statistics. These have been manipulated by officials in order to produce figures which are more acceptable to the government of the day. For example, between 1980 and 1991 the definition of unemployment was altered more than 20 times and each time the unemployment figure shrank. At the time an opposition MP asked in Parliament: 'Now that the government has succeeded in getting the unemployment statistics down, can it tell us when unemployment is going to come down?'

Even when not misusing official statistics, politicians sometimes use dodgy data drawn from other sources to back up their opinions. In a famous case in May 2013, education minister Michael Gove wrote an article in the *Daily Mail* about the failure of the education system in teaching historical facts. Gove wrote: 'Survey after survey has revealed disturbing historical ignorance, with one teenager in five believing Winston Churchill was a fictional character while 58 per cent think Sherlock Holmes was real.' Gove based his claims on a handful of PR surveys, including polls by Premier Inn and the Sea Cadets.

Originally the Department of Education could only find one survey that backed up Gove's views. The survey, commissioned by TV Gold in May 2008, asked all ages, not just teenagers, about supposed historical events. The survey itself contained inaccuracies, for example claiming that 12% of people thought Lady Godiva did exist when she was a fictional character. While the famous legend of Lady Godiva riding through the town of Coventry naked has not been proven, the woman herself did exist.

After further prompting, the Department came up with a second list of surveys. They quoted a Premier Inn survey in which children apparently believed Delia Smith,

Michael Gove

Jerry Hall and Camilla Duchess of Cornwall were among Henry VIII's wives, while William Shakespeare was the chairman of the BBC. However, a glance at the hotel company's findings suggests that teenagers were taking the mickey out of the survey at Premier Inn's expense.

Tristram Hunt MP, Labour's shadow education minister, slammed the education secretary's use of surveys, saying: 'Any good historian will tell you that it is critical to base your analysis on multiple, credible sources. Before he rushes to judgment about young people, Michael Gove should make sure he has researched the evidence thoroughly. Otherwise he risks coming across as Mr Sloppy.'

Follow-up questions

1 The publication by government of inaccurate statistics may result from conspiracy or it may result from incompetence or 'cock-up'. Explain the difference between a 'conspiracy theory' and a 'cock-up' theory.

2 Try and find other examples of the inaccurate publication of statistics by governments.

Practising drawing graphs at A2

At AS, you should have got plenty of practice in drawing supply and demand diagrams and marginal cost and benefit diagrams (for Unit 1) and *AD/AS* diagrams (for Unit 2). At A2, supply and demand diagrams are still needed, but largely in the context of the **labour market** (in Unit 3) and the **foreign exchange market** for a currency (in Unit 4). However, you must also learn to draw completely new graphs. For Unit 3 (Business economics and the distribution of income), it is extremely important to learn and practise drawing graphs which show costs, revenues and profit in the different market structures of **perfect competition, monopoly and oligopoly**. You may also have to plot cost curves or revenue curves from a table of data presented in an exam question. Labour market diagrams are also important, particularly those relating to the supply of labour, and to perfectly competitive labour markets and monopsony labour markets. (*Monopsony* means a single *buyer* in a market, whereas *monopoly* is a single *seller* in a market.)

Fortunately, the diagrams you learnt at AS to show the market failures of negative and positive externalities, and demerit goods and merit goods, don't need adding to for Unit 3. Likewise, the *AD/AS* diagrams learnt for Unit 2 are quite sufficient for answering Unit 4 (The national and international economy) questions. In both these cases, the diagrams you learnt at AS don't really need any further development. The main difference is that at A2, you will be applying the diagrams in a more sophisticated way, so as to display the 'higher order' skills of analysis and evaluation in answers of greater depth and breadth.

As is the case with Unit 3, new diagrams have to be learnt for Unit 4. Perhaps the most important set of new diagrams relate to **Phillips curve analysis** (see Case Study 1.1), which brings together relationships between unemployment and inflation at A2.

Many students who underachieve in economics exams appear to rote learn diagrams, without understanding how the graphs they draw are constructed. Usually this means that the unfortunate student makes mistakes when drawing from memory a complicated diagram in an exam answer. To prevent this happening, your teacher has probably gone through the building blocks of the diagram when first teaching you the diagram. In this situation, providing you have understood what your teacher has said, you have a greater chance of properly understanding the diagram and its mechanics, which in turn means you are less likely to make mistakes when drawing the diagram in exam conditions.

In the later chapters of this book, I have used the building-block approach to explain how each new diagram is constructed. However, there is a danger here. It is seldom if ever relevant to explain to the examiner all of the building blocks of a diagram. If you do this, your answer will drift into irrelevancy and waste valuable examination time. Instead, you should draw the finished diagram, and then get on with the job of using it as a visual aid in addressing the issue posed by the question.

Remember also the good habits you learnt at AS, namely labelling axes and curves accurately, drawing horizontal and vertical coordinates, explaining the short-hand you are using (such as *AD* for aggregate demand), and drawing diagrams of a reasonable size. If you can't remember a diagram, and if its inclusion is not necessary for your answer, then 'if in doubt, leave out'.

However, if a question explicitly requires a diagram, one must be drawn. Don't unnecessarily repeat the same diagram in an answer, but remember that relevant diagrams make it easier for examiners to read your answers. Examiners are put off by pages of turgid text, unbroken either by new paragraphs or by diagrams.

Interpreting economic policy and performance indicators

To become an *even better economist*, you should develop an understanding of the meaning of, and the difference between, economic policy indicators and economic performance indicators.

A **policy indicator** (such as the money supply) provides policy-makers with information about the recent success or lack of success in achieving the target set for a particular type of economic policy such as monetary policy or fiscal policy. Policy indicators also provide information about whether current policy is on course to hit the future target set for the stated policy.

> **KEY TERMS**
>
> **policy indicator:** provides information about whether a particular policy is on course to achieve a desired policy objective.
>
> **performance indicator:** provides information about what is happening in the economy.

Performance indicators are much the same as policy indicators, though they tend to be more general and are not necessarily focused on a particular type of economic policy such as monetary policy or fiscal policy. Performance indicators, such as information about **labour productivity** and **productivity gaps**, can also be used to compare the performance of the UK economy with that of competitor countries.

Performance indicators can be divided into *lead* and *lag* indicators. **Lead indicators** provide information about the future state of the economy (stemming from the way people are currently forming their expectations). Surveys of consumer and business confidence and investment intentions indicate the existence of a feel-good or feel-bad factor and provide information about the likely state of aggregate demand a few months ahead. Statistics for house-building starts and the number of people who have booked expensive summer or skiing holidays several months in advance also provide information about future spending, while data on commodity and input prices can signal future changes in retail price inflation.

> **KEY TERMS**
>
> **lead indicator:** provides information about the likely future state of the economy.
>
> **lag indicator:** provides information about past events that have already taken place in the economy.

By contrast, **lag indicators** provide information about *past* economic performance and the extent to which policy objectives such as economic growth and control of inflation have been achieved. Data on the level of GDP, and current and recent employment and unemployment figures are examples of lag indicators that provide information about current and recent economic performance.

The usefulness of a performance indicator depends of course on whether it provides accurate information about the state of the economy. Likewise, a policy indicator is only useful if it provides accurate information about a variable relevant to achieving the policy's objective(s). Performance and policy indicators are, however, almost always presented in the form of statistical data, e.g. unemployment and growth figures in the case of lagged indicators, and projections about the number of house-building starts in the case of lead indicators. The accuracy of the information provided by performance and policy indicators is thus highly dependent on the accuracy of the statistics available from the government and other sources.

CASE STUDY 1.3

David Smith's skip index and other confidence indicators

Every Sunday David Smith, the Economics Editor of the *Sunday Times*, writes an Economic Outlook column, which I thoroughly recommend you to read if you want to become a good economist. (You don't have to buy the *Sunday Times*; highlights of the Economic Outlook column can be accessed on David Smith's ECONOMICS UK.COM website on the internet.)

A few years ago, David Smith came up with the idea of a 'skip index', as an informal **lead indicator** of what might happen to the economy in the future. However, the accuracy of a skip index can be questioned. While an increase in the number of builder's skips might mean people are more affluent and spending the money on their houses, it might also mean that people cannot afford to move but their family is still growing and therefore they have to upgrade their house. A 'scaffolding index' might suffer from the same problem as a skip index

Another possibility is a 'crane index'. It is a way to gauge prosperity by counting the cranes on the urban skyline. However, it is also possible to turn a crane index on its head. An increase in the number of tower cranes

A 'crane index' is a way to gauge prosperity by counting the cranes on the urban skyline

may indicate over-expansion or over-confidence — not necessarily economic growth. Another confidence indicator is frequency of receipt of unsolicited letters from estate agents, claiming for example that a 'Mr Jones' is desperate to buy a house in your road if you'll just give the agent a call.

Follow-up question

Can you think of any other things that could be used to gauge the state of consumer or business confidence in the economy?

SUMMARY

- Understanding and applying economic models lies at the heart of becoming an *even better economist*.
- An economic model is a small-scale replica of real-world phenomena.
- At AS, you learnt about the supply and demand model, the circular flow model and the *AD/AS* model.
- AS models remain important at A2, but new models also need to be learned.
- The models of perfect competition, monopoly, oligopoly and the labour market are important A2 microeconomic models.
- The *AD/AS* model remains important at A2, and needs relatively little further development.
- The Phillips curve model and the international trade model are new macro models at A2.
- At A2 as at AS, it is important to understand and apply a range of economic statistics.
- You should not always rely on the accuracy of UK government statistics.
- Poorly drawn graphs contribute to under-achievement in exams.
- At A2 as at AS, it is important to understand and apply economic policy and performance indicators.

Unit 3

Business economics and the distribution of income

Chapter 2

Introduction to business economics

In 1925, American President Calvin Coolidge allegedly said 'The business of America is business'. This quote, true or not, serves to introduce the notion that businesses are central to modern economies. Business economics covers some of the most important topics in the Unit 3 specification. This chapter provides an introductory survey of the different topics included in business economics.

LEARNING OUTCOMES

This chapter will:
- provide an introduction to the theory of the firm
- explain the meaning of industrial policy
- address the question: what is a business?
- describe the different types of business in the UK today

The building blocks of business economics

At the heart of business economics is a body of theory that economists call the **theory of the firm**. The theory of the firm comprises a number of theoretical building blocks, which are:
- Production theory
- Cost theory
- Revenue theory and market structure
- Profit maximisation in perfectly competitive and monopoly market structures
- Using efficiency and welfare criteria to evaluate the good and bad features of perfect competition and monopoly
- Applying these criteria to evaluate a third market structure: oligopoly

Business economics also includes a number of other topics. These are: how and why firms grow; the divorce between ownership and control; business objectives other than profit maximisation; and the government's industrial policy in areas such as the ownership of businesses (private ownership versus public ownership), competition policy and the regulation or deregulation of industries, markets and business behaviour.

Introducing production theory

Figure 2.1 introduces the links between the first four of the building blocks that make up the theory of the firm. At the top of the chart is production theory. As I explain in the next chapter, **production**

KEY TERM

production: a process or set of processes that converts inputs into outputs.

is simply a process or set of processes that convert inputs into outputs. Production theory divides into **short-run** production theory and **long-run** production theory. The key concept in short-run production theory, which is shown along the upper left-hand flow arrow in Figure 2.1, is the **law of diminishing returns** (which is also known as the **law of diminishing marginal productivity**). The law explains what happens to output when more and more labour is added to the fixed capital employed by a business. The key concept in long-run production theory (located along the upper right-hand arrow in Figure 2.1) is **returns to scale.** Here there are three possibilities: increasing returns to scale; decreasing returns to scale; and constant returns to scale. For example, increasing returns to scale depict a situation in which output increases at a faster rate than total inputs when the scale of all the factors of production employed by the firm increases.

KEY TERMS

short run: the time period in which at least one factor of production is fixed.

long run: the time period in which the scale of all factors of production can be changed.

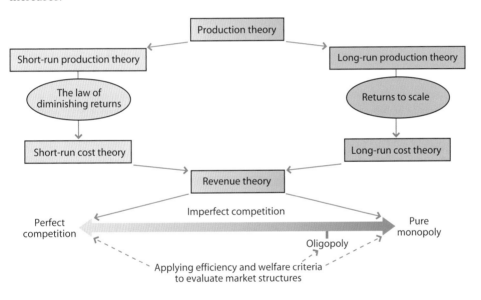

Figure 2.1 The building blocks of the theory of the firm

Introducing cost theory

The vertical flow lines located below the short-run and long-run production theory boxes in Figure 2.1 show how cost curves (and cost theory) are derived from short- and long-run production theory. The left-hand arrow links short-run production theory (and the law of diminishing returns) to short-run cost curves. Likewise, the right-hand arrow depicts the link between long-run production theory (and returns to scale) and long-run cost curves.

In examination answers, students often confuse production theory with cost theory. The important difference to note is that production theory does not include any mention of the money costs that a business incurs when it changes the level of output it produces. In contrast, as the name itself indicates, cost theory is all about money costs of production.

EXAM TIP

Make sure you don't confuse cost theory with production theory.

Production theory and cost theory are, however, related. As I explain in the next chapter, the impact of the law of diminishing returns (short-run production theory) leads to an increase in a firm's short-run **marginal costs** of production, and thence to the 'U' shape of the **average cost** of production curve.

Likewise increasing returns to scale followed by decreasing returns to scale cause a firm's long-run average cost curve also to have a 'U' shape, though other assumptions about the nature of returns to scale lead to other shapes for the long-run average cost curve. Falling long-run average costs are known as **economies of scale**, whereas rising long-run average costs show **diseconomies of scale**.

Introducing revenue theory and market structure

EXAM TIP

Make sure you don't confuse revenue with returns (as in production theory).

Besides confusing production theory with cost theory, another common trap that students fall into when learning about the theory of the firm centres on the two words: **returns** and **revenue**. The word 'returns', as in the *law of diminishing returns* and *returns to scale,* refers to the units of output such as cars or TV sets that a firm produces. By contrast, *revenue* (or *sales* revenue) is the money a firm earns when selling its output.

The nature of a firm's sales revenue depends on the competitiveness of the market structure in which the firm sells its output. Here, there are two extremes, which are shown at opposite ends of the double-headed arrow drawn towards the bottom of Figure 2.1. The two extreme market structures are **perfect competition** and **pure monopoly**. In perfect competition there are very large numbers of buyers and sellers, each of whom is a price-taker, passively accepting the ruling market price determined by the interaction of all the many market participants. By contrast, a pure monopolist, who faces no competition at all, is a price-maker who uses monopoly power or market power to determine the price at which it sells. These and other conditions facing a perfectly competitive firm and a monopoly are explained in more detail in Chapter 6.

EXAM TIP

Perfect competition, monopoly and oligopoly are the three market structures you need to know.

All the markets lying along the spectrum separating perfect competition and pure monopoly in Figure 2.1 are examples of **imperfect competition**. Imperfect competition varies from highly competitive markets towards the left-hand part of the spectrum to much less competitive markets that resemble pure monopoly at the other end of the range of market structures. Here, the main market structure is **oligopoly**, or imperfect competition among the few.

Profit maximisation and the objectives of a firm

EXAM TIP

You should be aware of business objectives other than profit maximisation.

When studying AS economics, you learnt that economists usually assume that all economic agents, e.g. households, firms and the government, have an objective that they wish to maximise. For firms, economists assume that the objective is profit (though as I explain in Chapter 8, there are a number of other possible business objectives, such as maximising sales revenue and the firm's rate of growth). **Profit** is defined as sales revenue minus costs of production.

Profit in perfectly competitive and monopoly market structures

The ability of a firm to make profit depends on the competitiveness of the market in which it sells its output. In Chapter 5, I explain how perfectly competitive firms make very little profit in the long run because the absence of **barriers to entry** means that significant profits made by incumbent firms (firms already in the market) attract new firms into the market. The market price falls, which reduces the profit made by firms that decide to stay in the market. Monopoly, by contrast, is protected by barriers to entry. As you learnt at AS, unless regulated by the government, a monopoly can use its market power to restrict output and raise the price at which it sells its output. As a result, monopoly profit is much higher than the rate of profit earned by firms producing in highly competitive markets. For similar reasons, oligopoly profits also tend to be high.

Evaluating the strengths and weaknesses of different market structures

Having surveyed the building blocks of the theory of the firm, I have arrived at the final but most important of the topics which relate to market structure and business behaviour. This is evaluation of the 'good' and 'bad' elements of perfect competition, monopoly and oligopoly.

Economists evaluate the strengths and weaknesses of the different market structures by applying two sets of criteria to address the questions:
■ Which market structure is 'best' and why?
■ Is it 'best' in all circumstances?

Efficiency concepts provide the first set of criteria. We must ask 'Is perfect competition more efficient than monopoly and oligopoly?' At AS, you used just one measure of economic efficiency: **productive efficiency**. To this, I must add: **allocative efficiency**, **static efficiency** and **dynamic efficiency**. Along with a recap of the meaning of productive efficiency, these are explained in Chapter 6.

Welfare concepts provide the second set of criteria. In Chapter 6, I explain the meaning of two measures of economic welfare, **consumer surplus** and **producer surplus**, which I then apply, along with the efficiency criteria just mentioned, to evaluate the desirable and less desirable characteristics of perfect competition and monopoly. In a similar way in Chapter 7, I evaluate the strengths and weaknesses of imperfect competition and oligopoly.

Industrial policy

During your AS studies, you learnt that monopoly can be a form of **market failure**, but that it can also be a source of economies of scale that may lead to falling average costs and prices from which consumers benefit. You also learnt that governments can intervene in markets to try to eliminate or reduce the various failures associated with monopoly, such as restricting output and raising the price that consumers pay and restricting consumer choice. At A2, you study **competition policy** in depth, evaluating the costs and benefits of monopoly and different policies governments can undertake with regard to established monopolies, mergers that might create new monopolies, and anti-competitive trading restrictive practices. Chapter 9 on **industrial policy** also analyses and evaluates state ownership of firms (**nationalisation**) and its opposite, **privatisation**, together with the **regulation** and **deregulation** of markets and industries.

What is a firm?

A **firm** is a business enterprise which either produces or deals in and exchanges goods or services. Unlike non-business productive organisations, for example a central government department such as HM Revenue and Customs (HMRC), firms are commercial, earning revenue to cover the production costs they incur.

Firms operate in both the private sector and the public sector of the economy. Public sector business enterprises include nationalised industries and certain municipally owned trading enterprises. The dividing line between private and public sector business enterprise is not always clear cut. In the past, some businesses were joint ventures, owned in part by both the private sector and by the state, whilst others were state-majority shareholdings, in which the state owned a controlling interest in a nominally private sector company. Since around 1980, these and other nationalised industries have mostly been privatised. Privatisation occurs when industries or firms are transferred from the public sector to the private sector. Before being sold to the private sector in 2013, the Royal Mail was the UK's largest nationalised or state-owned industry.

Businesses and their legal status

In terms of legal status, firms in the private sector of the UK economy include sole traders (or individual proprietors), partnerships and companies.

Sole traders

In the private sector, there are more than a million small businesses, many of which are sole traders or individual proprietorships. Sole traders are common in the labour-intensive provision of personal services, where not much capital is needed. Along with other forms of small business such as partnerships and smaller private companies, sole traders often occupy specialised market niches, sometimes providing services to much larger companies in the same or related markets. But although there are many of them, small size means that sole traders produce only a small proportion of national output.

Partnerships

A partnership is formed whenever two or more people agree to undertake a business or trading activity together, instead of operating separately as sole traders. There are in fact two rather different kinds of partnership. On the one hand, there are many thousands of small informal partnerships, usually with just two or three partners functioning much as if they were sole traders. (See Case Study 2.2 on the history of Marks & Spencer.)

The second type of partnership is more formal and often much larger than the small informal partnerships just described. Formal partnerships dominate the supply of professional services, such as architects, accountants and solicitors. Some partnerships in the accountancy and legal professions are very large, with scores of partners providing funds for the business. In these and other professions, professional ethic, which requires a member of the profession to be fully liable to clients for the service provided, prevents members of the profession from forming companies. Along with sole traders, partners traditionally had unlimited liability, which meant that the partners were personally liable for any loss incurred by the firm. As Case Study 2.1 explains, the law was changed in 2001 and the members of large partnerships now enjoy an element of limited liability.

CASE STUDY 2.1

Partnerships in the accountancy profession

A partnership is the main form of business organisation in professions such as accountancy, law and architecture. In accountancy, the 'big four' firms — PricewaterhouseCoopers (PwC), Ernst & Young, KPMG and Deloitte — are huge multinational partnerships that act as auditors, consultants, insolvency practitioners, and advisers for tax, business and corporate finance to all the leading public and private companies in the UK.

Partnerships are private businesses owned completely by the member partners. Until quite recently, each and every partner had unlimited liability. In 2001 the government created a new legal entity, the Limited Liability Partnership (LLP). Many accountancy firms changed their legal status to become Limited Liability Partnerships.

Follow-up questions

1 What is meant by limited liability and what is its main advantage?
2 Compared to companies, partnerships face difficulties in raising capital. Explain why.

CASE STUDY 2.2

The growth of Marks & Spencer

Michael Marks started in business as a sole trader in Kirkgate open market in Leeds in 1884. Ten years later, Marks formed a partnership with Tom Spencer and Marks & Spencer was born. The growth of the business that followed, including the transformation of M&S into first a private company and then a public company, is portrayed in the business's 'time line' shown below.

- **1884** Michael Marks, a Russian-born Polish refugee, opened a stall at Leeds Kirkgate Market. Goods sold included nails, screws, soap, wooden spoons and luggage labels.
- **1894** Michael formed a partnership with Tom Spencer, a former cashier from the wholesale company I. J. Dewhirst.
- **1903** Marks & Spencer Ltd was incorporated. The partnership was converted into a limited company with £30,000 in £1 ordinary shares of which 14,996 each were allotted to Marks and to Spencer.
- **1924–31** In 1924 Marks & Spencer's head office moved from Manchester to the City of London. In 1931 the M&S headquarters moved again to Baker Street in the West End.

Marks & Spencer store, Marble Arch

In 1926 the company, needing an injection of cash, was converted into a public company to raise new capital.

- **2004** Marks & Spencer moved its headquarters to Paddington Basin near Paddington Station. To update its image, in recent years M&S has replaced its old St Michael trade mark with brand names such as Autograph.

Follow-up questions

1 Explain why a growing business such as Marks & Spencer decided over time to change its legal status to eventually become a public limited company (plc).
2 Sometimes public companies such as Virgin change and revert to private company status. What are the disadvantages of public company status that lead to such decisions?

Companies

Outside the professions, the owners of growing and successful small businesses usually prefer to run their businesses as **companies** rather than as sole traders or partnerships. Companies are owned by shareholders who benefit from limited liability. This limits the shareholder's financial risk to the amount invested in the company. Without limited liability, only the safest and most risk-free business ventures could attract the large-scale supply of funds or savings required to finance large-scale capital investment.

There are two main types of company: private companies and public companies. A **private company** has the word 'limited' in its business name, whereas a public

> **KEY TERMS**
>
> **company:** an incorporated business enterprise.
>
> **private company:** issues shares that are not for sale on a market.

company can be recognised by the letters 'plc' in its business name. Most private companies are small or medium sized, though a few are quite large. Some private companies are wholly owned subsidiaries of public companies. For example, Lever Brothers Ltd is owned by Unilever plc, which is an Anglo-Dutch public company. Household-name public companies such as Tesco plc and Marks & Spencer plc are usually much larger than private companies.

Due to their large size, **public companies** are the most important form of business organisation in the UK, despite the fact that there are considerably fewer public companies than private companies. In recent years, however, there has been a move in the opposite direction, converting companies that used to be plcs back into private company ownership. The first reason for this is that a company's dominant shareholders don't want the company to be vulnerable to a hostile takeover bid. Only public companies and not private companies can be taken over against the will of major shareholders, unless of course a private company is forced out of business into receivership or liquidation. The second reason is that the company's dominant shareholders may also prefer the greater secrecy that private companies enjoy. Thirdly, the emergence of a new financial industry called **private equity finance** provides a source of capital both for companies converting back from plc to ltd status and for 'start-up' private companies that wish to grow without having to 'go public' to raise finance.

> **KEY TERM**
>
> **public company:** issues shares that the general public can buy on a market or stock exchange.

Plants and firms

In microeconomic theory, it is often assumed that a typical firm operates a single manufacturing plant to produce a specific product within a well-defined industry. Though single plant/single product firms certainly exist, particularly amongst small businesses, large firms tend to be much more diverse. A **plant** is an individual productive unit within the firm, such as a factory, office or shop. Many big firms operate a large number of plants producing a range of products. Such multi-plant and multi-product firms, often organised as holding companies owning subsidiary companies in each of the industries they operate in, are much more typical amongst big business than the single product/single plant firm.

The largest business corporations are **multinational companies** owning subsidiary enterprises throughout the world. Some multinationals such as BP and GlaxoSmithKline (GSK) are British owned, with their headquarters and many of their shareholders located in the UK. However, many of the multinational corporations operating subsidiary companies and branch factories in the UK are overseas owned. Nissan, Toyota and Honda are Japanese-owned multinationals that built factories in Britain when the UK joined the European Union, while Ford, General Motors and IBM are US multinationals that located in the UK at earlier dates.

> **KEY TERM**
>
> **multinational company:** a business with headquarters in one country that owns and operates subsidiary companies in other countries.

A BP-owned garage in Poland. This is an example of a plant.

SUMMARY

- The theory of the firm is the main part of business economics.
- The building blocks of the theory of the firm include production theory, cost theory and revenue theory.
- Production and cost theory divide into short-run and long-run theory.
- A firm's sales revenue is influenced by the market structure in which the firm sells its output.
- Perfect competition, monopoly and oligopoly are the three market structures you need to know, and you must be aware of the meaning of imperfect competition.
- Economists usually assume that maximising profit is a firm's main business objective.
- Profit is total sales revenue minus total costs of production.
- The government uses industrial policy to promote competition and to reduce the harmful effects of monopoly and oligopoly.
- Competition policy, privatisation and regulation and deregulation form the main parts of industrial policy.
- Firms can be defined according to their legal status as sole traders, partnerships and private and public companies.

Exam-style questions

1 Explain the difference, in microeconomic theory, between the short run and the long run. **(15 marks)**

2 Explain **three** business objectives a firm may have other than profit maximisation. **(15 marks)**

3 Do you agree that under all circumstances firms should be free to set their own business objectives without interference from the government or anyone else? Justify your answer. **(25 marks)**

4 Multinational companies such as Google and Starbucks have paid very little tax to the UK government on the profits they make in Britain. Evaluate the case for taxing such companies in the same way that UK firms such as Sainsbury's are taxed. **(25 marks)**

Extra resources to help you revise are available online at www.hodderplus.co.uk/philipallan

Production and cost theory

Chapter 3

Throughout this book you will be reminded that the ultimate purpose of economic activity is to increase economic welfare. (The economic welfare enjoyed by consumers is also known as utility.) For most people, most of the time, increased welfare means higher levels of demand for and consumption of consumer goods and services. But before goods and services can be consumed, they first have to be produced. This chapter explains two important parts of microeconomic theory: production theory and cost theory. Production theory centres on the relationship between inputs into the production process and the output of goods or services produced. Cost theory then links production theory to the money costs of production that firms incur when purchasing labour and the other factor services necessary for production to take place.

LEARNING OUTCOMES

This chapter will:
- explain the meaning of production
- compare short-run and long-run production
- derive short-run cost curves from short-run production theory
- derive long-run cost curves from long-run production theory
- remind you of economies of scale and diseconomies of scale

WHAT YOU SHOULD ALREADY KNOW

Unit 1 at AS introduced a number of production and cost terms and concepts. You learnt that production converts inputs, or the services of factors of production such as capital and labour, into final output. You should also understand the meanings of productivity (including labour productivity) and productive efficiency. You should be familiar with production possibility and average cost curve diagrams. However, at AS you were not expected to know the distinction between short-run and long-run cost curves or to give a detailed explanation of the shape of cost curves.

At AS you also came across economies and diseconomies of scale and learnt how they affect average costs and the growth of firms. You should be able to give examples of types or causes of economy and diseconomy of scale.

Production and costs

Production, which is depicted in Figure 3.1, involves processes that convert inputs into outputs. The inputs into production processes (land, labour, capital and enterprise) are also called **factors of production**. The nature of production depends to a great extent on the time period in which production is taking place. In microeconomics, there are three time periods: the market period, the short run and the long run.

The market period is a period so short that production cannot be changed at all. This chapter examines how firms can increase production, and thence incur **costs of production**, in the short run and in the long run.

Figure 3.1 Production

Short-run production theory

In microeconomic theory, the **short run** is the time period in which at least one of the inputs or factors of production is fixed and cannot be changed. (By contrast, in the **long run**, the scale of all the factors of production can be changed.) As a simplification, I shall pretend that only two inputs or factors of production are needed for production to take place — capital and labour. I shall also assume that in the short run, capital is fixed. It follows that the only way the firm can increase output in the short run is by adding more of the variable factor of production, labour, to the fixed capital.

Table 3.1 Short-run production with fixed capital

Number of workers (fixed capital)	0	1	2	3	4	5	6	7	8	9
Total output, product or returns	0	1	4	9	16	25	32	35	36	34
Average output, product or returns	–	1	2	3	4	5	5.3	5	4.5	3.8
Marginal output, product or returns		1	3	5	7	9	7	3	1	–2

Table 3.1 shows what might happen to car production in a small luxury sports car factory when the number of workers employed increases from 0 to 9. The first worker employed builds one car a year, and the second and third workers respectively add three and five cars to total production. These figures measure the marginal product (or marginal returns) of the first three workers employed. **Marginal product** is the addition to total output brought about by adding one more worker to the labour force.

In Table 3.1, the first five workers benefit from increasing marginal productivity (or increasing marginal returns). An additional worker increases total output by *more* than the amount added by the previous worker. Increasing marginal productivity is indeed very likely when the labour force is small. In this situation, employing an extra worker allows the workforce to be organised more efficiently. By dividing the various tasks of production among a greater number of workers, the firm benefits from **specialisation** and the **division of labour**. Workers become better and more efficient in performing the particular tasks in which they specialise, and time is saved that otherwise would be lost as a result of workers switching between tasks.

But as the firm adds labour to fixed capital, eventually the **law of diminishing marginal productivity** (or **law of diminishing marginal returns**) sets in. In this example, the law sets in when the sixth worker is employed. The fifth worker's marginal product is nine cars, but the sixth worker adds only seven cars to total output. Diminishing marginal productivity sets in because labour is being added to fixed capital. When more and more labour is added to fixed plant and machinery, eventually the marginal product of labour must fall, though not often at a labour force as small as six workers.

> **KEY TERM**
>
> **law of diminishing marginal returns:** a short-term law which states that as a variable factor of production is added to fixed factors, eventually the marginal returns (or marginal product) of the variable factor will begin to fall.

Note that diminishing marginal productivity does not mean that an extra worker joining the labour force is any less hardworking or motivated than his or her predecessors. (In microeconomic theory we often assume that workers and other factors of production are completely interchangeable and homogeneous.) The law sets in because the benefits resulting from any further specialisation and division of labour eventually become exhausted as more labour is added to a fixed amount of capital or machinery.

> **EXAM TIP**
>
> In production theory, students often confuse the law of diminishing returns, which is a short-run law, with returns to scale, which relate to the long run when firms change the scale of *all* the factors of production. You must avoid this mistake. The law of diminishing returns is important for explaining short-run cost curves, and likewise, returns to scale explain long-run cost curves, and the concepts of economies and diseconomies of scale.

Product curves

Figure 3.2 illustrates the law of diminishing marginal returns. In the upper panel of the diagram, the law begins to operate at point *A*, where the slope of the total product curve begins to change. With increasing marginal productivity, the slope of the total product curve increases, moving from point to point up the curve. When diminishing returns set in, the total product curve continues to rise as more workers are combined with capital, but the curve becomes less steep from point to point up the curve. Point *Y* shows where *total* product begins to fall. Beyond this point, additional workers begin to get in the way of other workers, so the marginal product of labour becomes negative. However, you must avoid explaining negative marginal productivity in terms of workers' hostility or their tendency to throw a spanner in the works.

The total product curve in the upper panel of Figure 3.2 plots the information in the top row of Table 3.1. By contrast, the lower panel of the diagram plots the marginal product of labour (from the information in the bottom row of Table 3.1) and the average product of labour (from the information in the middle row of Table 3.1).

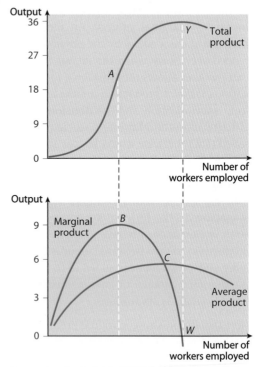

It is important to understand that all three curves (and all three rows in Table 3.1) contain the same information, but used differently in each curve (and row). The total product curve plots the information cumulatively, adding the marginal product of the last worker to the total product before the worker joined the labour force. By contrast, the marginal product curve plots the same information non-cumulatively, or as separate observations. Finally, at each level of employment, the average product curve shows the total product of the labour force divided by the number of workers employed.

Figure 3.2 Total, marginal and average product curves

In the lower panel of Figure 3.2, the law of diminishing marginal productivity sets in at point *B*, at the highest point on the marginal product curve. Before this point, increasing marginal productivity is shown by the rising (or positively sloped) marginal product curve, while beyond this point, diminishing marginal productivity is depicted by the falling (or negatively sloped) marginal product curve. Likewise, the point of diminishing *average* productivity sets in at the highest point of the average product curve at point *C*. Finally, marginal product becomes negative beyond point *W*.

The relationship between marginal product and average product
The relationship between the marginal productivity and the average productivity of labour is an example of a more general relationship that you need to know. Shortly, I shall provide a second example, namely marginal cost and its relationship to average cost.

Marginal and average curves plotted from the same set of data always display the following relationship:

- When the marginal is greater than the average, the average rises.
- When the marginal is less than the average, the average falls.
- When the marginal equals the average, the average is constant, neither rising nor falling.

EXAM TIP

Make sure you understand the relationship between the marginal and average values of an economic variable.

CASE STUDY 3.1

Adam Smith was an eighteenth-century Scottish philosophy professor, and later customs commissioner, who is often said to be the founder of modern economics. In his great book, An Inquiry into the Nature and Causes of the Wealth of Nations, *which was published in 1776, Adam Smith used the example of a local pin factory to explain how the division of labour amongst workers greatly increases their ability to produce. Here is a slightly abridged version of what Adam Smith wrote.*

Adam Smith's pin factory

A workman not educated in the business of pin making could scarce, perhaps, with his utmost industry, make one pin in a day, and certainly could not make twenty. But in the way in which this business is now carried on, one man draws out the wire, another straights it, a third cuts it, a fourth points it, a fifth grinds it at the top for receiving the pin head. The business of making a pin is divided into about eighteen distinct operations. Ten persons could make among them upwards of forty-eight thousand pins in a day. Each person, therefore, making a tenth part of forty-eight thousand pins, might be considered as making four thousand eight hundred pins in a day. But if they had all wrought separately and independently, and without any of them having been educated to this peculiar business, they certainly could not each of them have made twenty, perhaps not one pin in a day.

This great increase in the quantity of work is a consequence of the division of labour. There are three different aspects of this: first, the increase of dexterity in every particular workman; secondly, the saving of the time which is commonly lost in passing from one species of work to another; and lastly, the invention of a great number of machines which enable one man to do the work of many.

Follow-up questions

1 What is meant by the division of labour?

2 What effects does the division of labour have on production and costs?

Short-run costs

Cost curves measure the costs that firms have to pay to hire the inputs or factors of production needed to produce output. In the short run, when the inputs divide into fixed and variable factors of production, the costs of production can likewise be divided into fixed and variable costs. This can be written as:

total cost = total fixed cost + total variable cost

or:

$TC = TFC + TVC$

Likewise, average total cost per unit can be written as:

average total cost = average fixed cost + average variable cost

or:

$ATC = AFC + AVC$

To explain how total costs of production vary with output in the short run, I shall look first at fixed costs and then at variable costs.

Fixed costs

Fixed costs of production are overheads, such as the rent on land and the maintenance costs of buildings, which a firm must pay in the short run. Suppose, for example, that a car manufacturing company incurs overheads of £1 million

a year from an assembly plant it operates. I can represent these costs both as the horizontal total fixed cost curve in Figure 3.3(a) and as the downward-sloping average fixed cost curve in Figure 3.3(b). If the plant only managed to produce one automobile a year, *AFC* per car would be £1 million — the single car would bear all the overheads. But if the company were to increase production, average fixed costs would fall to £500,000 when two cars are produced, £333,333 when three cars are produced and so on. Average fixed costs per unit of output fall as output increases, since overheads are spread over a larger output.

Figure 3.3 Fixed costs of production

Variable costs

Variable costs are the costs that the firm incurs when it hires variable factors of production such as labour and raw materials. For simplicity, I shall assume that labour is the only variable factor of production. The upper panel of Figure

3.4 shows the marginal and average productivity of labour. Diminishing marginal returns begin at point *A*. Increasing marginal productivity of labour (or increasing marginal returns) is shown by the positive (or rising) slope of the marginal product curve, while diminishing marginal returns are represented, beyond point *A*, by the curve's negative (or falling) slope.

When labour is the only variable factor of production, variable costs are simply wage costs. If all workers receive the same hourly wage, total wage costs rise in exact proportion to the number of workers employed. However, with increasing marginal labour productivity, the total variable cost of production rises at a slower rate than output. This causes the marginal cost (MC) of producing an extra unit of output to fall. In Figure 3.4, the increasing marginal productivity of labour (shown by the positive slope of the marginal product curve in the upper of the two diagrams) causes marginal cost (shown in the lower of the two diagrams) to fall.

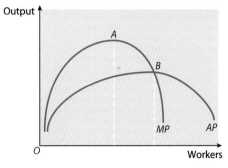

However, once the law of diminishing marginal productivity sets in, marginal cost rises with output. The wage cost of employing an extra worker is still the same, but each extra worker is now less productive than the previous worker. Variable costs rise faster than output, so marginal cost also rises.

Just as the *MC* curve is derived from the marginal returns or marginal productivity of the variable inputs, so the average variable cost (*AVC*) curve (illustrated in the lower panel of Figure 3.4) is explained by the average returns or productivity curve (shown in the upper panel). When

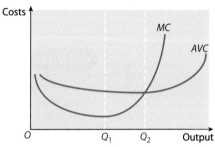

Figure 3.4 Deriving the *MC* and *AVC* curves from short-run production theory

increasing average returns are experienced, with the labour force on average becoming more efficient and productive, the *AVC* per unit of output must fall as output rises. But once diminishing average returns set in at point *B*, the *AVC* curve begins to rise with output.

EXAM TIP

Make sure you understand the relationship between marginal product curves (or marginal return curves) and marginal cost curves, in the economic short run.

Average total costs

The firm's average total cost (*ATC*) curve is obtained from the addition of the *AFC* and *AVC* curves, as shown in Figure 3.5(a). Figure 3.5(b) shows the *ATC* curve on its own, without showing its two components (*AFC* and *AVC*). You should note that the *ATC* curve is typically U-shaped, showing that average total costs per unit of output first fall and later rise as output is increased. In the short run, average total costs must eventually rise because, at high levels of output, any further spreading of fixed costs becomes insufficient to offset the impact of diminishing returns upon variable costs of production. Sooner or later, rising marginal costs (which, as I have explained, result from diminishing marginal returns) must cut through and 'pull up' the *ATC* curve.

(a) Adding *AFC* to *AVC* to obtain the *ATC* curve

(b) The U-shaped *ATC* curve

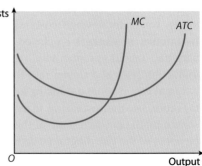

Figure 3.5 The average total cost (*ATC*) curve

EXAM TIP

You must understand that in the short run, the law of diminishing returns leads to rising marginal costs, which in turn cause a firm's average total cost curve to be U-shaped. Note also that the *MC* curve cuts both the *AVC* and the *ATC* curves at their lowest points (at the bottom of the 'U').

Long-run production theory

The only way a firm can increase output in the short run is by adding more variable factors of production (such as labour) to its fixed capital. But eventually the law of diminishing productivity sets in, which causes short-run marginal costs to rise. When the *MC* curve rises through the firm's *ATC* curve, average total costs of production also rise.

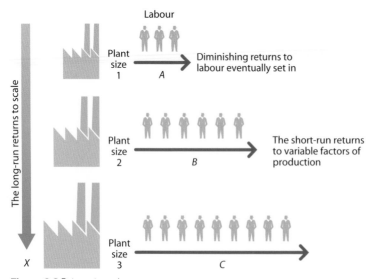

Figure 3.6 Returns to scale

To escape the adverse effect of rising short-run costs upon profit, in the economic long run a firm may decide to change the *scale* of its operations. In the long run there are no fixed factors of production. In this time period, the firm can change the scale of all its factors of production, including its capital or production plant, which is normally assumed to be fixed in the short run.

Returns to scale

Figure 3.6 illustrates the important distinction between returns to a variable factor of production, which occur in the short run, and **returns to scale**, which operate only in the economic long run. Suppose that initially a firm's fixed capital is represented by plant size 1 in the diagram. Initially, the firm can increase production in the short run, by moving along the horizontal arrow *A*, employing more variable factors of production such as labour. However, the only way the firm can further increase profits once the short-run profit-maximising output has been reached is to change the scale of its operations, assuming that the firm cannot operate its existing plant more efficiently. In the long run, the firm can invest in a larger production plant, such as plant size 2, shown as the move along the vertical arrow *X* in the diagram. Once plant size 2 is in operation, the firm is in a new short-run situation, able to increase output by moving along arrow *B*. But again, the impact of diminishing returns may eventually cause the firm to expand the scale of its operations to plant size 3 in the long run.

KEY TERM

returns to scale: describes how output changes when the scale of *all* the factors of production changes in the long run. They divide into increasing returns to scale, decreasing returns to scale and constant returns to scale.

The law of diminishing marginal productivity, explained earlier in the context of short-run production, is a short-run law that does not operate in the long run when a firm increases the scale of all its inputs or factors of production. With returns to scale there are three possibilities:

- **Increasing returns to scale.** If an increase in the scale of all the factors of production causes a more than proportionate increase in output, there are increasing returns to scale.
- **Constant returns to scale.** If an increase in the scale of all the factors of production causes a proportionate increase in output, there are constant returns to scale.
- **Decreasing returns to scale.** If an increase in the scale of all the factors of production causes a less than proportionate increase in output, there are decreasing (or diminishing) returns to scale.

It is important not to confuse returns to scale, which occur in the long run when the scale of all the factors of production can be altered, with the short-run returns that occur when at least one factor is fixed. We have already seen how short-run returns affect the shape of a firm's short-run cost curves. I shall now explain how returns to scale affect the shape of a firm's long-run average costs (*LRAC*) of production.

Long-run costs

In the long run, a firm can change the scale of all its factors of production, moving from one size of plant to another. Figure 3.7 shows a number of short-run average total cost (*SRATC*) curves, each representing a particular size or scale of firm. In the long run, a firm can move from one short-run cost curve to another, with each curve associated with a different scale of capacity that is fixed in the short run. The line drawn as a tangent to the family or set of *SRATC* curves is the long-run average cost (*LRAC*) curve.

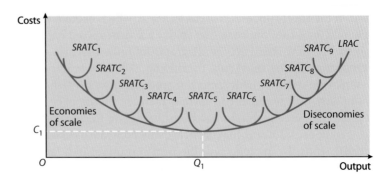

Figure 3.7 A U-shaped *LRAC* curve and its related *SRATC* curves

Economies of scale and diseconomies of scale

Just as it is important to avoid confusing short-run returns or productivity with long-run returns to scale, so **returns to scale** must be distinguished from a closely related concept: **economies and diseconomies of scale**. Returns to scale refer to the technical relationship in production between inputs and outputs measured in physical units. For example, increasing returns to scale occur if a doubling of a car firm's factory size and its labour force enables the firm to more than double its output of cars. There is no mention of money costs of production in this example of increasing returns to scale. Returns to scale are part of long-run production theory, but economies and diseconomies of scale are part of long-run cost theory. Economies of scale occur when long-run average costs (*LRAC*) fall as output increases. Diseconomies of scale occur when *LRAC* rise as output increases.

> **EXAM TIP**
>
> You must develop your understanding of economies and diseconomies of scale from the knowledge you learnt at AS. In particular, you must know that economies of scale reduce a firm's long-run average costs. At A2 you must thoroughly understand cost theory, especially the difference between short-run and long-run cost curves.

There is, however, a link between returns to scale and economies and diseconomies of scale. Increasing returns to scale lead to falling long-run average costs or **economies of scale**, and likewise decreasing returns to scale bring about rising long-run average costs or **diseconomies of scale**.

> **KEY TERMS**
>
> **economies of scale:** falling long-run average costs as the size or scale of the firm increases.
>
> **diseconomies of scale:** rising long-run average costs as the size or scale of the firm increases.

The shape of the long-run average cost curve

Figure 3.7 illustrates a U-shaped long-run average cost curve in which economies of scale are eventually followed by diseconomies. An increase in all the inputs or factors of production causes *LRAC* to fall to C_1, at output Q_1, but after this point, diseconomies of scale set in.

However, the long-run average cost curve need not be U-shaped, in which economies of scale are followed symmetrically by diseconomies of scale. Some industries, including many personal services such as hairdressing, exhibit **economies of small-scale production**. In such industries, diseconomies of scale may set in at a relatively small size of production plant or fixed capacity, resulting in the rising *LRAC* curve illustrated in Figure 3.8.

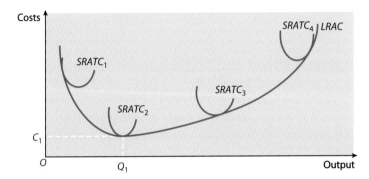

Figure 3.8 Economies of small-scale production

In other industries, which lack significant economies or diseconomies of scale, the horizontal *LRAC* curve depicted in Figure 3.9 may be more typical, allowing firms or plants of many different sizes to exist within the same industry.

Figure 3.9 A horizontal *LRAC* curve

In much of the manufacturing industry, however, statistical studies suggest that the *LRAC* curve is L-shaped, as illustrated in Figure 3.10. Beyond output Q_1 the *LRAC* curve is horizontal. No further economies of scale are possible, but likewise there are no diseconomies of scale. In industries such as automobile and aircraft building, for which the L-shaped curve may be typical, size of firm is limited by market constraints rather than by the onset of diseconomies of scale.

Figure 3.10 An
L-shaped *LRAC* curve
and the minimum
efficient scale (*MES*)

The optimum size of firm and minimum efficient scale

The size of plant at the lowest point on the firm's *LRAC* curve is known as the **optimum plant size**. When the long-run average cost curve is U-shaped, as in Figure 3.7, we can identify a single optimum plant size level of output, occurring after economies of scale have been gained, but before diseconomies of scale set in. In Figure 3.7, optimum plant size is shown by the short-run cost curve $SRATC_5$, with optimum output at Q_1. In the case of the horizontal *LRAC* curve illustrated in Figure 3.9, where there are no economies or diseconomies of scale, it is not possible to identify an optimal plant size.

EXAM TIP

A firm's long-run
average cost curve
may be U-shaped, but
it does not have to be
U-shaped. Various
shapes are possible.

However, when the *LRAC* curve is L-shaped, as in Figure 3.10, the long-run average cost curve flattens out. Plant size 3 is therefore known as the **minimum efficient scale (MES)**, indicating the smallest size of plant that can benefit from minimum long-run average costs. Some economies of scale may still be possible, for example technical economies, but these would be offset by diseconomies of scale emerging elsewhere

KEY TERM

minimum efficient scale (MES): the smallest size of plant that can benefit from minimum long-run average costs.

Engine construction at a
Rolls-Royce manufacturing
plant

within the business, for example managerial diseconomies of scale. (I explain technical economies of scale and managerial diseconomies of scale in Chapter 8.)

CASE STUDY 3.2

Economies of scale and mergers in the airline industry

In the recession which hit the global economy in 2008, airlines suffered badly from a collapse in passenger numbers. Many airlines concluded that the only way to reduce their losses was to merge with other airlines. In the USA, United Airlines merged with Continental to form the world's biggest carrier. In Europe, British Airways (BA) joined up with the Spanish flag-carrier, Iberia.

Why were mergers now such an attractive option? The simple answer is that airlines urgently needed to cut their costs, and mergers were seen as the easiest way to do it, without the airlines losing out to the competition.

Airlines operate very similar businesses. As well as flying the planes, they run significant back-office functions including administration and support services for planes. By merging these together, they can effectively halve their costs. Within the air transport industry there are significant economies of scale. Savings can also be made through cutting capacity by reducing the number of flights. For example, where Continental and United routes overlapped or competed with each other, the merged company cut some of these flights, thereby reducing competition for its remaining services, and saving the firm many thousands of pounds a day in the process. Additionally, the company sought to increase its revenues by using the landing and take-off slots freed up by the cuts to fly to new destinations.

Despite the obvious benefits, it took the worst crisis in the history of the airline industry to underline the urgent need for consolidation and the pursuit of further economies of scale.

However, consolidation through merger may be more trouble than it's worth. There may be significant cultural differences — even between two similar airlines — that can be difficult to overcome. There are also anti-monopoly issues, with governments increasingly concerned over the impact that large-scale consolidation could have on competition. Labour disputes with staff and trade unions — in BA's case in particular — have also made reducing costs through staff cuts more difficult than the airlines would like.

Follow-up questions
1 Outline two technical economies of scale that benefit airlines, in addition to the economies of scale that might result from mergers.
2 Describe two diseconomies of scale that may affect airlines as they grow in size.

SUMMARY

- Production is a process or set of processes for converting inputs into outputs.
- The key concept in short-run production theory is the law of diminishing returns.
- This law is also known as the law of diminishing marginal productivity.
- In the short run, the marginal cost curve and the average variable cost curve are derived from the law of diminishing marginal returns.
- The short-run average cost curve is U-shaped.
- The key concept in long-run production theory is returns to scale.
- Increasing returns to scale, constant returns to scale and decreasing returns to scale are all possible.
- Increasing returns to scale lead to economies of scale and falling long-run average costs.
- Decreasing returns to scale lead to diseconomies of scale and rising long-run average costs.
- The long-run average cost curve may be U-shaped, but other shapes are possible.
- Minimum efficient scale (*MES*) is illustrated on an L-shaped *LRAC* curve.

Exam-style questions

1 Explain the difference between the law of diminishing returns and decreasing returns to scale.
How do these affect a firm's cost curves in both the short run and the long run? **(15 marks)**

2 What is the relationship between returns to scale and economies and diseconomies of scale? **(15 marks)**

3 Evaluate the view that large firms are always better than small firms. **(25 marks)**

4 'Mergers in the global airline industry must be bad because they significantly reduce competition.'
To what extent do you agree with this view? Justify your answer. **(25 marks)**

Extra resources to help you revise are available online at www.hodderplus.co.uk/philipallan

Revenue theory and market structures

Chapter 4

Chapter 3 explains how production takes place, and how the nature of production affects a firm's costs of production, in both the short run and the long run. This chapter develops two further elements in the theory of the firm, namely the market structures in which firms sell their output, which in turn affect the sales revenue that firms earn when they increase the quantity of output they sell.

LEARNING OUTCOMES

This chapter will:
- develop the explanation of market structures first mentioned in Chapter 2
- explain how the competitiveness of a market structure affects a firm's revenue curves
- explain the difference between average revenue and marginal revenue
- compare a perfectly competitive firm's revenue curves with those of a monopoly

WHAT YOU SHOULD ALREADY KNOW

At AS, you learnt very little about the subject matter of this chapter. Having studied Unit 1: Markets and market failure, all you are required to know at the beginning of the A2 course is that profit is the difference between revenue and cost. Prior knowledge of revenue curves in the different market structures is not expected at the beginning of the A2 course.

However, an understanding of price elasticity of demand is very useful when learning about monopoly revenue curves. Elasticity is one of the key Unit 1 topics that is tested synoptically in the Unit 3 exam at A2.

The different market structures

In Chapter 2, I briefly mentioned that the nature of a firm's sales revenue depends on the competitiveness of the **market structure** in which the firm sells its output. Figure 2.1 on page 13 introduced the main market structures covered in this and the next three chapters, namely **perfect competition**, **monopoly** and **oligopoly**. These are shown in greater detail in Figure 4.1.

KEY TERM

market structure: the framework within which a firm sells its output.

EXAM TIP

For the Unit 3 examination, candidates must expect data-response and essay questions to be set on perfect competition, monopoly or oligopoly. Questions will *not* be set on monopolistic competition.

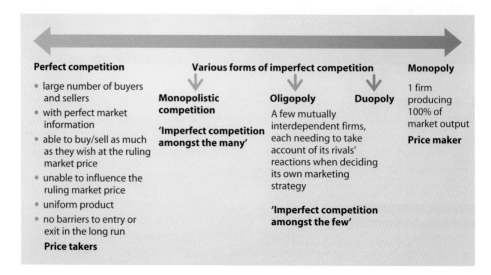

Figure 4.1 The main market structures

Market structures are defined by the number of firms in the market. However, this leads to other important aspects of the market, such as the competitiveness of the market, and the ways in which firms behave and conduct themselves in the market. Perfect competition and monopoly are at the opposite extremes of the spectrum of market structure shown in Figure 4.1. The market structures that lie between these extremes provide examples of **imperfect competition**.

EXAM TIP

While you should know the six conditions of perfect competition, it is seldom if ever relevant to regurgitate this list in an examination answer. Rather, you must learn the skills of applying one or more of the conditions of perfect competition to explain, analyse or evaluate the characteristics of a perfectly competitive market, or to compare perfect competition with monopoly or oligopoly.

Pure monopoly, in which a single firm produces the whole of the output of a market or industry, is the most extreme form of imperfect competition. Indeed, a pure monopolist faces no competition at

KEY TERM

pure monopoly: exists where there is only one firm in a market.

all, since there are no other firms to compete against. Usually, however, monopoly is a *relative* rather than an *absolute* concept. Until quite recently, the British Gas Corporation was the single producer of piped gas to households and most industrial customers, but it experienced competition from other sources of energy such as electricity and oil. British Gas's monopoly power was further reduced in 1998 when other companies, including electricity companies, were allowed to sell gas to customers via the pipelines previously owned by British Gas. Monopolists do, therefore, face competitive pressures, both from substitute products and sometimes also from outside firms trying to enter the market to destroy their monopoly position.

At the other end of the spectrum, **perfect competition** is actually non-existent. It is best to regard perfect competition as an unreal or abstract economic model defined by the conditions listed in Figure 4.1. In Chapter 5, I explain that real-world markets cannot display simultaneously *all* the conditions necessary for perfect competition. Since any violation of the conditions of perfect competition immediately renders a market imperfectly competitive, even the most competitive markets in the real economy are examples of imperfect competition rather than perfect competition.

But despite the lack of perfect markets in the real world, the theory of perfect competition is perhaps the most important and fundamental of all conventional economic theories. Critics of orthodox microeconomic theory strongly argue that economists pay undue attention to perfect competition as a market structure and that this encourages a false belief that a perfect market is an attainable ideal. As you read this and the next few chapters, remember at all times that perfect competition is an unrealistic market structure. (It would be clearer for students if perfect and imperfect competition were respectively called *unrealistic competition* and *realistic competition*.)

Nevertheless, perfect competition performs a very useful function. It serves as a standard or benchmark against which we may judge the desirable or undesirable properties of the imperfectly competitive market structures of the world we live in.

As I have mentioned, all markets between the polar extremes of perfect competition and monopoly are labelled as **imperfectly competitive**. There are two main imperfectly competitive market structures, **monopolistic competition** and **oligopoly**. If you use another textbook, alongside this one, that covers the requirements of all the GCE examining boards, you will find a chapter there on monopolistic competition. However, monopolist competition is not in the AQA economics specification, so don't bother learning about it, at least beyond knowing that monopolistic competition is, as Figure 4.1 indicates, imperfect competition amongst the many. This means that there are a large number of firms in the market. By contrast, in oligopoly, which Figure 4.1 describes as imperfect competition amongst the few, there are generally only a handful of firms. (Indeed in **duopoly**, which is a special case of oligopoly, there are only two firms in the market.)

Microsoft, Sony and Nintendo form an oligopoly in the video games console market

Almost all real-world markets, certainly in developed economies such as the United Kingdom, are imperfectly competitive, and some of them, such as the video games console market, are oligopolies. Chapter 7 explains how oligopoly and concentrated markets divide into **competitive oligopoly**, in which firms compete actively against each other, and **collusive oligopoly**, in which firms cooperate with each other.

Revenue

Revenue is the sales revenue or money that a firm earns when selling its output. As I emphasise in Chapter 2, you must not confuse a firm's *revenue* with the *returns* or output that the firm produces.

> **KEY TERM**
>
> **revenue:** the money income a firm receives from selling its output.

Likewise, you must not confuse **total revenue**, **average revenue** and **marginal revenue**. Total revenue is *all* the money a firm earns from selling the total output of a product. It is cumulative. Selling one more unit of a product or good usually causes total revenue to rise. By contrast, at any level of output, average revenue is calculated by dividing total revenue by the size of output:

$$\text{average revenue} = \frac{\text{total revenue}}{\text{output}} \text{ or } AR = \frac{TR}{Q}$$

> **EXAM TIP**
>
> Make sure you don't confuse revenue with returns or with profit.

where TR, AR and Q are the symbols I use for total revenue, average revenue and the level of output.

Marginal revenue is the addition to total revenue resulting from the sale of one more unit of output. Marginal revenue can be calculated by using the equation:

$$\text{marginal revenue} = \frac{\Delta \text{total revenue}}{\Delta \text{output}} \text{ or } MR = \frac{\Delta TR}{\Delta Q}$$

where MR means marginal revenue and Δ indicates a change in total revenue and output.

The Greek delta symbol Δ is used by mathematicians as the symbol for a change in the value of a variable over a range of observations. The word 'marginal' means the change in the value of a variable when there is one more unit of the variable, so Δ is the symbol that indicates this change. It is used in the formulae for marginal product and marginal cost, as well as marginal revenue.

How the competitiveness of a market structure affects a firm's revenue curves

Having explained the meaning of total, average and marginal revenue, in the final two sections of this chapter I shall explain how a firm's average revenue curve and its marginal revenue curve are derived, first in perfect competition and then in monopoly. (I explain oligopoly revenue curves in Chapter 7, rather than in this chapter.)

Revenue curves in perfect competition

I shall use the conditions of perfect competition, listed at the left-hand side of Figure 4.1, to derive the revenue curves facing a firm in a perfectly competitive market. The first four of the conditions of perfect competition are:

- a large number of buyers and sellers
- buyers and sellers possessing perfect information about the market
- possible to buy and sell as much as needed at the ruling market price set by market forces in the market as a whole
- individual market transactions unable to influence the ruling market price

Taken together, the four conditions I have listed tell us that a perfectly competitive firm, which is depicted in panel (a) of Figure 4.2, faces a perfectly elastic demand curve for its product. The demand curve facing the firm is located at the ruling market price, P_1, which itself is determined through the interaction of market demand and market supply in panel (b) of the diagram.

The assumption that a perfectly competitive firm can sell whatever quantity it wishes at the ruling market price P_1, but that it cannot influence the ruling market price by its own action, means that the firm is a passive **price-taker**.

The labels 'No sales' and 'No sense' that I have placed on Figure 4.2(a), respectively above and below the price line P_1, help to explain why a perfectly competitive firm is a price-taker. 'No sales' indicates that if the firm raises its selling price above the ruling market price, customers desert the firm to buy the identical products (perfect substitutes) available from other firms at the ruling market price. 'No sense' refers to the fact that although a perfectly competitive firm can sell its output below the price P_1, doing so is irrational. No extra sales can result, so selling below the ruling market price inevitably reduces both total sales revenue and profit. Such a pricing policy therefore conflicts with the profit-maximising objective that firms are assumed to have.

Figure 4.2 Deriving a perfectly competitive firm's average and marginal revenue curves

The horizontal price line facing a perfectly competitive firm is also the firm's **average revenue (AR)** and its **marginal revenue (MR)** curves. Suppose for example that the firm sells 100 units of a good, with each unit of the good priced at £1.00. The firm's total sales revenue (TR) is obviously £100.00.

$$AR = \frac{TR}{Q} \text{ or } \frac{£100.00}{100} = £1.00$$

$$MR = \frac{\Delta TR}{\Delta Q} \text{ or } \frac{£1.00}{1} = £1.00$$

The price or average revenue is £1.00, as is the marginal revenue the firm earns when it sells one more unit.

$$\text{price} = AR = MR$$

Revenue curves in monopoly

It is worth repeating that the demand curve facing a perfectly competitive firm, besides being located at the ruling market price, is also the firm's average revenue (AR) curve and its marginal revenue (MR) curve. By contrast, for monopoly the demand curve for the firm's output is also its AR curve, *but not* its MR curve.

This is because the demand curve facing a monopolist differs from the demand curve facing a firm in a perfectly competitive market. The industry demand curve and the demand curve for the monopolist's output are the same because the monopoly *is* the industry. This means that a monopolist faces a downward-sloping demand curve, whose elasticity is determined by the nature of consumer demand for the monopolist's product.

The downward-sloping demand curve affects the monopolist in one of two different ways. If the monopolist is a **price-maker**, choosing to set the price at which the product is sold, the demand curve dictates the maximum output that can be sold at this price. For example, if the price is set at P_1 in Figure 4.3, the maximum quantity that can be sold at this price is Q_1. And if the monopolist raises the price to P_2, sales fall to Q_2, unless the monopolist successfully uses advertising or other forms of marketing to shift the demand curve to the right. Alternatively, if the monopolist is a **quantity-setter** rather than a price-maker, the demand curve dictates the maximum price at which the chosen quantity can be sold. The fact that the demand curve is downward-sloping means that the monopolist faces a trade-off. A monopoly cannot set price and quantity independently of each other.

The demand curve is the monopolist's average revenue (AR) curve because the demand curve shows the price the monopolist charges at each level of output. However, unlike in perfect competition, marginal revenue and average revenue are *not* the same in monopoly. To explain this, I shall re-introduce the second statement in the mathematical relationship between a marginal variable and the average to which it is related:

when the marginal < the average, the average falls

(The full relationship is on page 25.)

Figure 4.3 The trade-off facing a monopolist

Since the monopolist's average revenue curve falls as output or sales rise, marginal revenue *must* be below average revenue. This relationship is shown in Figure 4.4, which depicts a monopolist's *AR* and *MR* curves, with the *MR* curve drawn twice as steep as the *AR* curve. This is always the case whenever the *AR* curve is a straight line or linear. (This property does not apply, however, when the *AR* curve is non-linear, though the *MR* curve will always be below the *AR* curve as long as the *AR* curve is falling.)

Figure 4.4 Monopoly average revenue and marginal revenue curves

SYNOPTIC LINK: ELASTICITY AND REVENUE CURVES

Earlier in the chapter, I mentioned that the horizontal price line facing a perfectly competitive firm is also the **perfectly elastic** demand curve for the firm's output. The explanation for this lies in the word **substitutability**. In AS microeconomics you learnt that the availability of substitutes is the main determinant of price elasticity of demand. Now in perfect competition, because of the assumptions of a uniform product and perfect information, the output of every other firm in the market is a perfect substitute for the firm's own product. If the firm tries to raise its price above the ruling market price, it loses all its customers.

In monopoly, by contrast, providing the demand curve is a straight line as well as downward sloping, price elasticity of demand falls moving down the demand curve. Demand for the monopolist's output is elastic in the top half of the curve, falling to be unit elastic exactly half way down the curve, and inelastic in the bottom half of the curve. This is shown in Figure 4.5. Demand is elastic between *A* and *B*, unit elastic at *B*, and inelastic between *B* and *C*.

I shall revisit the significance of elasticity in the next chapter, when comparing profit maximisation with revenue maximisation.

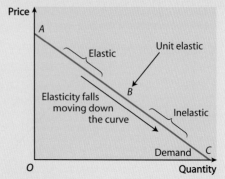

Figure 4.5 Price elasticity of demand for a monopoly

The next diagram, Figure 4.6, explains the relationship between a monopolist's *AR* and *MR* curves. The firm can only sell an extra unit of output by reducing the price at which *all* units of output are sold because the demand curve (or *AR* curve) facing the monopolist is downward-sloping. Total sales revenue increases by the area *k* in Figure 4.6, but decreases by the area *h*. Areas *k* and *h* respectively show the revenue gain (namely the extra unit sold multiplied by its price) and the revenue loss resulting from the sale of an extra unit of output. The revenue loss results from the fact that in order to sell one more unit of output, the price has to be reduced for *all* units of output, not just the extra unit sold. Marginal revenue, which is the revenue gain minus the revenue loss (or *k* – *h*), must be less than price or average revenue (area *k*).

Figure 4.6 Explaining the monopolist's *MR* curve

- Market structures provide the framework in which businesses exist.
- Different market structures display different degrees of competitiveness.
- Perfect competition, monopoly and oligopoly are three main market structures.
- In pure monopoly there is only one firm in the market.
- There would be a very large number of firms (and also buyers) in a perfectly competitive market.
- But no real-world market is perfectly competitive because not all the conditions of perfect competition can be met at the same time.
- Perfect competition provides a yardstick or benchmark against which the desirable and undesirable properties of real-world markets can be measured.
- A perfectly competitive firm is a passive price-taker in the market in which it exists.
- A perfectly competitive firm's average and marginal revenue curve is located along the horizontal ruling market price line, determined in the market as a whole.
- The ruling market price in perfect competition is also the perfectly elastic demand curve facing each firm in the market.
- A monopolist's demand curve is the market demand curve for the industry.
- A monopolist can be a price-maker or a quantity-setter, but not both at the same time.
- A monopolist's marginal revenue curve lies below its average revenue curve.
- Price elasticity of demand falls moving down a (linear) demand or AR curve facing a monopolist.

Exam-style questions

1 Explain why the average and marginal revenue curves of a monopoly slope downward, while those of a perfectly competitive firm are horizontal. **(15 marks)**

2 Explain the mathematical relationships between the average and marginal values of an economic variable. **(15 marks)**

3 'As it can sell as much as it wants to at the ruling market price, a perfectly competitive firm should always try to sell more of the good it produces.' Evaluate this view. **(25 marks)**

4 Evaluate the view that a monopoly can simultaneously increase both the price of the good it produces and the quantity of the good it sells. **(25 marks)**

Extra resources to help you revise are available online at www.hodderplus.co.uk/philipallan

Chapter 5

Perfect competition and monopoly

Chapters 2 and 4 have already introduced you to the two market structures of perfect competition and monopoly. Arguably, these are the two most essential topics you need to know when answering Unit 3 exam questions on business economics, though oligopoly, covered in Chapter 7, is also very important. This chapter draws on the information about cost and revenue curves explained in Chapters 3 and 4 to explain how profit maximisation occurs in perfect competition and monopoly. Chapter 6 then evaluates the desirable and less desirable features of the two market structures.

LEARNING OUTCOMES

This chapter will:
- explain how profit maximisation occurs
- analyse perfect competition equilibrium in the short run and the long run
- analyse monopoly equilibrium

WHAT YOU SHOULD ALREADY KNOW

At AS, there is a section of Unit 1 called 'Resource allocation in competitive markets'. However, candidates are not expected to know about perfect competition at AS. This means that at the beginning of the A2 course, you should understand how a competitive market works in a supply and demand context. Chapters 2–4 introduced you to perfect competition.

Monopoly is mentioned in the AS specification in the section on market failure. You are expected to 'understand that monopolies have market power and that the basic model of monopoly suggests that higher prices, inefficiency and a misallocation of resources may result in monopoly, compared to the outcome in a competitive market'. Besides understanding that monopoly is a type of market failure, you should also know about the sources or causes of monopoly power, and the possible benefits of monopoly such as economies of scale.

Profit-maximising behaviour

When I briefly mentioned how firms behave in Chapter 2, I stated that all economic agents, e.g. households, firms and the government, have an objective that they wish to maximise. I then said that for firms, economists assume that the objective is profit maximisation. This assumption is fundamental to the traditional (or neoclassical) theory of the firm. At any level of output:

total profit = total revenue – total cost

Providing we assume that it wishes to make the largest possible **profit,** a firm therefore aims to produce the level of output at which *TR – TC* is maximised. The maximisation of *TR – TC* is the **equilibrium condition** (or **optimising condition**) for a profit-maximising firm, for if the firm succeeds in producing and selling the output yielding the biggest possible profit, it has no incentive to change its level of output.

However, it is generally more convenient to state the equilibrium condition for profit maximisation as:

marginal revenue = marginal cost, or *MR = MC*

KEY TERM

MR = MC means that a firm's profits are greatest when the addition to sales revenue received from the last unit sold (marginal revenue) equals exactly the addition to total cost incurred from the production of the last unit of output (marginal cost).

MR = MC: the marginalist condition that must be met if profits are to be maximised.

Imagine, for example, a market gardener producing tomatoes for sale in a local market, but unable to influence the ruling market price of 50p per kilo. At any size of sales, average revenue is 50p, which also equals marginal revenue. Suppose that when the horticulturalist markets 300 kilos of tomatoes, the cost of producing and marketing the 300th kilo is 48p. If the tomato grower decides not to market the 300th kilo, 2p of profit is sacrificed. Suppose now that total costs rise by 50p and 52p respectively when a 301st kilo and a 302nd kilo are marketed. The marketing of the 302nd kilo causes profits to fall by 2p, but the 301st kilo of tomatoes leaves total profits unchanged: it represents the level of sales at which profits are exactly maximised.

To sum up, when:

MR > MC, profits rise when output increases

MR < MC, profits rise when output reduces

So only when *MR = MC* are profits maximised.

When *MR > MC* or *MR < MC* the firm fails to maximise profit. These are examples of **disequilibrium**. To maximise profit, the firm must change its level of output until it reaches the point at which *MR = MC*. Once this is reached, the firm has no incentive to change output, unless some event disturbs either costs or revenues.

It is important to understand that firms in *all* market structures (perfect competition, monopoly and imperfectly competitive markets such as oligopoly) can only maximise profit when marginal revenue equals marginal cost. *MR = MC* is a universal equilibrium or profit-maximising condition relevant to all market structures.

EXAM TIP

You must understand that profit is maximised in *all* market structures (perfect competition, monopoly and oligopoly) when *MR = MC*.

Normal and supernormal profit

Before explaining the concept of the profit-maximising firm in perfect competition, I must first introduce **normal profit** and **supernormal profit**. (Supernormal profit is also known as abnormal profit and above-normal profit.) Normal profit is the minimum level of profit necessary to keep incumbent firms in the market (i.e. firms that are already in the market). However, the normal profit made by incumbent firms is insufficient to attract new firms into the market. Economists treat normal profit as a cost of production, including it in a firm's average cost curve because a firm must make normal profit to stay in production. In the long run, firms unable to make normal profit leave the market. Supernormal profit is extra profit over and above normal profit. In the long run, and in the absence of entry barriers, supernormal profit performs the important economic function of attracting new firms into the market.

> **KEY TERMS**
>
> **normal profit:** the minimum profit a firm must make to stay in business, while being insufficient to attract new firms into the market.
>
> **supernormal profit:** profit over and above normal profit.

> **EXAM TIP**
>
> It is easy to confuse normal profit with a normal good, a good for which demand increases as income increases.

The conditions of perfect competition

You first came across the conditions of **perfect competition** in Figure 4.1 in Chapter 4. To remind you, the six conditions that must be present in a perfectly competitive market are:

1 a large number of buyers and sellers
2 perfect information about what is going on in the market, including prices of goods and their costs of production
3 firms being able to sell as much as they wish to at the ruling price established by demand and supply in the whole market
4 independent action by firms will not influence the ruling market price
5 a uniform, identical or homogeneous product
6 complete freedom for firms to enter or leave the market, but only in the long run

Short-run equilibrium in perfect competition

At this stage, you should refer back to page 39 and look again at Figure 4.2. The diagrams illustrate how each firm in a perfectly competitive market passively accepts the ruling market price, which becomes each firm's average revenue (*AR*) and marginal revenue (*MR*) curve. The third condition of perfect competition tells us that a perfectly competitive firm can sell as much as it wishes at the market's ruling price. But how much will it actually wish to produce and sell? Providing we assume that each firm's business objective is solely to maximise profit, the answer is shown in Figure 5.1.

(a) One firm in the market

(b) The whole market

Figure 5.1 Perfect competition in short-run equilibrium

Panel (a) of Figure 5.1 adds the perfectly competitive firm's average total cost (ATC) and its marginal cost (MC) to the revenue curves shown in Figure 4.2. Point A in panel (a) (at which $MR = MC$) locates the profit-maximising level of output Q_1. At this level of output, total sales revenue is shown by the area OQ_1AP_1. Total cost is shown by the area OQ_1BC_1. Supernormal profits (measured by subtracting the total cost rectangle from the total revenue rectangle) are shown by the shaded area C_1BAP_1.

Figure 5.2 A perfectly competitive firm in short-run equilibrium

---

EXAM TIP

A competitive market is in equilibrium when planned demand equals planned supply. A firm is in equilibrium when profit is maximised and $MR = MC$. True equilibrium is long-run equilibrium. By contrast, short-run equilibrium is really a constrained equilibrium which lasts only as long as new entrants are kept out of the market.

Figure 5.2 is the same as panel (a) of Figure 5.1, but presented without any information about what is going on in the market as a whole. The diagram enables you to focus on the short-run equilibrium of a perfectly competitive firm, especially the positions of the cost and revenue curves and the supernormal profit rectangle.

Long-run equilibrium in perfect competition

Referring back again to the list of the conditions of perfect competition, you will see that although firms cannot enter or leave the market in the short run, they can do so in the long run (condition 6). Suppose that in the short run, firms make supernormal profit, as illustrated in Figures 5.1 and 5.2. In this situation, the ruling market price signals to firms outside the market that supernormal profits can be made, which provides an incentive for new firms to enter the market. Figure 5.3 shows what might happen next. Initially, too many new firms enter the market, causing the supply curve to shift to the right to S_2 in panel (b) of the diagram. This causes the price line to fall to P_2, which lies below each firm's ATC curve. When this happens, firms make a loss (or **subnormal profit**). However, just as supernormal profit creates the incentive for new firms to enter the market, subnormal profit provides the incentive for marginal firms to leave the market. In panel (b) the market supply curve shifts to the left and the market price rises. Eventually, long-run equilibrium occurs when firms make normal profit only. For the market as a whole, this is shown at output Q''' and price P_3 in Figure 5.3.

Figure 5.3 Perfect competition in long-run equilibrium

Panel (a) of Figure 5.3 shows a perfectly competitive firm in long-run equilibrium. The price the firm faces is of course P_3, but its output is Q_3, which is immediately below the point at which $MR = MC$. This is shown more clearly in the next diagram, Figure 5.4, which shows the perfectly competitive firm in long-run equilibrium.

In Figure 5.4, the firm's total revenue and also its total cost are shown by the rectangle bounded by the points OQ_3XP_3. The entry of new firms into the market, attracted by short-run supernormal profits, has whittled away supernormal profit until in long-run equilibrium surviving firms make normal profit only. (Remember, normal profit is treated as a cost of production,

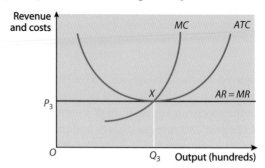

Figure 5.4 A perfectly competitive firm in long-run equilibrium minimising average costs of production

EXAM TIP

Make sure you understand and can draw the diagram shown in Figure 5.4. The previous diagram is less important to learn.

and is not shown explicitly in the diagram.) For the firm, output Q_3 is the long-run or true equilibrium. Total revenue equals the total cost of production, normal profit only is made, and there are no incentives for firms to enter or leave the market.

SYNOPTIC LINK: SOURCES OF MONOPOLY POWER

Section 3.1.4 of the AS specification states that candidates should be aware of the various sources of monopoly power which affect the behaviour and performance of firms. These include:

- **Natural monopoly**. This occurs when there is only room in the market for one firm benefiting to the full from **economies of scale**. In the past, **utility industries** such as water, gas, electricity and the telephone industries were regarded as natural monopolies. Because of the nature of their product, utility industries experience a particular marketing problem. The industries produce a service that is delivered through a distribution network or grid of pipes and cables into millions of separate businesses and homes. Competition in the provision of distribution grids is extremely wasteful, since it requires the duplication of fixed capacity, therefore causing each supplier to incur unnecessarily high fixed costs.

- **Geographical causes of monopoly**. A pure natural monopoly can occur when, for climatic or geological reasons, a particular country or location is the only source of supply of a raw material or foodstuff. Geographical or spatial factors also give rise to another type of monopoly, for example a single grocery store in an isolated village. Entry to the market by a second store is restricted by the fact that the local market is too small. Monopoly does not exist in an absolute sense, since the villagers can travel to the nearest town to buy their groceries. Nevertheless, the grocery store can still exercise considerable market power, stemming from the fact that for many villagers it is both costly and inconvenient to shop elsewhere. Prices charged are likely to be higher than they would be if competition existed nearby.

- **Government-created monopoly**. Governments sometimes create monopoly in markets they believe are too important to leave to competition. 'National flag' airlines are an example and trade mark and patent legislation also creates monopoly to protect intellectual copyright. Some governments also have a monopoly over broadcasting.

- **Advertising as a source of monopoly power**. Monopolies and other large firms can prevent small firms entering the market with devices such as saturation advertising. The small firms are unable to enter the industry because they cannot afford the minimum level of advertising and other forms of promotion for their goods which are necessary to persuade retailers to stock their products. The mass-advertising, brand-imaging and other marketing strategies of large established firms effectively crowd out newcomers from the market place.

Monopoly equilibrium

The profit-maximising or equilibrium level of output in monopoly is shown in Figure 5.5. As in perfect competition, the equilibrium output Q_1 is located at point A, where $MR = MC$. It is worth repeating that providing the firm is a profit maximiser, the equilibrium equation $MR = MC$ applies to *any* firm, whatever the market structure. However, in monopoly, point A does *not* show the equilibrium price, which is located at point B on the demand curve or AR curve above point A. The equilibrium price is P_1, which is the *maximum* price the monopolist can charge and succeed in selling output Q_1.

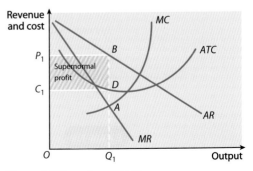

Figure 5.5 Monopoly equilibrium

You will notice that Figure 5.5 does not distinguish between *short-run* and *long-run* equilibrium in monopoly. This is because a monopoly is protected by barriers to entry, which prevent new firms entering the market to share in the supernormal profit made by the monopolist. Entry barriers enable the monopolist to preserve supernormal profits in the long run as well as in the short run. By contrast, in perfect competition supernormal profits are temporary, being restricted to the short run. Indeed in monopoly, supernormal profits are often called **monopoly profit**. A monopolist has the market power to preserve profit by keeping competitors out.

KEY TERM

monopoly profit: the supernormal profit a monopoly or imperfectly competitive firm makes in the long run as well as in the short run.

EXAM TIP

Make sure you understand and can draw Figure 5.5, and that you can compare it to the diagram showing perfect competition long-run equilibrium.

EXTENSION MATERIAL

Profit maximisation versus revenue maximisation

Students often confuse profit maximisation with revenue maximisation, but the two concepts are different. Profit maximisation occurs at the level of output at which the difference between a firm's total sales revenue (*TR*) and its total costs of production (*TC*) is greatest. This is also the level of output at which marginal revenue equals marginal cost (*MR* = *MC*). By contrast, revenue maximisation occurs at the level of output at which marginal revenue is zero. The difference between profit maximisation and revenue maximisation is shown in Figure 5.6.

Figure 5.6 Profit maximisation and revenue maximisation

The profit-maximising level of output Q_1 is located below point *X* where *MR* = *MC*. By contrast, the revenue-maximising level of output Q_2 is located at point *Z*, where *MR* = 0. Providing the *AR* and *MR* curves slope downward to the right and are linear (straight lines), the profit-maximising level of output is *always* below the revenue-maximising level of output.

EXAM TIP

Make sure you don't confuse profit maximisation with revenue maximisation.

EXTENSION MATERIAL

Marginal private benefit and marginal private cost

Provided that a firm's sole business objective is to maximise profit, marginal revenue can be thought of as the firm's **marginal private benefit**. Similarly, the marginal cost it incurs when producing output is its **marginal private cost**.

This is just a special case of the general proposition that all maximising economic agents, be they firms, consumers or workers, should undertake the activity they wish to maximise up to the point at which:

marginal private benefit = marginal private cost

or:

$MPB = MPC$

This generalisation covers the possibility that a firm may wish to maximise an objective other than profit, such as: sales revenue, the growth of the firm or managerial objectives (e.g. status or managers' pay). These possibilities are explored further in Chapter 7.

At AS you also came across the idea of equating marginal private benefit and marginal private cost in your study of market failure and externalities. This will be revisited in Chapter 10.

SYNOPTIC LINK: MONOPOLY AND ELASTICITY OF DEMAND

It is often said that a monopolist's ability to exploit consumers is greatest when demand is price inelastic and consumers are captive in the sense that no substitutes are available. It is obviously true that a monopolist may choose to produce a level of output for which demand is price inelastic. But to maximise profit, a monopoly must produce within the *elastic* section of the demand curve facing the firm. Figure 5.7 shows why.

As in Figure 5.5, profit maximisation occurs at output Q_1, drawn below point A on the diagram, where $MR = MC$. Now, because marginal cost is positive at point A, marginal revenue must also be positive. Yet, whenever MR is positive, demand is price-elastic. When the demand curve slopes downward and is linear (a straight line), the monopolist's MR curve is twice as steep as the AR or demand curve. In the diagram, the MR curve intersects the

Figure 5.7 Elasticity of demand and profit maximisation

quantity axis at point Z, which is exactly half way between the origin and point V, where the AR curve meets the quantity axis. The vertical line above point Z cuts the average revenue curve at point W, which is also half way along the AR curve. You should remember from your AS studies that demand is elastic at all points on the top half of a linear downward-sloping demand curve, and inelastic at all points on the bottom half. Bringing all these points together, the profit-maximising level of output Q_1 must lie below the top half of the average revenue curve. If it wishes to maximise profit, the monopoly must produce within the elastic section of the demand curve, even though monopoly power may appear to be greater when demand is inelastic.

- Profit is total sales revenue minus total costs of production.
- Profit maximisation occurs at the level of output at which marginal revenue equals marginal cost ($MR = MC$).
- The $MR = MC$ profit-maximising condition applies to all market structures: monopoly, oligopoly and perfect competition.
- Normal profit is just sufficient to keep incumbent firms in the market but is insufficient to attract new firms into the market.
- Normal profit is treated as a cost of production, and is included in a firm's cost curves.
- Supernormal profit is any profit over and above normal profit. On a graph it is shown by a profit rectangle.
- In a perfectly competitive market, supernormal profit attracts new firms into the market, until it has been competed away.
- A perfectly competitive firm is a price-taker, but a monopoly is a price-maker or quantity-setter.
- Perfectly competitive firms can make supernormal profit in short-run equilibrium, but not in long-run or true equilibrium.
- In monopoly, entry barriers prevent the entry of new firms from competing away supernormal profit. Supernormal profit exists in monopoly in the long run as well as in the short run.
- The point at which $MR = MC$ lies below the AR curve in a monopoly diagram, but not in a perfect competition diagram.

Exam-style questions

1 Explain why profit is maximised when $MR = MC$ in both perfect competition and monopoly. (15 marks)

2 Explain four different circumstances in which monopoly may occur. (15 marks)

3 'Since perfect competition does not exist in real-world markets, there are no lessons to learn from this market structure.' Critically evaluate this statement. (25 marks)

4 Do you agree that for a monopoly to exist and survive, demand for the monopolist's product must be inelastic? Justify your answer. (25 marks)

Extra resources to help you revise are available online at www.hodderplus.co.uk/philipallan

Evaluating perfect competition and monopoly

Chapter 6

Evaluation is the most demanding of the four skills tested in the Unit 3 and 4 examinations. Evaluation is tested when answering part 03 of your chosen question in the exam paper, and part 02 of the essay questions. In the context of perfect competition and monopoly, Unit 3 essay questions are likely to ask: which is the best market structure? To answer this question you need to be able to apply efficiency and welfare criteria. This chapter explains how.

LEARNING OUTCOMES

This chapter will:
- explain the meaning of economic efficiency and of efficiency concepts such as allocative efficiency and dynamic efficiency
- ask whether perfect competition is more efficient than monopoly
- introduce two welfare criteria: consumer surplus and producer surplus
- use these criteria to evaluate perfect competition and monopoly

WHAT YOU SHOULD ALREADY KNOW

Monopoly, but not perfect competition, is introduced in Unit 1. This means that, although you should be able to evaluate one weakness and one strength of monopoly, you cannot at this point in the course do the same for perfect competition.

Although the idea of improving economic welfare is in the Unit 1 specification, welfare concepts such as consumer surplus and producer surplus are not in the AS specification.

How do economists evaluate perfect competition and monopoly?

Economists use two sets of concepts to answer questions such as: is perfect competition preferable to monopoly? First, they apply efficiency concepts, such as productive efficiency, X-efficiency, allocative efficiency, and static and dynamic efficiency. Second, they ask how perfect competition and monopoly affect the consumer surplus and producer surplus that households and firms respectively enjoy, and hence the effect on general economic welfare.

EXAM TIP

You must learn to evaluate in order to display the skills needed to achieve an A grade.

Economic efficiency

I have already stated several times in previous chapters that a fundamental purpose of any economic system is to achieve the highest possible state of human happiness or welfare. Within a market economy, perfect competition and monopoly must ultimately be judged on the extent to which they contribute to improving human wellbeing, while remembering, of course, that perfect competition is an abstract and unreal market structure.

KEY TERM

economic efficiency: in general terms, economic efficiency minimises costs incurred, with minimum undesired side effects.

In order to judge the contribution of a market structure to human welfare, we must first assess the extent to which the market structure is efficient or inefficient. In terms of private self-interest, any decision made by an individual, a firm or a government is **economically efficient** if it achieves the economic agent's desired objective at minimum cost to the agent itself, and with minimum undesired side effects. However, in terms of the whole community, the social costs incurred and the social benefits received need also to be considered.

EXAM TIP

Economic efficiency is a key concept that can be used in the analysis of a wide range of economic topics, for example taxation and market failures.

Before discussing the extent to which perfect competition and monopoly can be considered efficient or inefficient, below are some of the meanings economists attach to the word 'efficiency'.

Technical efficiency

A production process is **technically efficient** if it maximises the output produced from the available inputs or factors of production. Alternatively, we may say, that at any level of output, production is technically efficient if it minimises the inputs of capital and labour needed to produce that level of output.

KEY TERM

technical efficiency: maximises output from the available inputs.

Productive efficiency or cost efficiency

To achieve **productive efficiency**, a firm must use the techniques and factors of production which are available, at lowest possible cost per unit of output. In the short run, the lowest point on the relevant short-run average total cost curve locates the most productively efficient level of output for the particular scale of operation. Short-run productive efficiency is shown in Figure 6.1.

KEY TERM

productive efficiency: involves minimising the average costs of production.

However, *true* productive efficiency is a long-run rather than a short-run concept. A firm's long-run average cost curve shows the lowest unit cost of producing different levels of output at all the different possible scales of production. The most productively efficient of all the levels of output occurs at the lowest point on

Figure 6.1 Productive efficiency in the short run

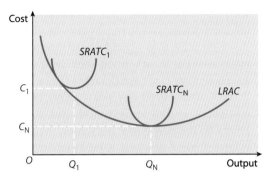

Figure 6.2 Short-run and long-run productive efficiency

the firm's *long-run* average cost curve. This is shown at output Q_N in Figure 6.2. Output Q_1 is also productively efficient, but only for the short-run cost curve $SRATC_1$.

Figure 6.3 illustrates another application of the concept of productive efficiency which you came across at AS. All points such as *A* and *B* on the production possibility frontier drawn for the whole economy are productively (and also technically) efficient. When the economy is on its production possibility frontier, it is only possible to increase output of capital goods by reducing output of consumer goods (and vice versa). By contrast, a point such as *C* inside the frontier is productively and technically inefficient. Output of capital goods could be increased by using inputs in a technically more efficient way, without reducing output of consumer goods.

X-efficiency

In the 1960s, the American economist Harvey Liebenstein argued that, due to organisational slack resulting from the absence of competitive pressures, monopolies are always likely to be technically and productively inefficient. This happens at all levels of output. Liebenstein introduced the term **X-inefficiency** to explain organisational slack.

Consider the short-run average total cost curve illustrated in Figure 6.4, which shows the lowest possible unit costs of producing various levels of output, given such conditions of production as the scale of the firm's fixed capacity and the prices of the factors of production used to produce the good. According to the cost curve, it is impossible for the firm to produce output Q_1 at a level of unit costs or average costs below C_1 (e.g. at a point such as *A*), unless of course the cost curve shifts downward over time. Conversely, if factors of production are combined in a technically inefficient

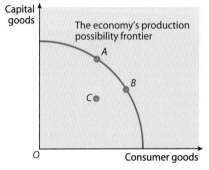

Figure 6.3 Productive and technical efficiency illustrated on a production possibility frontier

> **KEY TERM**
>
> **productive efficiency:** for the economy as a whole, productive efficiency can also be defined in terms of producing on the economy's production possibility frontier.

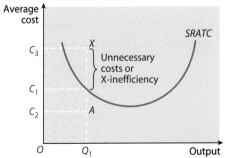

Figure 6.4 X-inefficiency occurring when a firm incurs unnecessary costs

way, unit costs *greater* than C_1 would be incurred when producing output Q_1. In this case, the firm would be producing off its cost curve, at a point such as X, at which average costs are C_3 rather than C_1. Point X, and indeed any point above the cost curve, is said to be X-inefficient. All

EXAM TIP

While X-efficiency is not in the AQA specification, it is an extremely useful concept to apply when analysing and evaluating market structures.

points on the cost curve (including the productively efficient point where unit cost is lowest) are X-efficient. X-inefficiency occurs whenever, for the level of output it is producing, the firm incurs unnecessary production costs, i.e. if the firm wished, it could reduce its costs.

There are two main causes of X-inefficiency. First, a firm may simply be technically inefficient: for example, employing too many workers (over-manning) or investing in machines it never uses. Second, X-inefficiency can be caused by the firm paying its workers or managers unnecessarily high wages or salaries, or by buying raw materials or capital at unnecessarily high prices. X-efficiency requires that the lowest possible prices are paid for inputs or factors of production.

Allocative efficiency

This rather abstract concept is of great importance to the understanding of economic efficiency. **Allocative efficiency** occurs when $P = MC$ in all industries and markets in the economy. To explain this further, we must examine closely both P and MC. The price of a good, P, is a measure of the value in consumption placed by buyers on the last unit consumed. P indicates the utility or welfare obtained at the margin in consumption. This is the good's opportunity cost in consumption. For example, a consumer spending £1 on a bar of chocolate cannot spend the pound on other goods. At

KEY TERM

allocative efficiency: occurs when it is *impossible* to improve overall economic welfare by reallocating resources between industries or markets (assuming an initial distribution of income and wealth). For resource allocation in the whole economy to be allocatively efficient, price must equal marginal cost in each and every market in the economy.

the same time, MC measures the good's opportunity cost in production, i.e. the value of the resources which go into the production of the last unit, in their best alternative uses.

Suppose that all the economy's markets divide into two categories: those in which $P > MC$ and those in which $P < MC$. In the markets where $P > MC$, households pay a price for the last unit consumed, which is greater than the cost of producing the last unit of the good. The high price discourages consumption, so we conclude that at this price the good is under-produced and under-consumed. Conversely, in the second set of markets in which $P < MC$, the value (P) placed on the last unit consumed by households is less than the MC of the resources used to produce the last unit. The price is too low, encouraging too much consumption of the good; thus at this price the good is over-produced and over-consumed.

Suppose resources can be taken from the second group of markets where $P < MC$ and reallocated to the former group of markets in which $P > MC$. Arguably, total consumer welfare or utility will increase as reallocation of resources takes place. As the reallocation proceeds, prices tend to fall in those markets *into which* resources are being shifted and prices tend to increase in the markets *from which* resources are being moved. Eventually, as prices adjust, P equals MC in all markets simultaneously. Beyond the point at which $P = MC$ in all markets, no further reallocation of resources between markets can improve consumer welfare (assuming, of course, that all the other factors which influence welfare, such as the distribution of income, remain unchanged). The outcome in which $P = MC$ in all markets is allocatively efficient.

It follows that **allocative inefficiency** occurs when $P > MC$ or $P < MC$. For any given employment of resources and any initial distribution of income and wealth amongst the population, total consumer welfare can increase if resources are reallocated from markets where $P < MC$ into those where $P > MC$, until allocative efficiency is achieved when $P = MC$ in all markets.

> **KEY TERM**
>
> **allocative inefficiency:** occurs when it is *possible* to improve overall economic welfare by reallocating resources between industries or markets. Resource allocation is allocatively inefficient when price is less than or greater than marginal cost in each and every market in the economy.

CASE STUDY 6.1

Microsoft's pricing policy, allocative efficiency and resource allocation

Economists often judge the monopoly power of a firm by the extent to which the price of the product is above marginal cost. The greater the gap between the marginal cost of production and the price, they argue, the greater the monopoly power. They also argue that when prices exceed marginal costs, economic inefficiency and resource misallocation occur.

It can readily be conceded that the price of Windows, whether $40 or $89, is substantially above the marginal cost of producing an extra copy of Windows, and that this makes Microsoft's operating system very profitable. The marginal cost of producing and supplying one extra copy of Windows is very close to zero, but the price charged must be higher so that Microsoft can recover the very significant development cost of Windows. Much of the price of a copy of Windows is unrelated to the marginal cost of producing

Microsoft's Redmond campus

an extra copy. But the price is still substantially below the price Microsoft could and would charge if it had the vast monopoly power the US Justice Department has claimed Microsoft possesses.

Follow-up questions
1 Explain the meaning of marginal cost.
2 Explain the statement: 'Much of the price of a copy of Windows is unrelated to the marginal cost of producing an extra copy.'

Dynamic efficiency

All the forms of efficiency so far considered are examples of **static efficiency**, i.e. efficiency measured at a particular point in time. By contrast, **dynamic efficiency** measures improvements in technical and productive efficiency that occur over time. Improvements in dynamic efficiency result from the introduction of better methods of producing existing products, including firms' ability to benefit to a greater extent from economies of scale and also from developing and marketing completely new products. In both cases, invention, innovation and research and development (R&D) improve dynamic efficiency. (**Invention** refers to advancements in pure science, whereas **innovation** is the application of scientific developments to production.)

Perfect competition and economic efficiency

Figure 6.5 shows the long-run equilibrium of a perfectly competitive firm. The diagram clearly shows that a perfectly competitive firm achieves both productive and allocative efficiency in the long run, provided there are no economies of scale. The firm is productively efficient because it produces the optimum output at the lowest point on the ATC curve, and it is allocatively efficient because $P = MC$. (Strictly,

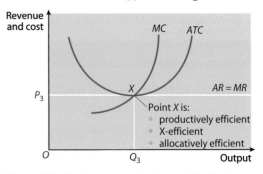

Figure 6.5 In the long run a perfectly competitive firm is productively, allocatively and X-efficient

I should qualify this conclusion by stating that the firm is allocatively efficient only if *all* markets in the economy are perfectly competitive and in long-run equilibrium, which means that every firm in every market is producing where $P = MC$.)

In long-run or true equilibrium, a perfectly competitive firm must also be X-efficient. The reason is simple. If the firm is X-inefficient, producing at a level of unit costs above its ATC curve, the firm could not make normal profits in the long run. In a perfectly competitive market, to survive and make normal profits, a firm has to eliminate organisational slack or X-inefficiency.

Monopoly and economic efficiency

In contrast to perfect competition — and once again assuming an absence of economies of scale — monopoly equilibrium is both productively and allocatively inefficient. Figure 6.6 shows that at the profit-maximising level of output Q_1, the monopolist's average costs are above the minimum level and that $P > MC$. Thus, compared to perfect competition, a monopoly produces too low an output which it sells at too high a price.

The absence of competitive pressures, which in perfect competition serve to eliminate supernormal profit, means that a monopoly is also likely to be X-inefficient, incurring average costs at a point such as X which is above the average cost curve. A monopoly may be able to survive, perfectly happily and enjoying an 'easy life', incurring unnecessary production costs and making satisfactory rather than maximum profits. This is because **barriers to entry** protect monopolies. As a result, the absence or weakness of competitive forces means there is no mechanism in monopoly to eliminate organisational slack.

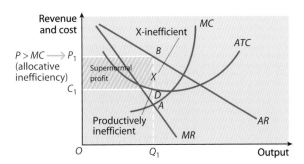

Figure 6.6 A monopoly is productively and allocatively inefficient, and it is likely to be X-inefficient

Natural monopoly and economies of scale

On the basis of the above analysis, it seems we can conclude that perfect competition is both productively and allocatively efficient whereas monopoly is neither. Monopoly is also likely to be X-inefficient. However, the conclusion that perfect competition is productively more efficient than monopoly depends on an assumption that there are no economies of scale. When substantial economies of scale are possible in an industry, monopoly may be more productively efficient than competition.

Figure 6.7 illustrates a natural monopoly where, because of limited market size, there is insufficient room in the market for more than one firm benefiting from full economies of scale. The monopoly may of course be producing above the lowest point on short-run average cost curve $SRATC_N$, hence exhibiting a degree of productive inefficiency. However, *all* points on $SRATC_N$ incur lower unit costs — and are productively *more* efficient — than any point on $SRATC_1$, which is the relevant cost curve for each firm if the monopoly is broken into a number of smaller competitive enterprises.

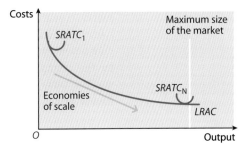

Figure 6.7 The justification of monopoly when economies of scale are possible

Dynamic efficiency in monopoly

Under certain circumstances, monopolies may also be more *dynamically efficient* than a perfectly competitive firm. Protected by entry barriers, a monopoly earns monopoly profit without facing the threat that the profit disappears when new firms enter the market. This allows an innovating monopoly to enjoy, in the form of monopoly profit, the fruits of successful R&D and product development. By contrast, in perfect competition, there is little or no incentive to innovate because other firms can free-ride and gain costless access to the results of any successful research. This argument justifies patent legislation, which grants a firm the right to exploit the monopoly position created by innovation for a number of years before the patent expires.

However, there is a counter-argument that monopoly reduces rather than promotes innovation and dynamic efficiency. Protected from competitive pressures, as I have noted, a monopoly may *profit-satisfice* rather than *profit-maximise*, content with satisfactory profits and an easy life.

Evaluating perfect competition and monopoly in terms of economic welfare

In order to analyse how market structures affect economic welfare, I must first explain the concepts of **consumer surplus** and **producer surplus**. These are both measures of **economic welfare**, as their names imply respectively for consumers and firms. Both are illustrated in Figure 6.8.

Consumer surplus is the difference between the *maximum price* a consumer is prepared to pay and the *actual price* he or she need pay. In a competitive market such as Figure 6.8 (a), the total consumer surplus enjoyed by all the consumers in the market is measured by the triangular area P_1EA. Consumer welfare increases whenever consumer surplus increases, for example when market prices fall. Conversely, however, higher prices reduce consumer surplus and welfare.

KEY TERMS

consumer surplus: a measure of the economic welfare enjoyed by consumers: surplus utility received over and above the price paid for a good.

producer surplus: a measure of the economic welfare enjoyed by firms or producers: the difference between the price a firm succeeds in charging and the minimum price it would be prepared to accept.

economic welfare: human happiness or utility.

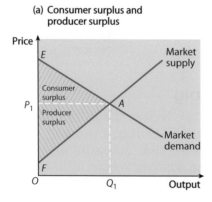

(a) Consumer surplus and producer surplus

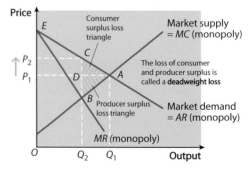

(b) How the formation of a monopoly results in a loss of economic welfare

Figure 6.8 How monopoly reduces economic welfare

Producer surplus, which is a measure of producers' welfare, is the difference between the *minimum price* a firm is prepared to charge for a good and the *actual price* charged. In Figure 6.8 (a), the producer surplus enjoyed by all the firms in the market is measured by the triangular area FP_1A.

Figure 6.8 (b) illustrates what happens to economic welfare when monopoly replaces perfect competition (again, assuming there are no economies of scale). Market equilibrium in perfect competition is determined at point A; output is Q_1 and price is P_1. However, monopoly equilibrium is determined at point B where $MR = MC$. (*Note that the marginal cost curve in monopoly is the same curve as market supply in perfect competition.*) The diagram illustrates the standard case against monopoly, namely that compared to perfect competition, monopoly restricts output (to Q_2) and raises price (to P_2).

But I can take the analysis one stage further and investigate how consumer surplus and producer surplus (and hence economic welfare) are affected. If a monopoly raises the price from P_1 to P_2 it gains the consumer surplus equal to the rectangular area P_1P_2CD. This means that producer surplus (in the form of monopoly profit) increases at the expense of consumer surplus. Over and above this transfer, however, there is a net loss of economic welfare caused by the fact that the amount bought and sold falls to Q_2. The welfare loss or **deadweight loss** is shown by the two shaded triangular areas in Figure 6.8 (b), which respectively depict the loss of consumer surplus (the top triangle) and the loss of producer surplus (the bottom triangle).

Consumer sovereignty and producer sovereignty

Arguably, perfect competition has the advantage of promoting **consumer sovereignty**, in the sense that the goods and services produced are those that consumers have voted for when spending the pounds in their pockets. When consumer sovereignty exists, the 'consumer is king'. (However, the extent to which consumer choice would exist in a perfectly competitive world is extremely limited. All the firms in a particular market would sell identical goods at an identical price, namely the ruling market price.) Firms and industries that produce goods other than those for which consumers are prepared to pay, do not survive in perfect competition.

By contrast, a monopoly may enjoy **producer sovereignty**. The goods and services available for consumers to buy are determined by the monopolist rather than by consumer preferences expressed in the market place. Even if producer sovereignty is not exercised on a 'take-it-or-leave-it' basis by a monopoly, the monopolist may still possess sufficient market power to manipulate consumer wants through such marketing devices as persuasive advertising. In these situations, the 'producer is king'.

Why firms like to become monopolies

Economists generally regard perfect competition as more desirable than monopoly. However, the desirable properties of perfect competition (namely economic efficiency, welfare maximisation and consumer sovereignty) do not result from any assumption that businesspeople or entrepreneurs in competitive industries are more highly motivated or public-spirited than monopolists. Economic theory assumes that everyone is motivated by self-interest and by self-interest alone. This applies just as much to firms in competitive markets as it does to monopolies. Entrepreneurs in competitive industries would very much like to become monopolists, both to gain an easier life and also to make bigger profits. Indeed, from a firm's point of view, successful competition means eliminating competition and becoming a monopoly. But in perfect markets, market forces (Adam Smith referred to the *invisible hand* of the market) and the absence of barriers to entry and exit prevent this happening.

Imagine, for example, a situation in which a firm in a perfectly competitive industry makes a technical breakthrough which reduces production costs. For a short time the firm can make supernormal profits. But because in perfect competition, perfect market information is available to all firms, other firms within the market and new entrants attracted to the market can also enjoy the lower production costs. A new long-run equilibrium will soon be brought about — at the lower level of costs resulting from the breakthrough — with all firms once again making normal profits only.

Ultimately, of course, consumers benefit from lower prices brought about by technical progress and the forces of competition, but it is market forces, and not some socially benign motive or public spirit assumed on the part of entrepreneurs, that accounts for the optimality of perfect competition as a market structure.

How competitive is perfect competition?

Although perfect competition is an abstract and unreal market structure, it is interesting to consider the forms competition might take in a perfectly competitive market economy. The first point to note is that price competition, in the form of price wars or price-cutting by individual firms, would not take place. In perfect competition, all firms are passive price-takers, able to sell all the output they produce at the ruling market price determined in the market as a whole. In this situation, firms cannot gain sales or market share by price-cutting. Other forms of competition, involving the use of advertising, packaging, brand-imaging or the provision of after-sales service to differentiate a firm's product from those of its competitors, simply destroy the conditions of perfect competition. These are the forms of competition which are prevalent, together with price competition, in the imperfectly competitive markets of the real economy in which we live.

So the only form of competition, both available to firms and also compatible with maintaining the conditions of perfect competition, is cost-cutting competition. Cost-cutting competition is likely in perfect competition because each firm has an incentive to reduce costs in order to make supernormal profit. But even the existence of cost-cutting competition in a perfect market can be questioned. Why should firms finance research into cost-cutting technical progress when they know that other firms have instant access to all market information and that any supernormal profits resulting from successful cost-cutting can only be temporary?

Think also of the nature of competition in a perfect market, from the perspective of a typical consumer. The choice is simultaneously very broad and very narrow. The consumer has the doubtful luxury of maximum choice in terms of the number of firms or suppliers from which to purchase a product. Yet each firm is supplying an identical good or service at exactly the same price. In this sense, there is no choice at all in perfect competition.

SUMMARY

- Economists evaluate perfect competition and monopoly using efficiency and welfare criteria.
- The main efficiency concepts are technical efficiency, productive efficiency, X-efficiency, allocative efficiency and static and dynamic efficiency.
- Providing we ignore dynamic efficiency considerations, perfect competition wins over monopoly in terms of being productively and allocatively efficient, and also X-efficient.
- However, monopoly can be justified by dynamic considerations, particularly through its ability to reduce prices over time as a result of benefiting from economies of scale and innovation in new products and methods of production.
- By restricting output and raising prices, monopolies transfer consumer surplus to producer surplus, and also trigger a net welfare loss.

Exam-style questions

1 Explain the main efficiency concepts economists use when analysing and evaluating perfect competition and monopoly. (15 marks)

2 Explain how economies of scale and technical progress affect economic efficiency. (15 marks)

3 'Increasing consumer surplus is always good but increasing producer surplus is always bad.' Evaluate this statement. (25 marks)

4 Evaluate the view that perfect competition is always preferable to monopoly. (25 marks)

Extra resources to help you revise are available online at www.hodderplus.co.uk/philipallan

Chapter 7

Oligopoly and concentrated markets

Almost all real-world markets are imperfectly competitive, lying between the extremes of monopoly and perfect competition. Imperfect competition is a wide-ranging term, covering all market structures from duopoly (two firms only in a market) to highly competitive markets which are very close to being perfectly competitive. This chapter explains one of the most important forms of imperfect competition: oligopoly. I shall look first at competitive oligopoly, in which a relatively small number of firms compete against each other. I shall then examine conditions in which competitive oligopolists may be tempted to collude or cooperate with each other, and form cartels.

LEARNING OUTCOMES

This chapter will:
- explain how oligopoly is a form of imperfect competition
- use a concentration ratio to define oligopoly in terms of market structure
- define oligopoly in terms of market behaviour or conduct
- distinguish between competitive and collusive oligopoly
- apply the kinked demand curve theory to illustrate competitive oligopoly
- explain a cartel as a form of collusive oligopoly
- introduce game theory as a way of modelling oligopoly

WHAT YOU SHOULD ALREADY KNOW

As oligopoly and concentrated markets are not in the AS specification, you are unlikely to be familiar with these concepts, except to the extent that brief mention of oligopoly has been made in some of the earlier chapters of this book.

Imperfect competition

I have mentioned in previous chapters that **perfect competition** does not actually exist in real-world economies. The label itself is extremely misleading, since the word *perfect* suggests a state of competition that cannot be bettered. This in turn implies that any form of competition that does not meet the six conditions of perfect competition must be somehow second rate or inferior. This implication is reinforced by the fact that all market structures lying between the extremes of perfect competition and monopoly are described by economists as *imperfectly* competitive.

Just as perfect competition is better described as *unrealistic* competition, so **imperfect competition** could more

KEY TERM

imperfect competition: describes the range of market structures lying between perfect competition and pure monopoly.

accurately be called *realistic* competition. Imperfect competition covers a wide range of real-world market structures. At one end of the spectrum are markets such as the stock exchange that approximate to perfect competition, without nevertheless meeting all six of the defining criteria. At the other extreme is **duopoly**, which is the market structure closest to pure monopoly. Duopoly is a special case of **oligopoly**. In a pure duopoly, there are just two firms in the market, each with considerable monopoly power. Oligopoly is a more general term, covering markets where there are several firms, which I define in more detail in the next two sections of this chapter.

> **KEY TERMS**
>
> **duopoly:** describes a market in which there are two dominant firms.
>
> **oligopoly:** an imperfectly competitive market containing only a few firms.

Oligopoly and market structure

To recap, **market structure** is defined according to the number of firms in a market. Oligopoly, which is a market structure in which there is a relatively small number of firms, is sometimes called *imperfect competition amongst the few*. Oligopolistic firms are not pure monopolies, but they possess monopoly power. You must avoid confusing *monopoly power* with *monopoly*. Pure monopoly is a precise market structure, but firms in all imperfectly competitive markets can exercise a greater or lesser degree of monopoly power: for example, by imposing **entry barriers** that enable firms to raise the price of a good. Whenever firms exercise **producer sovereignty** in this way, monopoly power exists.

Concentration ratios

Concentration ratios provide a good indicator of oligopolistic market structures. For example, a five-firm concentration ratio shows the percentage of output in an industry produced by the five largest firms in the industry. The five-firm concentration ratio in the UK supermarket industry in March 2013 can be calculated from the market share data shown in Figure 7.1. The five-firm concentration ratio of 82.1 indicates that the supermarket industry is an oligopoly.

> **KEY TERM**
>
> **concentration ratio:** measures the market share of the biggest firms in the market.

Oligopoly and market behaviour or conduct

However, oligopoly is best defined, not by market structure or the number of firms in the market, but by **market conduct**, or the behaviour of the firms within the market. An oligopolistic firm affects its rivals through its price and output decisions, but its own profit can also be affected by how rivals behave and react to the firm's decisions. Suppose, for example, the firm reduces its price in order to increase market share and boost profit. Whether the price reduction increases the firm's profit depends on the likely reactions of

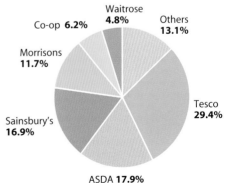

Figure 7.1 Market shares in the UK supermarket industry, March 2013

the other firms. So, when deciding whether or not to lower its price, the firm must make assumptions about likely responses by other firms. Competitive oligopoly displays reactive market behaviour and *strategic interdependence* amongst firms.

> **EXAM TIP**
>
> For many purposes, oligopoly is better defined by market behaviour or conduct than by the number of firms in the market or by concentration ratios.

Perfect and imperfect oligopoly

Perfect oligopoly exists when the oligopolists produce a uniform or homogeneous product such as petrol. One brand of petrol is really a perfect substitute for any other brand, though a petrol company such as Shell may use advertising to try to persuade motorists that Shell petrol is different from and better than other brands. By contrast, **imperfect oligopoly** occurs when the products produced by the firms are by their nature differentiated and imperfect substitutes: for example, automobiles.

Competitive oligopoly

Competitive oligopoly exists when the rival firms are *interdependent* in the sense that they must take account of the reactions of one another when forming a market strategy, but *independent* in the sense that they decide their market strategies without cooperation or collusion. The existence of uncertainty is a characteristic of competitive oligopoly; a firm can never be completely certain of how rivals will react to its marketing strategy. If the firm raises its price, will the rivals follow suit or will they hold their prices steady in the hope of gaining sales and market share?

> **EXAM TIP**
>
> Examination questions may ask you to explain why interdependence and uncertainty exist in markets dominated by a few firms. Oligopoly itself may not be mentioned in the question.

The kinked demand curve theory

The kinked demand curve theory can be used to illustrate how a competitive oligopolist may be affected by rivals' reaction to its price and output decisions. The theory was originally developed to explain alleged price rigidity and an absence of price wars in oligopolistic markets.

Suppose an oligopolist initially produces output Q_1 in Figure 7.2, selling this output at price P_1. In order to anticipate how sales might change following a price change, firms need to know the position and shape of the demand and revenue curves for their products. But in imperfectly competitive markets, firms lack accurate information about these curves, particularly at outputs significantly different from those currently being produced. This means that the demand curve or *AR* curve in Figure 7.2 is not necessarily the correct or *actual* demand curve for the oligopolist's output. Instead, it represents the firm's *estimate* of how demand changes when the firm changes the price it is charging.

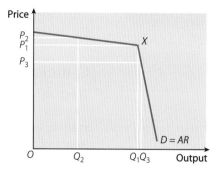

Figure 7.2 The kinked demand curve

When *increasing* price from P_1 to P_2, the oligopolist expects rivals to react by keeping their own prices stable and not following suit. By holding their prices steady, rivals try to gain profit and market share at the firm's expense. This means that the oligopolist expects demand to be *relatively elastic* in response to a price increase. The rise in price from P_1 to P_2 is likely to result in a *more than proportionate fall in demand* from Q_1 to Q_2.

Conversely, when *cutting* its price from P_1 to P_3, the oligopolist expects rivals to react in a very different way, namely by following suit immediately with a matching price cut. In this situation, because the market demand curve for the products of all the firms slopes downward, each firm will benefit from *some* increase in demand. However, the oligopolist fails to gain sales from rivals *within* the market. This means the oligopolist expects demand to be less elastic, and possibly *relatively inelastic* in response to a price cut. The fall in price from P_1 to P_3 may result in a *less than proportionate increase in demand* from Q_1 to Q_3. The oligopolist therefore expects rivals to react *asymmetrically* when price is raised or lowered.

In Figure 7.2, the oligopolist's initial price and output of P_1 and Q_1 intersect at point X, or at the kink at the junction of two demand curves of different elasticity, each reflecting a different assumption about how rivals may react to a change in price. In this situation, the oligopolist fears that both a price increase and a price cut may reduce total profit. Given this fear, the best policy may be to leave price unchanged.

The theory provides a second reason why prices may tend to be stable in oligopoly. As Figure 7.3 illustrates, there is a vertical section in the *MR* curve at output Q_1 shown by the distance B to C. This links the marginal revenue curves associated respectively with the relatively elastic and relatively less elastic demand (or average revenue) curves.

Suppose initially the firm's marginal cost curve is MC_1, intersecting the *MR* curve at point A, which is positioned in the middle of the vertical section. The diagram shows that the *MC* curve can rise or fall within the range of the vertical section of the *MR* curve, without altering the profit-maximising output Q_1 or price P_1. But if marginal costs rise above MC_2 at point B or fall below MC_3 at point C, the profit-maximising output changes. In either of these circumstances, the oligopolist would have to set a different price to maximise profits, providing of course that the *AR* curve accurately measures demand for the firm's product at different prices. Nevertheless, the oligopolist's selling price remains stable at P_1 as long as the marginal cost curve lies between MC_2 and MC_3.

Figure 7.3 The kinked demand curve and stable prices in oligopoly

The result is that the oligopolist's price remains stable, despite quite considerable changes in marginal costs.

Criticisms of the kinked demand curve theory

There are a number of weaknesses in the theory I have just described. Although at first sight it is attractive as a neat and apparently plausible explanation of price stability in conditions of oligopoly, few economists now accept the kinked demand theory of oligopoly pricing.

> **EXAM TIP**
>
> Students often wrongly believe that the kinked demand curve provides a complete theory of oligopoly. It is actually a very doubtful theory, but it does illustrate how oligopolists are interdependent and affected by uncertainty.

First, it is an incomplete theory, since it does not explain *how* and *why* a firm chooses in the first place to be at point *X*. Second, the evidence provided by the pricing decisions of real-world firms gives little support to the theory. Competitive oligopolists seldom respond to price changes in the manner assumed in the kinked demand curve theory. It is more reasonable to expect a firm to test the market, i.e. raise or lower its selling price to see if rivals react in the manner expected. If rivals do not, then the firm must surely revise its estimate of the shape of the demand curve facing it. Research has shown fairly conclusively that oligopoly prices tend to be stable or sticky when demand conditions change in a predictable or cyclical way, but that oligopolists usually raise or lower prices quickly and by significant amounts, both when production costs change substantially, and when unexpected shifts in demand occur.

Other aspects of pricing in oligopolistic markets

The ways in which prices are set can be quite complicated in oligopolistic markets. Some of the ways in which prices are set are explained below.

Cost-plus pricing

Cost-plus pricing, also known as **mark-up pricing** and **full-cost pricing**, is the most common pricing procedure used by firms in imperfectly competitive markets. Cost-plus pricing means that a firm sets its selling price by adding a standard percentage profit margin to average or unit costs:

$$P = AFC + AVC + \text{profit margin}$$

When customers are captive and willing to pay high prices, the profit mark-up can be high; for fashionable goods that may quickly go out of style, often over 100%. But when markets are more competitive, firms can find it much more difficult to charge a mark-up. Indeed in a very competitive market, the mark-up may be limited to a size which gives firms normal profit only, which then deters the entrance of new firms into the market. (See my later reference to limit pricing.)

EXAM TIP

Firms in real-world markets seldom use the $MR = MC$ rule when setting prices. They are much more likely to undertake cost-plus pricing. The $MR = MC$ rule is best regarded as a necessary condition for profit maximisation rather than as a decision-making rule.

Price parallelism

Price parallelism occurs when there are identical prices and price movements within an industry or market. Price parallelism can be caused by two different sets of circumstances, which make it difficult to decide whether the market is highly competitive or collusive. On the one hand, price parallelism can occur in a very competitive market, resembling perfect competition, where firms all charge a ruling market price determined by demand and supply in the market as a whole. But on the other hand, price parallelism results from price leadership in tightly oligopolistic industries, where overt or tacit price collusion occurs.

Price leadership

Because overt collusive agreements to fix the market price, such as cartel agreements, are usually illegal, imperfectly competitive firms often use less formal or tacit ways to coordinate their pricing decisions. An example of covert collusion is **price leadership**, which occurs when one firm becomes the market leader and other firms in the industry follow its pricing example.

Limit pricing

When natural barriers to market entry are low or non-existent, incumbent firms (i.e. firms already in the market) may set low prices, known as limit prices, to deter new firms from entering the market. Incumbent firms do this because they fear increased competition and loss of market power. With limit pricing, firms already in the market sacrifice short-run profit maximisation in order to maximise long-run profits, achieved through deterring the entry of new firms.

Should limit pricing be regarded as an example of a competitive pricing strategy, which reduces prices and the supernormal profits enjoyed by the established firms in the market? Or is limit pricing basically anti-competitive and best regarded as an unjustifiable restrictive practice? The answer probably depends on circumstances, but when limit pricing extends into predatory pricing, there is a much clearer case that such a pricing strategy is anti-competitive and against consumers' interest.

Predatory pricing

Whereas limit pricing deters market entry, successful **predatory pricing** removes recent entrants to the market. Predatory pricing occurs when an established or incumbent firm deliberately sets prices below costs to force new market entrants out of business. Once the new entrants have left the market, the established firm may decide to restore prices to their previous levels.

Price discrimination

Price discrimination involves firms charging different prices to different customers based on differences in the customers' ability and willingness to pay. Those customers who are prepared to pay more are charged a higher price than those who are only willing to pay a lower price. In the main form of price discrimination, the different prices charged are not based on any differences in costs of production or supply. However, in one form of price discrimination, **bulk-buying**, consumers are charged lower prices than consumers purchasing smaller quantities of the good. When this happens, different costs of supply may be involved. Bulk purchases generally have lower average costs of production than smaller purchases.

KEY TERM

price discrimination: charging different prices to different customers with the prices based on different willingness to pay.

EXAM TIP

It is only usually necessary to learn about one form of price discrimination. You must also learn how to illustrate it on a diagram.

CASE STUDY 7.1

Newspapers and predatory pricing

In 1993, Rupert Murdoch, owner of one of Britain's most upmarket newspapers — The Times — and one of its most downmarket — the Sun — slashed the price of The Times from 45p to 30p, undercutting the prices charged by the UK's other 'quality' newspapers.

Journalists, media analysts and especially the rival Daily Telegraph, the largest-selling broadsheet in England, waited anxiously to see what would happen next. They found out. Murdoch's plan was simple: lower the price and people will buy. Sure enough, The Times' circulation began climbing and that of others began falling. The Daily Telegraph, panicked at seeing its circulation dip below 1 million for the first time since the 1950s, quickly cut its price from 48p to 30p.

The Times immediately responded by putting a 20p price tag on its paper, a move the Daily Telegraph could not afford to follow. In fact, The Times couldn't have afforded its price cut if it had not been subsidised by Murdoch's vast media empire.

What exactly was Murdoch trying to do? To some, it was simple: he hoped to kill off his rivals. In an editorial

headlined, 'A Price War with Murder in its Sights', the Daily Mirror launched a full-page attack on Murdoch, asserting that he was practising nothing less than 'predatory pricing — selling his newspaper at a loss, at a figure that his rivals could not match'.

'Originally he wanted to prove that the newspaper market was price-sensitive', said a spokesperson for Murdoch's UK publishing company. 'People were saying it wasn't true that people bought newspapers based on price.'

But the Independent, another quality newspaper, which initially resisted cutting its price, did not believe Murdoch's aims were so benign. The Independent filed two complaints with the Office of Fair Trading (now merged into the Competition and Markets Authority), charging that The Times' price cuts were anticompetitive and amounted to predatory pricing. However, the OFT rejected both claims. Proof that even Murdoch couldn't maintain lower prices indefinitely was his decision a few months later to raise the Sun's price again.

Follow-up questions

1 Explain the difference between predatory pricing and limit pricing.
2 Do you believe that Rupert Murdoch's price cuts were anticompetitive and against the public interest? Justify your answer.

Perfect price discrimination

Perfect price discrimination occurs when a firm charges each customer the maximum price the customer is prepared to pay. With perfect price discrimination, which is technically known as first-degree price discrimination, consumers end up with zero consumer surplus — it has all been transferred to the seller of the good as extra profit. An outcome approaching perfect price discrimination occurs when potential customers haggle with street sellers about the price they are prepared to pay for the good.

If you go online you can watch the haggle scene in the Monty Python film, *The Life of Brian*, on YouTube at http://uk.youtube.com/watch?v=3n3LL338aGA

Indian bazaars provide prime examples of perfect price discrimination

Follow-up questions

1 Why do firms charge discriminatory prices?
2 Why are street sellers more likely to price discriminate than supermarket companies such as Tesco? Can you think of any ways in which supermarkets price discriminate?

A closer look at price discrimination

The case of two sub-markets or market segments

In Figure 7.4 a night club divides its market into male and female customers, each with a different elasticity of demand at each price of admission. At all the prices that could be charged for entry into the club, female demand is more elastic than male demand — indicating perhaps that women are less enthusiastic about the entertainment offered by the club. For both men and women, the downward-sloping demand curves in Figure 7.4 show average revenue (*AR*), but not marginal revenue (*MR*). In each case, the *MR* curve is twice as steep as the *AR* curve. The diagrams also assume that the marginal cost (*MC*) incurred when an extra person enters the club is always the same. This is shown by the horizontal *MC* curve.

Figure 7.4 Price discrimination when a firm charges different prices to two groups of customers

To maximise profit, *MR* must equal *MC* in both male and female sub-markets. As the diagrams show, this means that men pay a higher price for admission than women, namely P_M, with women paying the lower entry price of P_F. With the different prices being charged, Q_M males and Q_F females are allowed into the club. The point to note is that the different prices charged result from the different male and female price elasticities of demand. Profit is maximised when more price-sensitive female customers pay less to enter the club than the less sensitive males. Note that the *MR* received from the last man and woman admitted are the same. If this were not the case, the club could increase profit by changing the numbers of men and women admitted.

The conditions necessary for successful price discrimination

Successful price discrimination requires that the following conditions are met:

- It must be possible to identify different groups of customers or sub-markets for the product. This is possible when customers differ in their knowledge of the market or in their ability to shop around. Some customers may have special needs for a product and competition among oligopolists may vary in different parts of the market. In some geographical areas and for some products, a firm may face many competitors, whereas in other parts of the market the firm may be the sole supplier.
- At any particular price, the different groups of customers must have different elasticities of demand. Total profits can be maximised by charging a higher price in a market in which demand is less elastic.
- The markets must be separated to prevent seepage. Seepage takes place when customers buying at the lower price in one sub-market resell in another sub-market at a price which undercuts the oligopolist's own selling price in that market. In the European car market, car manufacturers have often charged higher prices for a vehicle in the UK market than in mainland Europe. Seepage has occurred when specialist car importers have bought cars on the Continent to resell in the British market, thereby undercutting the car manufacturers' recommended prices.

Why do firms price discriminate?

To understand why firms undertake price discrimination, I must re-introduce the concept of **consumer surplus** which I explained in the previous chapter. To remind you, consumer surplus, which is a measure of the economic welfare enjoyed by consumers, is the difference between the *maximum* price consumers are prepared to pay and the *actual* price they need pay. The greater the quantity of consumer surplus enjoyed by consumers, the greater their 'happiness' or economic welfare.

As Figures 7.5 and 7.6 illustrate, price discrimination allows firms to increase profit by taking consumer surplus away from consumers and converting it into extra monopoly profit or supernormal profit. Figures 7.5 (a) and (b) are basically the same as Figure 7.4, but Figure 7.5 (c) has been added to show the combined market with the male and female average revenue curves added together. The male and female marginal revenue curves have also been added together. Note that for the combined market (but *not* the male and female sub-markets considered separately), the marginal cost curve slopes upward, depicting the impact of the law of diminishing returns.

Figure 7.5 Price discrimination and the transfer of consumer surplus

In the absence of price discrimination, all consumers pay the same price, namely P_{CM} shown in Figure 7.5 (c). Without price discrimination, consumer surplus is shown by the shaded area (labelled 1) above P_{CM} in Figure 7.5 (c). But with price discrimination, when male customers are charged price P_M and female customers P_F, consumer surplus falls to equal the shaded areas labelled 3 and 2 in Figures 7.5 (a) and (b). The firm's profit has increased by transferring consumer surplus from consumers to the producer. **Producer welfare** (or producer surplus) has increased at the expense of **consumer welfare** (or consumer surplus).

Figure 7.6 illustrates a situation in which *all* the consumer surplus is transferred into producer surplus or producer welfare. Every customer is charged the maximum price

Figure 7.6 Price discrimination: the limiting case, when each consumer is charged the maximum price he or she is prepared to pay

he or she is prepared to pay. Figure 7.6 is basically the same diagram used in Chapter 5 to show monopoly equilibrium. In the absence of price discrimination, the firm produces the level of output Q_1 where $MR = MC$ and all customers are charged the price P_1. Supernormal profit is shown by the rectangle C_1P_1AB, and consumer surplus by the triangular area P_1ZA.

Now consider what happens when the firm charges each customer the maximum price he or she is prepared to pay. Customer Q_V depicted in the diagram is charged price P_V, customer Q_W is charged P_W, and so on. In this situation, there may be as many prices as there are customers. Because each customer is paying the maximum price he or she is prepared to pay, all the consumer surplus is transferred away from consumers to the firm, thereby boosting monopoly or oligopoly profit.

> **EXAM TIP**
>
> Make sure you understand why firms price discriminate and the necessary conditions for successful price discrimination, and that you can apply the concept of consumer surplus to price discrimination. You must also be able to explain how some consumers (often the poor), as well as producers, can benefit from price discrimination.

Can consumers benefit from price discrimination?

Price discrimination leads to a loss of consumer surplus or consumer welfare. Firms exploit producer sovereignty and monopoly power, and charge *most* consumers higher prices than would be charged in the absence of price discrimination. For these reasons price discrimination is usually regarded as undesirable.

Nevertheless, *some* consumers (who may also be the poorest consumers) can benefit from price discrimination. Each time the firm sells to one more customer, total sales revenue rises by the extra units sold multiplied by the price the customer pays. Because different customers are charged different prices, charging a high (or low) price to one customer does not affect the prices charged to other customers. In the absence of price discrimination, the firm's AR curve continues to be the demand curve the firm faces, with the firm's MR curve located below the demand (and AR) curve. But when each customer is charged the maximum price he or she is prepared to pay, the demand curve now functions as the firm's MR curve. It is no longer possible to locate an AR curve. The profit-maximising level of output, where $MR = MC$, shifts to Q_2, located at point Y in Figure 7.6. Customers who would refuse to buy the good at price P_1 buy the extra output because the prices they are charged are lower than P_1. As a result, most consumers end up paying a price which is higher than P_1 (the equilibrium price in the absence of price discrimination), but some consumers pay a lower price. The lowest of all the prices charged is P_2, which is the price charged to the marginal, and perhaps the poorest, customer.

Consider also a situation in which a firm can't make enough profit to stay in business unless some consumer surplus is taken from consumers and transferred to the producer. Market provision of healthcare by a doctor in an isolated village or very small town is an example. When charging the same price to all her patients, a doctor can't earn enough income to continue to provide the service. Without an increase in income, the doctor will move to a larger city and local medical care will no longer be available in the village. But with price discrimination, the rich pay a higher price than the poor. Everybody gets some benefit, and a needed service is provided.

Prices involving cross-subsidy

Many students confuse *price discrimination* with *cross-subsidy*, but the two concepts are completely different. In the example of price discrimination, the marginal cost incurred by the firm was the same for all customers, but the firm charged different prices based on customers' different willingness to pay. By contrast, when cross-subsidy takes place, *all* customers pay the same price, but the marginal cost of supplying the good varies between different customers.

For example, the Royal Mail charges the same price for all first-class letters of standard weight and size, whether posted to a local or to a distant part of the UK. For local letters the marginal cost incurred by the Royal Mail delivering an extra letter is less than the price charged, but for letters delivered over a long distance, MC exceeds P. Customers posting local letters (for which $P > MC$) cross-subsidise letters mailed over greater distances (for which $P < MC$). The Post Office uses profits made on the former group to subsidise losses borne on letters posted over longer distances.

As price does not equal marginal cost, cross-subsidy results in allocative inefficiency. For firms, cross-subsidy is administratively convenient and it can maximise consumer goodwill, even though it fails to maximise profits. From the public interest point of view, cross-subsidy is sometimes justified for social or regional policy reasons — for example, the better off cross-subsidise the poor, or customers in the more prosperous parts of the UK cross-subsidise those living in depressed regions. The provision of a universal service in which the same price is charged to people wherever they live in the UK also involves cross-subsidy.

EXAM TIP

Firms may cross-subsidise because they want to charge administratively simple prices. Make sure you don't confuse cross-subsidy and price discrimination. Note that cross-subsidy promotes allocative inefficiency.

Marginal cost pricing and off-peak pricing

It is often argued that, to avoid cross-subsidy and to improve allocative efficiency, firms should charge customers different prices which reflect the marginal cost of providing the good or service consumed. This is called **marginal cost pricing**. In perfectly competitive markets, where firms would be passive price-takers, the market mechanism would automatically ensure that $P = MC$. But market pressures do not operate in this way in imperfectly competitive markets where $P > MC$.

Nevertheless, when demand varies on a daily, weekly or seasonal basis, firms operating in imperfect markets may charge off-peak prices, which are a special case of marginal cost pricing. Transport, energy and tourist industries provide good examples. Consider the demand for electricity, which is higher in winter than in summer. Suppose demand for electricity increases in winter months. To meet this demand, power station companies must invest in new fixed capacity. This is a long-run marginal cost. By contrast, the marginal cost involved when meeting a surge in off-peak demand in the summer months is much lower. It is the short-run marginal cost of additional raw materials or energy supplies and labour. In summer, the electricity industry meets an increase in seasonal demand by using existing fixed capacity, which would otherwise lie idle in the off-peak months.

Low off-peak prices and high peak prices are justified on the basis of differences in long-run and short-run marginal costs when providing a good or service at different times of day or year. By encouraging consumers to shift demand from the peak period of demand, off-peak pricing can achieve a better or more productively efficient utilisation of fixed capital throughout the day or year.

Non-price competition in oligopoly

As I have noted, the theory of the kinked demand curve provides a possible explanation of stable prices in oligopolistic markets. However, there is a much simpler explanation for the absence of price competition. Realising that a price-war will be self-defeating for all the firms involved, firms may tacitly agree not to indulge in aggressive price competition as a means of gaining extra profits or market share at the expense of each other. In the absence of keen price competition, oligopolistic firms are therefore likely to undertake various forms of **non-price competition**. These include:

> **EXAM TIP**
>
> Exam questions might ask you to explain why firms use various forms of non-price competition, and to describe and explain some of these forms, such as persuasive advertising.

- marketing competition, including obtaining exclusive outlets such as tied public houses and petrol stations through which breweries and oil companies sell their products
- the use of persuasive advertising, product differentiation, brand-imaging, packaging, fashion, style and design
- quality competition, including the provision of point-of-sale service and after-sale service

Barriers to entry

Monopolies and firms in oligopolistic markets use **entry barriers** to protect the firm's position in the market. There are two main types of entry barrier: natural barriers and artificial or man-made barriers.

> **EXAM TIP**
>
> Exam questions may ask how entry barriers protect oligopolists and monopolists, and influence the behaviour of firms in protected markets.

Natural barriers

Natural barriers, which are also known as **innocent barriers**, include economies of scale and indivisibilities. **Economies of scale** mean that established large firms produce at a lower long-run average cost, and are more productively efficient, than smaller new entrants, who become stranded on high-cost short-run average cost curves.

Indivisibilities prevent certain goods and services being produced in plant below a certain size. Indivisibilities occur in metal smelting and oil refining industries.

Artificial barriers

Artificial or man-made entry barriers, which are also known as **strategic barriers**, are the result of deliberate action by incumbent firms to prevent new firms from entering the market. Strategic entry barriers include:

- **Patents.** Incumbent firms acquire patents for all the variants of a product that they develop.
- **Limit pricing and predatory pricing.** As I have already explained, large firms often set limit prices to deter entry by new firms. Some firms also use predatory pricing to kill off small firms which have already entered the market. Predatory pricing is generally illegal, but a large firm may feel it can get away with it, as it is difficult to prove that predatory pricing has taken place.

CASE STUDY 7.3

Independent schools' cartel busted

In 2003, 50 top UK private schools, including Eton, Winchester and Rugby, were investigated by the UK competition authorities for restricting competition by exchanging information on the fees they charge, and in effect price-fixing. The investigation by the Office of Fair Trading (OFT), which has since been merged into the Competition and Markets Authority (CMA), was prompted by a student who hacked into his school's financial records and leaked the documents to the press.

Evidence researched by the Halifax showed that school fees had risen by more than three times the rate of inflation over the 20 years prior to 2003.

The OFT investigation focused on fee rises between 2001 and 2004 and found that in each year, schools swapped details of their intended fees. Sevenoaks School in Kent then 'collated that information and circulated it, in the form of tables, to the schools concerned. The information in the tables was updated and circulated between four and six times each year as schools developed their fee-increase proposals in the course of their annual budgetary processes'.

Bursars have freely admitted that they used to meet regularly and talk about fees, but they maintain that this swapping of information did not amount to a concerted plot to push up fees.

Speaking before the OFT findings were announced, Stephen Taylor, the bursar of a leading private school, said that, rather than colluding to drive up fees, the aim was to keep them down. He said that as the schools were facing similar costs, the bursars would swap ideas on the cheapest solutions.

The OFT decided that the 50 schools should pay fines of just £10,000 each as an acknowledgement that they broke competition law by exchanging details of proposed fee increases and other sensitive price information. The fines are far below the sums that the OFT could have levied. The schools breached the Competition Act 1998 by colluding against parents to fix their fees over three academic years between 2001 and 2004.

Bursars at the schools routinely swapped e-mails containing sensitive cost and price information as they prepared their fee recommendations to governors. One e-mail, containing details of fee increases at 20 other schools, was sent to Sir Andrew Large, deputy governor of the Bank of England and the warden of Winchester College. Sent by Bill Organ, Winchester's then bursar, it read 'Confidential please, so we aren't accused of being a cartel'.

Follow-up questions

1 Why do economists usually think that cartel agreements are bad?

2 Access the CMA website and find the details of other alleged cartel agreements the Authority has investigated.

Cartel agreements and collusive oligopoly

The uncertainty facing competitive oligopolists can be reduced and perhaps eliminated by the rival firms forming a **cartel** agreement or **price ring**. In Figure 7.7, five firms jointly agree to charge a price to keep Firm E, which is the least efficient firm, in the market. In a competitive market, Firm E would have to reduce costs or go out of business. Cartel agreements enable inefficient firms to stay in business, while other more efficient members of the price ring enjoy supernormal profit. By protecting the inefficient and enabling firms to enjoy an easy life protected from competition, cartels display the disadvantages of monopoly (high prices and restriction of choice). However, this is without the benefits that monopoly can sometimes bring, namely economies of scale and improvements in dynamic efficiency.

KEY TERM

cartel: a collusive agreement by firms, usually to fix prices. Sometimes output may also be fixed.

EXAM TIP

Collusive or cooperative behaviour enables firms to reduce the uncertainty they face in imperfectly competitive markets. However, some forms of collusion, for example on joint product development or ensuring industry safety standards, are in the public interest.

Figure 7.7
A cartel or price ring

EXAM TIP

Joint-profit maximisation illustrates how firms can make more profit by colluding and restricting competition than by acting independently.

Although cartels can achieve a better outcome for all firms concerned, they are unlikely to be good for the consumer. For this reason, cartel agreements are usually illegal and judged by governments as being anti-competitive and against the public interest. Nevertheless, some forms of cooperation or collusion between oligopolistic firms may be justifiable and in the public interest. These include joint product development (such as the multi-purpose vehicles, the Ford Galaxy, Seat Alhambra and VW Sharan, jointly developed by Ford and VW), and cooperation to improve health and safety within the industry or to ensure that product and labour standards are maintained. Such examples of industry collaboration are normally deemed good, in contrast to price *collusion*, which is regarded as bad.

EXTENSION MATERIAL

Collusive oligopoly: joint-profit maximisation

Joint-profit maximisation, which is illustrated in Figure 7.8, occurs when a number of firms decide to act as a single monopolist, yet keeping their separate identities. The monopoly *MC* curve depicted in the right-hand side of the diagram is the sum of the identical *MC* curves of three firms (one of which is shown on the left of the diagram). The three firms share an output of 750 units, determined on the right of the diagram where the industry *MR* and *MC* curves intersect.

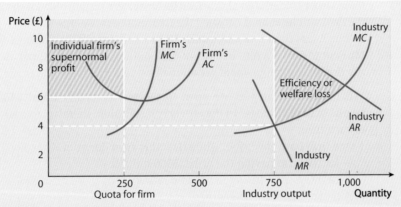

Figure 7.8 Joint-profit maximisation by members of a cartel

Each firm charges a price of £10, which, as the diagram shows, is the maximum price consumers are prepared to pay for 750 units of the good. The monopoly output of 750 units is well below 1,000 units, which would be the output if the industry were perfectly competitive. The shaded area in the right-hand panel shows the efficiency or welfare loss caused by the cartel raising the price to £10 and restricting output to 750 units. In this example, the members of the cartel split the 750 units equally, each firm producing 250 units. The shaded area on the left of the diagram shows the supernormal profit made by each firm.

The theory of joint-profit maximisation can be used to show how each member of the cartel has an incentive to cheat on the agreement. The marginal cost of producing the 250th unit of the good is only £4, yet for the firm (but not the whole industry) the marginal revenue received from selling one more unit is £10 (that is, the price set by the cartel). One member of the cartel can increase its profit at the expense of the other firms by secretly selling an output over and above its quota of 250 units at a price less than £10, but greater than the marginal cost incurred (£4). This is an example of a divergence between individual and collective interest. The firms' collective interest is to maintain the cartel so as to keep total sales down and the price up. But each firm can benefit by cheating on the agreement — providing all the others do not cheat.

Game theory and oligopoly

Game theory provides the most interesting and fruitful method of modelling the competitive behaviour of firms in oligopolistic markets. Most examples of game theory are mathematically complicated and beyond the requirements of an A-level economics course. However, there is one example of game theory, known as the **prisoner's dilemma** game, which I shall explain in detail as it provides a useful insight into both the *interdependence* of competitive oligopolists and the *incentive to collude* or cooperate. Consider the following situation in the international arms market, in which there are just two firms, a duopoly.

George W. Fixit IV is president of United States Arms Suppliers Inc. By paying bribes of $100 million to government ministers in the middle east he can be sure that they will purchase some of his weapons worth $600 million for their armed forces. However, his total sales to these governments depend on the actions of Sir Jasper Underhand, chairman of Exploitation Holdings plc, a British producer of similar weapons who is Mr Fixit's only serious rival.

> **KEY TERM**
>
> **game theory:** a mathematical approach to the study of conflict and decision-making which treats conflict as games with set tactics and strategies and rational players.

> **EXAM TIP**
>
> You should learn a relatively simple example of game theory, for example the prisoner's dilemma game, and apply it to explain why cartel agreements are made and sometimes broken.

If Sir Jasper Underhand also bribes the ministers responsible for the arms purchases, the deal will be shared between the two suppliers. George W. Fixit's profits will then be much less than if he alone pays bribes and gets all the business for his company. Mr Fixit thinks it a pity to pay out $100 million, but if he did not and Sir Jasper did, the British company would get all the business and he would make zero profit.

What market strategies are open to the two companies and what are the likely results of each strategy? In the absence of collusion, there are two strategies available to each firm:

1 One firm pays the bribe, while the other firm does not. Outcome:
   — for the firm paying the bribe: $500 million
   — for the firm refusing to bribe: nothing
2 Both pay the bribe. Outcome:
   — the sale is shared: each firm gets $200 million

By paying the bribe, United States Arms Suppliers Inc. earns $200m if Exploitation Holdings plc also bribes. If the American company bribes, but Sir Jasper refuses to bribe, the US company's earnings rise to $500m, but Exploitation Holdings plc makes no profit at all. The same options face the British company. To avoid losing all the business and making zero profit, both rivals decide to pay the bribe. In this scenario, paying the bribe is each firm's **dominant strategy:** that is the strategy to be pursued whatever rival firms do. Paying the bribe makes George W. Fixit better off, whatever Sir Jasper does, and vice versa.

However, the dominant strategy in a competitive market *does not* deliver the best possible outcome for both firms considered together. The best outcome is illustrated in the bottom right-hand panel of the **payoff matrix** in Figure 7.9, which shows all the possible outcomes facing the duopolists. If

Figure 7.9 Payoff matrix for the prisoner's dilemma game

both firms refuse to bribe, each receives $300 million — assuming the business is shared and that the middle-east government still wants to buy the arms. This outcome is unlikely in a competitive market because each firm fears bribery by its rival. The best way to overcome this fear is to agree not to pay the bribe: that is, to collude or cooperate. There is always the possibility, however, that one of the firms will cheat on the agreement and secretly bribe the government ministers. A collusive agreement can never completely get rid of uncertainty. If the firms really want to get rid of uncertainty, they would have to merge or be involved in a takeover.

You might be wondering how the prisoner's dilemma model obtained its name. In the original 'prisoner's dilemma', two prisoners are jointly charged with a serious crime such as armed robbery and are held in isolation from each other. The prosecutor,

AQA A2 Economics

hoping to have his task simplified, knows that a confession from one will convict the other, but he also knows that the available evidence is insufficient to ensure a conviction. If both prisoners plead not guilty, they are likely to go free. Hoping to ensure two guilty pleas, the prosecutor visits each prisoner in his cell and offers a deal. The prosecutor informs each prisoner that he will receive one of two possible punishments, depending on how he pleads:

- If both prisoners plead guilty, each will go to prison for 1 year.
- If one prisoner pleads guilty and the other not guilty, the prisoner pleading guilty will be freed and receive a reward (if he gives evidence to convict the other prisoner) whilst the other prisoner gets a 5-year jail sentence.

I shall leave it to you to work out what each prisoner should do. Would your answer be different if both prisoners were placed in the same cell and could cooperate? Or does the offer of a reward mean that both prisoners will be tempted to cheat on any deal they agree between them, thereby ensuring that the prosecutor obtains his two convictions?

SUMMARY

- Imperfect competition covers the range of market structures between perfect competition and pure monopoly.
- Oligopoly is a form of imperfect competition in which there are only a few firms in the market.
- Concentration ratios can be used to identify oligopoly market structures.
- Oligopoly can also be defined in terms of market conduct or behaviour.
- It is useful to distinguish between competitive and collusive oligopoly.
- The theory of the kinked demand curve is often used to model competitive oligopoly.
- The kinked demand curve theory illustrates uncertainty, interdependence and price stability in oligopoly, but the theory has a number of weaknesses.
- Oligopolies, and other firms with considerable market power, can set prices in a number of ways, which include cost-plus pricing, limit pricing, predatory pricing and discriminatory pricing.
- Price leadership is a common feature of oligopolistic markets.
- Oligopolists collude to reduce uncertainty and to increase monopoly profit.
- Game theory provides a fruitful way of modelling competitive and collusive oligopoly.

Exam-style questions

1 Explain why there is no general theory of oligopoly. (15 marks)

2 What are the requirements for successful price discrimination? (15 marks)

3 Evaluate the view that only producers, and not consumers, benefit when oligopolistic firms collude to try to reduce the uncertainty they experience. (25 marks)

4 Evaluate the view that the largest supermarket firms in the UK should be free to operate without any government interference. (25 marks)

Extra resources to help you revise are available online at www.hodderplus.co.uk/philipallan

Chapter 8

Further aspects of the growth of firms

Many of the most interesting aspects of business economics stem from how real-world firms actually behave. At university level, these topics are typically a part of a course in industrial economics. The aim of this chapter is to introduce you to some industrial economics topics, both those that are now in the AQA Unit 3 specification, and some that, though outside the specification, I consider it important for an economist to have some knowledge of.

LEARNING OUTCOMES

This chapter will:
- remind you of the meaning of a firm
- explain why firms grow
- relate the growth of firms to different possible business objectives
- explain the divorce between the ownership and the control of a business
- distinguish between the internal and external growth of firms, and between vertical, horizontal and lateral growth
- relate the concepts of economies and diseconomies of scale to the growth of firms
- explain the role of the capital market and banks in financing firms' growth

WHAT YOU SHOULD ALREADY KNOW

At AS you were introduced briefly to the different objectives a firm may have, and also to the meaning of economies of scale. Both of these are developed in greater detail in this chapter.

What is a firm?

I first explained the meaning of a **firm** in my Introduction to Business Economics in Chapter 2. I stated that a firm is a **business enterprise** which either *produces* or *deals in* and *exchanges* goods or services. Unlike non-business productive organisations, for example many charities, firms are commercial, earning revenue to cover the production costs they incur. It is also possible to classify different types of business or firm according to their **legal status**. There is an important difference between incorporated businesses such as private and public companies, and unincorporated sole traders and partnerships.

KEY TERM

firm: a business that sells its output commercially in a market.

EXAM TIP

Make sure you don't confuse *why* firms grow with *how* firms grow.

Why firms grow

Firms grow for all sorts of reasons. Quite often a firm grows without any deliberate intent on behalf of its owners or managers. This happens when demand for the goods or services that the firm is producing increases, and the firm increases its output and often its productive capacity or scale, simply to keep up with demand. This type of growth is particularly likely, first if it easy and relatively cheap to acquire more productive resources, and second if one of the firm's business objectives is to keep customers happy.

This brings me to the importance and significance of business objectives. Providing a good customer service is of course an important business objective, particularly for socially-minded owners and managers of businesses. However, usually it is a means to an end, the end being achieving some other business objective. *Growth for growth's sake* is another reason why firms grow (see the alternative theories of the firm below), while in some industries, business owners such as the proprietors of newspapers and TV stations sometimes believe that growth gives them not just **monopoly power**, but political influence as well. Case Study 8.1 describes a latter-day example: the media mogul Silvio Berlusconi in Italy.

CASE STUDY 8.1

Megalomania and political power as business objectives

Megalomania is a term for behaviour characterised by delusional fantasies of wealth, power, genius, or omnipotence, in other words delusions of grandeur. Over the last century or so, the media industry has thrown up many megalomaniac newspaper proprietors: Pulitzer and William Randolph Hearst in the USA, Lord Northcliffe, who built up the *Daily Mail* in the UK, and possibly Rupert Murdoch of Sky Television and News International, publisher of the *Sun*, the *News of the World* and *The Times* in the UK.

Silvio Berlusconi

A current example of a megalomaniac businessman and politician is Silvio Berlusconi, ex-cruise ship entertainer, media mogul, owner of AC Milan football club, and from 2008 to 2011, a third-time prime minister of Italy. In 2001 *The Economist* magazine argued that Berlusconi was unfit to lead Italy. According to *The Economist*, Berlusconi, while prime minister of Italy, retained effective control of 90% of all national television broadcasting. This figure included stations he owned directly as well as those over which he

had indirect control by dint of his position as prime minister and his ability to influence the choice of the management bodies of these stations. In June 2011, *The Economist* published an article on Berlusconi, titled 'The man who screwed an entire country'.

In his political career, Mr Berlusconi has commonly referred to himself in the third person as if he were already a historical figure, saying for example that 'If Italy entrusts itself to Berlusconi, it's the country's good fortune'. According to an article published in the *Financial Times*, Berlusconi has perfected a personal style that is a bizarre mix of megalomania, sexual braggadocio, off-colour jokes and outrageous claims, including, among his memorable antics: giving the sign of the horns over the head of the Spanish foreign minister in a group photograph of European leaders and calling a German member of the European parliament a concentration camp *kapo*.

Follow-up question

Using the example of Silvio Berlusconi in Italy, discuss why media moguls are particularly likely to have business objectives other than profit maximisation.

As the last few chapters have shown, in the traditional (and neoclassical) theory of the firm, economists assume that **profit maximisation** is a firm's ultimate business objective. If this is the case, then firms grow because their owners believe that growth leads to higher profits. Conversely, if the owners believe that growth reduces profits or indeed leads to losses, they will resist the temptation to pursue growth.

A complication that should be introduced at this point is the possible conflict between short-run and long-run profit maximisation. Long-run profits may require substantial investment in research and new capital. If a firm has a short time horizon, if it is worried about finance or about future risk and uncertainty, or if it fears that a lack of immediate profit will lower its share price and render it vulnerable to a hostile takeover raid, the firm may decide not to grow, even though it thinks that large profits could be made in the long run.

> **KEY TERM**
>
> **profit maximisation:** occurs when total sales revenue is furthest above total cost, which is when $MR = MC$.

> **EXAM TIP**
>
> Knowledge of the traditional profit-maximising theory is more important than knowledge of alternative theories of the firm.

Alternative theories of the firm

In real life, the people who own and run firms may have business objectives other than to make the biggest possible profit. There are two alternative theories of the firm: **managerial theories** and **organisational** or **behavioural theories**. Both claim to be more realistic in their assumptions, and hence better at explaining the actual behaviour of firms in the real economy, than the traditional profit-maximising theory of the firm.

> **KEY TERMS**
>
> **managerial theory:** assumes that firms wish to maximise managerial objectives rather than profit.
>
> **organisational theory:** assumes that a firm is a coalition of different groups such as shareholders, managers and workers.
>
> **principal/agent problem:** recognises that the principals (shareholders) have a different objective from that of the agents (managers).

Managerial theories

Managerial theories of the firm assume that a firm has a maximising objective, but they focus on a managerial objective rather than shareholders' profit. Managerial theories often take as their starting point the **principal/agent problem**, which stems from the split in a large public company between shareholders as owners, and managers as decision makers. Shareholders own companies, but they employ salaried managers or executives to make business decisions. In this situation, managers or business executives, who possess a monopoly of technical knowledge about the actual running of the company, concentrate on achieving managerial objectives such as sales maximisation, growth maximisation and maximising managerial career prospects or creature comforts.

Organisational or behavioural theories

Organisationalists or behaviouralists see the firm as an organisation comprising coalitions of different groups within the firm, each possessing different group objectives. These days, such coalitions are also regarded as company **stakeholders**: that is, groups of people with a vested interest in how the business performs.

Different stakeholders have different views on what the company should be doing. Managers form one coalition or stakeholder group, seeking prestige, power and high salaries. Other coalitions include production workers wanting higher wages and improved job security and working conditions, and shareholders desiring higher profits. Differing goals or aspirations can result in group conflict. Because of this, management may try to resolve conflict between the different interest groups within the organisation. However, attempting to satisfy the aspirations of as many groups within the organisation as possible means compromise and the possible setting of minimum rather than maximum targets.

For this reason, organisationalists introduce the concept of **satisficing** to replace the assumption of a maximising objective. Satisficing, or achieving a satisfactory outcome rather than the best possible outcome, is particularly likely for monopolies and firms in imperfectly competitive markets protected by entry barriers. In these circumstances, in seeking an easy life, a firm's managers may content themselves with satisfactory profit, combined with a degree of X-inefficiency (or unnecessary costs).

> **KEY TERM**
>
> **satisficing:** achieving a satisfactory objective acceptable to all the competing member groups of the coalition that makes up the firm.

Satisficing also helps to resolve the conflict between managers' and shareholders' objectives. While trying to maximise executive creature comforts such as managerial status, salaries, fringe benefits and career structures, a company's board of directors must keep shareholders happy. According to this theory, managers maximise their own objectives, subject to the constraint of delivering a satisfactory level of profit for shareholders.

EXTENSION MATERIAL

The theory of economic natural selection

The theory of economic natural selection, which is an example of **social Darwinism**, has provided a reason for supporting the traditional profit-maximising theory of the firm. Natural selection theory operates in two ways: through the economy's goods or **product markets** and through the **capital market** (described later in this chapter).

In the product market version of the theory, firms are assumed to sell their output in highly competitive goods markets. If managers make price and output decisions for reasons other than profit maximisation, they inevitably incur unnecessary production costs. But if goods or product markets are sufficiently competitive (perhaps approximating to perfect competition), the firms that stray from the profit-maximising path must mend their ways by reducing costs or go out of business. Whatever the conscious or deliberate aim of decision makers, the 'invisible hand' of the market means that only profit-maximising firms survive. To put it another way, decision makers who behave as if they are profit-maximisers survive, the rest fail to make normal profit and leave the market.

However, in many real-world goods markets, the forces of competition are not strong enough to allow this selection process to operate. Barriers to entry allow inefficient high-cost firms to survive. For large firms in imperfectly competitive goods markets, the second version of the theory of economic natural selection may be more significant. According to this theory, non-profit-maximising behaviour by firms is disciplined by competition in the capital market rather than by competition in the goods or product market. As I explain later in this chapter, the capital market is the financial market in which a modern large business corporation raises funds to finance investment by selling shares or ownership in the business. The **stock exchange** is an important part of the capital market.

When a firm's managers make decisions that are inconsistent with profit maximisation, the resulting low level of profit causes the company's share price to fall. This makes the company vulnerable to takeover on the stock exchange by a new owner (or **corporate raider**) who believes the company's assets can be managed better and more profitably. Even if the company is not taken over, fear of a possible takeover may prevent the corporate board and its managers from straying too far from the profit-maximising path.

The role of the entrepreneur and the divorce between ownership and control

In a firm, the **entrepreneur** is the decision maker and financial risk taker, providing answers to such standard economic questions as *what, how, how much, where* and *when* to produce. In many small firms, the owner of the business is the entrepreneur, so ownership and control lie in the same person. But this is not true for public companies, where ownership and control are almost always split. Medium-sized and large public companies are owned by thousands of shareholders, though the majority of shares are usually owned by a relatively small number of financial institutions such as pension funds and insurance companies. However, management decisions are made by executive directors, who are members of the company's corporate board, and by the salaried managers or executives whom the board employs.

> **KEY TERM**
>
> **entrepreneur:** a risk taker and decision maker within a firm.

In theory, the directors of a public company who exercise the entrepreneurial function are answerable to the shareholders. This means that, in the event of bad performance, the directors can be voted out of office. In practice, this seldom happens, although as I explained in the last section, institutional shareholders sometimes back hostile takeover bids, which, if successful, remove the incumbent board of directors.

> **EXAM TIP**
>
> Remember from your AS studies the functions of the four factors of production, including that of the entrepreneur.

Perhaps the most important problem resulting from the **divorce between ownership and control** is the possibility that directors and managers will pursue an agenda of their own, which is not in the interests of the shareholders as a body. This is an example of the principal/agent problem.

How firms grow

How firms grow involves issues such as the difference between internal and external growth, vertical, horizontal and lateral growth paths, and the pursuit of economies of scale.

Internal and external growth of firms

Internal growth (which is also known as **organic growth**) occurs when a business expands by investing in new capacity (for example, a new factory, office block or retail store) which it builds from scratch. By contrast, **external growth** involves **takeover** of, **merger** with, and **acquisition** of another, previously independent firm.

Whichever growth path a business follows — internal, external or a mix of the two — its growth may be vertical, horizontal or lateral, or again a mix of all three.

The vertical growth of firms

Vertical growth occurs when a firm grows backward along its supply chain, or forward along its distribution chain. The vertical line drawn above and below firm X in Figure 8.1 on the next page illustrates both processes. Backward vertical growth (illustrated by arrow 1) takes place when firm X (a car assembly firm) decides to produce for itself the engines, gear boxes and other components needed to make a car. Without such vertical growth, firm X would have to buy components from independent suppliers. Arrow 2 illustrates forward growth, namely firm X owning the distribution chain through which the company sells the cars that it manufactures.

In theory, vertical growth enables a firm to exercise greater control over its supply chain and/or its distribution chain: for example, in controlling the quality of components and the timing of their delivery. Often, however, it may be better to outsource component supply to independent suppliers, and to sell through independent retailers. Such a strategy can enhance competition, which in turn improves quality and drives down costs. These days, many large firms outsource a varied range of activities previously undertaken in-house. For example, ICT-provided customer service and other back office activities are increasingly being outsourced to countries with cheap labour, such as India.

In some circumstances, vertical growth creates monopoly power. A firm may deny competitors access to the supply of raw materials it has acquired. Likewise, by investing in market outlets, such as public houses and petrol stations, breweries and oil companies can prevent competitors selling through these outlets.

All the forms of growth illustrated in Figure 8.1 can be internal or external. For example, vertical internal growth could be illustrated by the car manufacturer investing from scratch in its own engine factory. By contrast, acquiring a previously independent engine manufacturer through takeover or merger illustrates vertical external growth.

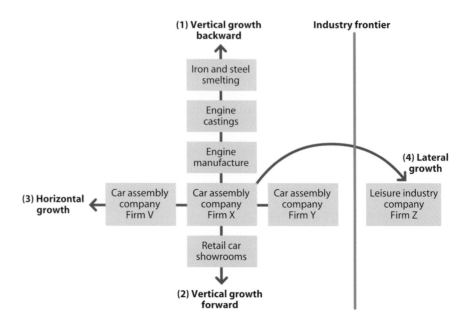

Figure 8.1 Vertical, horizontal and lateral growth of firms

Horizontal growth

Besides growing vertically, a firm can grow horizontally and laterally. **Horizontal growth** takes place when a firm expands by building or acquiring more plants at the same stage of production in the same industry. The possibility of achieving multi-plant economies of scale is an obvious motive for horizontal growth. A less benign motive might be to eliminate competitors so as to build up and exploit a monopoly position. Firm X acquiring firms V and Y in Figure 8.1 illustrates horizontal external growth. In the motor industry, Volkswagen's acquisition of Audi and the alliance between Peugeot and Citroën have both been successful. The newly merged companies were able to rationalise their production plant and product lines, and to exploit scale economies more fully. By contrast, BMW's takeover of Britain's Rover Group was less successful, leading to eventual demerger of the German company's UK acquisition and the creation of a new UK company. This in turn was unsuccessful. In 2005 MG Rover went bankrupt and the business was sold to a Chinese company which closed down most of the UK productive capacity.

Lateral growth

Lateral growth occurs when a firm diversifies into completely different industries. Figure 8.1 provides an example of lateral external growth, or **conglomeration**, when firm X acquires firm Z, a leisure industry firm operating cinemas and theme parks. Firms diversify in order to gain the scale

> **KEY TERM**
>
> **horizontal growth:** occurs when a firm undertakes more of the activities it is already involved in, which can lead to economies of scale.

> **KEY TERM**
>
> **lateral growth:** occurs when a firm diversifies into new types of production.

economies of massed resources and risk spreading. Lateral external growth may also allow the firm to benefit from financial and managerial economies. Lateral mergers, such as those undertaken by tobacco companies, can involve diversifying out of a declining market into what the firm believes to be markets with growth potential. However, managerial and organisational *diseconomies* may also result from the fact that the diversifying company lacks expertise in the fields into which it is expanding.

Economies of scale

Microeconomic theory generally assumes that a firm seeks to grow in order to enable more profit to be made. Profit depends on both demand conditions and supply conditions, with the latter depending, in the long run, on whether average costs of production fall or rise as the firm's scale of operations increases. In Chapter 3, I explained economies and diseconomies of scale in terms of a firm's long-run average cost curve. (At this stage, re-read Case Study 3.2 on page 33, which describes economies of scale in the airline industry.) In this chapter I examine the causes of the different types of economy of scale.

Internal and external economies of scale

Economies of scale are of two types: internal and external. **Internal economies of scale** occur when a firm's long-run average costs or unit costs fall as a result of an increase in the size of the firm itself, or of an increase in the size of a plant or various sites operated by the firm. By contrast, a firm benefits from **external economies of scale** when unit production costs fall because of the growth of the scale of the whole industry or market, rather than from the growth of the firm itself.

KEY TERM

internal economies of scale: lower long-run average production costs resulting from an increase in the size or scale of the firm in the long run.

Internal economies of scale

Sometimes firms grow larger but the plant sites they operate do not generally grow significantly in size. For this reason, it is useful to distinguish between those internal economies of scale that occur at the level of a single plant or establishment owned by a firm and those occurring at the level of the whole firm. In recent years, continued opportunities for further firm-level economies of scale have contributed to the growth of larger firms, but expansion of plant size has been less significant.

EXAM TIP

You don't need to rote learn all this information about economies and diseconomies of scale, but make sure you can explain at least two examples of each type of economy and diseconomy.

Plant-level economies of scale

Economies of scale that occur at the level of a single plant such as a factory or supermarket operated by a firm are largely technical economies of scale, though some management economies are also possible at plant level.

Technical economies of scale. Chapter 3 explains how some economies of scale are simply the translation of increasing returns to scale into money costs of production. Increasing returns to scale mean that as plant size increases, a firm can combine its inputs in a technically more efficient way. The resulting economies are called technical economies of scale. Increasing returns to scale therefore explain technical economies of scale. Technical economies affect the size of the typical plant or establishment, rather than the overall size of the firm, which may own and control several different plant sites. Where technical economies of scale are great, the typical plant or establishment is also large in size. The main types of technical economy of scale are as follows:

- **Indivisibilities.** Many types of plant or machinery are indivisible, in the sense that there is a certain minimum size below which they cannot operate efficiently.
- **The spreading of research and development costs.** With large plants, research and development (R&D) costs can be spread over a much longer production run, reducing unit costs in the long run.
- **Volume economies.** These are also known as economies of increased dimensions. With many types of capital equipment (for example, metal smelters, transport containers, storage tanks and warehouses), costs increase less rapidly than capacity. When a storage tank or boiler is doubled in dimension, its storage capacity actually increases eightfold. A large smelter or boiler is technically more efficient than a small one. Volume economies are thus very important in industries such as transport, storage and warehousing, as well as in metal and chemical industries.
- **Economies of massed resources.** The operation of a number of identical machines in a large plant means that proportionately fewer spare parts need be kept than when fewer machines are involved. This is an application of the law of large numbers, since we can assume that not all the machines will develop a fault at the same time.
- **Economies of vertically linked processes.** Much manufacturing activity involves a large number of vertically related tasks and processes, from the initial purchase of raw materials, components and energy, through to the completion and sale of the finished product. Within a single firm, these processes may be integrated through the links between the various plants owned by the firm. The linking of processes in a single plant can lead to a saving in time, transport costs and energy.

Managerial economies of scale. Managerial economies of scale can be achieved both by increasing the size of an individual plant or, at the level of the firm, by grouping a large number of establishments under one management. Both methods of expansion allow for increased managerial specialisation and the division of labour. This involves the delegation of detail to junior managers and supervisors and a 'functional division of labour', namely the employment of specialist managers (for example, in the fields of production, personnel and sales).

Multi-plant economies of scale

Multi-plant economies of scale occur when long-run average costs fall as a result of operating more than one plant.

Firm-level economies of scale

It is obviously in a firm's interest to benefit as much as possible from plant-level economies of scale. Firms will also try to take advantage of scale economies associated with the growth of the enterprise that are largely independent of plant size. Economies of scale at the firm level arise from the firm itself being large rather than from operating a single big plant or a number of large sites. As well as covering some of the R&D economies, massed resources economies and managerial economies already described, firm-level economies of scale also include marketing, financial and risk-bearing economies.

- **Marketing economies.** These are of two types: bulk buying and bulk marketing economies.
- **Financial or capital-raising economies of scale.** These are similar to the bulk-buying economies, except that they relate to the bulk buying or the bulk borrowing of funds required to finance the business's expansion. Large firms can often borrow from banks and other financial institutions at a lower rate of interest and on better terms than those available to small firms.
- **Risk-bearing economies of scale.** Large firms are usually less exposed to risk than small firms because risks can be grouped and spread. A bank can predict with some confidence the number of customers who will turn out to be bad debtors, but it is unlikely to know in advance which customers they will be. But because it knows that for each bad debt there will be many other solvent customers whose business is profitable for the bank, risks are spread and uncertainty is reduced.

Learning effects

When a firm increases the scale of its plant, it is quite likely that a new technology or new methods of working an old technology will be adopted. But if the firm's workers and managers are initially unfamiliar with the new methods, production is likely to be inefficient. A learning effect occurs when managers and workers learn from experience how to operate particular technologies and methods of production more effectively. Learning effects are usually associated with a change in the scale of a firm's operations, but they can also occur as a result of the reorganisation of existing capacity.

Economies of scope

In contrast to *economies of scale* which relate to reductions in the average costs resulting from increasing the scale of production for a single product type, *economies of scope* refers to lowering the average cost for a firm in producing two or more products.

External economies of scale

As I have noted earlier, **external economies of scale** are shared by a number of firms (or indeed by a number of industries) when the scale of production of the whole industry (or group of industries) increases. External economies are conferred on a firm, not as a result of its own growth, but because other firms have grown larger (although, of course, the firm's own growth may also contribute to the other firms benefiting from external economies). Indeed, if the firms were to

> **KEY TERM**
>
> **external economies of scale:** lower long-run average production costs resulting from the growth of the industry of which the firm is a part.

merge, external economies enjoyed by previously independent firms would become internal economies within the plants and subsidiaries of the combined enterprise. Thus takeovers and mergers internalise external economies (and diseconomies) of scale.

As with internal scale economies, it is possible to identify a number of different types of external economy of scale.

- **Economies of concentration.** When a number of firms in the same or related industries locate close together, they are able to gain mutual advantages through better transport facilities, the training of a pool of skilled labour and supplying each other with sources of components and market outlets. This is called a 'cluster effect'.
- **Economies of information.** In a large industry, it is worthwhile for specialist firms and for public bodies such as universities to undertake research and to provide information (for example, through technical and trade journals), from which all firms can benefit.
- **Economies of disintegration.** Although firms can often benefit from internal economies that result from linking processes internally, there may be circumstances when vertically linked production processes can be provided more efficiently by independent specialist firms. An obvious example occurs in the case of indivisibilities. If a firm is too small to use continuously plant or machinery that cannot be built on a smaller scale, it makes sense to buy supplies from an independent firm that can use the plant efficiently because it supplies a number of firms within the industry.

CASE STUDY 8.2

Does size matter? Economies and diseconomies of scale in the water industry

In January 2004, Ofwat, the government's regulatory agency for the water and sewage disposal industries, published a report entitled 'Investigation into evidence for economies of scale in the water and sewerage industry in England and Wales'. The objective of the study was to provide answers to three key questions:

- Whether the process of consolidation in the industry has resulted in an industry structure consistent with the least-cost production of water services in England and Wales.
- Whether the evidence on economies of scale presents a case for further horizontal integration in the industry.
- Whether there are opportunities for a more efficient industry structure through different types of restructuring (e.g. vertical separation).

The report was eagerly awaited by many in the UK water industry with the hope that it would conclude that there were economies of scale in the industry. This would have helped pave the way for future merger activity in the sector following a long period during which Ofwat had successfully blocked mergers between a number of water companies.

To the surprise of some, however, the report concluded amongst other things that there were significant diseconomies of scale for water and sewerage companies (WaSCs), i.e. the biggest water companies appear to be too big. The report also concluded that there were likely to be constant returns to scale for the water-only companies, i.e. they are about the right size.

Maybe, however, the findings of the study are not so surprising after all. Water is, as some argue, a localised industry — and water is heavy and expensive to move around. So having utilities based around urban areas is likely to be an efficient means of operating the sector. And optimal size will be determined by the characteristics of those urban areas.

Ofwat also concluded that the results were not hugely surprising to them: 'The conclusions do not surprise us — we regulate an industry that is a conglomerate of activities each with an optimum minimum scale that is related to human and physical geography. Beyond this level we see costs rising steadily.'

Follow-up questions

1 Why might evidence of economies of scale be used to justify further horizontal integration in an industry?
2 For a utility industry such as water, what is meant by 'vertical separation'?
3 Why might the 'localised' nature of the water industry lead to diseconomies of scale?

Internal and external diseconomies of scale

In many industries, particularly in manufacturing and in tertiary activities such as the provision of financial services, firms grow large in order to benefit from the falling long-run production costs brought about by economies of scale. However, a firm may eventually reach a size beyond which higher costs that result from **diseconomies of scale** exceed any further benefits that can be squeezed out of economies of scale.

For large firms, **managerial diseconomies** are probably the most significant type of **internal diseconomy of scale**. Managerial diseconomies can result from communication failure, which occurs when there are many layers of management between the top managers and ordinary production workers. In this situation, decision making and the ability to respond to customers' needs or to problems arising in the course of production, both suffer. As a result, the resources the business uses are not allocated as effectively as they could be. Top management loses touch with junior managers and employees, and with the problems facing the business.

External diseconomies of scale occur when a firm's long-run average costs of production increase, not because of the growth of the firm itself, but because of the growth of the industry or market of which the firm is a part. The firm may suffer from a 'negative cluster effect', for example when the close proximity of many firms increases the cost of negative externalities such as road congestion and pollution, which each firm dumps on its market co-members. Close geographical proximity can also lead to labour shortages caused by industry firms competing for labour, and higher resulting wage costs.

> **KEY TERMS**
>
> **internal diseconomies of scale:** higher long-run average production costs resulting from an increase in the size or scale of the firm in the long run.
>
> **external diseconomies of scale:** higher long-run average production costs resulting from the growth of the industry of which the firm is a part.

The capital market, banks and the growth of firms

All firms require finance to enable them to grow and to undertake production. Short-term finance is used to pay for the purchase of raw materials (circulating or working capital) and to pay wages. Long-term sources of funds are used to finance the internal or external growth of the firm via direct investment in new fixed plant, or through a process of takeover and merger. For all types of business enterprise, self-finance or the ploughing back in of profits (**internal finance**) is by far the most important source of finance, although the ability to engage successfully in self-finance depends upon profitability.

The main sources of **external finance** divide into borrowing (or debt) and the raising of capital by share issue. For public companies, this involves the capital market. Because private companies cannot generally raise funds on the capital market, the most important reason for private companies 'going public' (that is, becoming public companies) is to raise funds by selling new issues of shares and corporate bonds to whoever wishes to buy them. The government also raises funds on the capital market to finance its budget deficit and its borrowing requirement. The government does this by selling new issues of government bonds (called **gilt-edged securities** or **gilts**) to the general public.

Many students confuse the **capital market** with the **stock exchange**. The stock exchange is indeed an important part of the capital market, but it is only a part, and the capital market and stock exchange are not interchangeable terms. The capital market can be understood as comprising two elements: a new issues market or primary market; and a secondary market on which previously issued shares and bonds can be sold second-hand. The stock exchange is the most important part of the secondary or 'second-hand' market.

The relationship between the primary and the secondary parts of the main capital market is illustrated in Figure 8.2. The actual raising of new capital or long-term finance takes place in the primary market when public companies (in the private sector of the economy) or the government (in the public sector) decide to issue and sell new marketable securities. Companies can borrow long-term by selling **corporate bonds,** or they may sell an ownership stake in the company by issuing **shares** or **equity.** When selling corporate bonds, the company extends its debt, and the purchaser of the bond becomes a creditor of the company.

Figure 8.2 The role of capital markets in financing investment in British industry

By contrast, new issues of shares are sold when a company 'goes public' for the first time, or when an existing public company decides to raise extra capital with a new equity issue. In the latter case, the new share issue is most often a **rights issue**, in which the company's existing shareholders are given the right to buy the new issue of shares at a discount.

New issues of shares are seldom sold directly on the stock exchange. Instead, the direct sale of new issues to the general public takes place in the primary market, usually being arranged by specialised banks called **investment banks** via newspaper advertisements and the post. Nevertheless, by providing **liquidity** to the capital market, the stock exchange has an important role. Shares in private companies are illiquid and difficult to exchange for cash. By contrast, shares in listed public companies can be sold second-hand on the stock exchange. The stock exchange enables shares to be converted quickly into cash. Without the stock exchange, the general public would be reluctant to buy shares that could not easily be resold. An important source of funds necessary to finance the growth of a firm would be denied to public companies.

EXTENSION MATERIAL

The growth of venture capital or private equity finance

Until quite recently, it was not usually possible for a private company to finance expansion by extending significantly its share capital or equity, while still remaining a private company. When an ambitious private company wanted to raise a large capital sum, there were normally only two options. The company could either borrow and increase its debt or extend its share capital by going public with a flotation on the stock exchange. However, the 1980 Companies Act introduced a significant change in the financing of private companies which has led to the growth of the modern venture capital industry. The Act allows private companies to take on new shareholders who invest considerable stakes in the business without the necessity of converting to a plc.

Venture capital is finance provided, usually to young private companies and unquoted public companies, through the sale of shares or an equity ownership stake to specialist private equity finance institutions. In the boom years and enterprise culture of the 1980s, banks and other financial institutions such as insurance companies set up specialist venture capital subsidiaries. Typically, a venture capital firm invests a large sum of money in a private company, in return for an equity stake that is highly illiquid as long as the company remains private.

Part of the deal might be that the company — having successfully grown as a result of the capital injection provided by the venture capital firm — eventually goes public, either on the 'junior stock market' known as the **alternative investment market (AIM),** or on the main stock exchange. Going public provides an exit route for the venture capital firm. The private equity finance provider could then sell its stake in the client company and take its profit. The funds released may be used by the venture capital firm to invest in another start-up private company needing long-term funding.

The late 1990s and the early 2000s witnessed a massive growth of private equity finance in the USA and the UK. Most of this growth was fuelled by an activity very different from using venture capital to promote the growth of small start-up private companies. Instead, the private equity companies borrowed money from institutional investors and used the borrowed funds to finance leveraged (and often hostile) takeovers of established public companies. Once ownership had been transferred to the private equity company, the victim company might be broken up. Its assets would be sold and its workers sacked, to release the funds needed to pay back the borrowed funds that had financed the takeover.

For some, this represented asset-stripping, short-termism and the pursuit of private greed. But for others, private equity finance was simply a new and more efficient vehicle for engineering the restructuring of capitalism: that is, shifting productive assets from a less efficient to a more efficient use. Either way, this heyday of private equity finance was over by 2008, as a result of the credit crunch, which decimated financial businesses that had relied for their success on borrowed funds. However, recovery from recession may promote further growth of the venture capital industry.

The trade-off facing public companies

Except in a few special circumstances such as insolvency and boardroom disputes, the directors of an independent private company generally have complete control of the business. The directors own all the shares issued by the company. Complete control means, however, that no capital has been raised by selling shares on the capital market. Figure 8.3 illustrates what may happen when the directors decide to go public by converting the company into a plc.

EXAM TIP

Understanding the trade-off facing public companies is useful for understanding how victim companies may face hostile takeover bids.

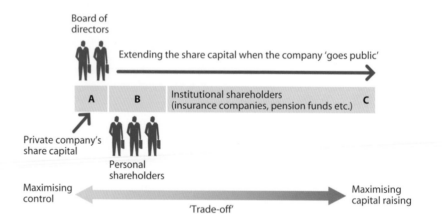

Figure 8.3 The trade-off facing a company's board of directors

The left-hand box (labelled A) in Figure 8.3 is the private company's share capital, all of which is owned by the directors. When the company goes public, new shares (shown by boxes B and C in Figure 8.3) are sold on the capital market. The people buying these shares comprise two very different groups of shareholders, namely small shareholders (or personal shareholders) and institutional shareholders. Small shareholders (shown by box B in Figure 8.3) are generally in the minority, particularly after selling the new issue 'second hand' to the institutions on the stock exchange. As a result of these sales, insurance companies, pension funds and other financial institutions end up owning most of the shares of plcs listed on the stock exchange. Institutional shareholdings are shown in box C in Figure 8.3.

Controlling most of the shares in public companies, the fund managers employed by pension funds and insurance companies can decide who runs these companies. The financial institutions are best regarded as sleeping owners of the companies in which they hold shares. Lacking specialised management expertise, fund managers prefer not to take an active entrepreneurial role in running the companies that their institutions effectively own. When a company's board does a good job, the financial institutions generally support the directors. However, if the board makes bad management decisions which reduce the company's profit and share price, fund managers may lose confidence in the directors. In these circumstances, fund managers can quickly switch allegiance and support a hostile takeover bid for the company.

SUMMARY

- Firms grow in order to achieve their business objectives.
- Profit maximisation is the assumed business objective in the traditional neoclassical theory of the firm.
- Alternative (managerial and organisational) theories assume different business objectives, including a satisficing objective.
- A divorce between ownership and control may occur in large public companies when the managers who make day-to-day decisions pursue business objectives which are not in the interests of the shareholders who own the company.
- This is an example of the principal/agent problem.
- You must avoid confusing why firms grow with how firms grow.
- Firms may grow internally (organically) or externally via takeover and merger.
- Growth may also be vertical, horizontal or lateral.
- Vertical and horizontal growth may lead to economies of scale, but lateral growth may be more likely to result in diseconomies of scale.
- Internal economies of scale divide into plant-level, multi plant-level and firm-level scale economies.
- External economies and diseconomies of scale result from the growth of the whole market or industry, rather than from the growth of the firm itself.
- Avoid confusing internal and external growth with internal and external sources of finance which fund a firm's growth.
- Internally financed growth involves ploughing back profit, whereas external finance may be raised by borrowing from banks or selling a new share issue on the capital market.
- However, a new share issue may render a public company vulnerable to a hostile takeover bid.

Exam-style questions

1 Explain why a firm may wish to pursue a satisficing objective rather than a maximising objective. **(15 marks)**

2 Explain how the divorce between ownership and control may affect a firm. **(15 marks)**

3 Do you agree that the objective of profit maximisation becomes less important than other possible objectives as a firm grows in size? Justify your answer. **(25 marks)**

4 Evaluate the view that the vertical growth of firms is much more in the public interest than horizontal or lateral growth. **(25 marks)**

Extra resources to help you revise are available online at www.hodderplus.co.uk/philipallan

Chapter 9

Industrial policy

Government economic policy divides into microeconomic policy and macroeconomic policy. In this and the next two chapters I explain microeconomic policy, which aims to make markets, industries and firms function more efficiently, more competitively, and in the public or national interest. Macroeconomic policy is, of course, covered in the third and final section of the book.

This chapter examines the meaning of industrial policy, describes its main elements, and assesses the effectiveness of the industrial policy implemented by UK governments in recent years. The three main elements of industrial policy are: competition policy; private versus public ownership of industry; and the regulation and deregulation of the UK economy.

LEARNING OUTCOMES

This chapter will:
- provide a short history of industrial policy
- outline the main elements of competition policy directed at monopoly, mergers and restrictive trading practices
- examine nationalisation and privatisation
- explain policies related to privatisation such as contractualisation and the private finance initiative
- distinguish between regulation and deregulation
- analyse policies such as price caps imposed by regulatory agencies such as Ofwat

WHAT YOU SHOULD ALREADY KNOW

Although Unit 1 covers government microeconomic policy with respect to issues such as the reduction of market failure, industrial policy is not in the AS specification. The elements of industrial policy which I explain in this chapter should therefore be completely new to you.

A short history of UK industrial policy

Industrial policy is part of the government's microeconomic policy. It aims to improve the economic performance of individual economic agents, firms and industries on the supply side of the economy. Since the 1930s, when industrial policy first began as a response to the Great Depression, all UK governments have had some sort of industrial policy. However, significant changes have occurred in the nature of the policy, and also in the importance attached by different governments to industrial policy in comparison to other aspects of economic policy. Far-reaching changes occurred in UK industrial policy when, from the late 1970s largely to the present day, free-market **supply-side economics** replaced **Keynesianism** as the prevailing economic orthodoxy.

Before this, for much of the period from 1945 until 1979, successive UK governments pursued an **interventionist** industrial policy. This reflected the Keynesian view that economic problems result from a failure of market forces, and that the problems can be cured (or at least reduced) by appropriate government intervention. During the Keynesian era (roughly the 1950s, 1960s and most of the 1970s), industrial policy in particular (and Keynesian economic policy in general) extended the roles of government and state planning in the economy. By contrast, the industrial policy pursued by governments since 1979 has mostly been **anti-interventionist** and based on the belief that the correct role of government is not to reduce the role of market forces, but to create the conditions in which market forces can work effectively and efficiently.

However, although recent governments have generally replaced interventionist industrial policy with a more free-market policy, the importance attached to industrial policy in the overall economic strategy has increased in one important way. During the Keynesian era, industrial policy and microeconomic policy were subordinate and subservient to macroeconomic policy. Keynesian macroeconomic policy was aimed overwhelmingly at the demand side of the economy, attempting to influence and control output and employment by managing the level of aggregate demand in the economy. But free-market economists believe that Keynesian demand management policies led to inflation rather than to full employment and economic growth. They also believe that the almost exclusive Keynesian concern with demand management served to divert attention away from the **supply side of the economy**, where the real problems that stand in the way of increased output and employment must be tackled. In recent years, therefore, industrial policy has been used to try to increase economic efficiency, productivity and competitiveness in goods markets and labour markets on the supply side of the UK economy.

Competition policy

For over 60 years, since its inception in 1948, competition policy has formed an important part of the UK government's wider industrial policy. **Competition policy** is the part of industrial policy that covers monopolies, mergers and restrictive trading practices, which I shall now look at in turn.

> **KEY TERM**
>
> **competition policy:** aims to make goods markets more competitive. It comprises policy toward monopoly, mergers and restrictive trading practices.

Monopoly policy

The USA was the first industrialised country to introduce a monopoly policy (anti-trust policy), with the 1890 Sherman Anti-Trust Act. (In the USA, monopolies are known as *trusts*.) Several decades then passed before the UK government decided that the problem of monopoly deserved special policy attention. Nevertheless, of the three main elements of competition policy I examine in this chapter, monopoly policy is the one with the longest history, dating back over half a century to the establishment of the Monopolies Commission in 1948. The Monopolies Commission later became the Competition Commission, which in turn in 2013 was rebranded as the

> **EXAM TIP**
>
> The label 'monopoly policy' is slightly misleading as very often the policy is aimed at oligopolies or concentrated markets rather than at pure monopoly.

Competition and Markets Authority (CMA). The CMA is not restricted solely to the investigation of *pure* monopoly. The commission investigates mergers that might create a new monopoly as well as established monopolies. But more generally, it investigates monopoly power in oligopolistic industries that are dominated by a few large firms.

Statutory monopoly

The UK government currently identifies two types of monopoly, known as **scale monopoly** and **complex monopoly**, which taken together are sometimes known as **statutory monopoly** (that is, monopoly as defined in law). A statutory monopoly exists in law if:

- one firm has at least 25% of the market for the supply or acquisition of particular goods or services (scale monopoly)
- a number of firms that together have a 25% share conduct their affairs so as to restrict competition (complex monopoly)

The theoretical background to monopoly policy

At this stage you should refer back to Chapter 6 and read through the sections that compare perfect competition and monopoly. The main points to note are:

- In the absence of economies of scale, perfect competition is more productively and allocatively efficient than monopoly, and it is also likely to be more X-efficient.
- In perfect competition, the 'consumer is king' and consumer sovereignty rules, whereas monopoly leads to the manipulation of consumers and the exploitation of producer sovereignty. By restricting output and raising prices, monopoly results in a net welfare loss as well as a transfer of consumer surplus into producer surplus and monopoly profit.

The model of perfect competition provides the theoretical justification for UK competition policy. However, there are two main circumstances in which monopoly may be preferable to small firms producing in a competitive market.

First, when the size of the market is limited but economies of scale are possible, monopolies can produce at a lower average cost than smaller, more competitive firms.

Second, under certain circumstances, firms with monopoly power may be more innovative than firms that are not protected by entry barriers. When this is the case, monopoly may be more dynamically efficient than a more competitive market.

Cartels versus fully integrated monopolies

Whether a monopoly promotes or reduces dynamic efficiency, and generally 'behaves itself', depends to a large extent upon the type of monopoly and upon the circumstances in which the monopoly power was created. With this in mind, it is useful to distinguish between two very different types of monopoly: cartels and fully integrated monopolies.

- **Cartels.** As I explained in Chapter 7, a cartel is usually regarded as the worst form of monopoly from the public interest point of view, since it is likely to exhibit most of the disadvantages of monopoly with few, if any, of the benefits. A cartel is a price ring formed when independent firms make a collective restrictive trading agreement to charge the same price, and possibly to limit output. A cartel acts as a monopoly in the marketing of goods, but the benefits of economies of scale are unlikely to occur because the physical or technical integration of the productive capacity of the members of the cartel does not take place. Consumer choice is restricted, and cartels tend to keep inefficient firms in business while the more efficient members of the cartel make monopoly profit. In these circumstances, it is probable that the incentive to innovate by developing new products and methods of production will be lacking. Cartels are thus likely to be dynamically inefficient. For all these reasons, cartels are generally made illegal.

- **Fully integrated monopoly.** A fully integrated monopoly (or fully unified monopoly) may result from accident rather than design. A dynamic firm grows and benefits from economies of scale, becoming a monopoly as the reward for successful competition. Monopoly is the end result of the firm's success in innovating, reducing costs and introducing new products — which are all factors indicating that the firm is dynamically efficient. A fully integrated monopoly may be the unintended spin-off of essentially benign motives for the firm's growth. Once established as a monopoly, the firm may continue to behave virtuously, retaining its innovating habits and using monopoly profit to finance new developments, though government regulation may be necessary to ensure continued good behaviour.

> **EXAM TIP**
>
> The influential Austrian-American economist Joseph Schumpeter argued that through a process he called **creative destruction**, monopolies are more dynamically efficient than firms unprotected by barriers to entry. This is one of the two main arguments used to justify monopoly, the other being related to economies of scale from which large firms benefit.

A cost–benefit approach to monopoly policy

Because economists recognise that monopoly can be either good or bad depending upon circumstances, UK policy has always been based on the view that each case must be judged on its merits. If the likely costs resulting from the reduction of competition exceed the benefits, monopoly should be prevented, but if the likely benefits exceed the costs, monopoly should be permitted. Ongoing regulation is needed to make sure the monopoly continues to act in the public interest.

The Competition and Markets Authority

As noted, UK monopoly policy is now implemented by the Competition and Markets Authority (CMA), formed in 2013 through the merger of the **Office of Fair Trading** and the **Competition Commission**. The CMA is responsible to a government ministry, the **Department for Business, Innovation and Skills (BIS)**.

> **EXAM TIP**
>
> You must understand the roles of the Competition and Markets Authority.

The CMA uses market structure, conduct and performance indicators to scan or screen the UK economy on a systematic basis for evidence of monopoly abuse. Concentration ratios provide evidence of monopolistic market structures. Market conduct indicators such as consumer and trade complaints allow the CMA to monitor anti-competitive business behaviour.

When the CMA discovers evidence of statutory monopoly that it believes is likely to be against the public interest, it investigates further. Until recently, the main issue to be decided was the relatively narrow one of whether particular trading practices undertaken by the investigated firm(s) were in the **public interest**. The public interest was fairly vaguely defined.

The 2002 Enterprise Act changed this, introducing **competition-based tests** to replace the public interest test. The tests centre on whether any features of the market (which include structural features and conduct by firms or customers in the market) prevent, restrict or distort competition.

Before the Enterprise Act was implemented, the government's competition agencies lacked direct power to implement or enforce their recommendations. Competition policy was criticised for lacking teeth. This has changed and the CMA's role is now *determinative* rather than just *advisory*. It can order firms to cease particular trading practices. Virtually all the decisions on markets or firms to be investigated and on policy enforcement are made by the CMA. In practice, recommendations don't need to be forced through very often. The CMA will talk with the firms involved to persuade them to alter business behaviour voluntarily. Typically, firms will be asked to drop undesirable trading practices and to give undertakings about future conduct.

Alternative approaches to the problem of monopoly

Ever since the initial establishment of the Monopolies Commission, the UK has adopted a regulatory and investigatory approach to the problem of monopoly. Relatively few firms and takeover bids are actually investigated. The policy rationale is that the possibility of a CMA investigation creates sufficient incentive for most large firms to behave well and to resist the temptation to exploit monopoly power.

However, although the CMA has adopted a 'watchdog investigatory/regulatory' role, a number of other strategic approaches could, in principle, be used to deal with the problem of monopoly. These include:

- **Compulsory breaking up of all monopolies ('monopoly busting').** Many free-market economists believe that the advantages of a free-market economy, namely economic efficiency and consumer sovereignty, can be achieved only when the economy is as close as possible to perfect competition. In itself, monopoly is bad and impossible to justify. The government should adopt an automatic policy rule to break up monopolies wherever they are found to exist. UK policy-makers have never adopted a monopoly-busting approach, although, as I have explained, powers do exist that allow the government to order the break-up of an established monopoly. By contrast, US anti-trust policy does require the break-up of firms with a very large share of the US market. However, the huge size of the US market has meant that most US firms can grow to a very large size by UK standards, without dominating the domestic market and running the risk of being broken up by the courts.

■ **Use of price controls to restrict monopoly abuse.** Although price controls have been used by UK governments at various times to restrict the freedom of UK firms to set their own prices, this has been part of an interventionist policy to control inflation, rather than a policy to control monopoly abuse. Under the influence of free-market economic theory, price controls have generally been abandoned in the UK in recent years. Nevertheless, as I explain later in this chapter, regulatory agencies have in the past required privatised monopolies such as British Telecom (BT) to keep price rises below the rate of inflation.

■ **Taxing monopoly profits.** As well as controlling prices directly, the government can tax monopoly profit to punish monopolistic firms for making excess profit. Monopoly taxes have not generally been used in the UK, except on a few occasions — for example, on the 'windfall' gain that landlords receive when the land they own is made available for property development. Similarly, windfall profits received by banks from high interest rates have been subject to a special tax. Also, in the late 1990s, the incoming Labour government imposed a windfall profit tax on the privatised utilities.

■ **Rate of return regulation.** In the USA, the regulators have imposed maximum rates of return on the capital that the utility companies employ. In principle, these act as a price cap, as the utilities are fined if they set prices too high and earn excessive rates of return. However, in practice, instead of increasing productive efficiency, rate of return regulation often has the opposite effect. This type of intervention has the unintended consequence of encouraging utility companies to raise costs (knowing they are protected by entry barriers), rather than to cut prices to comply with the rate of return regulation.

The BT Tower, London

■ **The public ownership of monopoly.** In the past, UK Labour governments have sometimes regarded the problem of monopoly as resulting solely from private ownership and the pursuit of private profit. At its most simplistic, this view leads to the conclusion that the problem of monopoly disappears when the firms are nationalised or taken into public ownership. Once in public ownership, the monopolies are assumed to act solely in the public interest.

■ **Privatising monopolies.** Opposing public ownership, past Conservative governments argued that state ownership produces particular forms of abuse that would not be experienced if the industries were privately owned. These include a general inefficiency and resistance to change, which stem from the belief by workers and management in the state-run monopolies that they will always be bailed out by government in the event of a loss. According to the Conservative view, monopoly abuse occurs in nationalised industries, not from the pursuit of private profit, but because the industries are run in the interest of a feather-bedded workforce that is protected from any form of market discipline. The Conservatives believe that the privatisation of state-owned monopolies should improve efficiency and commercial performance, because privatisation exposes the industry to the threat of takeover and the discipline of the capital market.

- **Deregulation and the removal of barriers to entry.** Most economists believe that privatisation alone cannot eliminate the problem of monopoly abuse; it merely changes the nature of the problem to private monopoly and the commercial exploitation of a monopoly position. The privatisation of the telecommunication and gas monopolies was accompanied by the setting up of regulatory bodies (now called Ofcom and Ofgem). This source of regulation, additional to that available from the Competition and Markets Authority, was a recognition of this problem. One method of exposing monopolies — including the privatised utility industries — to increased competition is to use deregulatory policies to remove artificial barriers to entry. I explain deregulation in greater detail later in the chapter.

Contestable market theory

EXAM TIP

Contestable market theory can be applied to a wide range of exam questions on competition policy and on monopoly and other market structures. Good answers will reflect this.

In recent years, much of the debate about the best way of dealing with monopoly abuse and regulating monopoly has centred upon the need to deregulate and remove barriers to market entry. This debate reflects the growing influence of **contestable market theory**. Before the free-market revival (of which the theory of contestable markets is a part), industrial policy involved an ever-increasing extension of regulation by government into the activities of private sector firms. Increased intervention was justified by the belief that regulatory powers must be strong enough, first, to countervail the growing power of large business organisations and, second, to make monopolies behave in a more competitive fashion.

At that time, monopoly was normally defined by the number of firms in the market and by the share of the leading firms, measured by a concentration ratio. The basic dilemma facing the policy-makers centred on how to reconcile the potential gains in large-scale productive efficiency with the fact that lack of competitive pressure can lead to monopoly abuse and consumer exploitation. But in contestable market theory, monopoly is defined neither by the number of firms in the market nor by concentration ratios, but rather by the potential ease or difficulty with which new firms may enter the market. Industrial concentration is not a problem, providing that an absence of barriers to entry and exit creates the potential for new firms to enter and contest the market. *Actual* competition in a market is not essential. The threat of entry by new firms or *potential* competition is quite enough, according to contestable market theory, to ensure efficient and non-exploitative behaviour by existing firms within the market.

For a market to be perfectly contestable, there must be no barriers to entry and no **sunk costs**. Sunk costs are costs incurred when entering a market that are irrecoverable should the firm decide to leave the market. *Sunk costs* must not be confused with *fixed costs*, although some sunk costs are also fixed costs. Suppose a firm invests in new machinery when it enters the market. This is a fixed cost, but if the machinery can be sold at a good price to another firm, it is not a sunk cost. In this situation, the cost can be recovered if the firm decides to leave the market. By contrast, if the machinery has no alternative use and a cost of disposal rather than a second-hand value, investment in the fixed capital is also a sunk cost. Another sunk cost might be expenditure on advertising to establish the firm in the market. If market entry is unsuccessful and the firm decides to leave, the expenditure cannot be recovered.

In recent years, contestable market theory has had a major impact upon UK monopoly policy. The theory implies that, providing there is adequate *potential* for competition, a conventional regulatory policy is superfluous. Instead of interfering with firms' pricing and output policies, the government should restrict the role of monopoly policy to discovering which industries and markets are potentially contestable. Deregulatory policies should be used to develop conditions in which there are no barriers to entry and exit, to ensure that reasonable contestability is possible. Appropriate policies suggested by the theory of contestable markets include:

- removal of licensing regimes for public transport and television and radio transmissions
- removal of controls over ownership, such as exclusive public ownership
- removal of pricing controls that act as a barrier to entry, such as those previously practised in the aviation industry

Merger policy

Whereas a government's monopoly policy deals with established monopoly, or markets already dominated by large firms, **merger policy** is concerned with takeovers and mergers that might create a *new* monopoly. Strictly, a **merger** involves the voluntary coming together of two or more firms, whereas a **takeover** is usually involuntary, at least for the victim being acquired through a **hostile takeover**. However, the term *merger policy* is used to cover all types of acquisition of firms, friendly or hostile, willing or unwilling.

Until quite recently, the government itself decided on whether to refer a merger to the authorities for investigation. This laid government open to the criticism that, when deciding against a merger reference, it was bending to the lobbying power of big business and engaging in political opportunism. However, the Competition and Markets Authority now makes virtually all merger references. The Authority keeps itself informed of all merger situations that might be eligible for investigation on public interest grounds. Currently, a takeover or merger is eligible for investigation if it is expected to lead to a **substantial lessening of competition (SLC).**

> **EXAM TIP**
>
> Mergers and takeovers, which occur when a firm grows *externally*, can be analysed in terms of the vertical, horizontal and lateral growth of firms.

In the 1990s, barely 100 mergers (out of a total of over 3,000) were in fact referred for investigation. Of these, only a minority were found to be against the public interest and banned. These figures give some support to the argument that UK governments were not serious in their attitude to mergers and the problem of growing industrial concentration. Governments tended to assume that all mergers were beneficial unless it could clearly be shown that the effects were likely to be adverse.

One effect of current legislation is that horizontal mergers are far more likely to be investigated than lateral mergers. This may be unfortunate because lateral mergers may produce managerial diseconomies of scale. By contrast, horizontal mergers, which tend to fall foul of current merger policy, may be **synergetic**. In this context, synergy means that when two firms merge the sum is greater than the two parts. However, lateral mergers may have the opposite result, with the sum being less than the two parts.

CASE STUDY 9.1

Overruling merger policy? Lloyds TSB's takeover of HBOS

In October 2008 the UK's banking system was in deep trouble in the financial meltdown triggered by the credit crunch. Halifax Bank of Scotland (HBOS) nearly went bankrupt. To rescue HBOS, the government waived through a takeover by another large bank, Lloyds TSB, without referring the takeover to the competition authorities as had been expected.

Sir John Vickers, the former chairman of the OFT wrote: 'It would appear to have been a mistake to waive normal merger law to address the HBOS problem once it was clear, as it was by early October 2008, that a systemic solvency problem existed. Relaxation of competition law was not a good way to help financial stability in this case, and as the subsequent problems of Lloyds have shown, it may have worsened it.' Vickers believes that nationalising HBOS instead of allowing Lloyds to take over the ailing lender 'would have had important economic advantages'.

By any measure, the takeover by Lloyds TSB of HBOS created a powerful monopoly. With 30% of current accounts and much the same share of the domestic mortgage market, the new 'super bank' had the potential to fleece customers. To prevent this happening, and to meet a European Union directive, Lloyds TSB was split up in 2013 into two separate banks.

Lloyds TSB took over HBOS

Follow-up questions

1 Why might Lloyds TSB's takeover of HBOS be deemed anti-competitive?
2 Do you agree that the takeover should have been investigated by the government's competition authorities? Justify your answer.

European Union merger policy

The **European Commission,** which is the executive body of the European Union (EU), has long had powers to prevent and control mergers in member countries of the EU, but before 1990, the commission did not apply these powers systematically. However, in 1990 a new EU merger policy came into operation to control the growing number of mergers involving companies active in more than one member country. The EU policy is based on the principle of **subsidiarity,** which delegates policy as much as possible to national governments. Member countries will continue to use national policy to deal with smaller mergers, but the European commission will adjudicate on larger mergers with a community dimension. As with UK merger policy, nearly all the commission's criteria for assessing whether a merger is justified are competition related, showing again the influence of contestable market theory.

> **EXAM TIP**
>
> The Unit 3 specification states that candidates should know the general features of both UK and EU competition policy. This is a fruitful topic for a data-response question on the impact of the EU upon the UK economy.

The European Commission justifies its policy as providing a one-stop regulatory system for mergers, in which the borderline between national and EU jurisdiction is clear-cut. However, many commentators believe that the opposite is the case. They criticise EU merger policy as an unclear, time-consuming lawyers' paradise. UK firms contemplating a merger or takeover bid have to register their plans with both UK and EU authorities to minimise the chance of falling foul of either.

Restrictive trading practice policy

Restrictive trading practices undertaken by firms in imperfect product markets can be divided into two broad kinds: those undertaken independently by a single firm, and collective restrictive practices that involve either a written or an implied agreement among two or more firms.

> **KEY TERM**
>
> **restrictive trading practice:** an activity undertaken by a firm on its own or in collusion with other firms that restricts competition.

Independent restrictive trading practices

Independently undertaken restrictive practices include:

- decisions to charge discriminatory prices
- the refusal to supply a particular resale outlet
- full-line forcing, whereby a supplier forces a distributor that wishes to sell one of its products to stock its full range of products

> **EXAM TIP**
>
> Avoid confusing *trading* restrictive practices with *labour* restrictive practices, which are mentioned in Chapter 12.

Collective restrictive trading practices

A cartel agreement, in which firms come together to fix or rig the price of a good, is the most commonly known example of a collective restrictive trading practice (see page 78 in Chapter 7). Collective restrictive agreements and practices used to be referred by the competition authorities to a court of law, the Restrictive Practice Court (RPC). However, both independently undertaken and collective restrictive trading practices are now dealt with directly by the Competition and Markets Authority. The CMA usually asks the firm or firms involved to drop the practice voluntarily on the ground that it is anti-competitive. A cartel agreement is usually banned, unless the firms involved persuade the CMA that the agreement is in the public interest — for example, to protect the public from injury.

Private versus public ownership of industry

Nationalised industries

A **nationalised industry** or business is one that is owned by the state. The history of nationalisation in the UK extends back to the middle of the nineteenth century, when the Post Office was established as a civil service department. Several nationalisations occurred in the 1920s when the Central Electricity Board, the London Passenger Transport Board and the BBC were established as public corporations (usually during Conservative governments) by Acts of Parliament. Most of the early public corporations represented what has been called *gas and water socialism*. This describes the regulation through public ownership of an essential utility or service regarded as too important to be left to the vagaries of private ownership and market forces.

In the mid-twentieth century, industries were nationalised in the UK by Labour governments for two main reasons: as an instrument of socialist planning and control of the economy; and as a method of regulating the problem of monopoly — in particular, the problem of natural monopoly in the utility industries.

The 1950s to the 1970s were the decades of the **mixed economy**, when the major political parties agreed that the mix of public and private enterprise worked and was 'right' for the UK. But with the election of a radical free-market-orientated administration under Margaret Thatcher in 1979, this consensus broke down. The Conservative governments of the 1980s and 1990s set about the task of breaking up the mixed economy and moving the UK economy closer to a pure market economy.

Privatisation

Privatisation involves the transfer of publicly owned assets to the private sector. In the UK this has usually involved the sale to private ownership of nationalised industries and businesses that were previously owned by the state and accountable to central government. The main privatisations are shown in Table 9.1. Although the main privatisations have involved the sale of nationalised industries, other state-owned assets such as land and council houses have also been privatised.

Before privatisation some state-owned industries, such as electricity, gas and the railways, were vertically integrated. When selling these industries to the private sector, their privatisation involved significant vertical disintegration. The industries were split into horizontal layers, with different companies in each layer buying or selling from companies above or below them in the supply or distribution chain.

Table 9.1 The main privatisations in the UK

British Aerospace	1981
National Freight Corporation	1982
British Leyland (Rover)	1984
British Telecom (BT)	1984
British Shipbuilders	1985
National Bus Company	1985
British Gas	1986
British Airports Authority	1987
British Airways	1987
British Steel	1989
Water authorities	1989
Electricity distribution (regional electricity boards — RECs)	1990
Electricity generation	1991
British Coal	1994–95
British Rail	1995–96
Royal Mail	2013

However, the gas industry was initially privatised in fully, vertically integrated form, with British Gas owning all the stages of production from purchasing natural gas to selling through regional marketing boards to the customer. The industry was split into separate layers a few years after the initial privatisation in order to weaken natural monopoly and promote competition.

For gas and electricity, this strategy has generally been successful. Consumers now choose between competing electricity and gas marketing companies, and the prices of electricity and gas fell in real terms, at least for a number of years. However, as Case Study 9.2 on pages 117–118 explains, by 2008 rapidly rising prices led to calls for the reintroduction of controls on gas and electricity prices. In 2013, the Labour Party said it would introduce such price controls if it wins the 2015 general election.

EXAM TIP

Several years ago, exam questions were set on the *reasons* for privatisation and on the *advantages* and *disadvantages* of privatisation. While such questions are still possible, modern questions are more likely to be set on evaluating the success or failure of a privatisation, for example that of the gas industry, on its *track record*.

Privatisation and the free-market revival

The general case for privatisation can only be properly understood when seen as part of the revolution (or counter-revolution) in economic thinking known as the **free-market revival.** In the past, socialists often regarded nationalisation as an end in itself, apparently believing that by taking an industry into public ownership, efficiency and equity would automatically improve and the public interest be served. In much the same way, supporters of the free-market revival at the opposite end of the political and economic spectrum believe that private ownership and capitalism are always superior to public ownership. Whatever the circumstances, they believe that the privatisation of state-run industries must inevitably improve economic performance.

The advantages of privatisation

Specific arguments used to justify privatisation include:

- **Revenue raising.** Privatisation, or the sale of state-owned assets, provides the government with a short-term source of revenue, which at the height of privatisation was at least £3–4 billion a year. But obviously an asset cannot be sold twice.
- **Reducing public spending and the government's borrowing requirement.** After 1979, Conservative governments aimed to reduce public spending and government borrowing. By classifying the moneys received from asset sales as negative expenditure rather than as revenue, governments were able, from an accounting point of view, to reduce the level of public spending as well as government borrowing. In addition, when the state successfully sold loss-making industries such as the Rover Group, public spending on subsidies sometimes fell. Government borrowing can also fall if private ownership returns the industries to profitability, since corporation tax revenue is boosted and the state earns dividend income from any shares that it retains in the privatised company.
- **The promotion of competition.** Privatisation has been justified on the ground that it promotes competition through the break-up of monopoly. At the time of their privatisation, industries such as gas and electricity were natural monopolies. But as I explain later in the chapter, the growth of technology-driven competition, together with the removal of barriers to entry by regulating agencies such as Ofgem, has significantly increased competition.
- **The promotion of efficiency.** For free-market economists, this is perhaps the most important justification of privatisation. Supporters of privatisation believe that public ownership gives rise to special forms of inefficiency which disappear once an industry moves into the private sector — even if the industry remains a monopoly. The culture of public ownership makes nationalised industries resistant to change. Through exposure to the threat of takeover and the discipline of the capital market, the privatisation of a state-owned monopoly should improve the business's efficiency and commercial performance.
- **Popular capitalism.** The promotion of an **enterprise culture** was an important reason for privatisation in the UK. Privatisation extended share ownership to employees and other individuals who had not previously owned shares, and thus added to the incentive for the electorate to support the private enterprise economy.

Privatisation has generally proved popular with voters, so governments, both Conservative and then Labour, saw no point in abandoning a winning programme.

The disadvantages of privatisation

Privatisation has the following possible disadvantages:

- **Monopoly abuse.** Opponents of privatisation have argued that, far from promoting competition and efficiency, privatisation increases monopoly abuse by transferring socially owned and accountable public monopolies into weakly regulated and less accountable private monopolies.
- **Short-termism wins over long-termism.** Many of the investments that need to be undertaken by the previously nationalised industries can only be profitable in the long term. There is a danger that under private ownership, such investments will not be made because company boards concentrate on the short-termism of delivering dividends to keep shareholders and financial institutions happy. Under-investment in maintaining the rail track and in technically advanced trains by the privatised railway companies provides an example. However, there is a counter-argument: that under public ownership, the government starved the nationalised industries of investment funds in order to keep government borrowing down.
- **Selling the family silver.** Opponents of privatisation also argue that if a private sector business were to sell its capital assets simply in order to raise revenue to pay for current expenditure, it would rightly incur the wrath of its shareholders. The same should be true of the government and the sale of state-owned assets. Taxpayers should not sanction the sale of capital assets owned on their behalf by the UK government to raise revenue to finance current spending on items such as wages and salaries. In reply, supporters of the privatisation programme argue that, far from selling the family silver, privatisation merely returns the family's assets to the family: that is, from the custody of the state to direct ownership by private individuals.
- **The free-lunch syndrome.** Opponents of privatisation also claim that state-owned assets have been sold too cheaply, encouraging the belief among first-time share buyers that there is such a thing as a free lunch. This is because the offer-price of shares in newly privatised industries has normally been pitched at a level which has guaranteed a risk-free capital gain or one-way bet at the taxpayer's expense. This encourages the very opposite of an enterprise economy.

Economic liberalisation

So far, I have defined privatisation in a strictly narrow sense, as the transfer of assets from the public sector to the private sector. Some commentators extend the definition of privatisation to include other aspects of the programme of economic liberalisation pursued by UK governments since 1979. Policies that are closely related to privatisation include:

- contractualisation
- marketisation
- public–private partnerships (PPPs) and the private finance initiative (PFI)
- deregulation

Contractualisation

Contractualisation or **contracting out** takes place when services such as road cleaning and refuse collection are put to private sector tender, although the taxpayer still ultimately pays for the service. To try to get value for money for the taxpayer, services that were previously provided *in house* by public sector workers are provided *out of house* through **competitive tendering.**

Marketisation

Whereas privatisation (narrowly defined) involves transferring assets from the public sector to the private sector, **marketisation** (or **commercialisation**) shifts the provision of services from the non-market sector into the market sector. A price is charged for a service that consumers previously enjoyed 'free'. Governments have also experimented in creating internal markets, whereby one part of a state-owned enterprise charges a price to another part of the same enterprise for the service it provides within the organisation. This is a form of transfer pricing.

> **EXAM TIP**
>
> Avoid confusing privatisation with other policies that have reduced the role of the state in the economy, such as marketisation and deregulation. Note, however, how the policies are linked.

Public–private partnerships and the private finance initiative

As the name suggests, **public–private partnerships (PPPs)** are partnerships between the private and public sectors to provide public services. They include the contractualisation of services that I have already described, but also cover activities such as the transfer of council homes to housing associations using private loans. PPP has been particularly important in the provision of health services, but private sector providers are running prisons, local authority revenue and benefit services, the majority of residential homes for the elderly, and schools.

The **private finance initiative (PFI)**, which was introduced by the Conservative government in 1993 and enthusiastically taken up by the subsequent Labour government, is closely related to PPP. Before PFI, the government was involved in all stages of planning, building and then running a public investment project such as a new school. Under PFI, the government's role is restricted to deciding the service it requires and then seeking tenders from the private sector for designing, building, financing and running the project. The government becomes an *enabler* rather than a *provider*.

Recent governments have favoured PFI because public sector services can be provided, but government borrowing (or at least on-balance sheet borrowing) does not increase, at least in the short run. The capital costs of the project are paid for by the private sector provider, but the taxpayer pays if a subsidy is required if the project is not self-financing. Taxpayers also contribute towards the profit made by the private provider. The government hopes, however, that efficiency gains resulting from private sector provision will more than offset the payment of taxpayers' funds into private sector profits. Public service trade unions oppose PPPs, and especially the PFI, because they see them as the creeping privatisation of public services. By contrast, governments argue that PPPs can provide the public sector with the cultural values of the private sector, injecting a fresh, innovative and entrepreneurial 'can-do' approach. They believe that without PPP, public services have a tendency to be entrenched, reactive and conservative. However, a counter-argument is that PPP and PFI are creating massive bills that taxpayers will have to pay in the future.

Deregulation

The nature of economic regulation

Economic regulation involves the imposition of rules, controls and constraints, which restrict freedom of economic action in the marketplace. There are two types of regulation: external regulation and self-regulation.

- **External regulation**, as the name suggests, involves an external agency laying down and enforcing rules and restraints. The external agency may be a government department such as the BIS, or a special regulatory body or agency set up by government, for example the Competition and Market Authority.
- By contrast, **self-regulation** or **voluntary regulation** involves a group of individuals or firms regulating themselves, for example through a professional association such as the Law Society or the British Medical Association.

Regulation and market failure

Competition can sometimes bring about a situation in which social costs and benefits are not the same as the private costs and benefits incurred and received by the people actually undertaking the market activity. As I explain in Chapter 10, the over-production of externalities such as environmental pollution, and the under-consumption of education, healthcare and other merit goods, provide familiar examples of divergence between private and social costs and benefits. Governments use regulation to try to correct such market failures and to achieve a socially optimal level of production and consumption. Monopoly is also a form of market failure, and regulation is used to limit and deter monopoly exploitation of consumers.

EXAM TIP

Exam questions may require a justification for removing or keeping government regulation of markets and businesses. While there is a strong case for removing regulations that protect incumbent firms or which raise business's costs unnecessarily, many regulations can be justified on the ground that they protect people from the abuse of monopoly power and from harmful externalities.

Other examples of government regulation aimed largely at reducing the social costs of market activity include health and safety at work, anti-discrimination and safeguards of workers' rights, and consumer protection legislation. Much of this regulation is concerned with the adequate provision of information for customers and workers, and the setting of quality standards for the production of goods. Such regulation may affect advertising standards, consumers' rights of redress when purchasing faulty goods, and workers' rights in the event of discrimination or unfair dismissal.

Deregulation

Deregulation involves the removal of any previously imposed regulations that have adversely restricted competition and freedom of market activity. During the last 35 years, significant deregulation has taken place in the UK and the USA. Systems of regulation built up during the Keynesian era have on occasion been completely abandoned, while in other cases they have been watered down or modified. The UK government has removed the protected legal monopoly status enjoyed, for example, by bus companies, airlines and commercial television and radio companies. Access to BT's distribution network of land lines has been given to competitors in the telecommunications industry, and private power companies have been allowed to rent the services of the national electricity and gas distribution grids.

There are two main justifications of deregulation:

- the promotion of competition and market contestability through the removal of artificial barriers to market entry
- the removal of red tape and bureaucracy which imposes unnecessary costs on economic agents, particularly businesses

Deregulation and the free-market revival

The switch away from the imposition of ever-more stringent rules and regulations upon private sector economic activity, and towards the opposite policy of deregulation, reflects the decline of Keynesianism and the resurgence of free-market economics. Deregulation should be regarded as a part of an overall policy of economic liberalisation, which, as already explained, also involved the policies of privatisation, contractualisation and marketisation (or commercialisation). In recent years, governments in most industrialised countries, including most recently those in the formerly centrally planned economies of eastern Europe, have begun this process of economic liberalisation and rolling back the economic functions of the state. However, as the recent history of the financial services and banking industries shows, 'light-touch' regulation arguably was a major cause of the financial melt-down that began in 2007. Since then, there have been calls for much tougher regulation of banking and financial services.

Deregulation and the theory of contestable markets

Much of the justification for the policies of deregulation and economic liberalisation that have been pursued in recent years has been provided by the **theory of contestable markets,** which I explained earlier in the chapter. Contestable market theory argues that the most effective way to promote competitive behaviour within markets is not to impose ever-more regulation upon firms and industries, but to carry out the opposite process of deregulation.

According to this view, the main function of deregulation is to remove barriers to entry, thereby creating incentives both for new firms to enter and contest the market and for established firms to behave in a more competitive way so as to deter new market entrants. Under the influence of the theory of contestable markets, governments have sought to remove or loosen all regulations whose main effect has been to reduce competition and to promote unnecessary barriers to market entry.

Regulatory capture

Another theory that has had some influence upon the trend towards deregulation is the **theory of regulatory capture.** This theory argues that regulatory agencies created by government can be 'captured' by the industries or firms they are intended to oversee and regulate. Following capture, the regulatory agencies begin to operate in the industry's interest rather than on behalf of the consumers whom they are supposed to protect.

Even if regulatory capture does not take place, the supporters of deregulation argue that much regulatory activity is unnecessary and ultimately burdensome upon industry and consumers. Once established, the regulators have an incentive to extend their role by introducing ever-more rules and regulations, since in this way they justify their pay and their jobs. Regulation acts both as an informal tax upon the regulated, raising production costs and consumer prices, and also as an extra barrier to market entry, restricting competition within the regulated industry.

The regulation of the privatised utility industries

As I have explained, deregulatory policies have been implemented alongside privatisation in liberalising the UK economy. In the 1980s and 1990s, UK governments realised that once industries such as telecommunications, gas, water and electricity were privatised, there was a danger they might abuse their monopoly position and exploit the consumer. For this reason, special regulatory bodies such as **Ofgem**, which now regulates the gas and electricity industries, were set up at the time of privatisation to act as watchdogs over the performance of the utilities in the private sector. At the time of privatisation, industry-specific regulatory bodies were created. Some of these agencies have recently been merged and now cover more than one industry.

The paradox of deregulation

The establishment of regulatory agencies such as Ofgem at a time when governments have actively been pursuing a policy of deregulation and economic liberalisation has created a rather strange paradox and a source of possible conflict. On the one hand, by setting markets free, deregulation reduces the role of the state; on the other hand, new watchdog bodies such as Ofgem have extended the regulatory role of government and its agencies.

However, successive governments have argued that there need be no conflict between regulation and deregulation. This is because the regulatory bodies are themselves actively involved in deregulating the industries they oversee — for example, by enforcing the removal of barriers that prevent the entry of new firms. Recent technical progress has made it increasingly possible for new firms to enter the utility industries, particularly in the telecommunications industry. By contesting the market away from established companies such as BT and British Gas, new market entrants have eroded the natural monopoly position previously enjoyed by the privatised utilities.

Supporters of the liberalisation programme hope that the new watchdog agencies will prove so successful that eventually the new regulatory bodies can wither away, when the markets they oversee have become sufficiently competitive. However, this is likely to be a long process. Although new firms are beginning to compete in the markets previously completely dominated by state-owned utilities, established companies like British Gas are still dominant. Their continuing market power means that, certainly for the next few years, the regulatory bodies set up at the time of privatisation must continue as a surrogate for competition. Some commentators argue that, far from withering away, the new regulatory agencies may gradually extend their powers and functions. Free-market critics of economic regulation believe that the UK regulatory system provides a classic example of a growing bureaucracy.

Price-capping and the RPI minus X price formula

At the time of the state sell-off of the telecommunications, electricity and gas industries, it was realised that the newly privatised companies might use their monopoly power to raise the prices they charged and to exploit consumers. To prevent this, some form of price control was deemed necessary. The UK government decided against rate of return regulation (the system of price control used in the USA) for the reason I mentioned earlier in the chapter; namely that it raises costs and increases productive inefficiency. Instead, the UK government imposed **price caps** based on the **RPI minus X** formula. The formula limited a privatised utility's freedom to raise its prices, but encouraged it to reduce costs.

Average price increases were limited to X percentage points below the rate of inflation, as measured by the retail prices index. For example, a price cap of 'RPI minus 5', set when the rate of inflation was 4%, meant that the privatised company would actually have to reduce its average prices by 1%.

The X factor reflected the improvements in productive efficiency that the regulator believed the privatised utility could make and share with its consumers each year. Suppose, for example, that with an inflation rate of 4%, Ofgem believes that gas companies can cut costs by 10% a year. If factor X is set at 0%, the gas companies can raise prices by 4%, even though their costs are falling by 10%. This means that only the gas companies and their shareholders benefit from the efficiency gain, while consumers gain nothing. At the other extreme, if factor X is set at 10%, consumers rather than the gas companies benefit. This might destroy the incentive for gas companies to invest in new technology. Hence the case for pitching factor X somewhere between 0% and 10%. If set at 5%, the efficiency benefits are shared equally between consumers and producers. Consumers gain from lower prices, yet gas companies still have an incentive to invest and to increase productive efficiency. By improving efficiency by more than the factor X set by the regulator, utility companies can further increase their profits.

EXTENSION MATERIAL

The regulatory bargain and other issues

Two significant problems emerged with the RPI minus X price formula after the price cap was first imposed on BT in 1984.

- Initially, the utilities believed that, as a part of a **regulatory bargain**, they would be left alone for 5 years after factor X was set, to get on with the task of running their businesses. They also believed that, if they achieved an efficiency gain during that 5-year period over and above the factor X set by the regulator, they would not be punished when the regulator reset factor X at the end of 5 years. In practice, however, the regulators intervened throughout the 5-year licence period, and in the early years, they generally raised X every time they reviewed it. Critics of the way RPI minus X was implemented believed that this reduced a utility's incentive to improve efficiency and reduce costs. This is because the regulator clawed back the utility's share of any productivity gain by increasing factor X, on the ground that the utility was making excess profits.

- The RPI minus X pricing formula could only work properly if the regulator had a good idea of how efficient the privatised utility was, and of how efficient it might become. In order to set the X factor for 5 years ahead, the regulators needed to possess considerable technical information about the industries they oversaw. A regulator who failed to foresee the direction that technical progress was likely to take over the next 5 years might have to reset X before the 5 years was up, thus triggering the disadvantage I mentioned above. A regulator was most likely to set X accurately if the technology in the industry was fairly mature and not subject to sudden change. In these circumstances, the rate at which the regulator could learn about the industry was faster than the rate at which technology changed.

With the privatisation of gas and water, the RPI − X formula was modified to RPI − X + Y, and RPI + K. This was to allow unavoidable service improvement costs (such as infrastructure upgrades) to be passed through to customers. These unavoidable costs included new investment demanded by the government to upgrade the gas network and improve the quality of drinking water and wastewater treatment.

CASE STUDY 9.2

In recent years, gas and electricity prices more than doubled at the same time as Ofgem was supposedly imposing the RPI minus X formula on both energy industries. Consumers might well have asked 'Whatever has happened to gas and electricity price caps?' The answer is that the caps still exist, but only with regard to the transport of gas and electricity from one part of the country to another.

To make sense of this, you must understand that gas and electricity are vertically disintegrated industries. Import prices of natural gas and coal, over which the UK regulator has no control, are the result of the first stage of production. The gas and electricity we then use at home are 'manufactured' or processed, before being transported to the consuming regions. The final stage of production is distributing gas and electricity locally to the consumer. The different stages of production are undertaken by different firms. As stated, Ofgem has little or no control over import prices, and therein lies the most important reason for escalating prices. And as the extract below reveals, the UK government has removed price controls previously imposed on the energy distributing companies, from which we buy our gas and electricity. The RPI minus X price cap is imposed on the middle transporting stage of production (e.g. the National Grid) and this has little effect on retail gas and electricity prices.

Does removing price controls protect consumers?

When competition in a market is weak, price controls can help to protect consumers from the risk that companies might take advantage of their position to set excessive prices. Ofcom, Ofgem and Postcomm have statutory objectives requiring them to protect consumers through the introduction of competition, where appropriate. Between 2002 and 2006, Ofgem removed retail price controls from gas and electricity supply. The regulator felt that the market was sufficiently well developed for consumers to be protected by competition.

Once price controls have been removed, regulators rely on consumers to switch suppliers, thereby rewarding companies that offer good service and competitive prices, and punishing the inefficient. For this to work, consumers need to have good information about different suppliers, be able to switch supplier easily, have sufficient confidence in the market to believe that changing supplier can make a difference, and be able to obtain redress where a company behaves anti-competitively.

Prices of gas and electricity have risen rapidly in the recent past, and almost doubled since the start of the decade. Businesses and consumers need to be confident that markets without price controls are being effectively regulated and working well, especially at a time of rapidly rising prices. Regulators should regularly monitor business and consumer confidence in the market and its regulation so that they can respond quickly if confidence falls.

Source: Report of the House of Commons Public Accounts Committee, November 2008

Follow-up questions

1 Why have gas and electricity prices risen so rapidly in recent years?

2 Should price caps be reintroduced on retail gas and electricity prices? Justify your answer.

EXAM TIP

Technology-driven competition and yardstick competition provide examples of methods of competition firms can use in addition to, or in place of, price competition.

Technology-driven competition

Regulatory agencies have been able to lower and sometimes to remove barriers to market entry by promoting **technology-driven competition.** This type of competition occurs when technical progress enables new firms to enter markets that were previously natural monopolies. In the telecommunications industry, developments such as mobile telephony, satellite technology and the falling real cost of laying fibre-optic land lines have meant that new market entrants such as Vodafone and the cable television companies can invest in their own distribution networks. BT's distribution network is no longer a natural monopoly.

In the gas, water and electricity industries, new firms have entered the market by renting the services of the existing distribution network or grid. New electronic information and recording systems allow customers living, for example, in Manchester to buy electricity from a distribution company located in another region. These developments make it possible for customers to shop around and find the distributor that offers the most attractive price.

Technology-driven competition can be thwarted if the distribution network through which the service is delivered into people's homes is owned by an established utility company, which is a major producer of the good or service transported through the system. In this situation, there is an obvious danger that the vertically integrated company owning the network might prevent new market entrants from using the distribution grid. For example, a vertically integrated British Gas Corporation could charge new gas suppliers artificially high prices for using its distribution grid, to prevent the new firms gaining market share.

This explains why government and the regulators have forced previously vertically integrated utility companies to disintegrate. Separate companies now own different layers of the gas and electricity industries. This means that the distribution layer (owned by National Grid Gas plc) is free to carry the electricity or gas of as many suppliers as it wishes, and not just the energy supplied by E.on or British Gas.

Yardstick competition

The telecommunications industry offers the greatest scope for technology-driven competition, with new market entrants able to bypass BT's distribution network or pay fair rents for its use. However, at the other end of the spectrum, the water industry possesses the least scope for technology-driven competition to remove barriers to entry and break up the natural monopoly.

For this reason, the Office of Water Services (Ofwat) uses **yardstick competition** as the main regulatory device to promote efficient and competitive behaviour by the water companies. After comparing the performance and costs of all the water companies, Ofwat sets prices so that all the water companies have to match the standards achieved by the best in the industry. If and when the other utility watchdogs run up against the realistic limits to technology-driven competition in the industries they regulate, they may turn to yardstick competition to assess the efficiency of the companies they oversee.

SUMMARY

- Industrial policy is an important part of the government's microeconomic policy.
- Competition policy, policy toward private and public ownership and regulatory and deregulatory policy are the three main elements of industrial policy.
- The three elements of competition policy are monopoly policy, merger policy and policy toward restrictive trading practices.
- UK monopoly policy is based on a cost–benefit approach to large firms.
- Mergers are most likely to be prevented if they are viewed as potentially anti-competitive.
- Collective trading practices such as cartel agreements are deemed against the public interest and are generally illegal.
- From the 1980s onwards, UK governments have privatised rather than nationalised industries, though from 2008 onwards, some UK banks were effectively nationalised, at least on a temporary basis.
- Governments have established regulatory agencies such as Ofcom to regulate the privatised industries.
- Regulatory agencies also try to deregulate. If successful, the agencies can wither away.
- Regulatory agencies have imposed 'RPI minus X' price caps, but these have not prevented rapid price rises for goods such as electricity and gas in recent years.

Exam-style questions

1 Outline the three main elements of competition policy. **(15 marks)**

2 Explain three different ways in which a government can try to deal with the problems posed by monopoly. **(15 marks)**

3 Evaluate the advantages and disadvantages of privatisation. **(25 marks)**

4 'Attempts by governments to regulate private industries inevitably lead to adverse unintended consequences.' To what extent do you agree with this view? Justify your answer. **(25 marks)**

Extra resources to help you revise are available online at www.hodderplus.co.uk/philipallan

Market failure

Market failure occurs whenever the market mechanism or price mechanism performs unsatisfactorily. There are two main ways in which markets fail. Markets can function inequitably or they can function inefficiently. It is also useful to distinguish between complete market failure, when the market simply does not exist, and partial market failure, when the market functions but produces the wrong quantity of a good or service. In the former case, there is a missing market. In the latter case, the good or service may be provided too cheaply, in which case it is over-produced and over-consumed. Alternatively, as in monopoly, the good may be too expensive, in which case under-production and under-consumption result.

LEARNING OUTCOMES

This chapter will:
- contrast A2 and AS coverage of market failure
- explain the different ways of classifying market failure
- summarise the main market failures you learnt at AS
- examine a number of case studies of market failure

WHAT YOU SHOULD ALREADY KNOW

The section of the A2 specification that covers market failure and government failure starts with the statement: 'Candidates will be expected to develop the models of market failure introduced in Unit 1'. Thus, unlike Chapters 2–9 which introduce topics not included at AS, this chapter covers topics you studied a year ago in the AS course. To avoid undue repetition, parts of this chapter summarise the coverage of market failures included in my *AQA AS Economics* textbook, without providing detail. For example, many of the diagrams included in my AS textbook on marginal private, external and social cost and benefit have been omitted from this book. You should refer back to my AS textbook, or to the notes you made last year, to remind yourself of these diagrams.

Building on your AS knowledge of market failure

Given that 'Markets and market failure' is the title of AS Unit 1, it is not surprising that about half of your study of microeconomics last year focused on **market failure**. Indeed, if you used my *AQA AS Economics* textbook in your AS studies, four out of the eleven chapters on Unit 1 were devoted to market failures, together with a chapter on government intervention in markets that explained how government policies attempt to correct market failures.

KEY TERM

market failure: occurs when a market functions badly, unsatisfactorily, or not at all.

In this book, by contrast, only this chapter focuses specifically on market failure. However, you should appreciate that earlier chapters on monopoly and oligopoly, and the chapters that follow on from this chapter on cost–benefit analysis, poverty and income inequalities, also touch on market failure.

In this chapter, I have resisted the temptation simply to repeat what you learnt last year. Instead below is a summary of what you should already know in order for you to *develop* your knowledge and understanding, particularly by using the concept of **allocative efficiency** to analyse market failures.

> **KEY TERM**
>
> **allocative efficiency:** occurs when it is impossible to improve overall economic welfare by reallocating resources between industries or markets.

Inequity and market failure

In this chapter, I use the word **equity** to mean fairness or justness (though in other contexts, such as the housing market, equity has the very different meaning of *wealth*). As soon as considerations of equity are introduced into economic analysis, **normative** or **value judgements** are being made about, for example, 'socially fair' distributions of income and wealth.

> **KEY TERM**
>
> **inequitable:** unfair or unjust.

As the experience of many poor countries shows, unregulated market forces tend to produce highly unequal distributions of income and wealth. Some economists, usually of a free-market persuasion, dispute whether this is a market failure. They argue that people who end up rich deserve to be rich, and people who end up poor deserve to be poor. According to this view, the market does not fail; it simply creates incentives, which, if followed, cause people to generate income and wealth which end up benefiting most of the population.

However, most economists reject as too extreme the view that the market contains its own morality with regard to the distributions of income and wealth. They argue that markets are essentially 'value-neutral' with regard to income and wealth distribution. When unregulated markets produce gross inequalities that cannot be justified on social fairness grounds, the state should intervene to limit market freedom.

Nevertheless, few economists who accept this view believe that markets should be abolished and replaced with the command mechanism. Rather, governments should modify the market so that it operates in a way more equitable than would be the case in the absence of state intervention. Taxing the better-off and redistributing tax revenues as transfers to the less well-off is the obvious way of correcting market failure to ensure an equitable distribution of income and wealth. However, as I explain in Chapters 12 and 13, the redistributive policies of **progressive taxation** and **transfers** to the poor may promote new types of inefficiency and distortion within the economy.

Markets functioning inefficiently

As I have explained in earlier chapters, monopoly and other forms of imperfect competition provide examples of market failure resulting from markets performing inefficiently. The 'wrong' or allocatively inefficient quantity is produced in monopoly, particularly when there are no economies of scale, and the 'wrong' price is charged. Too little is produced and is sold at too high a price, and the market outcome is both allocatively and productively inefficient.

Complete versus partial market failure

When studying the AS course a few months ago, you learnt about **pure public goods** and externalities. Both of these can lead to complete market failure. In a market economy, markets may fail to provide any quantity at all of a pure public good such as national defence and they also fail to provide or encourage production of a positive externality such as a beautiful view. This leads to the emergence of **missing markets**.

> **KEY TERM**
>
> **missing markets:** occur when the incentive function of prices completely breaks down and a market fails to come into existence or disappears completely.

To understand a missing market, we have to return to the functions that prices perform in markets and in a market economy. The following **synoptic link** should remind you of the three functions of prices you learnt about at AS.

SYNOPTIC LINK: MARKET FAILURE AND THE THREE FUNCTIONS OF PRICES

The signalling function. Prices provide information that allows all the traders in the market to plan and coordinate their economic activities. Let me provide one example. In Chapter 5 of my AS textbook, I described how on most Friday afternoons, I visit my local street market to buy fruit and vegetables, including tomatoes and lettuce. The prices, which are shown on white plastic tabs stuck into each tray of produce, help me to decide what to buy. Of course, information about prices alone is not enough. I also need information about the quality of the goods on sale, which I try to get by looking carefully at the size of the produce and for blemishes such as bruising on apples or pears.

The incentive function. The information *signalled* by *relative prices*, such as the price of tomatoes relative to the price of lettuce, creates incentives for people to alter their economic behaviour. Suppose, for example, I go to my local market intending to buy, along with other vegetables, a kilo of tomatoes and one lettuce. It being Friday afternoon, by the time I arrive at the market, the street traders have cut the price of tomatoes by 50% to try to prevent unsold stock accumulating, whose quality might deteriorate overnight. A fall in the price of tomatoes, *relative* to the price of other goods that I could buy, creates an incentive for me to buy more tomatoes, provided of course I believe the quality hasn't deteriorated.

The rationing or allocative function of prices. Suppose I respond to a fall in the relative price of tomatoes by buying more, say 2 kilos rather than the single kilo I had intended to buy as I made my way to market. Because my income is limited, spending more on one good usually means I spend less on other goods. Prices, together with income, ration the way people spend their money. Suppose tomato prices fall, not only in my local street market on a Friday afternoon, but throughout the economy for a sustained period of time. Tomatoes are now cheaper *relative* to other goods in the economy. On the one hand, the lower relative price causes households to increase their demand for tomatoes, substituting tomatoes in place of other vegetables. But, on the other hand, a lower relative price may indicate that growing tomatoes is not a very profitable activity. In response, farmers grow fewer tomatoes. If these events happen, the information signalled by changing relative prices creates incentives for economic agents to alter their market behaviour, and changes the way scarce resources are **rationed** and **allocated** between competing uses.

When explaining the nature of a missing market, we need to focus on the second function of prices, the **incentive function.** As I have explained, prices create incentives for people to behave in certain ways. In a market economy, entrepreneurs are generally unwilling to produce goods unless the goods can be sold at a profit. But with public goods and externalities, **non-excludability** and the absence of enforceable property rights create a situation in which profit cannot be made within a market. The result is a **missing market.**

With partial market failure, markets do exist but they end up providing an **allocatively inefficient** quantity of the good, either too much (in the case of **demerit goods** such as narcotic drugs), or too little (in the case of a **merit good** such as healthcare).

In the next sections, I provide a brief summary of market failures and expand on what you learnt last year.

Public and private goods

Most goods are **private goods**, possessing two important characteristics. The owners can exercise private property rights, preventing other people from using the good or consuming its benefits. This is called **excludability**. The second characteristic possessed by a private good is **rivalry** or **diminishability**. When one person consumes a private good, less of its benefits are available for other people. Private goods also have a third characteristic: **rejectability**. People can opt out and refuse to purchase private goods.

> **KEY TERMS**
>
> **private good:** a good which exhibits the characteristics of **excludability** and **rivalry**.
>
> **public good:** a good which exhibits the characteristics of **non-excludability** and **non-rivalry**.

In contrast, pure **public goods** exhibit the opposite characteristics of **non-excludability, non-rivalry** and **non-rejectability.** It is particularly the first two of these which lead to market failure.

Non-excludability and public goods

The best example of a pure public good is nuclear defence. If prices are charged for the benefits provided by the ring of nuclear missiles protecting Britain, then, without coercion, people could refuse to pay but still

> **KEY TERM**
>
> **free-rider:** somebody who benefits without paying.

enjoy the benefits. Any attempt by the private provider to retaliate by preventing those who do not pay from receiving the service, will not work. Withdrawing the benefits from one person means withdrawing them from all. Nevertheless, all individuals face the temptation to consume without paying, or to **free-ride**. If enough people choose to free-ride, market provision of nuclear defence breaks down. The incentive to provide the service through the market disappears. Assuming that the majority of the country's inhabitants believe nuclear defence to be necessary (that is, a 'good' rather than a 'bad'), the market fails because it fails to provide a service for which there is a need.

Non-pure public goods or quasi-public goods

Most public goods are **non-pure public goods** or **quasi-public goods** rather than pure public goods. This is because various methods can be used to exclude free-riders. Non-pure public goods include roads, television and radio broadcasts, street lighting and lighthouses. In principle, roads can be converted into private goods, provided for profit through the market. This could be done by limiting points of access, by constructing toll gates or by introducing a scheme of electronic road pricing. But even though non-pure public goods such as roads can be provided through the market, the second characteristic of a public good, **non-rivalry**, creates a strong case for non-market provision. Such provision will normally be made by the state at zero price to the consumer, being financed collectively out of general taxation.

> **KEY TERM**
>
> **non-pure public good:** a good for which it may be possible to exclude free-riders, but for which there is a case for not doing so.

> **EXAM TIP**
>
> Make sure you understand the difference between a private good and a public good, and can give examples of both.

Non-rivalry and public goods

Non-rivalry (also known as non-diminishability and non-exhaustibility) means that when an extra person benefits from a public good, the benefits available to other people are not reduced. In turn, this means that the marginal cost incurred by the provider of the public good when an extra person benefits from the good is zero ($MC = 0$). For example, when a person switches on a television set, the availability and benefits of the broadcast programme are not diminished for people viewing the programme on other television sets. Equally, the broadcasting company incurs no extra cost.

CASE STUDY 10.1

Allocative efficiency and rail fares

Motorists in cities pay substantially less than the costs they create when driving their vehicles. The greater the congestion, the truer this is. The extra cost or, as economists would call it, the marginal social cost, of an extra vehicle coming onto a road is quantifiable. Wherever there is congestion, the marginal social cost will be greater than the actual cost to the individual road user (often called the marginal road user) since the costs to the motorist of using the road are vehicle costs and time. The motorist does not have to take into account the costs imposed on other road users and on pedestrians.

On the other hand, if rail transport in cities is required to cover costs, it will then be over-priced relative to users of urban roads, since rail users will be required to cover all the real costs they give rise to, while road users will not. The effect of this difference in pricing policy is an inefficient distribution of traffic between road and rail. Less traffic travels by rail, especially in the peak, than is efficient.

One way of getting prices right would be to raise the price of urban road use until both public and private road transport covered its real costs. But if we accept it is politically imprudent or undesirable to raise the cost of using roads to a level where marginal social costs are covered, one can attempt to get the allocatively efficient relationship between road and rail by the opposite course of action: by keeping rail fares lower than they would be if the railways charged what the market would bear rather than by raising real prices. This is the essence of the case for rail subsidies.

The essential case, if proven, must be that the traffic the railways divert from the roads reduces congestion by an amount sufficient to justify the rail subsidies required. Underlying this is the proposition that users of city roads pay less through taxation for using them than covers the real cost of their use.

Follow-up questions

1 Define the term 'marginal social cost'.
2 The passage states that subsidising rail fares can establish the allocatively efficient relationship between the prices paid for road and rail use. Explain this statement.
3 Outline the case against subsidising rail fares.

Public goods and allocative efficiency

The allocatively efficient or 'correct' quantity of any good produced and consumed is the quantity that people choose to consume when $P = MC$. But as just noted, assuming a public good is already being provided, the MC of providing the good to an extra consumer is zero. Allocative efficiency therefore occurs when $P = 0$ and the good is free for consumers. But private entrepreneurs only willingly provide goods if profits can be made, and for this to happen, the price must be above zero $(P > 0)$. In the case of public goods, this means that markets can only provide the goods, assuming free-riders have been excluded, if the price is set above the marginal cost of supply $(P > MC)$. This reduces consumption of the public good to below the allocatively efficient level. Market provision thus results in under-production and under-consumption of the good.

Government provision of public goods

Because markets either fail to provide or under-provide public goods, there is a strong case for the state providing the goods at zero price. Charities such as Trinity House, which is responsible for lighthouses in the UK, can also provide public goods. In theory, free provision achieves the allocatively efficient level of consumption of the public good: that is, the quantity that people wish to consume when the good is free.

Public goods and government goods

Students often wrongly define a public good as a good that is provided by the government. This is confusing *cause* with *effect*. The word *public* in public good refers to the fact that members of the general public cannot be excluded from enjoying the good's benefits. It is this that *causes* market failure. To correct the market failure, governments provide public goods. This is the *effect*. Government goods include public goods such as defence, police and roads, but they also include merit goods such as education and healthcare, which I explain later in this chapter.

EXAM TIP

Make sure you don't confuse merit goods with public goods.

Public bads

A **bad** is the opposite of a **good**. People are prepared to pay a price to gain the benefits of a good such as a bar of chocolate. Equally, they are prepared to pay a price to avoid consuming a bad such as the household sewage they produce. In this case, this is the price of the sanitation equipment installed in their houses, together with the water and sewage rates households pay to the water authority that removes the sewage from their homes.

But in the case of many bads, known as **public bads**, people can free-ride by dumping the bads they produce on others. Examples are the emission of pollution into the atmosphere and fly-tipping rubbish in public parks or in other people's gardens. If a private sector company tries to charge a price for rubbish removal, households may avoid paying the price by dumping their garbage. This is why local authorities empty dustbins free, financing rubbish removal through local taxation.

KEY TERMS

bad: the opposite of a good, yielding dissatisfaction or disutility when consumed. Consumption of bads reduces economic welfare.

public bad: bad for which the producers free-ride, dumping the bad on third parties.

Externalities

An **externality** is a special type of public good or public bad, which is dumped by those who produce it on other people who receive or consume it, whether or not they choose to. (These people are known as **third parties**, and the externality is sometimes called a **spin-off effect**.) Because externalities are generated and received outside the market, they also provide examples of **missing markets**.

KEY TERM

externality: a public good, in the case of an external benefit, or a public bad, in the case of an external cost that is dumped on third parties outside the market.

Externalities also exhibit the **free-rider problem**. The provider of an external benefit such as a beautiful view cannot charge a market price to any willing free-riders who enjoy it. Conversely, the unwilling free-riders who receive or consume external costs such as pollution and noise cannot charge a price to the polluter for the bad that they reluctantly consume.

Externalities are classified in two main ways:
- as external costs and external benefits, also known as negative externalities and positive externalities
- as pure production externalities, pure consumption externalities and externalities involving a mix of production and consumption

Suppose, for example, that brick dust infiltrates houses and a laundry located near a brick works emitting the pollution. The pollution that soils newly washed laundry and is breathed in by local householders is emitted in the course of production. For the laundry, brick-dust pollution is a pure production externality, emitted in the course of production and received by other producers. But for the households, the pollution is a mixed externality, generated in production and received in consumption. I shall leave it to you to think of examples of pure consumption externalities and mixed consumption externalities. If in doubt, refer back to page 101 of my *AQA AS Economics* textbook.

EXAM TIP

Make sure you can give examples of external costs and external benefits and are aware of the difference between production and consumption externalities.

Divergence between private and social cost and benefit

At the heart of microeconomic theory lies the assumption that, in a market situation, an economic agent considers only the private costs and benefits resulting from its market actions, ignoring any costs and benefits imposed on others. For the agent, **private benefit maximisation** occurs when:

KEY TERM

private benefit maximisation: occurs when $MPB = MPC$.

marginal private benefit = marginal private cost

or:

$MPB = MPC$

However, **social benefit maximisation**, which maximises the public interest or the welfare of the whole community, occurs when:

KEY TERM

social benefit maximisation: occurs when $MSB = MSC$.

marginal social benefit = marginal social cost

or:

$MSB = MSC$

Households and firms seek to maximise private benefit or private self-interest, and not the wider social interest of the whole community. They ignore the effects of their actions on other people. However, when externalities are generated, costs and benefits are inevitably imposed on others, so private benefit maximisation no longer coincides with social benefit maximisation.

Social benefit is defined as private benefit plus external benefit. As a result:

marginal social benefit = marginal private benefit + marginal external benefit

or:

$MSB = MPB + MEB$

Likewise, social cost is defined as private cost plus external cost, which means that

marginal social cost = marginal private cost + marginal external cost

or:

$MSC = MPC + MEC$

Negative externalities and allocative inefficiency

When the production of a good causes pollution, external costs are generated, with the result that $MSC > MPC$. I shall now explain how this results in allocative inefficiency. In Chapter 6, I explained how a perfectly competitive economy can achieve a state of allocative efficiency when $P = MC$ in all markets. However, allocative efficiency occurs only if:

- there are competitive markets for all goods and services, including future markets
- there are no economies of scale
- markets are simultaneously in equilibrium

I can now add a fourth requirement for allocative efficiency: there must be no externalities, negative or positive. Long-run equilibrium occurs in a perfect market at the price at which $P = MPC$, which, in the absence of externalities, means also that $P = MSC$. But if negative production externalities are present, $P < MSC$ when $P = MPC$. To achieve allocative efficiency, price must equal the true marginal cost of production: that is, the marginal social cost and not just the marginal private cost. But in a market situation, profit-maximising firms are assumed only to take account of private costs and benefits. When externalities exist, therefore, the market mechanism fails to achieve an allocatively efficient equilibrium.

To put it another way, firms evade part of the true or real cost of production by dumping the externality on third parties. The price that the consumer pays for the good reflects only the private cost of production, and not the true cost, which includes the external cost. In a market situation, the firm's output is thus under-priced, encouraging too much consumption. A misallocation of resources results because the wrong price is charged. Too much consumption, and hence too much production, means that too many scarce resources are being used by the industry that is producing the negative externalities.

Government policy and negative externalities

There are two main ways in which a government can intervene to try to correct the market failure caused by negative externalities. It can use quantity controls (or regulation) or it can use taxation. Regulation directly influences the quantity of the externality that a firm or household can generate. By contrast, taxation adjusts the market price at which a good is sold and creates an incentive for less of the negative externality to be generated.

Regulation or quantity controls

In its most extreme form, regulation can be used to ban completely, or criminalise, the discharge of negative externalities such as pollution and noise. It may be impossible to produce a good or service such as electricity in a coal-burning power station without generating at least some negative externality. In this situation, banning the externality has the perverse effect of preventing production of a *good* (for example, electricity) as well as the *bad* (pollution). Because of this, quantity controls rather than a complete ban may be more appropriate. These include **maximum emission limits**, and restrictions on the time of day or year during which the negative externality can legally be emitted.

Taxation

Completely banning a negative externality such as pollution is a form of market *replacement* rather than market *adjustment*. By contrast, because taxes placed on goods affect incentives that consumers and firms face, they provide a market-orientated solution to the problem of externalities. Taxation compensates for the fact that there is a missing market in the externality. In the case of pollution, the government calculates the money value of the negative externality and imposes this on the firm as a **pollution tax.** This is known as the **polluter must pay** principle. The pollution tax creates an incentive, which was previously lacking, for less of the bad to be dumped on others. By so doing, the tax **internalises the externality.** The polluting firm must now cover all the costs of production, including the cost of negative externalities, and include these in the price charged to customers. By setting the tax so that the price the consumer pays equals the marginal social cost of production ($P = MSC$), an allocatively efficient level of production and consumption could in theory be achieved.

CASE STUDY 10.2

Ten years of the London congestion charge

In February 2013, the London congestion charge was 10 years old. At the time of its introduction, many economists believed that the congestion charge marked the triumph of economic common sense over narrow self-interest. Economists confidently believed that many other cities, both in the UK and abroad, would rush to adopt London-style road pricing. In the event, this did not happen. In November 2008, Manchester voters were asked to approve the introduction of a city-centre congestion charge and they voted against it.

What have been the possible benefits and costs of the London congestion charge? In 2003 the idea of charging car users to drive around the capital was met with near-apocalyptic warnings from motoring groups and newspapers such as the *Daily Mail*. The charge would 'destroy' the city's commercial heart and cause 'total gridlock', warned some. It would 'cause misery to thousands of commuters across the capital', said Conservative Greater London Authority's transport spokesman. 'Londoners will suffer conditions worse than cattle trucks on their morning commute into work,' she added. Motoring groups, such as the AA, say the cost to drivers has actually adversely affected the London economy by around £2.6 billion. For every £2 taken from

The congestion charge was introduced to London in 2003

drivers, more than £1 was spent on running the scheme. The AA also pointed out that traffic has been getting steadily slower. AA president Edmund King said: 'London drivers have paid a heavy price for slower journeys over the last decade.'

Since it was introduced in 2003, however, the charge, which has risen from £5 through £8 to its present level of £10, has not caused gridlock. Rather it has resulted in a gradual reduction in traffic levels. The congestion charge has generated a net revenue of over £1 billion since 2003. The charge had an immediate environmental impact. Nitrous oxide fell 13.4% between 2002 and 2003, and there were similar falls for carbon dioxide and particulate matter. In terms of the effect the charge had on local businesses, despite the scaremongering which accompanied its introduction, certainly before 2009, business activity within the charge zone has been higher in both productivity and profitability since the charge was introduced. Transport for London claims that the charge had a 'broadly neutral impact' on the wider London economy. The charge is broadly supported by a majority of Londoners, with 45% for and 41% against. Conservative mayor Boris Johnson has described the congestion charge as a success which has benefited London.

Elliot Jacobs, managing director of office supplies firm UOE, says: 'Getting deliveries on time is really important and the congestion charge means we have a consistency of traffic flow and a reliability that we know where the traffic's going to be, and that's important. It means we can get there on time and that's worth £10 every day.' However, although the congestion charge — which was seen as a radical step a decade ago — has won over many of the original doubters, there are still those who claim it has not been a success.

Follow-up questions

1 Why have other cities, in Britain and the rest of the world, not rushed to follow London's example and introduce a congestion charge?

2 Do you agree that road use should be priced? Justify your answer.

Note, however, that we can only be certain that the firm or industry is allocatively efficient if every other market in the economy is simultaneously setting price equal to *MSC*. This is an impossible requirement. We should also note that the pollution tax, like any tax, will itself introduce new inefficiencies and distortions into the market, associated with the costs of collecting the tax and with incentives created to *avoid* the tax within the law or to *evade* the tax illegally. For example, firms may dump waste at night to escape detection.

Until recently, governments have been much more likely to use regulation rather than taxation to reduce negative externalities such as pollution and congestion. Indeed, in the past, it has been difficult to find examples of pollution taxes outside the pages of economics textbooks, possibly because politicians have feared that pollution taxes would be too unpopular. But in recent years, governments have become more prepared to use pollution and congestion taxes. This reflects growing concern, among governments and the public alike, of environmental issues such as global warming and the problems posed by fossil fuel emissions and other pollutants. It may also reflect the growing influence of green or environmental pressure groups such as Friends of the Earth and a growing preference to tackle environmental problems with market solutions rather than through regulation.

CASE STUDY 10.3

The European Union Directive on Carbon Emissions and the European Union Emission Trading System

In 2002 the **Kyoto Protocol** committed the UK and other EU countries to reduce greenhouse gas emissions by 12.5%, from their 1990 levels, between 2008 and 2012. To achieve this goal, the European Commission issued a *Directive on Carbon Emissions*. Each member government had to impose tough regulations on carbon emissions for energy, steel, cement, glass, brick making, paper and cardboard industries. Once the regulatory framework was established, a market in traded pollution permits took over, creating market-orientated incentives for industries to reduce pollution because they can make money out of it. The market, which is called the **European Union Emission Trading System (EU ETS)**, is a major pillar of EU climate policy. As of January 2013, the EU ETS covered more than 11,000 factories, power stations and other installations in 31 countries — all 28 EU-member states plus Iceland, Norway and Liechtenstein. The installations regulated by the EU ETS are collectively responsible for close to half of the EU's emissions of carbon dioxide and 40% of its total greenhouse gas emissions. The EU

ETS remains the largest multinational, emissions trading scheme in the world.

The EU ETS works on the 'cap and trade' principle. A 'cap', or limit, is set on the total amount of certain greenhouse gases that can be emitted by the factories, power plants and other installations in the system. The cap is reduced over time so that total emissions fall. In 2020, emissions from sectors covered by the EU ETS will be 21% lower than in 2005. Within the cap, companies receive or buy emission allowances which they can trade with one another as needed. They can also buy limited amounts of international credits from emission-saving projects around the world. The limit on the total number of allowances available ensures that they have a value.

After each year a company must surrender enough allowances to cover all its emissions, otherwise heavy fines are imposed. If a company reduces its emissions, it can keep the spare allowances to cover its future needs or else sell them to another company that is short of allowances. The flexibility that trading brings ensures that emissions are cut where it costs least to do so.

Follow-up question

Research up-to-date details of the performance of the EU ETS since 2013.

Pollution permits

Again until recently, the main choice of policy for dealing with the problem of pollution was between regulation and taxation. As I have explained, the former is an interventionist solution, whereas taxation, based on the principle that the polluter must pay, has been seen as a more market-orientated solution. But nevertheless it is a solution which requires the government to levy and collect the pollution tax.

In the 1990s, another market-orientated solution started in the USA, based on a trading market in **permits** or **licences to pollute.** This still involves regulation, namely imposing maximum limits on the amount of pollution that coal-burning power stations are allowed to emit, followed by a steady reduction in each subsequent year (say, by 5%) of the maximum amount. But once this regulatory framework has been established, a market in **traded pollution permits** takes over, creating market-orientated incentives for the power station companies to reduce pollution because they can make money out of it.

> **KEY TERM**
>
> **traded pollution permits:** these allow governments to give companies licences to pollute at a certain level. Companies can buy, sell and trade these permits on a market.

A tradable market in permits to pollute works in the following way. Energy companies able to reduce pollution by more than the law requires sell their spare permits to other power stations, which, for technical or other reasons, decide not to, or cannot, reduce pollution below the maximum limit. The latter still comply with the law, even when exceeding the maximum emission limit, because they buy the spare permits sold by the former group of power stations. But in the long run, even power stations that find it difficult to comply with the law have an incentive to reduce pollution. By doing so, they avoid the extra costs that otherwise result from the requirement to buy pollution permits.

Establishing markets for trading private property rights

In 1960, Professor Ronald Coase, who died in 2013 aged 92, argued that if markets can be created for private property rights, government intervention to correct market failures may not be necessary. Coase used the example of wood-burning locomotives, which in nineteenth-century America frequently set fire to farmers' fields. If farmers possess the property right to prevent crops being destroyed, they can sell the rights to the railway companies. By contrast, if the railway companies possess the property right to emit sparks, farmers could pay the companies to reduce emissions.

Coase argued that in both cases the outcome might be the same. If farmers have a right to stop the sparks, but emitting sparks is worth more to the railway than stopping the sparks is worth to the farmers, the railway will buy the right to emit sparks from the farmers, and the damage continues. But if the railway companies have the right to emit sparks, and this right is worth more to them than to the farmers, the right will not be sold, and the damage again continues. In this example, initial ownership of property rights has no effect on the amount of resources devoted to suppressing sparks. Trading of property rights ensures the same outcome in either case.

This theory, which is known as the **Coase theorem**, has greatly influenced the free-market approach to market failures. Indeed, most economists now accept that governments should try to work *with the market* rather than *against the market* through regulation.

EXTENSION MATERIAL

Road pricing

Case Study 10.2 highlights that the issue of whether or not to charge motorists for the use of roads has entered public debate. The issue centres largely on road *congestion,* rather than on pollution, because fuel taxes are a better way of reducing the environmental pollution caused by vehicles burning fossil fuels. Motorists are now charged for driving in central London during business hours, and a private sector firm owns and runs a section of toll motorway north of Birmingham. Electronic pricing has become technically possible and is likely to be used in future road charging schemes.

The case for and against road pricing brings together issues concerning both public goods and negative externalities. Roads are a good example of a quasi-public good, since toll booths or electronic pricing can be used to exclude free-riders. Road use also results in the discharge of negative externalities. The extent to which negative externalities are produced depends upon whether the road is congested or uncongested. The two situations are shown in Figure 10.1, which measures the flow of traffic (for example, the number of cars travelling on the road per hour) on the horizontal axis and the cost per journey on the vertical axis.

When the traffic flow is less than F_1, an extra motorist driving along the road imposes no negative externalities or external costs upon other road users — if we ignore the pollution emitted by cars. In this situation, road use should be free, to encourage the allocatively efficient or socially optimal level of use. For levels of traffic flow between zero and F_1, the marginal social cost of road use equals the marginal private cost borne by motorists ($MSC = MPC$). But once the road becomes congested (at flows of traffic greater than F_1), this is no longer the case, and there is a case for road pricing to provide the incentive to reduce road use.

For traffic flows above F_1, each motorist who drives on the road adds to traffic congestion, which all motorists using the road then suffer. Beyond F_1, the marginal social cost of motoring is greater than the marginal private cost incurred by the motorist ($MSC > MPC$). But in the absence of road pricing, when deciding whether or not to drive on the road, motorists consider only the private cost of motoring and not the external cost dumped on other road users. Providing there is no charge for road use, motorists use their cars up to traffic flow F_2 (at point h). At F_2, the marginal private benefit of motoring equals the marginal private cost ($MPB = MPC$). At this point, the private cost incurred by the marginal motorist is C_1, but this is less than the social cost of the marginal journey, which includes the marginal cost of congestion caused by the marginal motorist but suffered by other road users. At traffic flow F_2, the marginal external cost of congestion imposed on other road users is shown by the distance $(k - h)$.

Figure 10.1 The benefits and costs of using an uncongested and a congested road

Resource misallocation results. Motorists make more journeys than they would, had they to bear the full social cost resulting from the use of their cars. The shaded triangle bounded by the points n, k and h measures the welfare loss suffered by society at the privately optimal traffic flow F_2, at which $MPB = MPC$.

Arguably, there is a case for road pricing when roads become congested. Allocative efficiency is improved when a motorist is charged a price equal to the marginal external cost imposed on other road users, as a result of the journey. The optimal congestion charge would be $(n - m)$, which measures the marginal external cost of a journey at the socially optimal level of road use, F_3. Some congestion still occurs at F_3, but it is less than at F_2, and motorists pay for the congestion they generate. The congestion charge or road price internalises the externality. Journeys that are worth undertaking in the absence of a congestion charge are not worthwhile once the appropriate charge is imposed.

Government policy and positive externalities

Just as governments *discourage* the production of negative externalities, in much the same way they try to *encourage* the production of positive externalities. As with negative externalities, the government can choose to regulate and/or try to change the prices of goods and activities that yield external benefits. In the latter case, subsidies rather than taxes are used to encourage production and consumption.

Regulation

Just as regulations can ban the omission of negative externalities, so the generation of positive externalities may be made compulsory. In this situation, it is illegal not to provide external benefits for others. For example, local authority bylaws can require households to maintain the appearance of properties, and the state may order landowners to plant trees.

Subsidies

A subsidy is the opposite of a tax: that is, money paid by the government to people or firms undertaking certain activities. **Producer subsidies**, given to firms, shift a good's supply curve rightward, increasing both the quantity produced of the good and the quantity of positive externalities generated from the production of the good. By contrast, a **consumer subsidy**, which is paid directly to consumers for spending on a particular good, shifts the demand curve for the good rightward. For example, a government can use both types of subsidy to encourage use of public transport. It can give money to railway or bus companies, or it can provide subsidised travel passes for passengers.

Demerit goods

Cigarettes, alcoholic drinks and narcotic drugs such as heroin are examples of **demerit goods**. People who consume these goods do so for the pleasure the goods yield. But demerit goods are often addictive, leading to an outcome in which short-term pleasure eventually turns into long-term health problems. However, the short-term pleasure that consumption yields means that a *demerit good* such as a cigarette should not be confused with a *bad* such as pollution. A bad yields displeasure, dissatisfaction or nastiness to the person unwillingly 'consuming' it. As a result, people are prepared to pay to get rid of a bad, though as I explained earlier in this chapter, public bads such as rubbish and pollution can be dumped on others so that the person or firm that creates the bad avoids paying for its removal.

> **KEY TERM**
>
> **demerit good:** a good, such as tobacco, for which the social costs of consumption exceed the private costs.

Examples, of course, are not the same as definitions. There are two ways of defining a demerit good, and both are acceptable in an examination answer. The first definition centres on negative externalities, whereas the second definition focuses on **information problems** that affect consumption of demerit goods. In the case of the first definition, the marginal social costs suffered by the wider community are greater than the marginal private costs incurred by a smoker or drinker. By contrast, the second definition ignores externalities, but distinguishes between the short-term and long-term *private* costs incurred by the person consuming the demerit good.

> **KEY TERM**
>
> **information problem:** occurs when people make poor decisions because they don't possess, or ignore, the relevant information.

- **Demerit goods and negative externalities.** When a person consumes a demerit good such as tobacco, negative externalities are generated which are unpleasant or harmful for other people. People unwillingly breathe in the fumes the smoker discharges, with eventual harmful effects on their health. (This is the problem of passive smoking.) Smelly clothing is a more trivial example of a negative externality caused by smoking.
- **Demerit goods and information problems.** When teenagers first get the 'habit' of smoking, drinking or drug-taking, they may either ignore the long-term private costs they may suffer later in life, or downplay the significance of these costs. Either way, young people tend to be myopic or short sighted with respect to the costs of consuming demerit goods. A person who started drinking as a teenager may regret the decision later in life when suffering an alcohol-related illness. But when he or she started to drink, the private costs that only emerge many years later are ignored or undervalued.

Demerit goods and allocative inefficiency

Earlier in this chapter, when discussing negative externalities, I explained that price must equal the marginal social cost of production ($P = MSC$) if the level of output in a market is to be allocatively efficient. From this it follows that the allocatively efficient level of production and consumption of a demerit good occurs when $P = MSC$. But when a demerit good is bought and sold in a free market, unaffected by taxes or regulation to discourage consumption, too much of the good is consumed. The privately optimal level of consumption occurs where $P = MPC$, but at this level of consumption $P < MSC$. The good is too cheap. The result is allocatively inefficient, with the demerit good ending up being over-consumed.

Merit goods

Education and healthcare provide examples of **merit goods**, which, as I stated earlier, must not be confused with public goods. (I also mentioned that both are examples of government goods, which leads to the possible confusion.) As is the case with demerit goods, merit goods can be defined in two ways: in terms of externalities (in this case *positive* externalities) and in relation to information problems.

> **KEY TERM**
>
> **merit good:** a good, such as health care, for which the social benefits of consumption exceed the private benefits.

- **Merit goods and positive externalities.** When a person consumes a merit good such as healthcare, the resulting positive externalities benefit other people. An obvious example is that healthy people seldom spread diseases. The social benefit enjoyed by the wider community is greater than the private benefit enjoyed by the healthy person.
- **Merit goods and information problems.** For a merit good such as healthcare, the long-term private benefit of consumption exceeds the short-term private benefit of consumption. But when deciding how much to consume, individuals take account of short-term costs and benefits, ignoring or undervaluing the long-term private costs and benefits. For many years, I taught in the Open University, where students' ages range from 22 to over 70. On numerous occasions adult students said to me: 'If only I had got my qualifications when I was younger; unfortunately I did not value education when I was at school.'

> **EXAM TIP**
>
> Students often confuse *merit goods* with *public goods*. Like public goods, merit goods such as education are often provided by the state, but the reason for doing so is different. Students also confuse demerit goods with bads or nuisance goods. A bad, such as rubbish, yields only disutility to any unlucky individual consuming it. By contrast, a demerit good such as tobacco certainly fulfils a need and provides satisfaction (in the short run at least) to an addicted smoker.

Merit goods and allocative inefficiency

In a market situation, and given the absence of subsidies or regulations designed to encourage consumption, people under-consume a merit good such as education. Figure 10.2 shows positive consumption externalities being generated when students 'consume' education. This means that the marginal social benefit curve (which shows the benefits received by the whole community) is positioned above the marginal private benefit curve (which shows the benefits enjoyed by the students themselves). However, in a free market in which the price reflects only the private

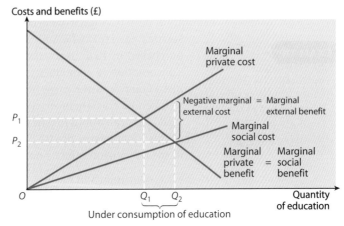

benefits and costs, the price of education is set at P_1 in Figure 10.2. This is the price at which $P = MPC$, but it is not the price at which $P = MSC$. At P_1, education is too expensive, too little is consumed, and the outcome is allocatively inefficient. To achieve the allocatively efficient level of consumption, Q_2, the price must be reduced to P_2. To understand this fully, you must understand that the *positive* marginal external benefit generated when a merit good is consumed can also be regarded as a *negative* marginal external cost. Viewed in this way, price P_2 is the price at which $P = MSC$. Hence, the outcome at which Q_2 is consumed, with price P_2 being charged, is allocatively efficient. The distance between Q_2 and Q_1 shows under-consumption of education at the higher free-market price P_1.

Figure 10.2 How charging a market price leads to allocative inefficiency in the case of a merit good such as education

Government policy and demerit goods

I explained earlier in this chapter how regulation, taxation and subsidies can be used to limit the production of negative externalities. Similar policies can be used to discourage consumption of demerit goods. Governments can use regulation (including making consumption illegal), taxation or both to prevent or limit consumption of a good such as tobacco or alcohol.

Regulation directly influences the level of consumption of a demerit good such as tobacco. By contrast, taxation adjusts the market price of the demerit good. In its most extreme form, regulation can be used to ban completely the sale and consumption of a demerit good such as heroin. However, this may have the perverse effect of driving consumption underground into a criminalised market in which, arguably, the social costs of consumption are greater than in a legal 'above-ground' market. For 'milder' demerit goods such as tobacco and alcoholic drink, smoking and drinking can be banned in public places, while shops can be banned from selling tobacco and alcohol to younger teenagers.

Completely banning consumption and/or production of demerit goods is a form of market replacement rather than market adjustment. By contrast, because taxes placed on goods affect incentives which consumers and firms face, they provide a market-orientated solution to the problems posed by demerit goods.

Government policy and merit goods

As with other examples of positive externalities, governments can use regulation, subsidy or both to enforce or encourage consumption of merit goods. For merit goods such as car seat belts and motorcycle crash helmets, which are infrequently purchased by road users, the UK government uses regulation but not subsidy. Consumption is compulsory, but road users must pay a market price for the merit good. In these cases, the government has decided that, as spending on a seat belt or crash helmet forms only a small part of total consumer spending, road users can afford to pay. By contrast, other merit goods, such as vaccination against contagious diseases, are completely subsidised and provided free, but in the UK consumption is not compulsory.

EXAM TIP

Many exam candidates assert that any good that is 'good for you' is a merit good. This assertion is wrong.

In the UK, education and healthcare are provided by the state and form an important part of public spending. Nevertheless, private sector provision also exists, and is growing. One reason for growing private sector provision of merit goods lay in the fact that free state provision does not necessarily mean good-quality provision.

Merit goods and uncertainty, moral hazard and adverse selection

Uncertainty about future long-term benefits and costs contributes to under-consumption of merit goods. For example, a person does not know in advance when, if ever, the services of a specialist surgeon might be needed. Sudden illness may lead to a situation in which a person cannot afford to pay for costly surgery, if provided solely through a conventional market. One market-orientated solution is for private medical insurance to pay for the cost of treatment at the time when it is needed. However, private medical insurance often fails to pay for treatment for the chronically ill or for the poor. Private insurance may also fail to provide medical care for risk takers in society who decide not to buy insurance, as distinct from risk-averters, who are always the most ready customers for insurance.

Like all private insurance schemes, healthcare insurance suffers from two further problems, both of which lead to market failure. These are the problems of moral hazard and adverse selection. **Moral hazard** is demonstrated by the tendency of people covered by health insurance to be less careful about their health because they know that, in the event of accident or illness, the insurance company will pick up the bill. **Adverse selection** relates to the fact that people whose health risks are greatest are also the people most likely to try to buy insurance policies. Insurance companies react by refusing to sell health policies to those who most need private health insurance. For those to whom they do sell policies, premium levels are set sufficiently high to enable the companies to remain profitable when settling the claims of customers facing moral hazard or who have been adversely selected.

KEY TERMS

moral hazard: describes the tendency of individuals and firms, once insured against some contingency, to behave so as to make that contingency more likely.

adverse selection: describes a situation in which people who buy insurance often have a better idea of the risks they face than do the sellers of insurance. People who know they face large risks are more likely to buy insurance than people who face small risks.

Public collective provision, perhaps organised by private sector companies but guaranteed by the state and funded by compulsory insurance, may be a better solution. Both private and public collective-provision schemes are a response to the fact that the demand or need for medical care is much more predictable for a large group of people than for an individual.

Value judgements and merit and demerit goods

Many people believe that an external authority, such as the state or a religious body, is a better judge than individuals of what is good for them. The state and religious bodies should therefore encourage the consumption of merit goods and discourage and sometimes completely ban the consumption of demerit goods.

Whether one agrees with this rather paternalistic view depends on one's own personal value judgement. Indeed, whether a good is regarded in the first place as a merit good or as a demerit good depends upon similar personal value judgements. Goods regarded by some people as merit goods are regarded by others as demerit goods. Examples include birth control, sterilisation and abortion, which, depending on ethical or religious standpoints, are regarded by some people as good for society, but by others as bad. The question of deciding whether, and to what extent, a good is a merit or a demerit good, or indeed neither, depends on value judgements that are likely to vary greatly from individual to individual, and between societies.

> **EXAM TIP**
>
> Make sure you don't confuse a demerit good with an economic bad. When consumed, a bad yields disutility, whereas a demerit good provides utility to the consumer, at least in the short run.

CASE STUDY 10.4

Should narcotic drugs be legalised?

Fed up by the growth of deaths, crime and corruption generated by the world's illicit drug trade, a growing number of government officials and academic experts have begun to debate whether the consumption and sale of narcotic drugs such as heroin and cocaine should be made legal. Prohibition of these drugs may have failed.

The legalisation argument rests on the assumption that drug laws, not drugs themselves, cause the most damage to society. If drugs were legal, the argument goes, drug black markets worth tens of billions of dollars would evaporate, the empires of drug gangsters would collapse, addicts would stop committing street crimes to support their habit, and the police, courts and prisons would no longer be overwhelmed by a problem they cannot hope to defeat.

But most politicians and policy-makers disagree, arguing that highly damaging substances would be cheaper, purer and far more widely available, and that legislation would cause a sharp jump in private costs to the drug users and external costs imposed on society in general. They say the losses would far outweigh the gains.

A key question is how much does society pay because drugs are illegal and how much does society pay because drugs themselves are harmful? Drug-related crime, such as child abuse and assaults by people experiencing drug-induced psychosis, will still exist, even if consumption is legalised.

Follow-up questions

1 Explain why a narcotic drug such as heroin is usually viewed as a demerit good.

2 Should the problem of drugs be treated as a health concern rather than a criminal justice problem?

3 Do you agree that narcotic drugs should be legalised? Justify your argument.

SUMMARY

- Markets can fail because they function inequitably or because they function inefficiently.
- A highly unequal distribution of income may result from a market functioning inequitably.
- Allocative inefficiency provides evidence of a market functioning inefficiently.
- Monopoly, public goods (and public bads), externalities, merit goods and demerit goods all lead to market failure and allocative inefficiency.
- Complete market failure leads to missing markets.
- Partial market failure results in too much, or too little, of a good being provided and/or consumed.
- Market failure is associated with resource misallocation.
- Regulation, taxation and markets in permits to pollute are used to reduce negative externalities and the consumption of demerit goods.
- Regulation and subsidies are used to encourage the production of positive externalities and consumption of merit goods.
- Extending the legal entitlement to property rights is another method of reducing negative externalities and encouraging production of positive externalities.
- Uncertainty, moral hazard and adverse selection all contribute to under-consumption of merit goods.
- Lack of accurate information about what might happen in the future, or down-playing of known information, contribute to under-consumption of merit goods and over-consumption of demerit goods.

Exam-style questions

1 With examples, explain the difference between market failures resulting from inefficiency and those resulting from inequity. **(15 marks)**

2 Explain the free-rider problem in the context of public goods and externalities. **(15 marks)**

3 Evaluate the case for using taxes and subsidies to promote the allocatively efficient level of consumption of merit goods and demerit goods. **(25 marks)**

4 Do you agree that markets on their own can be relied upon to reduce the problems of environmental pollution? Justify your answer. **(25 marks)**

Extra resources to help you revise are available online at www.hodderplus.co.uk/philipallan

Government failure and cost–benefit analysis

Chapter 11

One of the main functions of government microeconomic policy is to correct market failure. Often, however, such intervention leads to government failure. Government failure occurs whenever government intervention in markets or the direct provision by government of goods or services leads to an unsatisfactory outcome.

Governments often try to pre-empt and minimise the possibility of government failure by considering the costs and benefits for society as a whole that might result from government intervention in the economy. But cost–benefit analysis (CBA) need not be restricted to analysing the effects of government policy and intervention in the economy. It can be applied to private sector investment decisions, and indeed to any decision, however grand or trivial, made by an ordinary member of society such as you or me.

LEARNING OUTCOMES

This chapter will:
- link government failure to attempts to correct market failures
- relate government failure to public interest theory and public choice theory
- distinguish between cost–benefit analysis and private sector investment appraisal
- discuss the problems that arise when undertaking a cost–benefit analysis

WHAT YOU SHOULD ALREADY KNOW

At AS you learnt that government failure occurs when government intervention in the economy leads to a misallocation of resources. You also learnt that government intervention in the economy, for example to try to correct market failure, does not necessarily result in an improvement in economic welfare. The Unit 1 AS specification states: 'Governments may create, rather than remove, market distortions and inadequate information, conflicting objectives and administrative costs should be recognised as possible sources of government failure.'

Cost–benefit analysis is not mentioned in the AS specification. However, you may have come across the concept when evaluating at AS the various ways in which government intervention affects the economy, particularly with respect to attempting to correct market failures.

The possibility of government failure

Economics students sometimes assume that once a government intervenes to reduce or to eliminate a market failure, the policy is immediately effective, and that everyone can then live happily ever after. But there is another possibility. When the government intervenes to try to deal with a problem, far from curing or ameliorating the problem, intervention actually makes matters worse. When this happens, the problem of **government failure** replaces the problem of market failure.

KEY TERM

government failure: occurs when government intervention in the economy is ineffective, wasteful or damaging.

Government failure and the law of unintended consequences

The **law of unintended consequences**, which applies in almost all fields of human behaviour, predicts that, whenever the government intervenes in the market economy, effects will be unleashed which the policy-makers had not foreseen or intended. Sometimes of course, the unintended effects may be advantageous to the economy, while in other instances they may be harmful but relatively innocuous. In either of these circumstances, government intervention can be justified on the ground that the social benefits of intervention exceed the social costs and therefore contribute to a net gain in economic welfare. But if government activity — however well intentioned — triggers harmful consequences, which are greater than the benefits that the government intervention is supposed to promote, government failure will result.

EXAM TIP

Merit goods, demerit goods and externalities provide a link between market failure and government failure.

Public choice theory and government failure

Economists of a free-market persuasion argue that governments should be wary of intervening to try to correct any alleged market failures, including those related to the environment. This approach to markets and market failure is associated with a wider body of theory about the role of government in the economy, known as **public choice theory**.

The free-market advocates of public choice theory regard a market economy as a calm and orderly place in which the price mechanism, working through the incentives signalled by price changes in competitive markets, achieves a more optimal and efficient outcome than could result from a policy of government intervention. They believe that risk-taking businesspeople or entrepreneurs, who lose or gain through the correctness of their decisions in the market place, know better what to produce than civil servants and planners employed by the government on risk-free salaries with secured pensions. Providing that markets are sufficiently competitive, what is produced is ultimately determined by consumer sovereignty, with consumers knowing better than governments what is good for them.

EXAM TIP

Government failure often results from the failure of interventionist policies to correct market failure.

According to the free-market philosophy, the correct function of government is to reduce to a minimum its economic activities and interference with private economic agents. Thus government should be restricted to a **night-watchman** role, maintaining law and order, providing public goods and possibly offering other minor corrections when markets fail. Generally, government is there to ensure a suitable environment in which wealth-creating entrepreneurship can function in competitive markets subject to minimum regulation. This philosophy of the correct role of markets and of government leads free-market economists to reject government intervention in the economy, including policies that aim to correct alleged market failures. They believe that, at best, such intervention will be ineffective; at worst it will be damaging, destabilising and inefficient.

Should government intervene in the economy?

Public interest theory and government failure

Public interest theory is very different to the public choice theory I have just explained. Public interest theory is favoured by Keynesian economists who generally support government intervention in a market economy. They believe that governments intervene in a benevolent fashion in the economy in order to eliminate waste and to achieve an efficient and socially desirable resource allocation. Public interest theory, applied at the *microeconomic* level in the economy to correct market failure, is matched at the *macroeconomic* level by Keynesian economic management of the economy. Keynesians believe that government intervention at the macro level can anticipate and counter the destabilising forces existent in the market economy, achieving a better outcome than could be achieved in an economy subject to unregulated market forces. Keynesians justify discretionary government intervention in the economy on the ground that, provided the intervention is 'smart' and sensible, government activity stabilises an otherwise inherently unstable market economy.

Government failure and cost–benefit analysis

Governments, of course, want to prevent their policies, both those currently in progress, and those they are considering undertaking in the future, being cast as government failures. To prevent or at least to minimise the possibility of government failure, governments use cost–benefit analysis (CBA). However, CBA contains its own problems, and the large amounts of taxpayers' money governments spend on CBA may themselves be regarded as a form of government failure.

EXAM TIP

CBA is used by governments to try to prevent future government failures.

What is cost–benefit analysis?

Cost–benefit analysis (CBA) is a method of decision making that takes account of external as well as private costs and benefits. CBA undertaken by a government usually assesses whether a particular decision, for example an investment project, is socially optimal and in the public interest, and not just privately optimal and in the interest of the economic agent undertaking the activity.

KEY TERM

cost–benefit analysis (CBA): a technique for assessing *all* the costs and benefits likely to result from an economic decision, i.e. the social costs and benefits and not just the private costs and benefits.

In the past, CBA has most often been used by governments to help decide whether to invest in a major public project such as a motorway, an airport, or a major investment by a nationalised industry. However, there is no reason in principle why a private sector investment such as the Channel Tunnel, or indeed any action by a private economic agent or by the government (e.g. a tax change), cannot be examined by CBA. For example, a cost–benefit analysis of the proposed decision to extend Stansted Airport would take into account costs such as building and maintenance costs of the extension and of improved road and train links, compensation paid to local landowners and households, and environmental damage caused by the extension and by additional flights that will use the airport. Benefits would include any time saved by travellers, possible reductions in congestion near other airports, and the additional jobs created by the expansion.

CASE STUDY 11.1

More than 40 years ago in 1971, the economist Edward Mishan wrote a very good introductory article explaining cost–benefit analysis The passage below has been adapted from Mishan's article published in the Lloyds Bank Review.

The ABC of cost–benefit analysis

Cost–benefit analyses are in high fashion. Scarcely a week goes by without an authoritative voice asserting that, in connection with some proposed project or other, a thorough cost–benefit study is needed. No matter how heated a controversy, a government can still the protests of the critics and be assured of a respectful silence simply by announcing that a cost–benefit analysis is in progress.

The popular belief is that this novel technique provides a scientific assessment of the social value of a project, or at least an objective assessment.

True, if every benefit and every cost associated with a proposed project of investment is properly evaluated and brought into the calculus in a systematic way, the resulting sum — whether an excess of benefit over cost or the other way round — can hardly be challenged. Yet such a statement is not much more than a tautology. The fact is that evaluating 'properly' all relevant data is a guiding ideal, not a current practice. For although the procedure used in cost–benefit analysis follows certain conventions, the outcome may vary according to the economist in charge of the study, because of differences in judgement with respect both to *what* is to be included and *how* it is to be evaluated. In the absence of consensus, the individual judgement of whoever is in charge is an important factor in the outcome.

Judgements differ in the choice of which items are to be valued at market prices and which are to be valued at shadow prices; in the range of intangibles to be included in the study; in the methods used to evaluate these intangibles; in the choice of an investment criterion; and in the devices used to make allowances for future uncertainty. It is well to bear in mind that, in the present stage of its development, cost–benefit analysis is an imperfect calculus, as much an art as a matter of science, or more precisely, as much a matter of judgement as a technique.

Follow-up questions

1 Do you agree that cost–benefit analysis is more of an 'art' than a 'science'? Justify your answer.
2 What is meant by a 'shadow price', and what 'investment criterion' might be applied in a cost–benefit analysis? (Hint: read the Extension material that follows shortly and the paragraph after it.)

Why cost–benefit analysis is needed

Suppose the economy in which we live displayed the following conditions:
- perfect competition in all economic activities
- all effects relevant to the welfare of individuals are priced through the market
- no economies of scale and no externalities

Over 200 years ago, using the *invisible hand* metaphor, the great classical economist Adam Smith described such an economy. If such an economy actually existed, cost–benefit analysis would not be needed. Individuals pursuing private greed to maximise self-interest would at the same time ensure that the social benefit of the whole community was also achieved.

But, for good or for bad, real-world economies are not like this. As we have seen in previous chapters, market imperfections, economies of scale, missing markets and externalities mean that instead of maximising the social welfare of the whole community, the price mechanism misallocates resources and produces unjustifiable inequality in the distributions of income and wealth. Cost–benefit analysis is a technique for evaluating all the costs and benefits of any economic action or decision: that is, the *social costs and benefits* to the whole community and not just the *private costs and benefits* accruing to the economic agent undertaking the action.

The differences between private sector investment appraisal and CBA

Social cost–benefit analysis is really just an extension of private sector investment appraisal in that CBA assesses *all* the costs and benefits (*external* as well as *private*), for society as a whole, of making particular economic decisions. A private sector business deciding whether or not to invest in new capacity has to estimate the initial cost of the investment, the size, shape and length of its future income stream, and how to place monetary values on future private costs and benefits.

EXAM TIP

Exam questions will not be set on the techniques of private sector investment appraisal, but knowledge of the topic helps to build up an understanding of CBA.

However, social cost–benefit analysis has to go further, calculating expected future *external* costs and benefits. Many of the social costs and benefits resulting in the future from an action undertaken now take the form of externalities that are difficult to quantify. How does one put a monetary value on the saving of a human life resulting from fewer accidents on a proposed motorway? What is the social cost of the destruction of a beautiful view? It is extremely difficult to decide on all the likely costs and benefits, to draw a line on which to include and exclude, and to put monetary values on all the chosen costs and benefits accruing immediately and those which will only be received in the distant future.

EXTENSION MATERIAL

How a business makes investment decisions

Investment in fixed-capital projects, such as building a new factory, involves calculating all the future costs the project will incur and all the future benefits it will yield. A business has to put a monetary value on the project's expected net future income stream (i.e. future benefits minus future costs).

The central problem is guessing and putting money values on an unknown and uncertain future. If a firm is to maximise profit after investing in a capital project, the following condition must be met:

the rate of return per year expected over the life of the investment	>	the expected rate of interest per year which must be paid on borrowed funds to finance the investment

This requires the firm to estimate the initial fixed cost of the investment, together with details of its expected future income stream. The firm may be reasonably sure of the initial fixed cost of an investment. It also knows the current rate of interest or cost of borrowing which has to be paid to raise the funds to finance the investment. However, some of the most important features of an investment are not known, and these have to be estimated or guessed. The firm must estimate the expected life of the investment, together with the size and shape of the income stream which the investment is expected to yield over the years of its life.

Figure 11.1 illustrates some of the problems facing a business when deciding whether or not to invest in particular fixed-capital projects. The diagram assumes that, because of a shortage of investment funds, the business is choosing between two investment projects. These are a fleet of trucks to transport the firm's goods to customers, and a computer system for organising business activities such as customer orders, payments to suppliers and the company's wage bill.

Estimating the size and shape of the expected income stream (future revenues less future costs) is fraught with uncertainty. Not only must the investment's physical output be calculated for each year in the asset's expected economic life, so also must the prices at which the output is sold and the running costs of the investment. This includes future interest rates or borrowing costs, and future prices of other inputs such as labour and raw materials.

For the sake of simplicity, Figure 11.1 assumes both investment projects are identical in all respects except one. Each investment costs £1 million and takes a year to complete (Year 0 in the diagram), before the investment can be used by the firm. Each investment has an expected economic life of 10 years (Years 1–10 in the diagram), and the business expects each investment to deliver exactly the same total income stream over the 10-year period. Expected income is shown by the wedge-shaped area drawn for each investment project. Finally, at the end of 10 years, neither investment has a second-hand or scrap value, but equally, no disposal costs are incurred.

Figure 11.1 Two alternative investment projects available to a business

Although both investment projects are expected to earn exactly the same *total* income, the key difference between the two projects lies in the *shape* of the expected income streams, which are mirror images of each other. The business expects the trucks to suffer breakdown and mechanical problems as they get older. This means the trucks earn most of their income early in the 10-year period. However, the computer system is expected to yield most of its income late in the 10-year period. A possible reason for this lies in the fact that it takes time for a business to make full use of an ICT system.

Given all the information about the two competing projects, which project should be chosen by a profit-maximising business? The answer is the fleet of trucks. Two reasons justify this decision. First, the future is always uncertain, and the further we go into the future, the greater the uncertainty. Businesses must face the possibility that an investment's *economic life* (or *business life*) will be much shorter than its *technical life*. The development of new technologies, or changes in the price of labour or energy, may render an investment productively inefficient long before it actually wears out or permanently breaks down. This is particularly true in the case of computer systems. The firm may have to write off the computer system long before the 10 years are up, and replace it with a new system that was not around at the time of the initial investment.

Second, and even more importantly, income received early in a project's life can be reinvested, either in another project, or to earn the rate of interest when deposited in a bank or financial institution. This is true for all projects, but projects that earn most of their income early in life have much more potential for earning income in this way than projects earning income mostly late in life. Because the trucks deliver most of their income early in the 10-year period, they have a greater scope for earning such income.

The techniques used in cost–benefit analysis

Cost–benefit analysis is really an extension of methods that are used by private sector businesses to decide whether particular investment projects are worthwhile. To find out more about **private sector investment appraisal** read the Extension material included above. Two of the techniques used both in social cost–benefit analysis and by private businesses when choosing whether to invest are: discounting the future and shadow pricing.

Discounting the future

An important feature of both private sector investment appraisal and of social cost–benefit analysis is the method of placing monetary values, not only on current and expected future private costs and benefits, but on external costs and benefits as well. Costs and benefits occurring many years ahead must have lower monetary values placed on them than similar costs and benefits occurring in the near future. A mathematical technique known as **discounting the future** is generally used to place appropriate monetary values on costs and benefits expected in the future. Discounting the future enables both firms appraising their own investments, and the government undertaking a social cost–benefit analysis, to calculate the monetary value *now* of costs and benefits *expected in the future*. The further we go into the future, the lower the *current value* of expected future costs and benefits.

Shadow pricing

The prices charged for traded goods and services do not always reflect the true social marginal cost of resources in alternative uses. Market failure may produce this result, as may taxes and subsidies that do not reflect the correction of market failure. For these reasons, cost–benefit analysis sometimes uses prices which are different from the prices actually charged for goods and services. The artificial set of prices used in CBA are known as **shadow prices**. Shadow prices are *imputed prices* designed to reflect the true social costs and benefits of a particular course of action. For example, the extra journey time spent by people travelling from central London to Stansted rather than Heathrow might be valued at an appropriate hourly wage rate, as would the time saved by travellers living closer to Stansted.

Some difficulties involved in CBA

I have already mentioned some of the problems involved when undertaking a cost–benefit analysis. These include the problem of placing a monetary value on externalities, which by their nature are delivered and received outside the market; the problem of choosing an appropriate rate at which to discount the future; and the problem of setting shadow prices accurately. In addition to these problems, CBA also suffers from the following difficulties and limitations.

Forecasting

It is difficult to forecast all the costs and benefits that might occur in the future. Supply and demand patterns must be predicted, together with the development of completely new technologies that at the time of the CBA can only be guessed. Population distributions may change, and different rates of inflation can have different impacts on future costs and benefits.

Objectives

CBA helps policy-makers to choose between different ways of achieving a particular objective, but it cannot be used to choose between alternative objectives. For example, CBA can be used to choose between expanding, or not expanding, Stansted, Gatwick and Heathrow airports, but it cannot be used to choose between investing more in transport or investing in hospitals, schools and universities.

Social welfare

The value of CBA is limited by a definition of an increase in social welfare, which is implicitly included in cost–benefit analysis. In CBA, an increase in social welfare is defined according to the Hicks–Kaldor test. In this test, devised more than 60 years ago by two eminent UK economists, Sir John Hicks and Lord Kaldor, social welfare improves if the welfare gain enjoyed by the 'winners' from a policy measure is greater than the welfare loss suffered by the 'losers'. To put it another way, if part of the welfare gain is paid by the 'winners' to compensate the 'losers', there is still a net welfare gain, even though in practice, such compensation is seldom paid. CBA has often justified a particular project on the grounds that, when all costs and benefits have been evaluated, there is a net welfare gain using the Hicks–Kaldor test. However, a cost–benefit analysis can reach this conclusion by effectively bypassing the distributional consequences of the project. In the case of some projects, most of the 'winners' are the already better-off, and most of the 'losers' are the already disadvantaged.

CASE STUDY 11.2

The benefits and costs of HS2

At present, 13 countries operate modern high-speed rail lines. A further 26 countries are either adding to their existing network or building high-speed rail for the first time.

The UK government has decided to invest £32.7 billion in a high-speed rail link (known as HS2) between London and Birmingham, and eventually beyond to Manchester and Leeds. However, by 2013, costs had already risen. The government believes the HS2 project will bring between £41.4 billion and £46.9 billion of economic benefits over a period of six decades, ranging from income from ticket sales to reduced congestion on the roads and the creation of hundreds of jobs. If this is the case, investing £32.7 billion to gain £46.9 billion obviously makes sense.

The project has the support of some of the country's most senior economists and business leaders. However, there are many who have challenged the government's assumptions and calculations.

Many who live along the proposed route are naturally opposed to the project, fearing years of disruptive construction work, followed by up to 28 trains an hour screaming past their homes and villages at speeds of up to 250mph (400km/h). Because the trains don't stop between major cities, those living along the train routes will suffer environmental degradation.

Many who live along the proposed route of HS2 are opposed to the project

But many of the so-called 'nimby' (not-in-my-back-yard) locals along the proposed railway lines are highlighting other — arguably rather more objective — reasons why it should not go ahead. This is because the government's case in favour of HS2 is based on a number of assumptions that opponents have worked hard to discredit. The Campaign to Protect Rural England has expressed doubts about the government's carbon forecasts for HS2. However, the main arguments relate to the economic assumptions behind the government's analysis of the costs and economic benefits. The Institute of Economic Affairs (IEA), which is arguably the most vocal think-tank opposed to HS2, predicts that costs will be greater while the economic benefits will be lower than the government has forecast.

The overall costs will allegedly be higher for a number of reasons, the IEA insists, ranging from minor costs such as compensation for disruption during the construction work being paid to season-ticket holders, to major expenses arising from a resulting need to expand and upgrade Euston station and transport links to and from the station. And the overall revenue from ticket sales is unlikely to exceed £27.2 billion, the IEA calculates. But the central argument against HS2 put forward by the IEA is that the business case is based on an overly optimistic prediction of how much and how fast demand for long-distance train travel will grow.

Follow-up questions
1 Should governments invest in 'flag-waving' projects such as HS2? Justify your answer.
2 Outline four factors that should be included in the opportunity cost of HS2.

A final criticism of cost–benefit analysis

Critics argue that CBA is pseudo-scientific. By this, they mean that CBA appears to be a scientific technique for evaluating projects, undertaken by impartial 'experts'. In practice, however, CBA is loaded with value judgments and arbitrary decisions disguised as objectivity. For example, different decisions on how to value an hour of a business executive's time, or for that matter a tourist's time, when travelling from London to Stansted might lead to different results in an analysis of the proposed airport extension. At best, CBA simply may be a costly waste of time and money, or to put it another way, a job-creation scheme for economists and planners. At worst, CBA may reach the wrong decisions. Some critics also argue that CBA is a cynical method whereby politicians distance themselves from, and induce delay in, unpopular decisions, deflecting the wrath of local communities away from themselves and onto the 'impartial experts' undertaking the CBA.

Supporters of CBA reject these arguments and counter that, for all its defects, it remains the best method of appraising public investment decisions because all the likely costs and benefits are exposed to public discussion. Whatever one's view, in recent years, UK governments have largely abandoned officially undertaken CBAs, tending instead to evaluate public investment projects largely on commercial or private profit criteria.

SUMMARY

- Government failure occurs when governments intervene in markets, often when attempting to cure market failure, but actually making matters worse.
- In some instances, the adverse effects of government intervention are relatively trivial and are less than the benefits of intervention.
- On other occasions government intervention may be extremely damaging, with the costs exceeding any benefits resulting from the intervention.
- Government intervention provides many examples of the effect of the law of unintended consequences.
- Public choice theory and public interest theory can both be used to analyse the effects of government intervention in markets.
- Cost–benefit analysis provides a method of assessing whether, for the whole community, the benefits of government intervention exceed the costs.
- Cost–benefit analysis takes account of external and social costs and benefits that might result from an investment decision or from any type of government policy.
- In principle, there is no reason why any decision, however great or small, or made by any economic agent such as a household or individual, cannot be subject to a cost–benefit analysis.
- Cost–benefit analysis must take account of future as well as current costs and benefits and quantify them.
- Discounting the future and using shadow prices are techniques used in cost–benefit analysis.
- One problem is knowing where to draw the line on which costs and benefits to include and exclude, and on how far into the future to go.
- Choice of discount rate is also critical to the result of an analysis.
- Cost–benefit analysis is more of an art than a science, and it provides a way for government ministers to put themselves at arm's length from potentially unpopular decisions.

Exam-style questions

1 Explain the difference between government failure and market failure. (15 marks)

2 Explain the difference between private sector investment appraisal and social cost–benefit analysis. (15 marks)

3 Assess the view that, in the light of the possibility of government failure, the state should not intervene in markets to try to correct market failures. (25 marks)

4 'Since it is impossible to correctly identify and evaluate all *future* costs and benefits, cost–benefit analysis should not be undertaken.' Evaluate this statement. (25 marks)

Extra resources to help you revise are available online at www.hodderplus.co.uk/philipallan

Labour markets

Chapter 12

In earlier chapters I explained and analysed the behaviour of households and firms in the economy's product markets. When explaining the price of a good, I assumed that the prices of inputs or factor services necessary for production to take place are generally given. This chapter reverses this assumption. When studying how wage rates and levels of employment are determined in the economy's labour markets, we generally assume that the prices of the goods that labour produces are given.

LEARNING OUTCOMES

This chapter will:

- discuss role reversal in labour markets and goods markets
- compare a perfectly competitive labour market with a perfectly competitive goods market
- explain the supply of labour, both for a worker and the market supply of labour in a perfectly competitive labour market
- explain the demand for labour, both for a firm and the market demand for labour in a perfectly competitive labour market
- compare a monopsony labour market with a monopoly goods market
- analyse wage discrimination and other forms of discrimination in labour markets
- examine the impact of trade unions and the national minimum wage on wage rates and employment

WHAT YOU SHOULD ALREADY KNOW

Because there is no mention of labour markets in the AS specification, it is more than likely that you started your A2 studies having undertaken no formal analysis of the markets for factors of production, including the economy's labour markets.

I am assuming, therefore, that at the start of your reading of this chapter, you know little or nothing about the functioning of labour markets at the microeconomic level in the economy.

Role reversal and labour markets

Much of the theory I explain in this chapter is really just the price theory you have already studied in the **goods markets** (or **product markets**) of an economy, operating in the **labour market**. A labour market is an example of a **factor market**, i.e. a market in which the services of a factor of production are bought and sold. Markets for land, capital goods and entrepreneurial skill are the other factor markets.

As Figure 12.1 shows, households and firms function simultaneously in both sets of markets, but their roles are reversed. Whereas firms are the source of supply in a goods market, in a factor market firms exercise demand for factor services supplied by households. The incomes received by households from the sale and supply of factor services contribute, of course, in large measure to the households' ability to demand the output supplied by firms in the goods market. To exercise **demand**, which requires an *ability* to pay as well as a *willingness* to pay, households need an income, which for most people requires the sale of labour in a labour market.

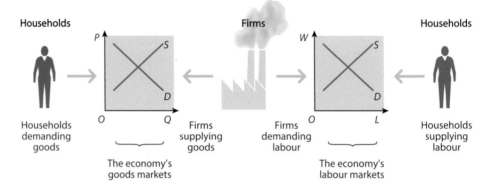

Figure 12.1 The goods market and the factor market

Indeed, the relationship between households and firms in the two markets is essentially circular, resembling the **circular flow of income** that you learnt at AS. In goods markets, finished goods and services flow from firms to households, who spend their incomes on the goods. In labour markets, members of households earn the incomes they spend on goods by selling labour to their employers.

EXTENSION MATERIAL

Marxist theory and labour markets

In this chapter, I use standard **price theory**, developed over 100 years ago by **neoclassical** economists such as Alfred Marshall, to explain how wage rates and levels of employment are determined.

There is, however, an alternative theory, which was developed by Karl Marx, one of the great nineteenth-century classical economists. **Marxist theory** argues that a class struggle between capitalists and workers determines the level of wages. By treating labour as a commodity and forcing their workers' wages down, capitalists extract **surplus value** from them. This chapter provides no further explanation of Marxist theory, but it does explain how, in imperfectly competitive labour markets without trade unions or minimum-wage legislation, monopsonistic employers can use market power to exploit the labour force.

Perfectly competitive labour markets

As in a perfectly competitive goods market, a perfectly competitive labour market contains a large number of buyers and sellers, each unable to influence the ruling market price (in this case the ruling market *wage*), and operating in conditions of perfect market information. Employers and workers are free to enter the market in the long run, but an individual employer or firm cannot influence the ruling market wage through its independent action.

In Chapter 4, I explained how a firm in a perfectly competitive goods market can sell as much as it wants at the ruling market price, which is also the perfectly elastic demand curve facing the firm and the firm's average and marginal revenue curve. Each firm is a passive price-taker at the ruling price which is determined in the market as a whole, choosing the quantity to sell, but not the price.

A very similar situation exists when a firm takes on workers in a perfectly competitive labour market, except that now the firm can buy as much labour as it wants at the ruling market wage. To state this another way, each employer faces a perfectly elastic supply of labour curve in a perfectly competitive labour market. Figure 12.2 illustrates why.

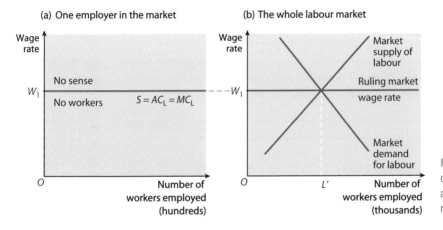

Figure 12.2 The supply curve of labour facing each firm in a perfectly competitive labour market

Figure 12.2 (b) shows demand and supply conditions in the whole of the labour market. The ruling market wage facing all employers and workers is W_1. Each firm, depicted in Figure 12.2 (a), *could* pay a wage higher than W_1, but there is no need to, since as many workers as the firm plans to employ are available at the ruling wage. In any case, such a course of action means that the firm incurs unnecessary production costs, leading to X-inefficiency and a failure to maximise profits. Hence the label 'no sense' positioned above W_1.

Conversely, any firm offering a wage below W_1 would lose all its workers. In a perfectly competitive labour market, workers regard all employers as perfect substitutes for each other. Why work for a firm paying below the market wage when work is available from employers offering the market wage?

EXAM TIP

Economic theory is easier to understand when you see how the same reasoning and way of thinking applies in different contexts. Compare Figure 12.2 with Figure 4.2 on page 39. The diagrams show perfect competition in a labour market and in a goods market. In Figure 12.2, the wage rate lies along the perfectly elastic *supply* curve of labour facing each employer. By contrast, in Figure 4.2 the price that each firm charges lies along the perfectly elastic *demand* curve for the firm's output.

Indeed, in a perfectly competitive labour market, each employer is just one among many in the market, able to hire whatever number of workers it wishes, providing only that the ruling market wage is offered to all employees taken on. This also means that W_1 (the ruling market wage rate) is each firm's **average cost of labour** curve (AC_L) and its **marginal cost of labour** curve (MC_L). Average costs of labour are calculated by dividing total wage costs by the number of workers employed. Likewise, marginal costs of labour are measured by the growth of the total wage bill whenever an extra worker is hired.

> **KEY TERMS**
>
> **average cost of labour:** total wage costs divided by the number of workers employed.
>
> **marginal cost of labour:** the addition to a firm's total cost of production resulting from employing one more worker.

The market supply of labour

I shall return to perfect competition in the labour market later in the chapter. However, before I do this, I first need to explain the market supply curve of labour, and then the market demand curve for labour.

If we add together the labour supply curves of all the workers in the labour market, we arrive at the **market supply curve of labour** illustrated in Figure 12.2 (b). To explain this curve, I must first explain an **individual worker's supply curve of labour**. This curve shows how many hours of labour the worker plans to supply at different hourly wage rates.

> **KEY TERMS**
>
> **market supply curve of labour:** planned supply of labour by all the workers in a labour market.
>
> **individual worker's supply curve of labour:** planned supply of labour by one worker.

My starting point is the assumption that a worker supplies more labour to increase personal economic welfare: that is, to maximise private benefit. The welfare that a worker derives from the supply of labour divides into two parts, which taken together are sometimes called **net advantage**.

Net advantage includes:

- welfare derived from the wage (or strictly from the goods and services bought with the money wage)
- welfare derived from work (popularly known as job satisfaction, or if negative, job dissatisfaction)

Different types of work yield different amounts of positive or negative welfare (job satisfaction and dissatisfaction). When a worker enjoys the job, the net advantage of work is greater than the welfare of the wage. In this situation, the worker is willing to work for a money wage lower than the wage that would be acceptable if there were no satisfaction from the work itself. But for some workers, work such as routine assembly-line work in factories and heavy manual labour is unpleasant, yielding job dissatisfaction. The supply of labour for this type of employment reflects the fact that the hourly wage rate must be high enough to compensate for the unpleasantness (or sometimes the danger) of the job.

CASE STUDY 12.1

Who should be paid more, MPs or news readers?

An essay question in an AQA exam paper once asked for an explanation of why workers employed in pleasant occupations, such as television celebrities, are paid more than those in disagreeable occupations, such as road sweepers. A good answer to the question might have argued that if job satisfaction or dissatisfaction were to be the only factor determining wages, the road sweeper would be paid more. However, the answer would then go on to argue that other factors, related to supply and demand, productivity, learned skills and innate ability tend to override the job satisfaction factor and explain why television celebrities are paid more than road sweepers.

In 2008, a government minister asked 'should MPs be paid more than television newsreaders?'. In a follow-up poll, 45% of the general public said 'yes' and 55% voted 'no'. Former Conservative MP Michael Portillo, now a TV presenter, argued that 'low pay will discourage good people from becoming MPs, especially if we are now going to denigrate their outside earnings too, even though that's how TV presenters boost their salaries. The present exchange rate is approximately one Jonathan Ross equals 100 MPs. It is a topsy-turvy world where we pay top journalists more to comment occasionally on what the Prime Minister does than we pay him to do his job 24/7.'

Replying 'no', Ken Livingstone, the Labour ex-mayor of London said: 'Far too many people are paid too much for what they do. In 1979, Britain's top 10% of earners were paid four times as much as the bottom 10%. In 2008 that figure had doubled to eight times as much. Is Britain twice as well run as it was 30 years ago? Is the output of television twice as good as in the 1970s? Are our politicians and bankers twice as honest? It's time for a dramatic reduction in top salaries across the board, not just those of TV presenters.'

Follow-up question

Do you believe that **both** MPs and TV newsreaders are paid too much? Use economic theory to justify your argument.

The upward-sloping supply curve of labour

As a simplification, I shall now assume that work yields neither job satisfaction nor dissatisfaction, and that a worker's net advantage derives solely from the wage. The worker must choose whether to supply an extra hour of labour time in order to earn money or whether to enjoy an extra hour of leisure time. The choice is illustrated in Figure 12.3.

There is an **opportunity cost** whenever a person decides to work. The opportunity cost of supplying one more hour of labour time (in order to earn money) is the hour of leisure time sacrificed. Because of the time constraint (there are only 24 hours in a day) a decision to supply one more hour of labour time means that the worker chooses 1 hour less of leisure time. Labour time and leisure time are substitutes for each other, and working longer hours eats into leisure time.

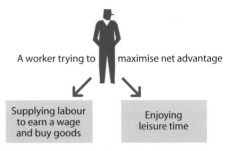

A worker trying to maximise net advantage

Supplying labour to earn a wage and buy goods

Enjoying leisure time

Figure 12.3 The choice between supplying labour and enjoying leisure time

But both the money wage and leisure time yield less and less extra welfare, the greater the quantity a person has. As more labour time is supplied at a particular hourly wage rate, the extra income yields less and less extra satisfaction. However, the decision to supply more labour simultaneously means the decision to enjoy less leisure time. In this situation, each extra hour of leisure sacrificed is accompanied by an increasing loss of economic welfare. At the margin, to maximise personal welfare, a worker must supply labour up to the point at which:

$$\frac{\text{welfare from the last}}{\text{unit of money earned}} = \frac{\text{welfare from the last unit}}{\text{of leisure time sacrificed}}$$

In this situation, the marginal private benefit received by a worker from supplying labour equals the marginal private cost incurred from giving up leisure time. Providing personal preferences remain stable, there is no incentive for the worker to supply more labour at the going hourly wage rate.

However, a higher hourly wage disturbs this equilibrium. With a higher wage rate, at the margin, the welfare derived from the wage becomes greater than the welfare derived from the last unit of leisure time enjoyed. To maximise personal welfare at the higher wage rate, the worker must supply more labour and enjoy less leisure time. The result is the upward-sloping individual supply curve of labour shown in Figure 12.4. An increase in the hourly wage rate from W_1 to W_2 means that the worker increases the hours of labour time supplied from L_1 to L_2.

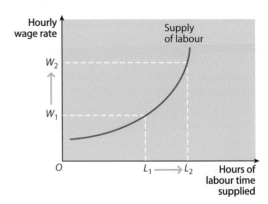

Figure 12.4 The upward-sloping supply curve of labour

The backward-bending supply curve of labour

Under some circumstances, however, a worker's labour supply curve may be backward bending, regressive or 'perverse', showing that as the wage rises, *less* labour is supplied. This is illustrated in Figure 12.5. When the wage rate rises from W_1 to W_2, the worker responds by working longer. The supply of labour increases from L_1 to L_2. But in Figure 12.5, the supply curve is upward-sloping for only part of the curve. At hourly wage rates higher than W_2, the supply curve bends back towards the vertical axis of the graph, and the curve's slope is negative rather than positive. Following an increase in the hourly wage rate from W_2 to W_3, a worker reduces the number of hours of labour supplied from L_2 to L_3.

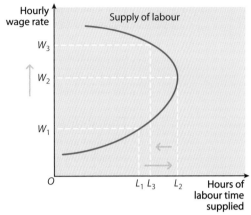

Figure 12.5 The backward-bending supply curve of labour

To explain the possibility of a backward-bending supply curve of labour, I must introduce two new concepts:

- **The substitution effect of an increase in the hourly wage rate.** To understand the idea of a substitution effect, think of the hourly wage rate as the price of an hour of leisure time. For example, at an hourly wage rate of £10, the price of an hour of leisure time is also £10, rising to £11 if the wage rate is increased by a pound. As the wage rate rises, an hour of leisure time becomes more expensive compared to the goods that the money wage can buy. Acting rationally, a worker responds to the rise in the hourly wage rate (and the price of leisure time) by substituting more labour time in place of leisure time.
- **The income effect of an increase in the hourly wage rate.** If the substitution effect is the only effect operating, a worker's supply curve slopes upward, showing labour time being substituted for leisure time as the hourly wage rate increases. However, matters can be complicated by the existence of an income effect resulting from the price change. The income effect of a wage-rate increase results from the fact that, for most people, leisure time is a normal good and not an inferior good. A rise in the hourly wage rate increases the worker's real income, and as real income rises, so does the demand for the normal good, leisure time.

Up to a wage rate of W_2 in Figure 12.5, the substitution effect of any wage increase exceeds the income effect. As a result, a worker chooses to work longer hours and to enjoy less leisure time. But when the wage rate rises above W_2, the income effect of a higher wage rate becomes more powerful than the substitution effect. As a result, a worker chooses to work fewer hours so as to enjoy more leisure time — and the worker's supply curve of labour slopes backward. Total money income may not fall. Given freedom of choice, a worker may, for example, decide to work 40 hours a week when the wage rate is £10 an hour, for a weekly income of £400. When the wage rate rises to £11, the worker may respond by working for only 38 hours, with a weekly income of £418.

A simpler approach to the backward-bending supply curve is to assume that a worker aspires to a target standard of living measured in the goods and services that the money wage can buy. When the money wage rate rises, a worker can meet the target and fulfil aspirations by working fewer hours, choosing more leisure time rather than more material goods and services. Workers are especially likely to behave in this way when the work itself is highly unpleasant or dangerous, yielding negative job satisfaction.

The shape of the supply curve of labour and government policy

Whether an individual's supply curve of labour is upward-sloping as in Figure 12.4, or backward-bending as depicted in Figure 12.5, is important for a government's tax and fiscal policies (and also for supply-side policy). An increase in the rate of income tax is equivalent to a fall in the hourly wage rate. With an upward-sloping supply curve of labour, a rise in income tax is a disincentive to work. When, however, the supply curve bends backward, a rise in income tax increases the supply of labour. The tax increase has a perverse incentive effect — a worker must now work longer to maintain a target material standard of living.

In real life, a tax increase may create an even greater need for laws to deal with tax avoidance and illegal tax evasion. In the second scenario, people may decide to supply their labour untaxed in the informal, underground economy, rather than formally, but subject to taxation.

Whatever the shape of an individual's supply curve of labour, the market supply curve of labour will probably slope upward. The explanation lies in the fact that more workers enter the labour market in response to a wage rise, attracted both from other labour markets and from unemployment.

A perfectly competitive firm's demand curve for labour

Just as the market supply curve of labour in a perfectly competitive labour market is the sum of the supply curves of all the individual workers in the labour market, so the market demand curve for labour is obtained by adding together each firm's demand curve for labour at different wage rates. We must therefore derive a perfectly competitive firm's demand curve for labour in order to understand the market demand curve for labour.

A firm demands labour only if profits can be increased by employing more workers. But this assumes that households in goods markets demand the goods and services that workers are employed to produce. This means that a firm's demand for labour is a **derived demand** — derived from the demand for goods. Assuming a profit-maximising objective on the part of firms, there can be no demand for labour in the long run unless the firms employing labour sell the outputs produced for at least a normal profit in the goods market. I shall now show that, in a perfectly competitive labour market, a firm's demand curve for labour is the **marginal revenue product** of labour (*MRP*) curve facing the firm.

> **KEY TERM**
>
> **marginal revenue product:** the monetary value of the addition to a firm's total output brought about by employing one more worker.

When deciding whether it is worthwhile employing one more worker, a firm needs to know the answers to three questions:
- How far will total output rise?
- How far will total sales revenue rise when the extra output is sold in the goods market?
- How far will total costs of production rise as a result of paying the worker a wage?

In a perfectly competitive labour market, a firm's demand curve for labour is derived from the answers to the first two of these questions. The answer to the third question is provided by the horizontal ruling market wage, illustrated earlier in Figure 12.2.

EXAM TIP

Exam questions on the demand for labour require knowledge of marginal productivity theory. However, marginal productivity theory cannot in itself explain different wage rates. Labour supply theory is also required, together with an appreciation that different labour markets differ in their competitiveness.

The marginal physical product of labour

When answering the first of the three questions posed above, a firm has to calculate the value of the **marginal physical product** of labour (*MPP*). The marginal physical product of labour is (rather confusingly) just another name for the **marginal returns** (or **marginal product**) of labour, which I explained in Chapter 3. *MPP* measures the amount by which a firm's total output rises in the short run (holding capital fixed), as a result of employing one more worker. In Chapter 3, I explained how the law of diminishing returns or diminishing marginal productivity operates as a firm employs more labour when capital is held fixed. In the context of labour market theory, it is usual to assume that the law of diminishing returns begins to operate as soon as a second worker is added to the labour force. This means that the possibility of increasing marginal returns at low levels of employment is ignored.

KEY TERM

marginal physical product: the addition to a firm's total output brought about by employing one more worker.

Given this simplifying assumption, the impact of the law of diminishing returns is illustrated in Figure 12.6 (a), which shows the marginal product of labour falling as additional workers are hired by the firm.

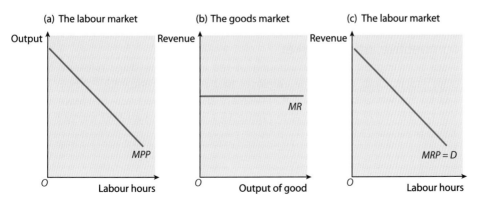

Figure 12.6 Deriving the *MRP* curve from the *MPP* curve

The marginal revenue product of labour

The falling *MPP* curve provides the answer to the first of the three questions I posed, showing how much total output will rise when an additional worker is employed. But as its name indicates, the *MPP* curve only shows the *physical* output produced by an extra worker — measured, for example, in automobiles or loaves of bread, or whatever goods the firm produces. To convert the marginal physical product of labour into a money value, the *MPP* of labour has to be multiplied by the addition to the firm's total sales revenue resulting from the sale in the goods market of the extra output produced by labour. We therefore multiply *MPP* by marginal revenue (*MR*) to answer the second of the three questions. When the economy's goods market is perfectly competitive, *MR* is identical to the good's price or average revenue, and is shown by the horizontal *MR* curve in Figure 12.6 (b).

Figure 12.6 (c), which shows the marginal revenue product curve of labour, can be explained with the use of the following equation:

$$\text{marginal physical product} \times \text{marginal revenue} = \text{marginal revenue product}$$

or:

$$MPP \times MR = MRP$$

As the equation shows, the marginal revenue product of labour is calculated by multiplying the *MPP* of labour in Figure 12.6 (a) by the horizontal *MR* curve in Figure 12.6 (b). When a firm sells its output in a perfectly competitive goods market, the falling diminishing marginal revenue productivity of labour is explained solely by the diminishing marginal physical product: that is, by the law of diminishing returns.

However, if output is sold in an imperfectly competitive goods market, marginal revenue product of labour declines faster than in a perfectly competitive goods market. This is because in imperfectly competitive goods markets, the marginal revenue earned from selling an extra worker's output also falls as output increases. In this situation, there are *two* reasons for the *MRP* curve to fall as employment increases.

The equilibrium wage rate and level of employment in a perfectly competitive labour market

I can now explain the determination of the equilibrium wage rate and level of employment, both for a single employer in a perfectly competitive labour market and for the whole labour market. These are shown respectively in Figure 12.7 (a) and (b). Figure 12.7 is identical to Figure 12.2, except that an *MRP* curve has been added in Figure 12.7 (a).

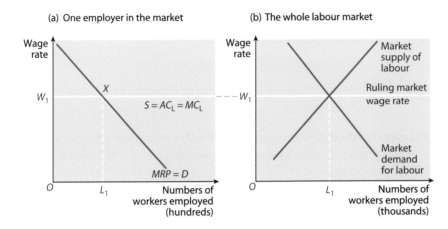

Figure 12.7
Equilibrium in a perfectly competitive labour market

A perfectly competitive firm's demand curve for labour

In a perfectly competitive labour market, each employer passively accepts the ruling market wage. At this wage, it is a passive price-taker. The ruling wage, determined in Figure 12.7 (b), is also the perfectly elastic supply curve of labour facing the firm, and the firm's AC_L and MC_L curve. Each firm can hire as many workers as it wishes at the ruling market wage, but cannot influence the ruling wage by its own actions. To maximise profit when selling the output produced by labour, the firm must choose the level of employment at which:

the addition to sales revenue resulting from the employment of an extra worker $=$ the addition to production costs resulting from hiring the services

or:

$MRP = MC_L$

The marginal revenue product of labour is the **marginal private benefit** accruing to the employer when hiring an extra worker. Likewise, the **marginal cost of labour** or MC_L is the marginal private cost incurred by the firm. Since, in a perfectly competitive labour market, the marginal cost of labour always equals the wage paid to the workers, the perfectly competitive firm's level of employment is where:

$MRP = W$

Point X in Figure 12.7 (a) shows the number of workers that a firm is willing to employ at the ruling wage of W_1. Consider what happens if the firm employs a labour force larger than L_1. Additional workers add more to total cost than to total revenue, and profit falls. Conversely, with a workforce below L_1, the MRP of the last worker is greater than the wage, and the profits that a larger labour force would generate are not made.

Summarising:

If $MRP > W$:   more workers should be hired

If $MRP < W$:   fewer workers should be employed

If $MRP = W$:   the firm is employing the number of workers consistent with profit maximisation

The market demand for labour in a perfectly competitive labour market

Earlier in the chapter, I explained that the market supply curve of labour is obtained by adding the individual supply curves of all the workers in the market at different possible wages. In a similar way, we add the demand curves for labour of all the firms in the market to obtain the market demand curve for labour shown in Figure 12.7 (b). Since each employer's demand for labour is shown by the MRP curve, the market demand curve for labour is the horizontal sum of the MRP curves.

Monopsony labour markets

Monopsony means a single buyer, just as **monopoly** means a single seller. In a monopsony labour market, workers cannot choose between alternative employers, since there is only one firm or employer available to hire them.

> **KEY TERM**
>
> **monopsony:** there is only one buyer in a market.

Although in some ways a monopsony labour market resembles a monopoly goods market, there are also significant differences. In much the same way that the market demand curve facing a monopoly supplier of a good is the monopolist's average revenue curve, so in a monopsony labour market, the market supply curve of labour is the firm's average cost of labour curve (AC_L). The AC_L curve shows the different wage rates that the monopsonist must pay to attract labour forces of different sizes. For example, Figure 12.8 shows a monopsony employer hiring five workers at an hourly wage rate or AC_L of £10. As the diagram shows, the hourly wage per week must rise to £11 to attract a sixth worker into the firm's labour force.

The supply or AC_L curve facing the monopsonist shows the wage that has to be paid to all workers at each size of the labour force, to persuade the workers to supply their services. However, in a monopsony labour market, the AC_L curve is *not* the marginal cost of labour curve (MC_L). To attract an extra worker, the monopsonist must raise the hourly wage rate and pay the higher wage to all the workers. In this situation, the marginal cost of labour incurred by employing an extra worker

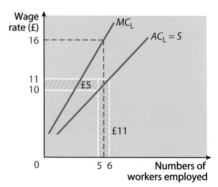

Figure 12.8 In a monopsony labour market, the MC_L curve lies above the AC_L or supply of labour curve

includes the total amount by which the wage bill rises, and not just the wage rate paid to the additional worker hired. The MC_L curve of labour illustrated in Figure 12.8 is positioned above the AC_L (or supply curve). Similarly, in the goods market, a monopolist's MR curve is below its AR curve. In Figure 12.8, the MC_L incurred per hour by employing the sixth worker is £16, made up of the £11 wage rate paid to the sixth worker, plus the £1 extra paid to each of the five workers already employed before the sixth worker joined the labour force.

> **EXAM TIP**
>
> It is important to realise that *all* real-world labour markets are imperfectly competitive to some extent. Perfect competition is as much a theoretical abstraction in labour markets as it is in goods markets.

The equilibrium wage rate and level of employment

Figure 12.9 shows how the equilibrium wage and the equilibrium level of employment are determined in a monopsony labour market. As in the case of a perfectly competitive employer in the labour market, the monopsonist's level of employment is determined by the point where $MRP = MC_L$. This occurs at point A in Figure 12.9, at which L_1 workers are employed.

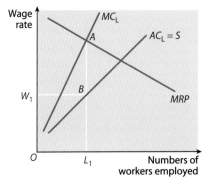

Figure 12.9 Equilibrium in a monopsony labour market

However, in a monopsony labour market, the equilibrium wage rate is determined at point B, which lies below A. The wage rate paid by the monopsonist (W_1 in Figure 12.9) is less than the value of the marginal revenue product of labour. Point B is positioned on the supply curve of labour facing the monopsonist. The supply curve shows that L_1 workers are willing to work for an hourly wage rate of W_1. Although the firm could pay a wage rate higher than W_1, the monopsonist has no need to pay a higher wage rate. Why pay more, when W_1 attracts all the workers the monopsonist requires? Indeed, if the monopsonist were to pay a wage higher than W_1, it would inevitably incur unnecessary production costs and end up being X-inefficient. It would fail to maximise profits when selling its output in the goods market. Profit maximisation requires that a wage no higher than W_1 is paid.

Wage equalisation in a perfectly competitive market economy

If all labour markets in the economy were perfectly competitive, there would be no barriers preventing workers moving between labour markets. In this situation, the forces of competition would reduce many of the differences in wages between different occupations. Some differences would probably remain because different types of work have different skill requirements, and innate abilities and skills would still vary between workers. Nevertheless, higher wages in one occupation would attract workers from other labour markets, causing the supply curve of labour to shift to the right in the high-wage labour market and to the left in the low-wage market.

At the same time, wage differentials would create incentives for firms in the high-wage market to reduce their demand for labour by substituting capital for labour, and for firms in the low-wage labour markets to adopt more **labour-intensive methods of production.** Demand and supply curves and wages would continue to adjust until there was no further incentive for firms to change their method of production or for workers to shift between labour markets. Wage differentials would diminish throughout the economy, but would not completely disappear.

Explanations of different wage levels

Wage differences in competitive labour markets

Even in highly competitive labour markets, wage differences exist, largely because labour demand and supply curves are in different positions in different labour markets, reflecting factors such as different labour productivities, abilities and required skills. We might also expect wage differentials to exist in highly competitive labour markets for two further reasons:

- **Different jobs have different non-monetary characteristics.** I have already explained how the net advantage of any type of work includes job satisfaction or dissatisfaction as well as economic welfare gained from the wage. Other things being equal, a firm must pay a worker a higher wage to compensate for any relative unpleasantness in the job. An equalising wage differential is the payment that must be made to compensate a worker for the different non-monetary characteristics of jobs. Following such a payment, there is no incentive for a worker to switch between jobs or labour markets.
- **Disequilibrium trading.** Economies are subject to constant change, such as the development of new goods and services and improved methods of production or technical progress. Patterns of demand also change. Because market conditions are always changing, labour markets — like other markets — are usually in disequilibrium rather than in equilibrium. Although market forces tend to equalise wages in competitive labour markets, at any point in time disparities exist, reflecting the disequilibrium conditions existent at the time.

Wage differences in imperfectly competitive labour markets

In imperfectly competitive labour markets, including monopsony labour markets, there are a number of other reasons why differences in wages occur. These include:

- immobility of labour
- different elasticities of demand for, and supply of, labour
- wage discrimination
- differences in pay between women and men
- the effect of trade unions
- the effect of different methods of pay determination, such as collective bargaining

Immobility of labour

There are two main types of labour immobility: **occupational immobility** and **geographical immobility**.

- **Occupational immobility of labour**. This occurs when workers are prevented, by either natural or artificial barriers, from moving between different types of job. Workers are obviously not homogeneous or uniform, so differences in natural ability may prevent or restrict movement between jobs. Some types of work require an innate ability, such as physical strength or perfect eyesight, which prevents a worker immediately switching between labour markets. Examples of artificial barriers include membership qualifications imposed by professional bodies such as accountancy associations, and trade union restrictive practices such as pre-entry closed shops, which restrict employment to those already belonging to the union. Various forms of racial, religious, age and gender discrimination are also artificial causes of occupational immobility of labour.

- **Geographical immobility of labour**. This occurs when factors such as ignorance of job opportunities, family and cultural ties, and the financial costs of moving or travel prevent a worker from filling a job vacancy located at a distance from his or her present place of residence. Perhaps the most significant cause of geographical immobility in the UK in recent years has been the state of the housing market, which itself reflects imperfections in other factor markets. During house price booms, low-paid and unemployed workers in the northern half of the UK have found it difficult or impossible to move south to fill job vacancies in the more prosperous southeast of England. The prices of owner-occupied housing have soared and there has been very little housing available at affordable rents in either the private or the public sectors. At the same time, workers living in their own houses in the southeast may be reluctant to apply for jobs elsewhere in the country, for fear that they will never be able to afford to move back to southern England.

Different elasticities of demand for, and supply of, labour

Both the mobility of labour and wage rates in different labour markets are affected by the elasticities of the supply of, and the demand for, labour. I shall now look briefly at factors affecting labour market elasticities.

Determinants of the wage elasticity of labour demand. If the wage rate increases, but nothing else that might affect the demand for labour changes, by how much will employment fall? The answer is affected by firms' elasticity of demand for labour. The demand for a particular type of labour is likely to be relatively inelastic:

- when the relevant wage cost forms only a small part of total production costs (this has been called the importance of being unimportant)
- when the demand for the good or service being produced by the labour is inelastic
- when it is difficult to substitute other factors of production, or other types of labour, for the labour currently employed
- in the short run, rather than the long run, since it often takes time for employers to adjust their production process

Determinants of the wage elasticity of labour supply. The supply of unskilled labour is usually more elastic than the supply of a particular type of skilled labour. The training period of unskilled labour is usually very short, and any innate abilities required are unlikely to be restricted to a small proportion of the total population. All the factors reducing the occupational and geographical mobility of labour tend to reduce the elasticity of labour supply. The supply of labour is also likely to be more elastic in the long run than in the short run. Finally, the availability of a pool of unemployed labour increases the elasticity of supply of labour, while full employment has the opposite effect.

EXAM TIP

Unit 3 exam questions are likely to require synoptic application of elasticity theory, learnt in the context of goods markets in Unit 1, to the demand for, and the supply of, labour.

Wage discrimination

In imperfectly competitive labour markets, employers often possess sufficient market power to reduce the total wage bill through **wage discrimination**.

KEY TERM

wage discrimination: paying different workers different wages for doing the same job.

Figure 12.10 illustrates the effect of wage discrimination introduced into a previously competitive labour market. However, in real life, discrimination is more likely in imperfectly competitive labour markets. In the absence of wage discrimination, all workers are paid the same wage, W_1, determined by supply and demand. Employers' total wage costs are shown by the rectangle OW_1AL_1.

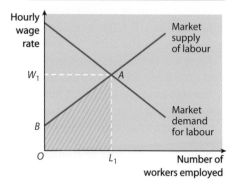

Figure 12.10 Wage discrimination

But if, instead of paying W_1 to all workers, employers pay each worker the minimum he or she is prepared to work for, the total wage bill falls to equal the shaded area $OBAL_1$. Employers thus gain at the expense of workers, which is why firms pay, and trade unions resist, discriminatory wages whenever possible.

EXAM TIP

You should understand the similarity between wage discrimination in the labour market where a firm hires its labour and price discrimination in the goods market where the firm sells its output.

EXTENSION MATERIAL

Bringing together wage discrimination and price discrimination

In the case of perfect price discrimination (first-degree price discrimination), a firm charges different prices to different customers for the same good, with the same marginal cost of production, so that each customer pays the maximum price he or she is prepared to pay. The entire consumer surplus that customers would otherwise enjoy is transferred to the firm, enlarging the firm's profit.

With perfect wage discrimination, the firm pays each worker the minimum wage the worker is prepared to accept, without transferring his or her employment elsewhere. Part of the wage that workers would otherwise get is transferred to the firm, once again boosting profit.

From an imperfectly competitive firm's point of view, the best possible outcome is simultaneous price discrimination in the goods market in which it sells its output and wage discrimination in the labour markets in which it hires its workers. Profit is boosted from two directions at once.

Can you think of reasons why such simultaneous exploitation seldom takes place?

CASE STUDY 12.2

The Unit 3 specification advises that candidates should be able to discuss the impact of gender, ethnic, age and other forms of discrimination on wages, levels and types of employment. The passage below argues that too little has been done to get rid of gender discrimination and glass ceilings that prevent women from rising to occupy top jobs.

Glass ceiling for women replaced by reinforced concrete as progress stalls

The so-called glass ceiling that prevents women progressing in the workplace is more like 'reinforced concrete', the chief executive of the Equality and Human Rights Commission (EHRC) has warned. Nicola Brewer, the chief executive of the Equality and Human Rights Commission, said:

'We always speak of a glass ceiling. These figures reveal that in some cases it appears to be made of reinforced concrete. We need radical change to support those who are doing great work and help those who want to work better and release talent.'

Young women's aspiration is in danger of giving way to frustration. Many of them are now excelling at school and achieving great things in higher education. And they are keen to balance a family with a rewarding career. But workplaces forged in an era of stay-at-home mums and breadwinner dads are putting too many barriers in the way — resulting in an avoidable loss of talent at the top.

Young women's aspiration is in danger of giving way to frustration

There are fewer women MPs in Westminster, where they make up just 19.3% of all MPs. Women's representation among FTSE 100 directors has improved slightly from 10.4 to 11.0%.

The Commission has likened women's progress to a snail's pace. A snail could crawl:

- nine times round the M25 in the 55 years it will take women to achieve equality in the senior judiciary
- from Land's End to John O'Groats and halfway back again in the 73 years it will take for equal numbers of women to become directors of FTSE 100 companies
- the entire length of the Great Wall of China in 212 years, only slightly longer than the 200 years it will take for women to be equally represented in Parliament

The Commission's report argues that its findings are not just a 'women's issue' but a powerful symptom of a wider failure. The report asks in what other ways old-fashioned, inflexible ways of working are preventing Britain from tapping into talent — whether that of women or other under-represented groups such as disabled people, ethnic minorities or those with caring responsibilities. Britain cannot afford to go on marginalising or rejecting talented people who fail to fit into traditional work patterns.

Source: Equality and Human Rights Commission, September 2008

Follow-up questions

1 What is meant by a 'glass ceiling'?
2 Do 'glass ceilings' affect adversely other groups in society, such as ethnic and religious minorities and old people, or does discrimination take different forms against these groups of people?

Differences in earnings between men and women

In recent years, although women have accounted for an increasing share of total employment in the UK, women's pay often continues to be lower than men's pay, despite the fact that equal pay legislation has been in place since 1972. The pay gap between men and women is at risk of widening for the first time on record, a leading pay equality campaign group has warned. The Fawcett Society has said that women still earn 14.9% less on average than men for the same job, and that this gap could widen as public sector cuts push women into the private sector, where the gap is wider. A second survey, the 2012 Gender Salary Survey, undertaken by the Chartered Management Institute (CMI) also finds that the average annual pay gap stands at £10,060. Women also lose out when it comes to bonuses, receiving less than half the average £7,496 that men receive.

There are two main reasons why women earn less than men:
- women work predominantly in low-paid industries and occupations
- in many occupational groups, women are paid less than men. This is often because women are under-represented in the higher-paid posts within an occupation, rather than because women are paid less for doing the same job

Discrimination against women in labour markets may contribute to both these sets of circumstances. In addition, women are disproportionately represented in industries where the average size of firm and plant is small. These industries tend to pay lower wages and offer fewer promotional prospects than large firms and large industries. Such industries are also seldom unionised. Indeed, within all industries, women workers traditionally have been less unionised than men.

This relates to another reason why women earn less than men: on average, their attachment to the labour force is weaker. Before the 2008 recession, each year of work experience raised the pay of both men and women by an average 3%. Yet when women leave the labour force, usually to look after young children, their potential pay falls by 3% for each year involved. For example, a man and woman enter employment with equal potential and after 8 years the woman leaves the workforce in order to raise a family. If she re-enters the labour force 8 years later she will be 16 years, in pay terms, behind the man.

The higher labour turnover of women also imposes costs on the employer — for example, the costs of training replacement workers. This may reduce the incentive for employers to train female workers. Similarly, women may have less incentive to spend time and money on their own education and training if they expect the benefits that they will eventually receive to be less than the costs initially incurred.

The effect of introducing a trade union into a perfectly competitive market

A **trade union** is an association of workers formed to protect and promote the interests of its members. A major function of a union is to bargain with employers to improve wages and other conditions of work. Many UK employers are now reluctant to recognise and bargain with the unions to which their employees belong. However, in my analysis, I shall regard a trade union as a monopoly supplier of labour, which is able to keep non-members out of the labour market and also to prevent its members from supplying labour at below the union wage rate. Of course, in real life a union may not necessarily have the objectives specified above, and even if it does, it may not be able to achieve them. I shall make one other increasingly unrealistic assumption, namely that a union can fix any wage rate it chooses, and that employment is then determined by the amount of labour that employers will hire at this wage.

> **KEY TERM**
>
> **trade union:** a collective association of workers whose aim is to improve the pay and other conditions of work of its members.

Given these assumptions, Figure 12.11 shows the possible effects resulting from workers organising a trade union in a labour market that had previously been perfectly competitive. Without a trade union, the competitive wage rate is W_1. The workers join a trade union, which raises the minimum wage rate acceptable to union members to W_2. Without the union, the market supply of labour curve is the upward-sloping line labelled $S = AC_L$. With the union, the market supply of labour curve is the kinked line W_2XS. For all sizes of labour force to the left of, or below, L_3, the supply curve of labour is horizontal or perfectly elastic, lying along the wage W_2 set by the trade union. If employers wish to hire a labour force larger than L_3 (and to the right of point X), a wage higher than W_2 has to be offered. Beyond L_3, the supply curve of labour slopes upward because higher wage rates are needed to attract more workers.

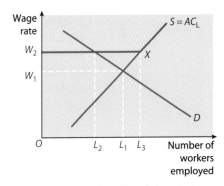

Figure 12.11 The effect of introducing a trade union into a previously perfectly competitive labour market

EXAM TIP

Note the effects shown in Figure 12.11 and in Figure 12.13 can also be used to explain the effect of a national minimum wage imposed above the wage rate that would otherwise be determined by market forces.

At the wage level set by the union, employers only wish to hire L_2 workers. However, L_3 workers are willing to work at this wage rate. This means there is excess supply of labour and unemployment in the labour market. More workers wish to work than there are jobs available. The resulting unemployment, called **classical unemployment**, is shown by the distance $L_3 - L_2$.

The effect described above is sometimes used to justify the argument that any attempt by a union to raise wages must inevitably be at the expense of jobs, and that if unions are really interested in reducing unemployment, they should accept wage cuts. However, many economists — especially those of a Keynesian and left-of-centre persuasion — dispute this conclusion. They argue, first, that it is unrealistic to assume that conditions of demand for labour are unchanged. By agreeing to accept technical progress, by working with new capital equipment and new methods of organising work and by improving the skills of their members, a union can ensure (with the cooperation of management) that the *MRP* curve of labour shifts to the right. In these circumstances, increased productivity creates scope for both increased wages and increased employment.

Second, both wages and employment can rise when a union negotiates for higher wages to be paid by firms producing in an expanding goods market. In these conditions, increased demand for output creates increased demand for labour to produce the output. Indeed, rising real wages throughout the economy are likely to increase the aggregate demand for the output of all firms producing consumer goods because wages are the most important source of consumption expenditure in the economy.

So far, I have assumed that trade unions try to increase pay by preventing union members supplying labour at wage rates below the rate set by the union. Figure 12.12 illustrates a second way in which much the same result can be achieved. In this case, the trade union establishes a **closed shop**, which keeps non-union workers out of the labour market. The union-controlled entry barrier shifts the supply curve of labour leftward, and increases the inelasticity of the curve. Employment falls from L_1 to L_2, and the wage rate is hiked up to W_2.

The word *shop* in the term 'closed shop' refers to the workshop or the shop floor, where manufacturing firms undertake the tasks involved in production. A closed shop is an example of a **labour restrictive practice**. There are two types of closed shop, both of which have been made illegal in the UK. Figure 12.12 illustrates the effect of a *pre-entry* closed shop, which requires workers to join the union before starting

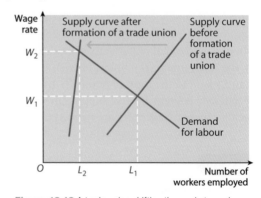

Figure 12.12 A trade union shifting the market supply curve of labour

employment. By imposing a quota or ceiling on the number of union members, a union uses a pre-entry closed shop to shift the supply curve of labour to the left. By contrast, a *post-entry* closed shop permits non-members to get jobs, but all workers have to join the union to keep their jobs. Post-entry closed shops have little effect on entry barriers, but they are a means of dealing with the free-rider problem in labour markets.

Free-riding occurs when workers decline to join a union while accepting pay rises that the union negotiates. Free-riders benefit from the union 'mark-up' — that is, the generally higher pay in unionised rather than non-unionised places of work — but save themselves the cost of paying union membership fees.

How a trade union can increase both the wage rate and employment in a monopsonistic labour market

The assertion that unions raise wages at the expense of jobs is heavily dependent on the assumption that, before the union was formed, the labour market was perfectly competitive. In the case of a monopsony labour market, it is possible for a union to raise *both* the wage rate and employment, even without the *MRP* curve shifting rightward. This is illustrated in Figure 12.13. If the labour market is non-unionised, the equilibrium wage rate is W_1 and the level of employment is L_1.

The introduction of a trade union into a monopsony labour market has the same effect on the labour supply curve as in perfect competition. In Figure 12.13, the kinked line W_2XS is the labour supply curve and the average cost of labour curve (AC_L) when the union sets the wage rate at W_2. But in monopsony, W_2XS is *not* the marginal cost of labour curve (MC_L). The MC_L curve is the double-kinked line W_2XZV. The double kink is explained in the following way. Providing the monopsonist employs a labour force smaller than or equal to L_2, the MC_L of employing an extra worker equals both the AC_L and the union-determined wage of W_2. But beyond L_2 and point X, the monopsonist must offer a higher wage in order to persuade additional workers to supply labour. In this situation, with all the workers now being paid the higher wage, the MC_L curve lies above the supply curve or AC_L curve. The upward-sloping line ZV drawn in Figure 12.13 shows the MC_L of increasing employment above L_2.

Figure 12.13 The effect of introducing a trade union into a monopsony labour market

This means there is a vertical gap between the horizontal section of the MC_L curve (for levels of employment at or below L_2 and point X) and the upward-sloping section of the curve (ZV). In the absence of a union, the level of employment is L_1, determined at point A (with point B determining the wage rate W_1). But when the union sets the wage rate at W_2, employment rises to L_2, which is the level of employment at which the MRP curve intersects the vertical section of the MC_L curve at point C, between X and Z. The union has managed to increase both the wage rate and the level of employment.

The national minimum wage

The explanation in the previous section, of how a trade union can increase both the wage rate and the level of employment, can also be used to analyse the effect of a national minimum wage set by the government. Under the unrealistic assumption that labour markets are perfectly competitive, Figure 12.11 can be adapted to show how a national minimum wage set above the market-clearing wage rate leads to a loss of jobs and unemployment. But if, more realistically, labour markets are imperfectly competitive, Figure 12.13 should be used. This figure can be adapted to show how a national minimum wage can increase both the wage rate and the level of employment.

KEY TERM

national minimum wage: a minimum wage or wage rate that must by law be paid to employees.

From 1979 until 1997, UK Conservative governments opposed the introduction of a minimum legal wage, believing that its main effect would be to increase unemployment.

CASE STUDY 12.3

Recession, recovery and the UK jobs market

In the third quarter of 2008, the UK economy entered recession. Many UK companies, including the plant manufacturers, JCB, had already begun to sack workers, and those still in jobs feared they would be made redundant. To try to prevent further lay-offs, union members at JCB offered to work for lower wages. However, wage reductions didn't work. In fact, JCB sacked more workers in the autumn of 2008, as orders for bulldozers and other construction plant dried up.

However, by 2013, JCB was creating jobs again as the UK economy showed signs of recovering from recession. The company announced it was creating 50 jobs at its Derbyshire factory. Having made a record profit of £365 million, JCB is investing £45 million in engine development. But many of the workers JCB hires are agency workers and lack the guarantee of continuous employment. However, JCB says that most of their full-time employees have entered through some period of temporary work and proved their worth. With an improving economy, the company has taken them on. And as a result of investing in its own training academy, JCB has recently created a hundred jobs for teenage apprentices. But JCB is creating far more jobs by investing in factories in Brazil and India. A company spokesman has said 'Growth for JCB anywhere is good for JCB and a significant number of the machines are still made here in the UK and shipped around the world.'

Follow-up questions

1 Why are companies such as JCB, whose clients are building companies, especially likely to lay off workers in a recession?

2 In what way does the information in the case study illustrate the globalisation process?

By contrast, the Labour Party and the trade union movement were both committed to the introduction of a national minimum wage, arguing that evidence from other European countries suggests that the benefits in terms of social fairness exceed any costs involved. The national minimum wage (NMW) introduced in April 1999 was set at a level of £3.60 per hour throughout the UK, or 45% of median earnings. But young workers below the age of 18 were excluded from its protection.

EXAM TIP

Exam questions may be set on different methods of pay determination and on reasons for the decline of *collective bargaining* as a method of pay determination.

The government decides the level of the national minimum wage, taking advice from the Low Pay Commission. The government does not guarantee to increase the NMW each year, although in recent years the NMW has been raised annually. There are four levels of minimum wage, and the rates from 1 October 2013 were:

- £6.31 per hour for workers aged 21 years and older (the adult rate)
- £5.03 per hour for workers aged 18–20 inclusive (the development rate)
- £3.72 per hour for all workers under the age of 18 (the rate for 16–17–year–olds)
- £2.68 per hour (the apprentice rate)

EXTENSION MATERIAL

Support for a legal minimum wage

In the 1970s and 1980s, many economists accepted that when government forces businesses to pay higher wages, businesses in turn hire fewer employees. It is a powerful argument against the minimum wage since it suggests that private businesses as a group, along with teenagers and low-wage employees, will be penalised by a mandatory raise.

This view came under attack in the mid-1990s following some work done by two Princeton economists, David Card and Alan Krueger. In 1992, New Jersey increased the state minimum wage to $5.05 an hour (applicable to both the public and the private sectors), which gave the two young professors an opportunity to study the comparative effects of that increase on fast-food restaurants and low-wage employment in New Jersey and Pennsylvania, where the minimum wage remained at the federal level of $4.25 an hour. Card and Krueger agreed that the hypothesis that a rise in wages would destroy jobs was one of the clearest and most widely appreciated in the field of economics. Both believed, at the start, that their work would reinforce that hypothesis. But in 1995, and again in 2000, the research of the two academics showed that the conventional wisdom was wrong. Their data demonstrated that a modest increase in wages did not appear to cause any significant harm to employment; in some cases, a rise in the minimum wage even resulted in a slight increase in employment. (See the earlier section on page 173 on how a trade union can increase both the wage rate and employment in a monopsonistic labour market.)

SUMMARY

- The price mechanism operates in the labour market in a similar way to how it operates in the goods market, but the roles of firms and households are reversed.
- In their role as employers, firms demand labour in the labour market.
- The demand for labour is a derived demand.
- Members of households supply labour to earn an income which then provides an effective demand for goods.
- A worker supplies labour to maximise net advantage, which may include job satisfaction.
- The opportunity cost of working is the leisure time forgone.
- An individual's supply curve of labour may slope upward or bend backward.
- The shape of the supply curve of labour affects labour market incentives.
- In a perfectly competitive labour market, the marginal revenue product (*MRP*) curve facing an employer is the employer's demand curve for labour.
- The supply curve of labour facing a firm in a perfectly competitive labour market is the perfectly elastic line determined by the interaction of market supply and demand.
- For a firm, this horizontal line is also the average cost of labour (AC_L) and the marginal cost of labour (MC_L).
- A monopsony is the only buyer of labour in a labour market.
- The wage rate and the level of employment are likely to be lower in monopsony than in a perfectly competitive labour market.
- In monopsony, a trade union may be able to increase both the wage rate and the level of employment toward the perfectly competitive levels. A national minimum wage can have the same effect.
- Likewise, the national minimum wage might result in both higher wages and higher employment because real-world labour markets are imperfectly competitive.
- Wage discrimination occurs if employers exert their power to pay workers the minimum wage rates they are prepared to accept.
- Gender discrimination means that women often earn less than men.

Exam-style questions

1 Explain why a worker's supply curve of labour may bend backward. **(15 marks)**

2 Explain three factors significant in determining a firm's demand for labour. **(15 marks)**

3 Assess the effects of the migration of workers from central Europe to the UK upon UK wage rates, levels of employment and the competitiveness of labour markets. **(25 marks)**

4 Evaluate the view that when trade unions raise wages they inevitably reduce levels of employment. **(25 marks)**

Extra resources to help you revise are available online at www.hodderplus.co.uk/philipallan

Poverty and the distribution of income and wealth

As the experience of many poor countries shows, unregulated market forces tend to produce highly unequal distributions of income and wealth, which are themselves a form of market failure. Of course, not all economists agree. Extreme free-market economists seem to think that people who end up poor deserve to be poor. According to this view the market does not fail; it simply creates incentives that cause people to generate income and wealth which end up benefiting most of the population. They also believe that attempts by governments to redistribute income and wealth from the rich to the poor usually end up, through the distortion of personal incentives, in government failure which harms national economic performance.

LEARNING OUTCOMES

This chapter will:
- discuss the meaning of poverty
- distinguish between absolute poverty and relative poverty
- explain the main causes of poverty in the UK
- examine inequalities in the distribution of income and wealth in the UK
- summarise how government policies such as progressive taxation, transfers and the national minimum wage attempt to reduce poverty and make the distribution of income more equal
- relate progressive taxation to fiscal drag and to the poverty and unemployment traps

WHAT YOU SHOULD ALREADY KNOW

Poverty is not mentioned in the AS specification, though the concept is implicit in the Unit 1 requirement that candidates should understand that inequalities in the distribution of income and wealth can lead to market failure. Apart from advice that candidates should be able to give examples of this cause of market failure, there is no other mention of income and wealth inequalities in the AS specifications. My advice is that you treat both poverty and income and wealth inequalities as A2 topics on which exam questions are likely to be set.

What is poverty?

Poverty is caused both by a low real national income relative to a country's total population size and by inequalities in the distributions of income and wealth. The former leads to **absolute poverty** for most of a country's inhabitants, whereas the latter causes **relative poverty**.

- Absolute poverty occurs when income is below a particular level. According to the charity Barnardo's:

KEY TERMS

absolute poverty: occurs when income is below a particular level.

relative poverty: occurs when income is below a specified proportion of average income.

Absolute poverty refers to a set standard which is consistent over time and between countries. Measuring poverty by an absolute threshold has the advantage of applying the same standard across different locations and time periods, making comparisons easier. However, it does not take into account that you need different levels of income in different places, for example, a cup of coffee is more expensive in England than it is in Brazil.

■ Relative poverty is suffered by a household if its income is below a specified proportion of average income for all households (for example, less than a third of average income). Barnardo's says:

Relative poverty defines 'poverty' as being below a relative poverty threshold. It classifies individuals or families as 'poor' not by comparing them to a fixed cut-off point, but by comparing them to others in the population under study.

CASE STUDY 13.1

Many UK charities try to pressure individuals to donate to their cause and governments to intervene more in the economy to reduce poverty. Shelter centres its activities on homelessness. Barnardo's is especially concerned with child poverty. The passage below has been taken from Barnardo's campaign sheets.

Barnardo's and the reality of child poverty

Many families living on a low income have only about £12 per day per person.

This needs to cover:

■ all their day-to-day expenditure, including necessities such as food and transport
■ occasional items such as new shoes and clothes, school trips and activities for children, and replacing broken household items such as washing machines and kitchen equipment
■ all household bills such as electricity, gas and water, telephone bills and TV licences

A family with two adults and two children needs to have £349 each week in order to be above the poverty line. In 2010, there were 3.6 million children living in poverty in the UK. That's almost a third of all children. Of these children, 1.6 million lived in severe poverty. In the UK 58% of children living in poverty are in a family where someone works; 24% of children in the poorest fifth of households are in families who can't afford to keep their house warm, compared to just 1% in the richest fifth.

Nearly half of all children in the poorest fifth of households were in families who couldn't afford to replace broken electrical goods, compared with just 3% of children in the richest households.

Sixty-two per cent of children in the poorest fifth of households had parents who would like to, but could not afford to take their children for a holiday away from home for one week a year. This only applies to 6% of children in the richest fifth.

Follow-up questions

1 Suppose you have to live on £12 a day. After finding out about prices, and assuming you have a partner and two children, what will you spend the £12 on?
2 Outline **two** ways in which child poverty could be reduced.

When all incomes grow, *absolute* poverty falls. However, *relative* poverty only falls if low incomes grow at a faster rate than average incomes. For the most part, the problem of poverty in the UK is one of relative poverty. Because the UK has been a high-income, developed economy in which welfare benefits provide a minimum income and safety net for the poor, very few people have suffered from absolute poverty — at least until the 2008 recession and the subsequent public spending cuts.

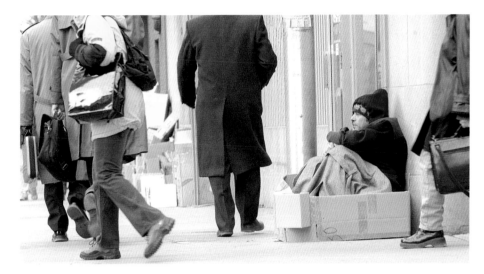

The gap between rich and poor is an issue in the UK

The main causes of poverty in the UK

Three of the main causes of poverty in the UK are old age, unemployment and the low wages of many of those in work.

Old age and poverty

Old age causes poverty largely because many old people rely on the state pension and lack a private pension. Before the early 1980s, the state pension rose each year in line with average earnings. This meant that pensioners, albeit from a lower base, shared in the increase in national prosperity delivered by economic growth and higher real earnings. However, pensions then moved from being index-linked to average earnings. Instead, they were linked to the rate of inflation, measured by changes in the **retail prices index (RPI)**. Pensions no longer rose in line with the general increase in standards of living and pensioners' living standards were in effect kept at their 1980 level. Old people reliant solely on the state for a source of income became increasingly worse off compared to people in work.

In 2011, the newly elected Coalition government introduced what has become known as the 'triple lock'. The government said that the state pension would now rise in line with *either* earnings, *or* CPI inflation *or* a 2.5% increase, *whichever is the greatest*. However, the 'triple lock' may well be abandoned after the 2015 general election, on the ground that it is costing too much. In 2013, the Coalition government was considering switching back to linking

> **EXAM TIP**
>
> Exam questions may ask you to distinguish between absolute and relative poverty and to explain their different causes.

> **EXAM TIP**
>
> The problem of poverty is a Unit 3 topic but candidates may be expected to apply knowledge learned when studying Units 2 and 4 to explain how fiscal policy can be used to reduce poverty.

pension increases solely to rises in average earnings, thus ending the annual inflation-linked rise in benefits. Ironically, the reason for this is to reduce the rate at which pensions have been rising. In contrast to the 1970s when the rate of increase in average earnings exceeded the rate of inflation, the recent 1% or so annual rise in average earnings has been considerably lower than the rate of inflation. But whatever happens, the state pension will continue to be very much a *poverty income*.

Unemployment and poverty

Unemployment benefits are generally lower than the pay workers received before losing their jobs. An increase in unemployment therefore increases poverty. In 2013, as part of the policy of cutting public spending, the Coalition government introduced a cap on a range of benefits received by the poor, including unemployment benefits. The cap will further increase poverty and widen income differentials. It follows that absolute poverty (and potentially relative poverty) can best be reduced by fast and sustained economic growth and by creating jobs. Economic growth can also create the wherewithal, if the electorate and state are so minded, to increase the real value of the state pension and unemployment benefits.

> **EXAM TIP**
>
> Exam questions may require an explanation of the causes of poverty and/or of the effects of poverty on the economy.

Low wages and poverty

When discussing the nature of both absolute and relative poverty in the UK, we must distinguish between the **low-waged** and the **un-waged**, who are unemployed. The *low*-waged, unlike the *un*-waged, are workers with jobs, albeit jobs in which their hourly and weekly earnings are low. The low-waged include many unskilled workers, together with skilled workers who have lost jobs in the manufacturing industry and who have had to trade down to employment in more menial unskilled activity. The low-waged poor are almost always *relatively* poor rather than *absolutely* poor. In contrast, some of the un-waged, including homeless people living on the street, fall into the category of the absolutely poor. As I shall explain later, the introduction of the **national minimum wage** was an attempt to reduce the poverty of the low-waged.

Beside those claiming unemployment benefits and pensioners, the un-waged includes people whose only sources of income are **income support** and the **Employment and Support Allowance (ESA)**. Income support can be claimed by those with no income or a low income, or who are working less than 16 hours a week or who haven't signed on as unemployed. It is often claimed by the elderly who would otherwise be completely reliant on the state pension, and by families otherwise dependent solely on the unemployment benefit paid to one family member. Many economists believe that the ESA, which was introduced in 2008 eventually to replace Incapacity Benefit, is aimed at reducing the number of people claiming benefits on the ground that they are medically unfit for paid work.

CASE STUDY 13.2

What is fuel poverty?

In recent years a supposedly new type of poverty has been identified. This is fuel poverty. In 2013 any household spending more than 10% of its income on fuel was said to be in fuel poverty. However, a new definition of fuel poverty is likely to replace the '10%' definition.

One of the main criticisms of the '10%' definition has been that it does not 'equivalise' incomes for household size and composition. Equivalisation means, for example, that a family of four with a household income of £30,000 is not deemed to be as well off as a retired couple with the same income.

The new definition, proposed to the government by Professor John Hills, does take account of equivalised income. It also measures income after the deduction of housing costs, which are usually higher for families with children. More families with children will be regarded as fuel poor if Hill's definition of fuel poverty is accepted by the government.

In cold winters, low-income households, especially pensioner households living in badly insulated properties, are likely to experience fuel poverty. The problem is made worse by the fact that many pensioners and other low-income families live in houses equipped with inefficient heating systems. In 2013, people suffering from fuel poverty needed an average of £448 more a year in order to heat their homes properly. This was an increase of £26 on 2012. Poor families with children also suffer fuel poverty. At the start of 2013, approximately 1.6 million children were in fuel poverty — 130,000 more than in 2010, the last year before 2013 in which an official estimate of fuel poverty had been made.

Pensioner households living in badly insulated properties are especially likely to experience fuel poverty

Follow-up questions

1 Do you think that fuel poverty is a new type of poverty that did not exist until quite recently? Justify your answer.

2 Evaluate *two* different policies which the UK government might use to eliminate or reduce fuel poverty.

Poverty and the tax and benefits system

Poverty is seldom caused directly and immediately by taxation and the benefits system. However, through a process known as **fiscal drag** (which I explain later in the chapter) and through cuts in welfare benefits, poverty can increase. Making taxation more **progressive** and increasing **welfare benefits** reduces poverty and inequalities in the distribution of income, at least in the short run. However, free-market and supply-side economists believe that, in the drive to reduce inequality, these changes worsen labour market incentives, competitiveness and economic growth. According to this view, in the long run, low incomes may fail to grow and poverty may increase. If true, government intervention in labour markets causes government failure.

Inequalities in the distribution of income and wealth in the UK

At AS you will have learnt that income is a **flow** while wealth is a **stock**. Personal wealth is the stock, or historical accumulation, of everything you own that has value. By contrast, your income is the flow of money you receive hourly, weekly, monthly or annually, some of which (the part that you *save*) can add to your personal wealth. This is one of the links between income and wealth. A second link operates in the opposite direction — the wealthier you are, the more investment income you are likely to earn, which adds to your total income. Indeed, the rich benefit from a virtuous circle: wealth increases income, which allows the wealthy to save, and saving adds to wealth, and so on. By contrast, many of the poor suffer a vicious circle: low income means the poor have to borrow, borrowing adds to personal debt, income is then spent on debt repayment, consumption falls, and any wealth the poor possess disappears.

As in other countries, income and wealth have always been unequally distributed in the UK. Even when economic growth creates full employment, the incomes of the rich tend to increase faster than those of the poor. For this reason, though absolute poverty declines, fast economic growth may actually increase relative poverty and widen income differences.

EXAM TIP

Exam questions may ask for an explanation of why inequalities in the distribution of income and wealth have changed in the UK economy in recent years. You are not required to know about events more than 10 years before the exam.

Inequality in the Keynesian era

Nevertheless, during the Keynesian era, from the 1950s to the late 1970s, a combination of sustained economic growth, low unemployment and state intervention reduced both poverty and inequalities in the distribution of income in the UK. State intervention made the tax system more progressive and transferred the resulting tax revenue in welfare benefits paid largely to the poor.

Inequality in the 1980s and early 1990s

Free-market and supply-side economics replaced Keynesianism in the 1980s and early to mid-1990s. (Chapter 15 of my *AQA AS Economics* book explains this in some detail.) These decades were marked by widening inequality in the distribution of income and wealth. The wealthy benefited from greater tax cuts than the poor and their income rose at a faster rate. Many commentators believe that in the 1980s, Margaret Thatcher's Conservative governments widened income and wealth inequalities quite deliberately. Thatcher believed that government policies such as progressive taxation and transfers to the poor destroy personal incentives, which in turn harms the economy. To make the poor better off in the long run, they must be made relatively worse off in the short run, in order to create the conditions in which hard work and the entrepreneurial spirit can deliver economic growth.

CASE STUDY 13.3

UK income inequality at the present day

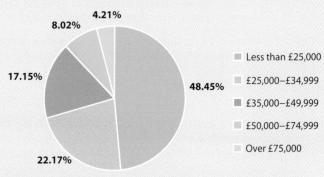

Figure 13. 1 Percentages of UK adults in different income groups, 2012

A study published in March 2013 by the High Pay Centre, a think-tank set up in the wake of an inquiry into escalating executive pay, shows that there are now 26,000 Britons taking home more in a month than those on average salaries earn in a year. According to the study, the UK has returned to levels of income inequality last seen in the 1930s, with the share of the national income going to the top 1% more than doubling since 1979, to 14.5%. In 2013, the 26,000 top-earning UK residents, who have salaries of more than half-a-million pounds a year, receive at least £21,500 a month after tax — more than the average annual wage of £20,500. At the other end of the spectrum, there are 6.75 million workers earning less than £800 a month. Figure 13.1 shows that in 2012, 4.21% of people in receipt of income enjoyed incomes of £75,000 or more a year, while at the other extreme, 48.45% had to live on incomes of £25,000 or less. The richest 1% of course received much more than £75,000 while the very poor made do with much less than £25,000.

Follow-up questions

1 Do you agree that the failure to redistribute income from rich to poor is *not* an example of government failure? Justify your answer.

2 Outline your view on whether governments should attempt to redistribute income.

Measuring inequality

Economists use **Lorenz curves** and the **Gini coefficient** to measure inequality. Exam questions will not require use of either measure, but as exam candidates frequently use one or both of these measures, I have included them in this chapter. Be warned, however: valuable exam time is easily wasted drawing a Lorenz curve that is not necessary for the answer.

The Lorenz curve and the Gini coefficient

A Lorenz curve measures the extent to which the distribution of income (or wealth) is equal or unequal. The degree of inequality is measured by a statistic known as a Gini coefficient.

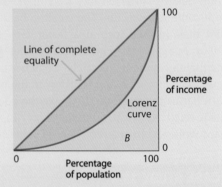

Figure 13.2 The Lorenz curve

The Lorenz curve in Figure 13.2 shows population on the horizontal axis, measured in cumulative percentages from 0% to 100%. The vertical axis shows the cumulative percentage of income received by the population. If incomes were distributed equally, the Lorenz curve would lie along the diagonal line in the diagram. The nearer the Lorenz curve is to the diagonal, the more equal is the distribution of income.

The Gini coefficient measures the area between the Lorenz curve and the diagonal as a ratio of the total area under the diagonal. In terms of the diagram, the Gini coefficient is calculated using the following formula:

$$\text{Gini coefficient} = \frac{\text{area } A}{\text{area } A + \text{area } B}$$

The lower the value of the Gini coefficient, the more equally household income is distributed. If the Lorenz curve were to lie along the 45-degree line in the above diagram, every household would have exactly the same income and the Gini coefficient would be zero. At the other extreme, if one person received all the income and everybody else no income, the Lorenz curve would be the reverse L-shape lying along, first the horizontal axis, and then the right-hand vertical axis in the diagram. Between these two extremes, Lorenz curves closer to the line of complete equality show greater equality (and Gini coefficients approaching zero), while Lorenz curves further away from the diagonal display greater inequality (and Gini coefficients approaching 1).

Will inequality increase in the future?

At the time of writing (July 2013), the UK economy is just about beginning to recover from the deep recession which hit the UK economy in 2008. Unemployment, which increased rapidly in the recession, stood at 2.51 million in May 2013 (or 7.8% of the economically active population). It is generally accepted that unemployment will remain high unless the growth rate improves significantly. If unemployment continues to grow, the low level at which unemployment benefits are set means that inequality will also increase. This will be exacerbated by the impact of draconian public spending cuts on the poor, both those in work as well as the jobless. Absolute poverty will increase, as will relative poverty, if low incomes fall while high incomes increase. (See the section on Revisiting output gaps on page 223.)

Government policies that aim to reduce poverty and income inequalities

The main policies UK governments have used to try to reduce poverty and to make the distribution of income and wealth more equal are progressive taxation, transfers to the poor, the tax credit system and the national minimum wage.

Progressive taxation

In a **progressive tax** system the proportion of a person's income paid in tax *increases* as income *rises*, while in a **regressive tax** system, the proportion paid in tax *falls*. A tax is proportionate if exactly the same proportion of income is paid in tax at all levels of income. Progressivity can be defined for a single tax or for the tax system as a whole.

The word 'progressive' is value-neutral, implying nothing about how the revenue raised by the government is spent. Nevertheless, progressive taxation has been used by governments, particularly during the Keynesian era and to a minor extent more recently by Labour governments (1997–2010), to achieve the social aim of a fairer distribution of income.

It is often assumed that the UK tax system is highly progressive, and is thus used to redistribute income and wealth to the poor. In fact, apart from capital gains tax and inheritance tax which are quite easily avoidable, wealth (and capital) is not taxed in the UK. This means that inequalities in the distribution of *wealth* have not really been reduced by the tax system.

Nevertheless, many people believe wrongly that income taxes are strongly progressive in the UK. Personal income tax is only slightly progressive for most income groups, becoming rather more progressive for the richest fifth of households. The progressivity of income tax was reduced by the abolition in 2013 of the highest 50% marginal rate of income tax, which was levied on those with taxable incomes over £150,000. National Insurance contributions (NICs) reduce the progressivity of the direct tax system for the top 20% of households. NICs are *regressive* on higher incomes because little or no further contributions are paid once a worker's income rises above a given ceiling. Because the council tax and indirect taxes (mostly expenditure taxes) are regressive, taking a declining proportion of the income of rich households, overall the UK tax system is at best only slightly progressive, and it may even be regressive.

Transfers to the poor

Progressive taxation cannot by itself redistribute income — a policy of **transfers** in the government's public expenditure programme is required for this. Progressive taxation used on its own merely reduces **post-tax income differentials** compared to **pre-tax differentials**. Currently, the main transfers directed at the poor in UK public spending are the old age pension, unemployment benefits, incapacity benefit and income support. These forms of income, paid by the state to individuals who fall into the relevant category, are meant to transfer income from taxpayers to people on low incomes. Income support is paid to low-waged families

> **KEY TERM**
>
> **progressive taxation:** a tax or tax system in which the rich pay a higher proportion of income in tax than the poor.

> **EXAM TIP**
>
> Make sure you can explain how progressive taxation and transfers have affected the economy and can evaluate whether the effects have been good or bad.

> **KEY TERM**
>
> **transfer:** an income paid by the state to benefit recipients and financed from taxation.

and the state pension can be claimed by people who stay on at work after the state retirement age. More often, however, transfers are paid to the *un-waged* poor.

Tax credits

Whereas *positive* income tax is paid by people whose total yearly income is higher than their personal tax allowance, tax credits are a form of *negative* income tax, paid by the government to people in employment whose incomes are very low. Many low-paid people who work, but earn low wages, qualify for **universal credit**, which was introduced in 2013 to replace **working tax credits**. Universal credit is meant to make work pay, in the sense that people will no longer see their income drop by moving off benefits and into low-paid work. The Coalition government intends that, by 2017, universal credit will have replaced jobseeker's allowance, the employment and support allowance, income support and housing benefit (but not child benefit).

EXAM TIP

You may be asked to evaluate the effects of the national minimum wage on the economy.

The national minimum wage

I have already described the UK national minimum wage in Chapter 12. Read again about the national minimum wage, and assess whether it has had any effect in reducing poverty and income inequalities.

Fiscal drag, poverty and low pay

The UK tax system has affected poverty partly through a process known as **fiscal drag**. Fiscal drag occurs in a progressive income tax system when the government fails to raise **tax thresholds** (or **personal tax allowances**) to keep pace with inflation. Figure 13.3 (a) shows an income pyramid with the rich at the top of the pyramid and the poor at the bottom and with the tax threshold fixed at an income of £5,000. In this example, a person with an income of £4,900 is just below the threshold and pays no income tax.

KEY TERM

fiscal drag: a failure to raise personal tax thresholds in line with inflation that brings the low paid into the tax net.

Suppose that both prices and all money incomes exactly double. If there are no taxes, real incomes will remain unchanged, with households no better off or worse off. But if there are taxes, and the government fails to increase personal tax allowances in line with inflation (that is, to raise the tax threshold to £10,000), a doubling of the person's money income to £9,800 means that £4,800 of income is now taxable. The individual concerned is now worse off in real terms.

The new situation is shown in Figure 13.3 (b). Inflation has dragged the low-paid worker across the basic tax threshold and into the tax net. In a similar way, higher-paid workers are dragged deeper into the tax net if the higher 40% marginal tax rate remains unadjusted for inflation.

Governments can reduce relative poverty among the low paid by raising income tax thresholds by more than the rate of inflation. This takes the low paid out of the income tax net and claws back the fiscal drag that has taken place in previous years. However, unless the government simultaneously reduces public spending (which generally benefits the low paid more than the high paid), taxes have to be raised elsewhere in the economy, which may also adversely affect the poor.

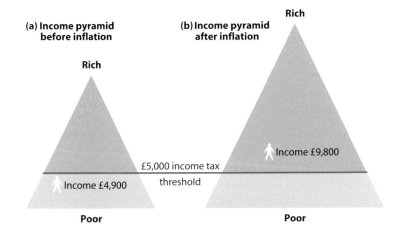

Figure 13. 3 How fiscal drag brings the low paid into the tax net

The earnings trap or poverty trap

Fiscal drag is one of the causes of the **poverty trap**. As there are a number of ways in which the poor can be trapped in poverty, this particular trap, which traps the low-waged in *relative* poverty, is better called the **earnings trap**. It affects people in employment on low rates of pay, rather than the unemployed who are un-waged. Another poverty trap contains the homeless, who are trapped in poverty because to get a job they need a home, but to get a home they first need a job.

The immediate cause of the earnings trap is the overlap, illustrated in Figure 13.4, between the income tax *threshold* (the level of income at which income tax starts to be paid) and the means-tested welfare benefits *ceiling* (the level of income at which means-tested transfer incomes cease to be paid). When **welfare benefits** are means-tested, a person's right to claim the benefit is reduced and eventually disappears

KEY TERM

poverty trap: also known as the earnings trap, the poverty trap describes a situation in which the low paid are trapped in relative poverty by having to pay income tax and NICs at the same time as losing welfare benefits.

EXAM TIP

Make sure you understand the difference between, but also the relationship between, the poverty trap (or earnings trap) and the unemployment trap.

Income pyramid

Rich

Means-tested benefits ceiling

Poverty trap in zone of overlap

Income tax threshold

Poor

Figure 13.4 The poverty trap or earnings trap

EXAM TIP

See page 287 of Chapter 19 for a description of the marginal tax rate.

completely, as income rises. By contrast, a **universal benefit** is claimed as of right and is not dependent on income, although the state can claw back universal benefits that are taxable.

A low-paid worker caught within the zone of overlap in Figure 13.4 not only pays income tax and national insurance contributions on each extra pound earned, he or she also loses part or all of the right to claim benefits. Thus low-paid workers and their families whose income falls within this zone of overlap become trapped in relative poverty, since any increase in their pay results in little or no increase (and in extreme cases a fall) in disposable income.

The *effective* marginal rate of taxation of workers in poorly paid occupations is high when the loss of means-tested benefits is added to deductions through income tax and NICs. Calculated in this way, the marginal tax rates of the low paid are much higher (often around 70% and in extreme cases over 100%) than the top 40% rate now paid by the better-off. Moreover, since the low paid are generally employed in occupations yielding little job satisfaction or scope for legal tax avoidance, disincentives to work imposed by the UK tax system affect the poor at the lower end of the income pyramid much more than they affect the better-off.

The poverty trap can be eliminated by getting rid of the zone of overlap in the income pyramid illustrated in Figure 13.4. The income tax threshold could be raised to take low-waged households out of the tax net. Means-tested benefits could be replaced by universal benefits, although, as taxes would have to increase to pay for any substantial increase in universal benefits, the poor might end up more heavily taxed. The national minimum wage might also reduce poverty by preventing employers paying 'poverty wages'. However, raising the NMW could be counter-productive if unemployment increases as a result.

CASE STUDY 13.4

The introduction of the universal credit may place more families in the poverty trap

The Coalition government has been accused of creating a poverty trap with recent changes to the tax and benefits system which risk penalising almost two million low earners trying to boost their income. A new report by the anti-poverty campaigning group, the Joseph Rowntree Foundation, suggests that universal credit, which in 2013 replaced the previous system of tax credits, could see people worse off in work and struggling to manage their finances, with many left to deal with a more complex benefits system than before. The report states that, while making work pay is the key aim for the universal credit, many households are set to be worse off, or only marginally better off.

Simplifying the benefits system is also undermined by a new complex system of helping families in crisis. Finally, the report raises serious concerns about a 'one-size-fits-all' IT-based delivery system and potential IT failures which could quickly lead to backlogs, poor service and complaints.

Follow-up questions

1 Why have income differentials widened in the UK in recent years?

2 Research whether the universal credit has actually increased poverty and drawn more families into the poverty trap.

The unemployment trap

The poverty trap I have just described affects the low-waged in jobs rather than the unemployed who are un-waged. It is important not to confuse the poverty trap or earnings trap with the **unemployment trap**. The unemployment trap is closely related to the earnings trap, since both affect the poor and result from the nature of the tax and benefits systems. But people caught in the unemployment trap are out of work — at least in terms of officially declared employment. The unemployment trap contains un-waged social security claimants who choose unemployment. This is because they decide they are better off out of work, living on benefits, than in low-paid jobs paying income tax and NICs and losing some or all of their right to claim means-tested benefits. In 2013, the Coalition government announced policies to force the long-term unemployed into undertaking community work or registering each day at a job center.

> **KEY TERM**
>
> **unemployment trap:** the unemployed are trapped in unemployment as they are better off living on benefits than in a low-waged job paying income tax and NICs, while losing the ability to claim means-tested benefits.

One link between the earnings trap and the unemployment trap is the **underground economy** — the hidden or informal economy in which people work, usually for cash payments, while failing to declare income and often fraudulently claiming social security benefits. Low-paid workers in employment can escape the earnings trap by giving up declared work in order to claim unemployment pay, while receiving income from undeclared work undertaken in the underground economy. The underground economy is sometimes called the 'black economy'.

Horizontal and vertical equity

Equity, which means fairness or justness, is a *normative* concept (a matter of opinion). The closely related but not quite identical concept of **equality** is a *positive* concept. Equality, but not equity, can be measured. Government intervention in the economy, which treats people in the same circumstances equally, obeys the principle of **horizontal equity**. Horizontal equity occurs when households with the same income and personal circumstances (for example, number of children) pay the same income tax and are eligible for the same welfare benefits. **Vertical equity** is much more controversial, since it justifies taking income from the rich (on the ground that they don't need it) and redistributing their income to the poor (on the ground that they do need it). The distribution of income *after* taxation and receipt of transfers is judged more equitable than original income before redistribution. Achieving greater vertical equity can conflict with another principle of intervention, the **benefit principle**, which argues that those who receive most benefit from government spending (for example, motorists benefiting from roads) should pay the most in taxes.

> **KEY TERMS**
>
> **horizontal equity:** describes households in similar circumstances paying similar taxes and receiving similar benefits.
>
> **vertical equity:** redistributes income from the rich to the poor on the basis of need.

SUMMARY

- It is important to distinguish between absolute and relative poverty.
- Absolute poverty occurs when income is below a particular specified level.
- A household is relatively poor if its income is below a specified proportion of average income for all households.
- Old age, unemployment and low wages are important causes of poverty in the UK.
- Fuel poverty is an important form of poverty.
- Government intervention to reduce poverty may lead to government failures that may make matters worse.
- Inequalities in the distribution of UK income and wealth widened after 1979.
- After 1997, Labour governments used progressive taxation, transfers to the poor, the introduction of a national minimum wage and a tax credits system to reduce both absolute and relative poverty.
- However, by 2013, income inequalities and poverty relative to the richest in society had widened, largely due to the rapid rise in the incomes of the well-off.
- Fiscal drag in the tax system has contributed to the existence of a poverty trap or earnings trap, and also to an unemployment trap.
- Horizontal equity occurs when households with the same income and personal circumstances pay the same income tax and are eligible for the same welfare benefits.
- Vertical equity increases when income taken from the rich is redistributed to the poor.

Exam-style questions

1 Explain the difference between absolute and relative poverty. (15 marks)

2 Explain why inequalities in the distribution of income and wealth have widened in recent years. (15 marks)

3 Evaluate the view that progressive taxation and transfers should not be used to reduce income inequalities and poverty. (25 marks)

4 Evaluate the view that the government should rely on market forces to determine the distribution of income and wealth in the UK, and should reduce direct intervention in the economy which has aimed at making the UK more equal. (25 marks)

Extra resources to help you revise are available online at www.hodderplus.co.uk/philipallan

Unit 3 key terms

absolute poverty: occurs when income is below a particular level.

adverse selection: describes a situation in which people who buy insurance often have a better idea of the risks they face than do the sellers of insurance. People who know they face large risks are more likely to buy insurance than people who face small risks.

allocative efficiency: occurs when it is impossible to improve overall economic welfare by reallocating resources between industries or markets (assuming an initial distribution of income and wealth). For resource allocation in the whole economy to be allocatively efficient, price must equal marginal cost in each and every market in the economy.

allocative inefficiency: occurs when it is possible to improve overall economic welfare by reallocating resources between industries or markets. Resource allocation is allocatively inefficient when price is less than or greater than marginal cost in each and every market in the economy.

average cost of labour: total wage costs divided by the number of workers employed.

average revenue (*AR*): equals total revenue divided by the size of output.

bad: the opposite of a good, yielding dissatisfaction or disutility when consumed. Consumption of bads reduces economic welfare.

cartel: a collusive agreement by firms, usually to fix prices. Sometimes output may also be fixed.

company: an incorporated business enterprise.

Competition and Markets Authority (CMA): the CMA began operating in October 2013, replacing the Competition Commission and the Office of Fair Trading (OFT). The CMA now implements UK competition policy.

competition policy: aims to make goods markets more competitive. It comprises policy toward monopoly, mergers and restrictive trading practices.

concentration ratio: measures the market share of the biggest firms in the market.

consumer surplus: a measure of the economic welfare enjoyed by consumers: surplus utility received over and above the price paid for a good.

cost–benefit analysis (CBA): a technique for assessing all the costs and benefits likely to result from an economic decision, i.e. the social costs and benefits and not just the private costs and benefits.

demerit good: a good, such as tobacco, for which the social costs of consumption exceed the private costs.

diseconomies of scale: rising long-run average costs as the size or scale of the firm increases.

duopoly: describes a market in which there are two dominant firms.

dynamic efficiency: measures the extent to which various forms of static efficiency improve over time.

economic efficiency: in general terms, economic efficiency minimises costs incurred, with minimum undesired side effects.

economic model: a small-scale replica of real-world phenomena.

economic welfare: human happiness or utility.

economies of scale: falling long-run average costs as the size or scale of the firm increases.

entrepreneur: a risk taker and decision maker within a firm.

external diseconomies of scale: higher long-run average production costs resulting from the growth of the industry of which the firm is a part.

external economies of scale: lower long-run average production costs resulting from the growth of the industry of which the firm is a part.

external growth: growth via acquisition, either takeover or merger.

externality: a public good, in the case of an external benefit, or a public bad, in the case of an external cost that is dumped on third parties outside the market.

firm: a business that sells its output commercially in a market.

fiscal drag: a failure to raise personal tax thresholds in line with inflation that brings the low paid into the tax net.

fixed costs: the costs of employing the fixed factors of production in the short run.

free-rider: somebody who benefits without paying.

game theory: a mathematical approach to the study of conflict and decision-making which treats conflict as games with set tactics and strategies and rational players.

geographical immobility of labour: describes the difficulty of moving from one location to another.

government failure: occurs when government intervention in the economy is ineffective, wasteful or damaging.

horizontal equity: describes households in similar circumstances paying similar taxes and receiving similar benefits.

horizontal growth: occurs when a firm undertakes more of the activities it is already involved in, which can lead to economies of scale.

imperfect competition: describes the range of market structures lying between perfect competition and pure monopoly.

individual worker's supply curve of labour: planned supply of labour by one worker.

industrial policy: the government's microeconomic policy towards firms and industry.

inequitable: unfair or unjust.

information problem: occurs when people make poor decisions because they don't possess, or ignore, the relevant information.

internal diseconomies of scale: higher long-run average production costs resulting from an increase in the size or scale of the firm in the long run.

internal economies of scale: lower long-run average production costs resulting from an increase in the size or scale of the firm in the long run.

internal growth: occurs when a firm invests from scratch in new capacity such as factories and offices, also known as organic growth.

lag indicator: provides information about past events that have already taken place in the economy.

lateral growth: occurs when a firm diversifies into new types of production.

law of diminishing marginal returns: a short-term law which states that as a variable factor of production is added to fixed factors, eventually the marginal returns (or marginal product) of the variable factor will begin to fall.

lead indicator: provides information about the likely future state of the economy.

long run: the time period in which the scale of *all* factors of production can be changed.

managerial theory: assumes that firms wish to maximise managerial objectives rather than profit.

marginal cost of labour: the addition to a firm's total cost of production resulting from employing one more worker.

marginal physical product: the addition to a firm's total output brought about by employing one more worker.

marginal revenue (*MR*): equals the change in total revenue divided by the change in the size of output.

marginal revenue product: the monetary value of the addition to a firm's total output brought about by employing one more worker.

market failure: occurs when a market functions badly, unsatisfactorily, or not at all.

market structure: the framework within which a firm sells its output.

market supply curve of labour: planned supply of labour by all the workers in a labour market.

merit good: a good, such as health care, for which the social benefits of consumption exceed the private benefits.

minimum efficient scale (MES): the smallest size of plant that can benefit from minimum long-run average costs.

missing markets: occur when the incentive function of prices completely breaks down and a market fails to come into existence or disappears completely.

monopoly profit: the supernormal profit a monopoly or imperfectly competitive firm makes in the long run as well as in the short run.

monopsony: there is only one buyer in a market.

moral hazard: describes the tendency of individuals and firms, once insured against some contingency, to behave so as to make that contingency more likely.

$MR = MC$: the marginalist condition that must be met if profits are to be maximised.

multinational company: a business with headquarters in one country that owns and operates subsidiary companies in other countries.

national minimum wage: a minimum wage or wage rate that must by law be paid to employees.

non-pure public good: a good for which it may be possible to exclude free-riders, but for which there is a case for not doing so.

normal profit: the minimum profit a firm must make to stay in business, while being insufficient to attract new firms into the market.

occupational immobility of labour: describes the difficulty of moving from one occupation to another.

oligopoly: an imperfectly competitive market containing only a few firms.

organisational theory: assumes that a firm is a coalition of different groups such as shareholders, managers and workers.

perfect competition: exists in a market containing a large number of firms and meets the six conditions that define the market structure.

performance indicator: provides information about what is happening in the economy.

policy indicator: provides information about whether a particular policy is on course to achieve a desired policy objective.

poverty trap: also known as the earnings trap, the poverty trap describes a situation in which the low paid are trapped in relative poverty by having to pay income tax and NICs at the same time as losing welfare benefits.

price discrimination: charging different prices to different customers with the prices based on different willingness to pay.

principal/agent problem: recognises that the principals (shareholders) have a different objective from that of the agents (managers).

private benefit maximisation: occurs when $MPB = MPC$.

private company: issues shares that are not for sale on a market.

private good: a good which exhibits the characteristics of excludability and rivalry.

producer surplus: a measure of the economic welfare enjoyed by firms or producers: the difference between the price a firm succeeds in charging and the minimum price it would be prepared to accept.

production: a process or set of processes that converts inputs into outputs.

productive efficiency: (1) involves minimising the average costs of production. (2) For the economy as a whole, productive efficiency can also be defined in terms of producing on the economy's production possibility frontier.

profit: revenue minus costs.

profit maximisation: occurs when total sales revenue is furthest above total cost, which is when $MR = MC$.

progressive taxation: a tax or tax system in which the rich pay a higher proportion of income in tax than the poor.

public bad: bad for which the producers free ride, dumping the bad on third parties.

public company: issues shares that the general public can buy on a market or stock exchange.

public good: a good which exhibits the characteristics of non-excludability and non-rivalry.

pure monopoly: exists where there is only one firm in a market.

relative poverty: occurs when income is below a specified proportion of average income.

restrictive trading practice: an activity undertaken by a firm on its own or in collusion with other firms that restricts competition.

returns to scale: describes how output changes when the scale of *all* the factors of production changes in the long run. They divide into increasing returns to scale, decreasing returns to scale and constant returns to scale.

revenue: the money income a firm receives from selling its output.

satisficing: achieving a satisfactory objective acceptable to all the competing member groups of the coalition that makes up the firm.

short run: the time period in which at least one factor of production is fixed.

social benefit maximisation: occurs when $MSB = MSC$.

static efficiency: measures technical, productive, X and allocative efficiency at a particular point in time.

supernormal profit: profit over and above normal profit.

technical efficiency: maximises output from the available inputs.

trade union: a collective association of workers whose aim is to improve the pay and other conditions of work of its members.

traded pollution permits: these allow governments to give companies licences to pollute at a certain level. Companies can buy, sell and trade these permits on a market.

transfer: an income paid by the state to benefit recipients and financed from taxation.

unemployment trap: the unemployed are trapped in unemployment as they are better off living on benefits than in a low-waged job paying income tax and NICs, while losing the ability to claim means-tested benefits.

variable costs: the costs of employing the variable factors of production in the short run.

vertical equity: redistributes income from the rich to the poor on the basis of need.

vertical growth: occurs when a firm grows by expanding back up its supply chain or forward along its distribution chain.

wage discrimination: paying different workers different wages for doing the same job.

welfare: basically means human happiness.

Unit 4

The national and international economy

Economic growth, development and standards of living

This chapter begins by explaining the difference between economic growth and economic development. Having reminded you of the difference between short-term and long-term economic growth, I shall investigate each in turn. I shall examine short-term growth in the context of the economic cycle or business cycle. Then, having surveyed the roles of investment and technical progress in causing long-term growth, I shall discuss the benefits and costs of economic growth and the issue of growth sustainability. I shall conclude the chapter by discussing whether measures of economic development such as the United Nation's Human Development Index (HDI) provide better indicators than gross domestic product (GDP) of standards of living and people's quality of life.

LEARNING OUTCOMES

This chapter will:
- define economic growth and remind you of the difference between short-run and long-run economic growth
- distinguish between economic growth and economic development
- link economic growth to the growth of productivity in the economy
- relate short-run growth to the economic cycle or business cycle
- discuss the causes of long-run economic growth or true growth
- survey the costs and benefits of growth and possible conflicts between growth and other macroeconomic policy objectives

WHAT YOU SHOULD ALREADY KNOW

At AS you learnt that economic growth, which is one of the government's most important macroeconomic objectives, occurs when the productive capacity of the economy is increasing. You learnt to illustrate both short-run and long-run economic growth on production possibility curves and *AD/AS* diagrams. The Unit 2 specification also required the ability to analyse and evaluate the various demand-side and supply-side determinants of both short-run growth and the long-run trend rate of economic growth. AS economics also introduced the link between short-run economic growth, the economic cycle and output gaps.

The meaning of economic growth

Economic growth can be defined as the increase, over time, of the potential level of output the economy can produce.

KEY TERM

economic growth: an increase in the potential output an economy can produce.

Strictly, this is **long-run economic growth**, which is not the same as **short-run economic growth**. Long-run and short-run economic growth are both illustrated in Figure 14.1. Short-run growth is shown by the movement from point *C* inside the economy's production possibility frontier, located at *PPF*₁, to point *A* on the frontier. Long-run growth is depicted by the shift from point *A* on *PPF*₁ to point *B* on *PPF*₂.

Long-run economic growth can also be thought of as *true* growth while short-run growth is best thought of as **economic recovery** from recession. Short-run growth makes use of spare capacity and takes up slack in the economy, whereas long-run growth increases total productive capacity.

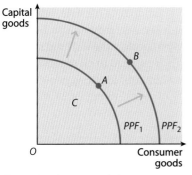

Figure 14.1 Long-run and short-run economic growth illustrated on a production possibility frontier diagram

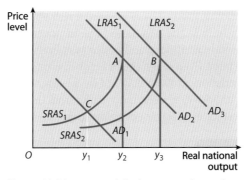

Figure 14.2 Long-run and short-run economic growth illustrated on an *AD/AS* diagram

In the next diagram, Figure 14.2, I illustrate the difference between long-run and short-run economic growth on an *AD/AS* graph. In the diagram I initially locate macroeconomic equilibrium at point *C*, where the aggregate demand curve *AD*₁ intersects the short-run aggregate supply curve *SRAS*₁. You should note that point *C* is to the left of the long-run aggregate supply curve *LRAS*₁. The level of real output *y*₁ lies below the full-employment level of output *y*₂, and there is both spare capacity and idle labour in the economy.

The initial macroeconomic equilibrium in Figure 14.2 results from deficient aggregate demand in the economy. In terms of Figure 14.1, the economy is producing *inside* its production possibility frontier. Keynesian unemployment or **cyclical unemployment** occurs as a result of this. If the government responds to this situation by using fiscal policy and/or monetary policy to increase aggregate demand (or if consumption, investment or exports increase), the aggregate demand curve may move to *AD*₂. Once again, the economy is in macroeconomic equilibrium, but at point *A* rather than point *C*, and the level of output *y*₂ is the full-employment level of output. The economy is now producing on the **long-run aggregate supply curve** *LRAS*₁ and on production possibility frontier *PPF*₁ in Figure 14.1. Short-run economic growth has moved the economy to this position.

As there is no longer any spare capacity or idle labour in the economy, for further growth to occur, both the long-run aggregate supply curve and the production possibility frontier must shift to the right (to $LRAS_2$ in Figure 14.2 and PPF_2 in Figure 14.1). Among the factors that can bring about long-term growth are investment in more and better capital goods, investment in human capital through education and training, and population growth, for example through immigration. Either way, a shift of the $LRAS$ curve from $LRAS_1$ to $LRAS_2$ means that the full-employment level of output has increased from y_2 to y_3.

Economic growth versus economic development

Economic growth does not *necessarily* improve the economic welfare of all or most of the people living in a country. On occasion, in some countries, the fruits of economic growth have allowed a rich elite to enjoy a champagne lifestyle, while the vast bulk of the population live in poverty. In such a society, growth also helps to maintain a military and police system used primarily to protect the rich and subdue the poor. Even when the benefits of economic growth are spread to all or most of the population, growth may not be sustainable. In this situation, future generations as yet unborn may eventually suffer from the profligacy of people living today and their quest for ever-faster economic growth.

EXAM TIP

Economic development is not in the AQA Economics specification, either at AS or at A2. Nevertheless, it is extremely useful to understand the difference between growth and development, particularly when discussing welfare and standards of living.

Economic development is a better indicator of improved human welfare, and the ability to continue to improve welfare, than economic growth. Economic development, which includes the quality and not just the quantity of growth, is measured by:

- general improvement in living standards, which reduces poverty and human suffering
- access to resources such as food and housing that are required to satisfy basic human needs
- access to opportunities for human development (for example, through education and training)
- sustainability and regeneration, through reducing resource depletion and degradation

EXAM TIP

Don't confuse *sustainable* economic growth with *sustained* growth, which is a particular growth rate maintained for a number of years.

Resource depletion occurs when finite resources such as oil are used up, and when soil fertility or fish stocks irreversibly decline. By contrast, **resource degradation** is best illustrated by pollution of air, water and land. To benefit people in the long run, growth (and development) must be sustainable. Sustainable economic growth requires the use of *renewable* rather than *non-renewable* resources that minimise pollution and other forms of resource degradation.

The causes of long-run economic growth

The cause of short-run economic growth, which occurs when the economy moves from a point *inside* its production possibility frontier to a point *on* the frontier, is an increase in aggregate demand. By contrast, **long-run economic growth** is explained by **supply-side factors** that shift the frontier outward. However, sufficient aggregate demand has to be generated to absorb the extra output produced by the growth process. The immediate supply-side cause of long-run growth is **increased labour productivity**, which itself results from investment in, and accumulation of, capital goods and human capital, and from technical progress. **Investment**, **technical progress** and **increased labour productivity** lie at the heart of long-run economic growth.

The importance of increasing productivity

Productivity is mentioned five times in the Unit 2 specification on The National Economy, but not once in the A2 Unit 4 specification on The National and International Economy. However, given the fact that the concept also surfaces in the Unit 3 specification on Business Economics and the Distribution of Income, productivity is important throughout the A-level economics course. Despite its lack of mention in the A2 macroeconomic specification, the synoptic nature of the Unit 4 exam means that you *must* know about productivity and all its implications.

KEY TERM

productivity: output per unit of input, e.g. labour productivity is output per worker.

To the layperson, the term 'productivity' usually means labour productivity. Labour productivity can be measured in terms of the **average product of labour**, or **output per worker**, and the **marginal product of labour**, which measures the addition to total output brought about by employing an extra worker. In general discussion, however, we usually mean average output per worker.

These definitions are *short-run* definitions that assume capital is fixed and technical progress remains unchanged. In much the same way, the productivity of capital can be measured by adding capital to a fixed labour force, once again with a given state of technical progress. In either case, by adding labour to fixed capital, or by adding capital to fixed labour, the **law of diminishing returns** sets in, eventually reducing the average productivity of the input being changed.

To escape the impact of diminishing returns to labour or capital, labour and capital must be changed together. In this situation, when **increasing returns to scale** may operate, the key concept is **total factor productivity (TFP)**. A change in TFP measures the change in total output when *all* the factors of production are changed in the economic long run.

EXAM TIP

Productivity is one of the most important concepts you need to understand, for Unit 3 as well as Unit 4.

Technical progress and productivity

Technical progress, or the rate of growth of technology, increases the rate of growth of total factor productivity. It measures how much more productive capital, labour and other factors of production have become in total over a period of time. There is general agreement among economists that technical progress is the main cause of economic growth, but there is considerable disagreement as to what causes technical progress itself.

Fluctuations in the level of economic activity

At AS you learnt that the level of economic activity fluctuates over a number of different time periods. These include seasonal fluctuations, taking place within a single 12-month period, and cyclical fluctuations that extend over a number of years. **Seasonal fluctuations** are largely caused by changes in climate and weather. Examples include the effect of cold winters closing down the building trade and seasonal employment in travel and tourism. Rather longer **cyclical fluctuations** divide into the short **economic cycle**, which lasts for just a few years, and **long cycles** (or long waves), which may extend over about 60 years.

> **KEY TERM**
>
> **economic cycle:** a period of between about 4 and 10 years in which actual output fluctuates above and below trend output.

The economic cycle

In an economic cycle (which is also known as a *trade cycle* or *business cycle*), the economy's growth rate fluctuates considerably from year to year. Figure 14.3 shows two complete economic cycles, together with a line showing the economy's **trend output**, from which the economy's **long-term growth rate** can be calculated. Actual growth, which is measured by the percentage change in real GDP over a 12-month period, varies in the different phases of the economic cycle. In the cycle's upswing, growth is positive, but as Figure 14.3 shows, 'growth' becomes negative if and when a recession occurs in the cyclical downturn. In the UK, a **recession** is defined as negative economic growth (or falling real GDP) for 6 months or more.

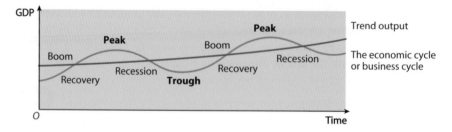

Figure 14.3 Changes in trend output and the economic cycle

> **EXAM TIP**
>
> You learnt about output gaps at AS. Your knowledge may be synoptically tested at A2.

Before the second quarter of 2008, when recession once again hit the British economy, the UK had suffered two big recessions in the previous 30 years. The first recession was between 1979 and 1981, followed a decade or so later by the second deep recession starting in 1990. Both recessions were followed by several years of recovery, unfortunately brought to an end by unsustainable booms and speculative 'bubbles'. Speculative bubbles occurred in housing, commodity and financial markets. When these bubbles were 'pricked', falling confidence, aggregate demand and asset prices led into the next recession.

Economic cycles can still, however, be identified even when there are no recessions. In this situation, the annual growth rate falls in the cycle's downswing, but still remains positive. This was the situation, which is illustrated in Figure 14.4, from the end of the 1990–92 recession until 2008. There were no recessions in these years, but actual output fluctuated above and below the UK's trend output line.

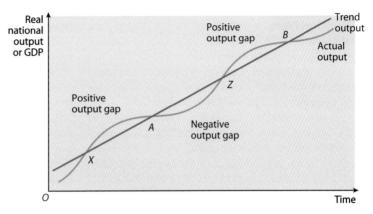

Figure 14.4 Identifying the beginning and end of economic cycles

The UK Treasury defines an economic cycle as starting and finishing at points when the economy is judged to be on-trend. At these points, there are no output gaps, positive or negative. In terms of Figure 14.4, an economic cycle starts at point X and ends at point Z. (Alternatively, a cycle could be dated from point A to point B.)

CASE STUDY 14.1

Double-dip recession: 'Now you see it, now you don't'

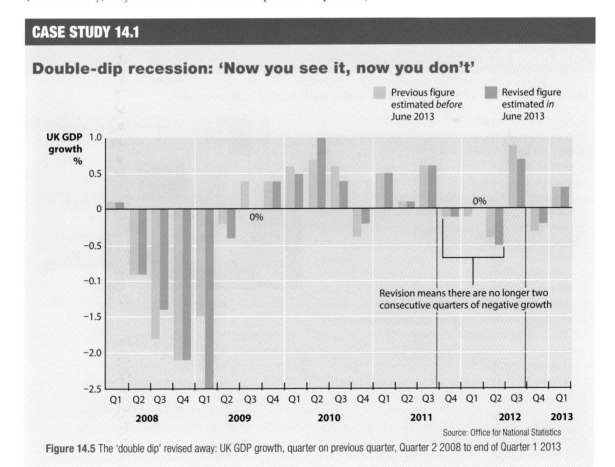

Figure 14.5 The 'double dip' revised away: UK GDP growth, quarter on previous quarter, Quarter 2 2008 to end of Quarter 1 2013

The data in Figure 14.5, published by the ONS in June 2013, shows what 'apparently' happened to quarterly UK economic growth between Quarter 2 of 2008 and Quarter 1 of 2013. The graph begins by showing the deep recession which lasted from Quarter 2 in 2008 until the end of Quarter 2 in 2009 (i.e. five quarters in total).

In fact, Figure 14.5 contains two sets of data. The light blue bars in the graph show the ONS's estimate of quarterly growth published *before* June 2013. These data show the 'second dip' of a 'double dip' recession occurring between Quarter 4 of 2011 and the end of Quarter 2 of 2012. But according to the revised data, shown by the dark blue bars in Figure 14.5, and published in June 2013, there was zero growth in Quarter 1 of 2012, i.e. neither positive nor negative. Hence the 'second dip'

never happened and there was no 'double-dip' recession. However, the revised data also show the 2008 recession being deeper than previously thought.

A conclusion you may draw from this story is *never to trust economic data*. The ONS follows the 'continuous revision' method of publishing economic statistics. When new information comes to light, the data are revised. (Hence the word 'apparently' in the first sentence of this case study.) Back in April 2013 the *Daily Telegraph* had published an article under the headline: 'Never mind the triple-dip recession, the double dip may have been an illusion too', which anticipated the data revision. At the time, many economists were anticipating a 'third dip', which of course did not happen.

Follow-up questions

1 Research what has happened to UK economic growth since this book was published.

2 Find out how a recession is defined in other countries, including the USA.

CASE STUDY 14.2

Has the UK's trend growth rate recently changed?

The economy's trend (or potential) growth rate is the rate at which output can grow, on a sustained basis, without putting upward or downward pressure on inflation. The trend growth rate is measured over a period covering more than one (and preferably several) economic cycles. Until quite recently, the UK's trend growth rate was judged to be about 2.25% a year. At first sight, this growth rate appears low, especially when compared to higher trend growth rates in newly industrialising countries. Nevertheless, the UK's trend growth rate is similar to the long-run growth rates of other developed economies in western Europe and North America. The absolute increase in real output delivered by a 2.25% growth rate may also exceed that delivered by a 10% growth rate in a much poorer country. Moreover, because of the compound interest effect, a 2.25% growth rate meant that average UK living standards doubled every generation or so. (The compound interest effect also explains why the trend output line in Figure 14.3 became steeper from year to year, moving along the line. For example, 2.25% of £1,000 billion is a larger absolute annual increase in GDP than 2.25% of £800 billion.)

In 2002, the Office for National Statistics (ONS) estimated that the trend growth rate in the UK had increased from 2.25% to about 2.75%. At the time, this

ICT has improved labour productivity

was explained by the impact of new technologies such as ICT and the internet improving labour productivity and causing structural change in the economy.

The UK government accepted this estimate, but was rather more cautious, building a 2.5% projected growth rate into its financial calculations. The government hoped that faster trend growth could deliver sufficient extra tax revenue to finance increased government spending on healthcare and education, without tax rates being raised.

However, by 2005 estimates of future growth were more pessimistic and tax revenues were also less than had been expected. The pessimism was fully justified, with the economy continuing to slow in 2006 and 2007, and eventually dipping into a full-blown recession in 2008.

In February 2013, Peter Dixon, a strategist at Commerzbank, argued that the UK's trend growth rate had fallen to be 'more like 1%'. Two months later, however, the OECD reported that the UK was on track to recover to its long-term growth rate of around 2% later in 2013. Due to this uncertainty, make sure you keep up to date about what is actually happening to UK growth and its future prospects.

Follow-up questions

1 Distinguish between actual growth and trend growth.
2 Research what has happened to UK economic growth in the period between the writing of this book (July 2013) and your reading of this chapter.

The recovery and boom phases of the economic cycle

The upswing of an economic cycle divides into a *recovery* phase and a *boom* phase. Real output or GDP grows in both phases, but the two phases differ according to whether real output is below or above the trend output line drawn in Figures 14.3 and 14.4. In the recovery phase real output is below trend output (a **negative output gap**). But when real output rises above trend output, recovery gives way to boom and a **positive output gap**.

Explanations of the economic cycle

In the 1930s, John Maynard Keynes argued that economic recessions are caused by fluctuations in aggregate demand. In Keynes's theory, investment and aggregate demand rise and fall as business confidence gives way to pessimism, and vice versa.

However, as Case Study 14.3 explains, it is now recognised that supply-side factors can also trigger economic cycles. A theory of real business cycles has recently been developed, which argues that in some circumstances, changes in technology on the supply side of the economy might be as important as changes in aggregate demand in explaining economic cycles. Among the factors that may cause or contribute to economic cycles are the following:

> **EXAM TIP**
>
> You may be asked to explain three or four causes of economic cycles. Make sure you don't confuse *causes* with possible *effects* of cyclical fluctuations.

Climate factors

The nineteenth-century neoclassical economist, Stanley Jevons, was one of the first economists to recognise the trade cycle as it was then known. Perhaps taking note of the Bible's reference to '7 years of plenty' followed by '7 years of famine', Jevons believed that a connection exists between the timing of economic crises and the solar cycle. Variations in sunspots affect the power of the sun's rays, influencing the quality of harvests and thus the price of grain, which, in turn, affects business confidence and gives rise to trade cycles.

Although Jevons's sunspot theory was never widely accepted, there is no doubt that climate changes do affect economic activity. The El Niño effect has renewed interest in Jevons's theory. El Niño is a severe atmospheric and oceanic disturbance in the

Pacific Ocean occurring every 7–14 years. The disturbance leads to a fall in the number of plankton that upsets the entire ocean food chain, which badly damages the fishing industry. The effect leads to a complete reversal of trade winds, bringing torrential rain, flooding and mudslides to the otherwise dry Pacific coastal areas of central South America. By contrast, droughts occur in much of Asia and in areas of Africa and central North America.

The role of speculative bubbles

Rapid economic growth leads to a rapid rise and speculative bubble in asset prices. When people realise that house prices or share prices have risen far above the assets' real values, asset selling replaces asset buying. This causes the speculative bubble to burst, which in turn destroys consumer and business confidence. People stop spending and the economy may fall into recession.

Changes in inventories

Besides investing in fixed capital, firms invest in stocks of raw materials and in stocks of finished goods waiting to be sold. This type of investment is called inventory investment or stock building. Although stock building accounts for less than 1% of GDP in a typical year, swings in inventories are often the single most important determinant of recessions. Firms hold stocks of raw materials and finished goods in order to smooth production and cope with swings in demand. But paradoxically, changes in stocks tend to trigger and exacerbate economic cycles. Stocks of unsold finished goods build up when firms over-anticipate demand for finished goods. Firms are then forced to cut production by more than the original fall in demand. The resultant de-stocking turns a slowdown into a recession. Swings in inventory investment accounted for about half of the reductions in GDP in the USA's past ten recessions. De-stocking has also made UK recessions worse.

Political business cycle theory

In democratic countries, general elections usually have to take place every 4 or 5 years. As an election approaches, the political party in power may 'buy votes' by engineering a pre-election boom. After the election, the party in power will normally then deflate aggregate demand to prevent the economy from overheating. However, when the next general election approaches, demand is once again expanded.

Outside shocks affecting the economy

Outside shocks can be divided into *demand shocks*, which affect aggregate demand, and *supply shocks*, which impact on aggregate supply. In some cases, an outside shock hitting the economy may affect both aggregate demand and aggregate supply. Thus the outbreak of a war in the Middle East may affect demand by causing a sudden collapse in consumer and business confidence and also aggregate supply through its effects on the supply of crude oil.

> **EXAM TIP**
>
> Recent exam questions reflect the fact that the UK economy entered recession in 2008, and this was followed by a weak recovery and the possibility of 'double-dip' recession.

Supply-side causes of recessions

Until quite recently, it was generally agreed that recessions are caused by a collapse of aggregate demand that shifts the *AD* curve to the left. However, as I explain in Case Study 14.3, it is now recognised that a fall in aggregate supply can also cause a recession.

CASE STUDY 14.3

Can supply-side factors cause recessions?

Economic ups and downs have always been a fact of human life. Since the Great Depression in the 1930s, Keynesian views of the causes of recession have dominated economic discourse. However, in 1982 Edward Prescott, of Arizona State University, and a Norwegian, Finn Kydland, of Carnegie Mellon University wrote a paper that fundamentally challenged the Keynesian view that changes in aggregate demand for goods and services drive the business cycle. Prescott and Kydland, who were awarded the Nobel Prize in economics, speculated that changes in technology could generate many of the fluctuations in employment and output that had been noted in the past. Changes in aggregate demand were not necessary to explain such fluctuations.

Rather than blaming recessions on the vagaries of aggregate demand, as Keynes had done, Prescott and Kydland asked whether changes in technology, or other supply shocks such as a rise in oil prices, might be as important. Might lulls in innovation be a prime cause of recessions, and surges a source of booms? This became known as the theory of 'real business cycles'. In particular, they showed that if the elasticity of supply of labour is 3, and if various 'shocks' (i.e. unanticipated changes) in total factor productivity (TFP) are persistent and of the right magnitude, their model could account for 70% of the fluctuation in output in the postwar United States.

Follow-up questions

1 What is meant by the words 'the elasticity of supply of labour is 3'?

2 Using *AD/AS* diagrams, explain how demand-side and supply-side factors may cause a recession.

Marxist theory

Marxist economists explain economic cycles as part of a restructuring process that increases the rate of profit in capitalist economies. Under normal production conditions, a fall in the rate of profit caused by competitive pressure threatens to bankrupt weaker capitalist firms. Marxists believe that recessions create conditions in which stronger firms either take over weaker competitors, or buy at rock-bottom prices the assets of rivals forced out of business. Either way, restructuring by takeover or bankruptcy means that the 'fittest' capitalist firms survive. (Note how this process is similar to the theory of economic natural selection explained in Chapter 8.) In Marxist analysis, business cycles are deemed necessary for the regeneration and survival of capitalism.

Marxists have also argued that, in the upswing of a cycle, high employment generates wage inflation. Labour's share of output increases, but at the expense of capitalists' profits and future investment and output. The reduction in output in turn reduces demand for labour and employment, leading to lower wage inflation or wage deflation, which reduces labour's share of output. As the workers' wage share declines, profits and investment increase. This increases the demand for labour, which improves workers' bargaining power. Wages once again rise at the expense of profit, and the cycle repeats itself.

Multiplier/accelerator interaction

Keynesian economists have argued that economic cycles may be caused by the interaction of two dynamic processes: the multiplier and the accelerator. You came across the multiplier and the accelerator at AS, though I shall be examining the multiplier in more detail in the next chapter. In short, via an increase in investment, the multiplier process leads to an increase in national income. The change in income then leads, via the accelerator, to a further change in investment, and the process repeats itself.

Stabilising the economic cycle

From the early 1950s to the 1970s, Keynesian-inspired governments attempted to manage the level of aggregate demand in the UK in order to stabilise the economic cycle. In the downswing, fiscal policy and monetary policy were used to increase or reflate aggregate demand. Conversely, in the upswing, governments contracted or deflated aggregate demand, before the economy overheated in the cycle's boom phase.

However, stable and milder business cycles may result more from the role of **automatic stabilisers** (which I explain in Chapter 19) than from demand-management policies. Demand management led to the stop–go problem. In successive economic cycles, periods of slow growth became longer, while periods of 'go' were quickly brought to a halt by the economy running into higher rates of inflation, or a balance of payments crisis.

Some economists argue that in the Keynesian era, government intervention actually destabilised business cycles, widening rather than reducing cyclical fluctuations and possibly reducing the economy's trend growth rate. There are three reasons why Keynesian demand-management policies may have done this. In the first place, the success of demand management depends on correct timing. By responding to changes in unemployment rather than to changes in output or GDP, governments may have got their timing wrong. (Changes in employment and unemployment often occur several months after changes in output.) Instead of expanding demand when the growth of output slowed, governments intervened too late, after output had already begun to recover. Likewise, governments contracted demand after the peak of the business cycle, thus worsening the downturn. Second, the timing of intervention may have resulted from the government's need to win votes rather than to manage the economy properly. Third, by causing the public sector to grow in size, expansionary fiscal policies may have crowded out the private sector, thereby reducing the economy's trend growth rate.

In the monetarist era in the early 1980s, stabilising the business cycle through the use of demand management policies went out of fashion. But in the early 1990s, managing aggregate demand came back into fashion, though at this time, monetary policy but not fiscal policy was used for this purpose. However, this changed again in the 2008 recession. The then Labour government cut taxes and increased government spending and the budget deficit in a policy known as the **fiscal stimulus**. The election of the Coalition government in 2010 brought a swift end to the fiscal stimulus, replacing it with the opposite policy of **fiscal consolidation** (known also as **fiscal restraint** and **fiscal austerity**). At the time of writing (July

2013), the Coalition government is managing aggregate demand by combining 'loose' monetary policy with 'tight' fiscal policy. Although there have been calls by bodies as eminent as the IMF for a return to fiscal stimulus, chancellor George Osborne is sticking to fiscal austerity (so-called Plan A) and refusing to introduce a more expansionary Plan B.

Using national income statistics to measure welfare and standards of living

EXAM TIP

At AS, you learnt about the meaning and measurement of national income, and other measures of national output such as GNI and GDP. Make sure you revise these concepts thoroughly.

Because GNI, GDP and other national income statistics are the main source of data on what has happened and what is happening in the economy, they are often used as indicators of economic growth, economic and social welfare, and changing living standards, and for comparison with other countries.

To see how living standards change over time, we must look at real per capita GNI figures (real GNI divided by the number of people living in the country). Rising real GNI per capita gives a general indication that living standards are rising, but it may conceal great and sometimes growing disparities in income *distribution*. This is especially significant in developing countries, where the income distribution is typically extremely unequal and where only a small fraction of the population may benefit materially from economic growth.

Besides the problem of income distribution, a number of other problems surface when using national income statistics to measure living standards.

The non-monetised economy

National income statistics underestimate the true level of economic activity because the non-monetised economy is under-represented. In the UK, housework and 'do-it-yourself' home improvement take place without money incomes being generated. When measuring national income, a decision has to be made on whether to estimate or to ignore the value of this production. The UK accounts can be criticised for estimating the value of some but not all of the non-monetised economy.

Imputed rents are estimated for the housing services delivered to owner-occupiers by the houses they live in, based on an estimate of the rent that would be paid if the house-owners were tenants of the same properties. But housekeeping allowances paid within households are not estimated, implying that housework — most of which is undertaken by women — is unproductive. Judgements such as these lead to the anomaly that national income appears to fall when a man marries his housekeeper or paints his own house, having previously employed a decorator.

The hidden economy

Economic activity undertaken illegally in the hidden economy may be omitted. The hidden economy (which is also known as the informal economy, the underground economy and the black economy) refers to all the economic transactions conducted in cash that are not recorded in the national income figures because of tax evasion. It is impossible to make a completely accurate estimate of the size of the hidden economy, but it can be approximated by the gap between the GNI total obtained by the income and expenditure methods of measurement. The hidden economy probably equals about 10% of the UK's measured GNI, while countries such as Greece, Spain and Portugal have hidden economies equal to 20% of GNI.

The quality of goods and services

Over time, the quality of goods changes for better or worse, presenting a particularly difficult problem in the construction and interpretation of national income figures. This is also true of services. When services such as public transport and healthcare deteriorate, GNI may rise even though welfare and real living standards decline.

Negative externalities

National income statistics overestimate living standards because of the effects of negative externalities such as pollution and congestion, and of activities such as crime. What is, in effect, a welfare loss may be shown as an increase in national output, falsely indicating an apparent welfare gain. For example, the stresses and strains of producing an ever-higher national output lead to a loss of leisure time and people become ill more often. Loss of leisure and poorer health cause welfare to fall. However, in the national accounts, these show up as extra production and as extra consumption of healthcare, both of which imply a welfare gain. Traffic congestion increases the cost of motoring, and hence the value of national income. Motorists would prefer uncongested roads and less spending on petrol and vehicle wear and tear.

Likewise, installing *regrettables* such as burglar alarms raises national income, but most people would prefer a crime-free environment and no burglar alarms. Along with the effects of divorce and other elements of social breakdown, national income statistics treat the effect of crime on economic activity as a welfare gain.

Comparing national income between countries

Comparisons of national income per head between countries are misleading if the relative importance of the non-monetised economy differs significantly. There are also differences in the degree of statistical sophistication in data collection, particularly between developed and developing countries, and a lack of international uniformity in methods of classifying and categorising the national accounts.

There are further problems in making comparisons when different commodities are consumed. Expenditure on fuel, clothing and building materials for cold winters is usually greater in developed countries than in much warmer developing economies. However, greater expenditure on these goods may not indicate higher real incomes and living standards.

Standards of living and the quality of life

For the national economy, the average standard of living can be defined as consumption per head of population of purchased goods and services. But because it focuses solely on material goods and services bought largely in the shops, this definition is really too narrow. More widely defined, the standard of living includes quality of life factors and general economic welfare, as well as narrow GNI-related consumption. A wider definition of living standards might include the three elements shown in the following equation:

$$
\begin{array}{c}
\text{standard} \\ \text{of living}
\end{array}
=
\begin{array}{c}
\text{economic} \\ \text{welfare derived} \\ \text{from goods} \\ \text{and services} \\ \text{purchased in the} \\ \text{market economy}
\end{array}
+
\begin{array}{c}
\text{economic welfare} \\ \text{derived from public} \\ \text{goods and merit} \\ \text{goods collectively} \\ \text{provided by the} \\ \text{state}
\end{array}
+
\begin{array}{c}
\text{economic welfare} \\ \text{derived from quality of} \\ \text{life factors, including} \\ \text{external benefits and} \\ \text{intangibles minus} \\ \text{external costs and} \\ \text{intangibles}
\end{array}
$$

If used carefully, national income figures can provide a reasonable estimate of economic welfare derived from the first two of these three elements, both of which relate to the direct consumption of material goods and services. However, national income figures fail to estimate how externalities and other quality of life factors affect economic welfare and living standards.

Additionally, national income fails to reflect the effect of resource depletion and environmental degradation resulting from producing *current* income on humankind's ability to produce *future* income. This means that national income and GDP do *not* address the issue of sustainability.

Education can be used as a measure of standard of living

CASE STUDY 14.4

What's wrong with GNI as a measure of economic welfare?

The gross national income includes air pollution and advertising for cigarettes, and ambulances to clear our highways of carnage. It counts special locks for our doors, and jails for the people who break them. GNI includes the destruction of the redwoods and the death of Lake Superior. It grows with the production of napalm and missiles and nuclear warheads... And if GNI includes all this, there is much that it does not comprehend. It does not allow for the health of our families, the quality of their education, or the joy of their play. It is indifferent to the decency of our factories and the safety of our streets alike. It does not include the beauty of our poetry or the strength of our marriages, or the intelligence of our public debate or the integrity of our public officials... GNI measures neither our wit nor our courage, neither our wisdom nor our learning, neither our compassion nor our devotion to our country. It measures everything, in short, except that which makes life worthwhile; and it can tell us everything about America — except whether we are proud to be Americans.

Source: adapted from a speech by US Senator Robert Kennedy, 1967

Follow-up question
Compare alternative measures of economic welfare.

Alternative measures of economic welfare

The environmental pressure group Friends of the Earth argues that measures of national income such as GDP were never intended to be indicators of progress or welfare. Indeed, in 1934, Simon Kuznets, the inventor of the GDP concept, argued that 'The welfare of a nation can scarcely be inferred from a measurement of national income'. Not surprisingly, therefore, other measures that are less dependent on raw GNI or GDP are increasingly used to place a value on economic and social progress.

One of the earliest of these was the **Measure of Economic Welfare (MEW)**, developed by Nordhaus and Tobin in 1972. The MEW showed that welfare in the USA grew, but at a slower rate than GDP, between 1950 and 1965. More recent attempts to adjust conventional national income figures include the **United Nations Human Development Index (HDI)**, the **Index of Sustainable Economic Welfare (ISEW)** and the **Genuine Progress Indicator**.

The United Nations Human Development Index (HDI)

As from 2010, the HDI combines three dimensions:

- **A long and healthy life:** life expectancy at birth.
- **Education index:** mean years of schooling and expected years of schooling.
- **A decent standard of living:** gross national income (GNI) per capita, measured in US dollars at purchasing power parity.

The maximum value of the HDI is 1 (or unity). The closer a country's HDI is to 1, then the greater its human development, measured in terms of the three indicators specified in the index.

The HDI is by no means a perfect index of economic welfare and human development, since it ignores the distribution of income and expenditure on healthcare.

Out of the 185 countries in the index published in 2013, Norway, Australia, the USA and Germany were ranked in the top five. Previous 'top-fivers' Iceland and Ireland had slipped down the list, their economies having greatly suffered from the global financial crisis. The UK was in 27th position. The Sub-Saharan African countries of Burkina Faso, Chad, Mozambique, Liberia, the Democratic Republic of Congo and Niger languished in the bottom five places.

The Index of Sustainable Economic Welfare (ISEW) and the Genuine Progress Indicator (GPI)

Both the ISEW and the GPI try to capture the effects of externalities and other intangibles upon human happiness and welfare. They take account of a number of aspects of economic life that GDP ignores. For the ISEW, these include pollution, noise, commuting costs, capital growth, health and education spending, urbanisation, and the loss of natural resources. The GPI distinguishes between 'good' or 'worthwhile' growth and 'bad' or 'uneconomic' growth. The latter is economic growth that reflects or creates a decline in the quality of life. The GPI takes into consideration indicators such as the value of voluntary work and unpaid work, the value of leisure time, the distribution of income, the impact of growth on the environment and the cost of crime.

Is economic growth sustainable?

Sustainable growth meets the needs of people living today without compromising the ability of future generations to meet their own needs. Environmentalists, ecologists and some economists predict that the pursuit of ever-growing GNI is unsustainable, arguing that growth will eventually lead to the depletion of non-renewable resources. However, many, although certainly not all, economists believe this is too simplistic. They question the environmentalists' assumptions of an ever-faster rate of resource usage accompanied by an ever-faster rate of decline of resource reserves.

You learnt at AS that prices perform three main functions in a market economy: signalling, creating incentives and allocating scarce resources between competing uses. Other things being equal, an increase in the rate of resource usage causes resource prices to rise. In their turn, rising resource prices create incentives for consumers and producers to alter economic behaviour — literally, to economise. Consumers buy less of goods and services whose relative prices are rising. Producers, meanwhile, respond to the changing relative prices of their inputs or factors of production. First they do this by altering methods of production. Second, producers explore the earth's crust for new supplies of minerals and fossil fuels, which would be uneconomic to search for and extract at a lower resource price.

Nevertheless, most economists have taken on board the environmentalists' belief that governments should aim for sustainable economic growth and development. R. K. Turner has defined an optimal sustainable growth policy as one that maintains 'an acceptable rate of growth in per capita incomes without depleting the national capital asset stock or the natural environment asset stock'.

The benefits and costs of economic growth

For many people and most economists, achieving a satisfactory and sustained rate of economic growth is arguably the most important of all the macroeconomic objectives that governments wish to achieve. Without growth, other objectives, particularly full employment and competitive export industries, may be impossible to attain. And when growth becomes negative, as in the recession that started in the UK in 2008, people become all too aware of the rapid disappearance of the fruits of growth. For most people, standards of living fall, with the most unfortunate losing their jobs as the industries that used to employ them collapse or slim down.

However, as I hinted at in earlier parts of the chapter, including the last section, in the long run, *sustained* economic growth may not be *sustainable*. With countries in the developing world, particularly the 'emerging market' countries, recently growing at a far faster rate than richer developed economies, maintaining global growth rates may not be sustainable. The rapid using-up of finite resources and the pollution and global warming that spin off from

EXAM TIP

Exam questions may ask you to analyse and evaluate the benefits and costs of economic growth.

economic growth will result increasingly in desertification, water shortages, declining crop yields, famines and wars.

Some economists argue an opposite effect, namely that one of the benefits of growth, at least as far as advanced developed countries are concerned, is the development of environmentally friendly technologies. These reduce the ratio of energy consumption to GDP. Nevertheless, rich developed economies, especially the USA, continue to be, at least for the time being, the world's biggest consumers of energy and the biggest polluters.

Benefits of economic growth

- Economic growth increases standards of living and people's welfare.
- Growth leads to more civilised communities who take action to improve the environment.
- Growth provides new more environmentally friendly technologies.
- Economic growth has increased the length of people's lives and has provided the means to reduce disease.
- Economic growth provides a route out of poverty for much of the world's population.
- Economic growth produces a 'fiscal dividend', namely the tax revenues that growth generates. Tax revenues can be used to correct market failures and to provide infrastructure, thereby increasing the economic welfare of the whole community.
- For a particular country, economic growth can generate a 'virtuous circle' of greater business confidence, increased investment in state-of-the-art technology, greater international competitiveness, higher profits, even more growth, and so on.

Costs of economic growth

- Economic growth uses up finite resources such as oil and minerals that cannot be replaced.
- Economic growth leads to pollution and other forms of environmental degradation, with the earth eventually reaching a tipping point, beyond which it cannot recover.
- Growth can destroy local cultures and communities and widen inequalities in the distribution of income and wealth.
- Economic growth leads to urbanisation and the spread of huge cities, which swallow up good agricultural land.
- In its early phases, economic growth leads to a rapid growth in population, more mouths to feed, and more people actually poor.
- Growth produces losers as well as winners. Countries suffering low growth may enter a vicious circle of declining business confidence, low profits, low investment, a lack of international competitiveness, even lower profits, zero growth, and so on.

SUMMARY

- Economic growth is the increase, over time, of the potential level of output the economy can produce.
- Short-run economic growth makes use of spare capacity and labour in the economy.
- Short-run economic growth is also known as economic recovery.
- Long-run economic growth shifts the economy's production possibility frontier outward.
- Economic growth should not be confused with economic development.
- Technical progress, investment and increased labour productivity are important causes of economic growth.
- Fluctuations in economic activity, known as the economic cycle, accompany short-run economic growth.
- Economic cycles are usually caused by fluctuations in aggregate demand, though supply-side factors can also lead to cycles.
- Changes in national income or GDP can be used to measure changes in living standards.
- Other indicators, such as the United Nations Human Development Index (HDI) provide better measures.
- Sustainable economic growth should not be confused with sustained economic growth.
- There are a number of benefits and costs of economic growth.

Exam-style questions

1 With the help of a *PPF* diagram, explain the difference between short-term and long-term economic growth. **(15 marks)**

2 Briefly explain three possible causes of economic cycles. **(15 marks)**

3 Evaluate the benefits and costs of economic growth. **(25 marks)**

4 Do you agree that recessions are always caused by a collapse of aggregate demand? Justify your answer. **(25 marks)**

Extra resources to help you revise are available online at www.hodderplus.co.uk/philipallan

Developing the aggregate demand and aggregate supply macroeconomic model

In this chapter, I start by reminding you of the meaning of aggregate demand (*AD*) and aggregate supply (*AS*) and by drawing the *AD* and *AS* curves that illustrate these important macroeconomic concepts.

In the last 30 years, the *AD/AS* model has become the preferred theoretical framework that many economists use for investigating macroeconomic issues. The model is particularly useful for analysing the effect of an increase in aggregate demand upon the economy. This addresses a key issue: will expansionary fiscal policy and/or monetary policy increase real output and jobs (i.e. will it be reflationary), or will the price level increase instead (i.e. will it be inflationary)? As this chapter explains, the answer to this key macroeconomic question depends on the shape of the *AS* curve, both in the short run and in the long run.

LEARNING OUTCOMES

This chapter will:

- provide a brief summary and reminder of the main features of the *AD/AS* model
- explain the nature of aggregate demand and short-run aggregate supply
- remind you of the meaning of macroeconomic equilibrium
- distinguish between short-run and long-run aggregate supply
- use an *AD/AS* diagram to illustrate output gaps
- revisit the Keynesian long-run aggregate supply curve
- develop your AS knowledge of the multiplier theory

WHAT YOU SHOULD ALREADY KNOW

At A2, you don't really need to know much more about aggregate demand and aggregate supply than you learnt a year ago at AS. To prepare for the Unit 4 data-response and essay questions, you must practise your skills in shifting *AD* curves to illustrate the effects of changes in any of the components of aggregate demand. You must also identify supply-side factors that influence the positions of the *SRAS* and *LRAS* curves, and understand how monetary and fiscal policies affect aggregate demand and supply.

The meaning of aggregate demand

Aggregate demand must not be confused with the national income concept of national expenditure. Aggregate demand is the total *planned* spending on the goods and services produced *within* the economy in a particular time period, for example a year. Aggregate demand

KEY TERM

aggregate demand: total planned spending on the goods and services produced within the economy in a particular time period.

measures *planned* spending, whereas national expenditure measures realised or actual spending, which has already taken place.

Four sources of spending are included in aggregate demand, each originating in a different sector of the economy: households, firms, the government sector and the overseas sector. These are shown in the following equation:

$$\text{aggregate demand} = \text{consumption} + \text{investment} + \text{government spending} + \text{exports (net of imports)}$$

or:

$$AD = C + I + G + (X - M)$$

where *C, I, G, X* and *M* are the symbols used respectively for planned consumption, investment, government spending, exports and imports.

EXAM TIP

At A2, as at AS, exam questions seldom instruct you to draw an *AD/AS* diagram, or to apply *AD/AS* analysis. Nevertheless, these are the key skills needed for answering many data-response and essay questions in the Unit 4 exam.

The London Olympic stadium was an example of a government spending project

EXAM TIP

Make sure you understand and can apply the aggregate demand equation:

$$AD = C + I + G + (X - M)$$

It is useful in a number of different contexts, such as monetary and fiscal policy. You may be tested synoptically on your understanding of the components of aggregate demand, consumption, investment and exports.

The AD curve

The aggregate demand curve is illustrated along with a short-run aggregate supply (*SRAS*) curve in Figure 15.1. This diagram shows the total quantities of real output that all economic agents plan to purchase at different price levels within the economy, when all the factors influencing aggregate demand other than the price level are held constant. If any of the determinants of aggregate demand change (apart from the price level), the *AD* curve shifts to the right or to the left, depending on whether there has been an increase or a decrease in aggregate demand. For example, an increase in consumer or business confidence shifts the *AD* curve to the right, via the effect on consumption or investment. An increase in net export demand ($X - M$) has a similar effect, as does expansionary monetary policy and expansionary fiscal policy. By contrast, an increase in imports, contractionary monetary or fiscal policy, or a collapse in consumer or business confidence, shift the *AD* curve to the left.

> **KEY TERM**
>
> **short-run aggregate supply:** shows the quantities of real output businesses plan to produce and sell at different price levels, assuming there is spare capacity in the economy.

> **EXAM TIP**
>
> The *slope* of the *AD* curve tells us what happens to aggregate demand when the price level changes. Don't make the mistake of asserting that a change in the price level *shifts* the *AD* curve.

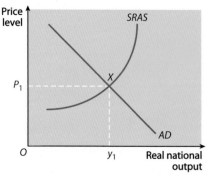

Figure 15.1 A downward-sloping *AD* curve and an upward-sloping *SRAS* curve

Explaining the shape of the aggregate demand curve

The *AD* curve slopes downward to the right, showing that as the price level falls, aggregate demand expands. A number of factors explain the *slope* of the *AD* curve, as distinct from a *shift* of the curve.

- One explanation lies in a **wealth effect** or **real balance effect**. Assuming a given nominal stock of money in the economy, a decrease in the price level increases people's *real* money balances, i.e. the same amount of money buys more goods and services. An increase in real money balances makes people wealthier because money is a part of peoples' wealth.
- The increase in real money balances I have just described also means that the real money supply has increased, relative to the demand to hold real money balances. Basic supply and demand analysis tells us that when the supply of *any* commodity

increases relative to demand for the commodity, its price tends to fall. Now, the *rate of interest* is the price of money. The increase in the supply of real money balances relative to demand reduces real interest rates, which in turn leads to higher levels of consumption and investment.

- A third factor relates to exports and imports. When the domestic price level falls (and assuming the exchange rate remains unchanged), demand increases for the country's exports. At the same time, consumers buy domestically produced goods instead of imports. Aggregate demand thus increases as the price level falls.

The *SRAS* curve

Just as the *AD* curve shows the total quantities of real output that economic agents plan to purchase at different levels of domestic prices, so the *SRAS* curve shows the quantities of **real output** that businesses plan to produce and sell at different price levels.

Before explaining the shape of the *SRAS* curve, I shall first explain the factors determining the *position* of the curve. If one of these factors changes, the *SRAS* curve shifts to the right or left to a new position. The factors are indeed virtually the same as those fixing the position of a market supply curve in a particular microeconomic market. The main determinants of the position of the *SRAS* curve are:

- costs of production
- taxes that firms have to pay
- technology
- productivity
- attitudes
- enterprise
- factor mobility
- economic incentives facing workers and firms
- the institutional structure of the economy

Explaining the shape of the short-run aggregate supply curve

Whereas the *AD* curve is almost always drawn downward-sloping, different assumptions about the nature of aggregate supply lead to different shapes and slopes of the *AS* curve. A short-run aggregate supply (*SRAS*) curve is illustrated in Figure 15.2.

The shape of the upward-sloping *AS* curve is explained by two assumptions of microeconomic theory of the firm (refer to Chapter 3), which are:

- all firms aim to maximise profits
- in the short run, the law of diminishing returns or diminishing marginal productivity operates

Following an increase in aggregate demand from AD_1 to AD_2 in Figure 15.2, which disturbs an initial macroeconomic equilibrium

Figure 15.2 The implications of an upward-sloping *SRAS* curve at point X, the price level rises to P_2 to create conditions in which profit-maximising firms are happy to supply more output.

If the prices firms could charge did not rise, it would not be profitable for firms to increase supply. The explanation for this is as follows. First, I assume that firms are already producing the profit-maximising level of output, which occurs when $MR = MC$. If firms increase output beyond this point, marginal costs rise, which leads to falling profit. This is because the marginal product of the workers needed to produce the extra output falls, which increases marginal costs. For profit-maximising firms to produce more output in the face of rising marginal costs, marginal revenues must also rise. This requires higher prices. Without a higher price level, profit-maximising firms will not voluntarily increase the supply of output.

It is important to emphasise that, because each short-run AS curve is drawn under the assumption that the money wage rate remains unchanged, there is a different short-run AS curve for each and every money wage rate. When the money wage rate rises, production costs increase and firms reduce the quantity of output they are willing to supply at the current price level. As a result, the short-run AS curve shifts to the left to a new position. Conversely, a fall in the money wage rate shifts the AS curve to the right.

Macroeconomic equilibrium

Macroeconomic equilibrium occurs when the aggregate demand for real output equals the aggregate supply of real output, i.e. where:

$AD = AS$

When $AD = AS$, households, firms, the government and the overseas sector plan to spend in real terms within the economy an amount exactly equal to the level of real output that firms are willing to produce. Referring back to Figure 15.1, macro-economic equilibrium occurs at point X, where the AD curve intersects the AS curve. The equilibrium level of real output is y_1, and the equilibrium price level is P_1.

Long-run aggregate supply

The aggregate supply curve I have considered so far in this chapter is a short-run AS curve. I shall now extend the analysis to explain the economy's **long-run aggregate supply** ($LRAS$) curve. Economists generally believe that the $LRAS$ curve is vertical, though there is an

KEY TERM

macroeconomic equilibrium: occurs when $AD = AS$ and when injections into the circular flow of income equal leakages from the flow.

EXAM TIP

You can also explain macroeconomic equilibrium by using a circular flow diagram. Equilibrium occurs when $S + T + M = I + G + X$. Do not, however, confuse *macro*economic equilibrium for the *whole* economy with *micro*economic equilibrium in a market *within* the economy.

KEY TERM

long-run aggregate supply: the real output that can be supplied when the economy is on its production possibility frontier and producing at full potential.

exception known as the **Keynesian LRAS curve**. A vertical *LRAS* curve, such as the curve illustrated in Figure 15.3, means that in the long run a rightward shift of aggregate demand increases the price level, but *not* real output.

The explanation for the vertical *LRAS* curve is quite simple. The *LRAS* curve in Figure 15.3 is located at the full-employment level of real output y_{FE}, with production taking place on the economy's production possibility frontier. Firms cannot produce more output to meet the increase in aggregate demand depicted by the shift of the *AD* curve from AD_1 to AD_2. In this situation, the excess demand for real output is met by an increase in the price level, with the point of macroeconomic equilibrium moving from point *X* to point *Z*.

Figure 15.3 A vertical long-run aggregate supply (*LRAS*) curve

Supply and demand in a busy supermarket

Long-run economic growth and a shift of the *LRAS* curve

At this point you should go back to Chapter 14 and reread the section at the beginning of the chapter on the meaning of economic growth. There you will see two diagrams, Figures 14.1 and 14.2, which show, respectively, the economy's production possibility frontier shifting outward, and the *LRAS* curve shifting to the right. Figure 15.4 shows similar diagrams.

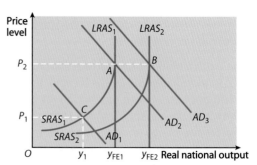

Figure 15.4 Economic growth, the economy's production possibility frontier and the *LRAS* curve

Suppose the economy is initially at point *C* in both panels of the diagram, producing output y_1. In this situation, an increase in aggregate demand from AD_1 to AD_2 in panel (b) takes up the slack in the economy, and short-run economic growth takes place. Output increases from y_1 to y_{FE1} in panel (b) of the diagram, and the economy moves from point *C* to point *A* in both panels. However, as I have explained, for firms to produce the extra output the price level must rise.

Once at point *A*, the economy is on production possibility frontier PPF_1, and also producing on long-run aggregate supply curve $LRAS_1$. The level of output is now y_{FE1}. Because there is no spare capacity, for output to increase on a permanent basis long-run economic growth must take place. Long-run growth shifts the economy's production possibility frontier outward from PPF_1 to PPF_2, and the *LRAS* curve rightward from $LRAS_1$ to $LRAS_2$. The economy now produces at point *B* rather than point *A* in both panels of the diagram. Note that panel (b) shows aggregate demand increasing from AD_2 to AD_3. In this situation aggregate demand increases just sufficiently to *absorb* the increase in aggregate supply without the price level rising or falling. Although output has increased to y_{FE2}, the price level has remained at P_2. If aggregate demand were to remain at AD_2, or if the *AD* curve were to shift by either more or less than is shown in panel (b), the price level would change.

The economy's natural level of output and long-run aggregate supply

For free-market, monetarist and supply-side economists, the full-employment level of real output y_{FE} is also the economy's natural level of output (y_N) toward which market forces and a flexible price mechanism eventually adjust. The **natural level of output** is the long-run equilibrium level of *potential* output associated with the economy's natural levels of employment and unemployment in the economy's aggregate labour market. For free-market economists the vertical *LRAS* curve carries the message that the short-run expansionary effect on output and employment of increasing aggregate demand may be negated in the long run by the way the supply side of the economy responds to the demand stimulus.

> **KEY TERM**
>
> **natural level of output:** the long-run equilibrium level of potential output.

Revisiting output gaps

You first came across **output gaps** at AS when learning, in the context of the economic cycle, how the economy's actual output usually differs from trend output. Negative and positive output gaps are illustrated in Figure 14.4 of Chapter 14. Before proceeding any further, go back to this diagram and make sure you understand the meaning of an output gap.

> **KEY TERM**
>
> **output gap:** the difference between actual output and trend output.

> **EXAM TIP**
>
> Don't confuse an *output* gap with a *productivity* gap, which is the gap between the productivity levels of two countries.

Positive output gaps occur when the economy temporarily produces at a point outside its current production possibility frontier. However, because this represents overuse of capacity, such a point cannot be sustained for long. In the context of the *AD/AS* model, this means that the economy temporarily produces a level of output to the right of the *LRAS* curve, and above the full-employment level of output, for example at point W in Figure 15.5. Note that I have drawn the diagram so that the *SRAS* curve extends to the right of the full-employment level of output y_{FE}, without becoming vertical at point X. For a short period, output can rise above y_{FE} to y_1, but eventually output falls back to the full-employment level.

By contrast, the economy suffers a **negative output gap** whenever the level of output is to the left of the *LRAS* curve and *below* the full-employment level of output y_{FE}. A negative output gap occurs at point V in Figure 15.5, with the short-run macroeconomic equilibrium level of output at y_2.

Figure 15.5 Positive and negative output gaps and the *LRAS* curve

> **KEY TERMS**
>
> **positive output gap:** the difference between actual output and the trend output when actual output is above trend output.
>
> **negative output gap:** the difference between actual output and trend output when actual output is below trend output.

Revisiting the Keynesian long-run aggregate supply curve

The vertical *LRAS* curve I have described is often called the *free-market* or *supply-side LRAS* curve. This label reflects the view commonly expressed by free-market economists that, provided markets function competitively and efficiently, the economy always operates at or close to full capacity. As I explained earlier, in the short run real output is influenced by the average price level, but in the long run aggregate supply is determined by maximum production capacity.

> **EXAM TIP**
>
> You should generally assume that the *LRAS* curve is vertical with its position determined by the full-capacity and full-employment level of output, but understand that there is a second 'Keynesian' version of the curve.

Most modern Keynesians (who are often called **New Keynesians**) agree that the *LRAS* curve is vertical. However, in the past some Keynesians were associated with the rather different *LRAS* curve illustrated in Figure 15.6. This curve is derived from Keynes's own views on how the economy operates.

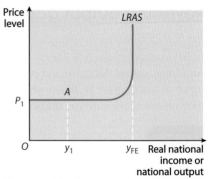

Figure 15.6 The Keynesian *LRAS* curve

The 'Keynesian' *LRAS* curve is based on Keynes's explanation of the Great Depression in the UK and US economies in the 1930s. Keynes argued that a depressed economy can settle into an under-full employment equilibrium, shown for example by point *A* on the horizontal section of the *LRAS* curve in Figure 15.6. At point *A*, the level of real national output is y_1. Keynes argued that without purposeful intervention by the government, an economy could display more or less permanent demand-deficiency. Market forces would fail to adjust automatically and achieve full employment. But if the government is able to shift the *AD* to the right along the horizontal section of the *LRAS* curve (mainly through expansionary fiscal policy), the existence of huge amounts of spare capacity would lead, in Keynes's view, to a growth in real output (and employment), without an increase in the price level.

The vertical long-run aggregate supply curve and economic policy

As I have mentioned, the vertical *LRAS* curve favoured by free-market and supply-side economists is located at the natural or equilibrium level of real output, which is the level of output consistent with the natural rate of unemployment in the labour market. Because output and employment are assumed to be at their natural or equilibrium levels, an increase of aggregate demand causes the price level to rise, but with no long-term effect upon the levels of real output and employment.

Free-market and supply-side economists therefore conclude that it is generally irresponsible for governments to use expansionary fiscal or monetary policies to try to increase national output and employment *above* their natural rates and levels. While such policies may succeed in the short run, though at the expense of inflation, they are doomed eventually to fail. In the long run, output and employment fall back to their equilibrium or natural rates and levels, which are determined by the economy's production potential or ability to supply. Thus, instead of increasing aggregate demand to reduce unemployment *below* its natural rate, supply-side economists believe that the responsible approach is for the government to use microeconomic supply-side policies to reduce the natural rate itself.

Market-orientated supply-side policies aim to improve incentives and the performance of individual economic agents and markets. They shift the economy's production possibility frontier outward and the *LRAS* curve rightward, thereby increasing the natural levels of output and employment in the economy.

In summary, in the *extreme* supply-side or free-market view, providing output, employment and unemployment are at their natural levels, there is no case for demand management. Instead, macroeconomic policy should be subordinated to the needs of a supply-side orientated microeconomic policy aimed at increasing the economy's production potential. Policy should focus on shifting the *LRAS* curve rightward.

However, more *moderate* free-market economists do these days accept that demand can legitimately be increased if the economy is suffering recession and a negative output gap. In this situation, with output and employment below their natural levels and unemployment above its natural level, there is a case, using expansionary monetary policy, for increasing aggregate demand. Free-market, but not Keynesian, economists generally reject the use of fiscal policy (a fiscal stimulus) for this purpose.

Aggregate demand and the national income multiplier

You first came across the **national income multiplier** when studying Unit 2 at AS, but at A2 it is useful to understand the multiplier process in more depth. A **multiplier** exists whenever a change in one variable induces or causes multiple and successive stages of change in a second variable. Each succeeding stage of change is usually smaller than the previous one so that the total change induced in the multiplier process comes effectively to an end when further stages of change approach zero. We can calculate the value of a multiplier by dividing the total change induced in the second variable by the size of the initial change in the first variable. For example, a multiplier of 8 tells us that an increase in the first variable will cause successive stages of change in the second variable, which are 8 times greater in total than the initial triggering change.

> **KEY TERM**
>
> **national income multiplier:** measures the relationship between a change in any of the components of aggregate demand and the resulting change in the equilibrium level of national income.

In macroeconomic theory, the national income multiplier (or Keynesian multiplier) measures the relationship between a change in aggregate demand in the economy and the resulting change in the equilibrium level of national income. The size of the national income multiplier is significant for fiscal policy.

Nested within the national income multiplier are a number of specific multipliers, each related to the particular component of aggregate demand that initially changes. These are the consumption multiplier, the investment multiplier, the government spending multiplier and the export multiplier. There are also *negative* multipliers for changes in taxation and imports. Taken together, the government spending and tax multipliers are fiscal policy multipliers. Likewise, the export and import multipliers are foreign trade multipliers.

The government spending multiplier

As Figure 15.7 illustrates, an increase in government spending (or in any component of aggregate demand) causes multiple successive changes in national income that are greater in total than the initial increase in government spending.

£10bn
£9bn
£8.1bn
£7.2bn...

ΔG
Initial increase
in government
spending on road
building £10bn

ΔY

Successive stages of increase
in national income £100bn

Figure 15.7 The government
spending multiplier

The multiplier process, which is essentially dynamic, taking place over time, resembles ripples spreading over a pond after a stone has been thrown in the water. However, the ripples in a pond last only a few seconds, whereas the ripples spreading through the economy following a change in aggregate demand can last for months and even years. Figure 15.7 illustrates the ripple effect. The diagram, which shows the government spending multiplier, can easily be adapted to illustrate the investment multiplier or any other national income multiplier.

In order to explain the government spending multiplier, I shall assume there is demand-deficient unemployment in the economy, and that the levels of taxation and imports do not change when aggregate demand increases. To reduce demand-deficient unemployment, the government decides to spend an extra £10 billion on road building.

KEY TERM

government spending multiplier: measures the relationship between a change in government spending and the resulting change in the equilibrium level of national income.

EXAM TIP

The multiplier is not mentioned explicitly in the Unit 4 specification at A2, but the synoptic nature of the specification means that good exam answers should make use of and apply the multiplier concept.

- In the first stage of the multiplier process, £10 billion is received as income by building workers who, like everybody in the economy, spend 90p of every pound of income on consumption. (I am also assuming the marginal propensity to consume (*MPC*) is 0.9 throughout the economy, which means that people plan to consume 90p out of an increase in income of £1.00. An *MPC* of 0.9 means that the marginal propensity to save (*MPS*) is 0.1. At each stage of the multiplier process, 10% of an extra pound of income leaks into saving and is not spent on consumption.
- At the second stage of the multiplier process, £9 billion of the £10 billion income is spent on consumer goods and services, with the remaining £1 billion leaking into unspent savings.
- At the next and third stage, consumer good sector employees spend £8.1 billion, or 0.9 of the £9 billion received at the second stage of income generation.

- Further stages of income generation then occur, with each successive stage being 0.9 of the previous stage. Each stage is smaller than the preceding stage due to the fact that part of income leaks into savings.

Assuming that nothing else changes in the time taken for the process to work through the economy, the eventual increase in income ΔY resulting from the initial injection of government spending is the sum of all the stages of income generation. ΔY is larger than ΔG, which triggered the initial growth in national income.

(Note: the formula for calculating the value of the multiplier in this numerical example is:

multiplier $= \dfrac{1}{s}$

where s is the marginal propensity to save, MPS.)

CASE STUDY 15.1

The government spending multiplier and the austerity programme

The larger the size of the government spending multiplier, the more powerful is fiscal policy for managing aggregate demand in the economy and the level of output. The smaller the multiplier, the less effective is fiscal policy used in this Keynesian way. Now, the multiplier illustrated in the previous section is highly misleading. Real-world government spending multipliers are much smaller than 10, being much closer to unity (i.e. 1). In the numerical example above, and in Figure 15.7, I assumed that the only leakage or withdrawal of spending out of the flow of income at each stage of the multiplier process is saving. If this is the case, as I explained, the government spending multiplier is large, in this case 10. But in real life, significant fractions of any new income generated by the multiplier process are paid in taxation to the government, and also leak into spending on imports. In this situation, the formula for the multiplier is:

$$\frac{1}{s + t + m}$$

where s is the marginal propensity to save, t is the marginal tax rate, and m is the marginal propensity to import.

The marginal tax rate (t) and the marginal propensity to import (m) respectively measure the proportion of a change in income paid in tax and the proportion people wish to spend on imports. Given a marginal propensity to save (s) of 0.15, and setting the marginal tax rate (t) at

0.4 and the marginal propensity to import (m) at 0.35, the value of the multiplier becomes:

$$\frac{1}{0.15 + 0.4 + 0.35}$$

or: 1.1

Before recession hit the UK economy in 2008, it was generally believed that the government spending multiplier was even smaller than 1.1, around 0.5. If the government spending multiplier is small, a cut in public spending does not cause much short-term damage to national output. If it is large, then the process can become self-defeating, at least in the short run, with each pound of government spending cuts, for example, costing the economy more than a pound in lost output and thus actually increasing the government debt-to-GDP ratio. Chancellor George Osborne used the low multiplier figure to justify his fiscal policy austerity programme. The Treasury argued that public spending cuts of £10 billion would depress UK national income by only a further £5 billion.

However, in 2012 the IMF said that it had seriously underestimated the size of the government spending multiplier. The IMF admitted that, in the early part of the recession at least, the multiplier was significantly higher, lying between 0.9 and 1.7; that is to say, between two and three times greater than previously estimated.

Follow-up questions
1 Explain why a government spending multiplier of 1.7 means that the government's austerity programme may have seriously damaged the UK economy.
2 Find out what has happened to the debate about the size of the government spending multiplier since this book was published.

EXTENSION MATERIAL

The multiplier and Keynesian theory

The national income multiplier first came into prominence as a key part of Keynesian economic theory. The multiplier concept was first stated in 1931 by R.F. Kahn, a colleague and former pupil of John Maynard Keynes at Cambridge University. In its early days, the multiplier theory was an **employment multiplier** showing how a change in public sector investment, for example in road building, might trigger a subsequent multiple growth in employment. Keynes made use of Kahn's employment multiplier for the first time in 1933 when discussing the effects of an increase in government spending of £500, a sum that he assumed to be just sufficient to employ one man for 1 year in road construction. Keynes wrote:

> If the new expenditure is additional and not merely in substitution for other expenditure, the increase of employment does not stop there. The additional wages and other incomes paid out are spent on additional purchases, which in turn lead to further employment…the newly employed who supply the increased purchases of those employed on the new capital works will, in their turn, spend more, thus adding to the employment of others and so on.

By 1936, when Keynes's *General Theory* was published, the multiplier had become a part of Keynes's explanation of how unemployment might be caused by deficient aggregate demand. In his *General Theory*, Keynes explained the investment multiplier, which suggests how a collapse in investment and business confidence might cause a multiple contraction in output, leading in turn to large-scale unemployment. Keynes then went on to argue that through an active fiscal policy, the government spending multiplier might reverse this process.

The multiplier and Keynesian demand management

Despite the possibility of a low multiplier effect during the Keynesian era, governments in many industrialised mixed economies (including the UK), based macroeconomic policy on the management of aggregate demand. This became known as **discretionary fiscal policy**. To achieve full employment, governments deliberately ran budget deficits (setting $G > T$). This increased aggregate demand, but sometimes too much demand 'overheated' the economy. Excess demand pulled up the price level in a demand-pull inflation or pulled imports into the country and caused a balance of payments crisis. In these circumstances, governments were forced to reverse the thrust of fiscal policy, cutting public spending or raising taxes to reduce the level of demand in the economy.

The Keynesians used fiscal policy in a discrete way, supplemented at times by monetary policy, to *fine-tune* the level of aggregate demand in the economy so as to stabilise the fluctuations in the economic cycle and to try to achieve the macroeconomic objectives of full employment and economic growth without excessive inflation or an unsustainable deterioration in the balance of payments.

The decline and rebirth, and then the further decline, of demand-side fiscal policy

Whatever the size of the multiplier, the multiplier process increases *nominal* national income, and not necessarily *real* national income. You must always remember that *nominal* national income can increase in two ways: through reflation of real output, or through inflation of the price level in a demand-pull inflation. Keynesians believed, providing the economy has spare capacity, expansionary fiscal policy stimulates real output more than inflation.

By contrast, free-market and supply-side economists believe that an increase in government spending stimulates *prices* rather than *real output,* and that government spending **crowds out** private sector investment. (Crowding out is explained in Chapter 19.) They also argue that the more fiscal policy is used to increase aggregate demand, the more it injects larger and larger doses of inflation into the economy, irrespective of whether the economy is in boom or recession.

In the 1970s this argument became more and more persuasive. Keynesian economics went into decline and was replaced by the free-market revival. Fiscal policy was no longer used to manage aggregate demand. Then, in 2008 the onset of recession and the introduction of a fiscal stimulus designed to tackle the recession brought about a revival in Keynesian demand management and with it renewed interest in the size of the government spending multiplier.

However, the Keynesian fiscal stimulus was short lived. In the UK it was abruptly abandoned in 2010 when the Coalition government replaced the previous Labour government. George Osborne, the new Conservative chancellor, is very much a supply-side and pro-free-market politician, disliking 'big government' and government intervention in the economy. Osborne replaced the Keynesian fiscal stimulus with the opposite programme of fiscal consolidation, fiscal restraint or fiscal austerity. There was, however, a second non-ideological reason for the new programme of fiscal austerity. This was the emergence of a completely new issue known as the **sovereign debt** problem, which is explained in Case Study 19.2 on page 301.

Using an *AD/AS* diagram to illustrate the government spending multiplier

Figure 15.8 shows the multiplier effect of an increase in government spending in an *AD/AS* diagram. The initial increase in government spending is shown by the horizontal distance between the curves AD_1 and AD_2, labelled ΔG. If the size of the multiplier is 1, there are no further stages in the multiplier process, and the story ends here. Real income increases from y_1 to y_2, and the price level rises from P_1 to P_2. However, with a multiplier greater than 1, the aggregate demand curve now shifts further to the right from AD_2 to AD_3. The larger the government spending multiplier, the greater the distance between the two *AD* curves. Real national income increases to y_3 and the price level rises to P_3.

In Figure 15.8, the effect of the multiplier on *real* national income depends on the shape and slope of the *AS* curve. With the upward-sloping *SRAS* curve depicted in Figure 15.8, real income increases from y_1 to y_3, but part of the multiplier effect is deflected into an increase in the price level (from P_1 to P_3). If I had drawn the diagram with a vertical *LRAS* curve, as opposed to an upward-sloping *SRAS* curve, an increase in government spending would not in the long run produce an increase in real output. Conversely, if the economy is in deep recession and operating on the horizontal section of the Keynesian *LRAS* curve illustrated in Figure 15.6, all of the multiplier effect falls on real output, until the upward-sloping and vertical sections of the curve are reached.

Figure 15.8 Illustrating the government spending multiplier on an *AD/AS* diagram

EXTENSION MATERIAL

A recent development in *AD/AS* analysis

Students are often puzzled by a particular feature of the *AD/AS* model as taught and learnt at A-level. If you look carefully at Figure 15.9, you will see that a leftward movement of the *AD* curve from AD_1 to AD_2 results in a *fall* in the price level, i.e. deflation. However, we all know that except in a deep recession, contractionary fiscal or monetary policy that shifts the *AD* curve to the left results not in falling prices but in a slowdown in the rate of inflation, or disinflation. Average prices still rise, but at a slower annual rate of increase.

Figure 15.9 The traditional *AD/AS* model

Figure 15.10 The Romer *AD/AS* model

This difference results from the fact that the original *AD/AS* model (i.e. the one you have learnt) is misleading. In a fairly recent development of the model, David Romer of the University of California explained why. Romer's explanation goes well beyond the requirements of A-level economics. If you are interested, it is in an academic paper called 'Keynesian Macroeconomics without the LM Curve', which you can find in the *Journal of Economic Perspectives*, Volume 14, Number 2, Spring 2000. You can also find the article on the internet at http://elsa.berkeley.edu/~dromer/papers/JEP_Spring00.pdf

For a simpler account of Romer's *AD/AS* model, look at the Bized PowerPoint presentation on aggregate demand and aggregate supply, which can also be found on the internet at **www.bized.co.uk/educators/16-19/economics/adas/presentation/adas.ppt**

Romer's central argument is as follows. The *AD/AS* model learnt at A-level assumes that when a central bank such as the Bank of England implements monetary policy it does not allow the money supply to change. Given this assumption, the shift to the left of the *AD* curve illustrated in Figure 15.9 is indeed correct. But in recent years, monetary policy has operated in a different way, through the raising or lowering of interest rates rather than tight control of the money supply. This leads to the outcome illustrated in Figure 15.10 and *not* in Figure 15.9. Contractionary fiscal or monetary policy, and indeed a fall in any of the components of aggregate demand, reduces the rate of inflation (shown in Figure 15.10 by the symbol $\dot{P}$), but not necessarily the price level.

EXAM TIP

For the most part, when answering exam questions you should use the original *AD/AS* model in which the aggregate demand for output and aggregate supply of output are functions of the average price level, rather than the newer model in which they are functions of the inflation rate. The older model is the model set out in the specification.

SUMMARY

- The aggregate demand/aggregate supply macroeconomic model provides the main theoretical framework for answering Unit 4 examination questions.
- Macroeconomic equilibrium occurs when $AD = AS$.
- Aggregate demand is the total planned spending on the goods and services produced within the economy, per period of time.
- The aggregate demand equation $AD = C + I + G + (X - M)$ includes the different components of aggregate demand.
- The aggregate demand curve slopes downward to the right, showing that at a lower price level, more real goods and services are demanded.
- The short-run aggregate supply (*SRAS*) curve shows the quantities of real output that businesses plan to produce and sell at different price levels.
- *SRAS* curves slope upward to the right, showing that at a higher price level more real goods and services are supplied.
- The long-run aggregate supply (*LRAS*) curve is generally assumed to be vertical.
- The vertical slope of the *LRAS* curve results from the fact that the curve is located at the full-capacity level of output. Firms cannot increase output in the short run following an increase in aggregate demand.
- Expansionary fiscal and monetary policy shifts the *AD* curve to the right. Contractionary fiscal and monetary policy shifts the *AD* curve to the left.
- Supply-side policies attempt to shift the *LRAS* curve to the right.
- Changes in aggregate demand induce multiplier effects in which nominal or money national income changes by a multiple of the initial change in aggregate demand.
- The government spending multiplier is likely to be small in size. This reduces the power of fiscal policy used as a means of demand management.
- A new version of the *AD/AS* model has been developed in which the level of real output is a function of the rate of inflation rather than the price level.

Exam-style questions

1 Briefly explain the different components of aggregate demand.   (15 marks)

2 Explain the stages of the multiplier process.   (15 marks)

3 Do you agree that, to get an economy out of recession, a government should rely solely on policies aimed
  at increasing aggregate demand, and ignore the supply side of the economy? Justify your answer.   (25 marks)

4 Evaluate different policies a government might use to try to shift the *LRAS* curve to the right.   (25 marks)

Extra resources to help you revise are available online at www.hodderplus.co.uk/philipallan

Employment and unemployment

Chapter 16

On numerous occasions in recent years, when writing about employment and unemployment, I usually started by asserting that unemployment, though serious in the past, had become less and less of a problem for UK macroeconomic policy-makers. The reason for such a confident assertion was simple: after the end of a deep recession in 1992, unemployment fell more or less continuously from a peak of around 3 million to half that amount by early 2008.

Unfortunately, by early 2009 the picture had radically changed. As recession once again hit the UK economy, unemployment climbed fast to reach 2.3 million by the end of March 2009. There was a similar growth in unemployment in virtually all high-income countries such as the USA, Germany, France, Italy and Australia. In much of the developing world, where joblessness and hidden unemployment have kept billions of people in poverty, unemployment never disappeared, even in good years. Granted, millions of new jobs have been created in emerging market economies such as China and India, but not nearly enough to absorb the tens of millions of peasants moving from rural areas to the towns.

In the UK, unemployment continued to grow, as it usually does, after the recession (measured by falling GDP) had ended in mid-2009. The Labour Force Survey (LFS) measure of unemployment peaked in October 2011 at 2.68 million, falling to 2.51 million in April 2013. The Coalition government points out that although unemployment remains very high, employment in the private sector has grown significantly, though many of the new jobs are part time.

LEARNING OUTCOMES

This chapter will:

- discuss the meaning of full employment
- explain equilibrium unemployment or the natural level or rate of unemployment
- describe how employment and unemployment are measured
- remind you of the types of unemployment learnt at AS
- explain the other types of unemployment you need to know at A2
- assess the costs unemployment imposes on the jobless, their families, wider society and the economy

At AS, you became aware of the main UK measures of unemployment: the claimant count and the Labour Force Survey measure. You developed an understanding of how employment and unemployment may be determined by both demand-side and supply-side factors. You practised using production possibility curves and *AD/AS* diagrams to analyse and evaluate demand-side and supply-side causes of unemployment. Finally, the AS specification required knowledge and understanding of cyclical, frictional, seasonal and structural unemployment.

The meaning of full employment

Along with economic growth and higher living standards, achieving **full employment** or low unemployment is a major objective of macroeconomic policy. Although economists do not have a formal definition of full employment, there are at least two definitions that are often used by

> **KEY TERM**
>
> **full employment:** according to the Beveridge definition, occurs when 3% of the labour force are unemployed.

economists and politicians. The first is known as the **Beveridge definition**. In 1944, a famous White Paper on employment policy, inspired by Keynes but largely written by William Beveridge, effectively committed postwar governments to achieving full employment. William Beveridge was an economist at the London School of Economics and University College London who later became Lord Beveridge. In the White Paper, Beveridge defined full employment as occurring when unemployment falls to 3% of the labour force.

During the 1950s and 1960s, unemployment was always below 3%, so full employment, according to Beveridge's definition, was achieved during the postwar Keynesian decades. However, during and after the crisis in Keynesian economics in the 1970s, UK unemployment rose considerably above 3%, peaking at 11.3% (with over 3 million workers unemployed) in 1986. High unemployment in the mid-1980s was the result of recession at the beginning of the decade.

Likewise, the second recession suffered by the UK economy from 1990 to 1992 led to unemployment rising again to 9.9% (and 2.9 million unemployed) in 1993. Between 1997 and 2009, UK unemployment was always less than 5%, falling to meet Beveridge's definition of full employment (at 2.8%) in 2007. However, the return of recession in 2008 led again to the growth of mass unemployment, though as stated at the beginning of the chapter unemployment peaked at 2.68 million, a lower total than in the earlier recessions, despite the fact that the size of the total labour force had been growing.

Free-market economists generally favour a second definition of full employment, partly because they regard Beveridge's 3% definition as too arbitrary. Free-market economists define full employment in terms of the aggregate demand for and the aggregate supply of labour in the economy, as illustrated in Figure 16.1. The downward-sloping aggregate demand curve for labour (AD_L) shows that as the *real wage rate* paid to workers falls, employers or entrepreneurs are willing to employ more labour. There are two main reasons for this:

- In the short run, labour's diminishing marginal product means that it is unprofitable for firms to take on more workers unless the cost of hiring labour falls.
- The real wage falls relative to the cost of capital, firms substitute labour for capital and adopt more labour-intensive methods of production.

In contrast to the aggregate demand curve for labour, the aggregate supply curve for labour (AS_L) slopes upward, showing that workers are prepared to supply more labour as the real wage rate rises. Again, there are two main reasons for this:

- As the real wage rate rises, workers with jobs are prepared to work longer hours.
- People who are unwilling to join the economically active labour force at lower real wage rates, such as family members with children, decide to supply labour at a higher real wage rate.

For free-market economists, full employment occurs at the market-clearing real wage rate at which the number of workers wishing to work equals the number of workers employers wish to hire. In Figure 16.1 this is shown at the level of employment E_{FE}, at the real wage rate of w_{FE}.

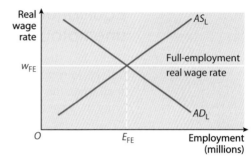

Figure 16.1 Full employment illustrated in the economy's aggregate labour market

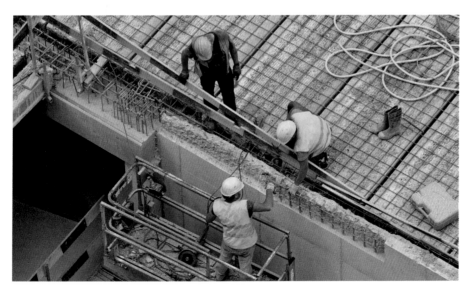

Labourers working on a building site

EXAM TIP

The natural rate of unemployment (NRU) is the unemployment rate when unemployment is restricted to its equilibrium level. I explain the NRU in detail in Chapter 17.

Equilibrium unemployment or the natural level of unemployment

Figure 16.1 shows the economy's aggregate labour market in a state of balance or rest, i.e. in *equilibrium*. It appears from the diagram that there is *no* unemployment at all when the labour market is in equilibrium. But as Figure 16.2 now shows, this is not the case.

For free-market economists, full employment does not necessarily mean that every single member of the working population is in work. Instead, it means a situation in which the number of people wishing to work at the going market real wage rate equals the number of workers that employers wish to hire at this real wage rate.

But even this definition needs qualifying, since in a dynamic economy change is constantly taking place, with some industries declining and others growing. Workers moving between jobs may decide to take a break between the two employments. This is called *frictional* unemployment. As new products are developed and demand and cost conditions change, firms demand more of some labour skills while the demand for other types of labour declines. This leads to *structural* unemployment. Frictional and structural unemployment make up what is called **equilibrium unemployment**. Equilibrium unemployment exists even with the real wage rate at its market-clearing level. Expressed as a *rate* of unemployment, rather than as a *level*, this is the **natural rate of unemployment (NRU)**. I explain and examine the NRU in more detail in the next chapter on inflation.

In Figure 16.2, the AS_{LN} curve represents all the workers available for work and not just those willing to work at different real wage rates. Full employment occurs at E_{FE}, depicted where the AD_L and AS_L curves intersect at point X. In this situation equilibrium unemployment, or the natural level of unemployment, is measured by the distance from X to Z, or E_1 minus E_{FE}.

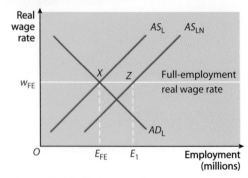

Figure 16.2 Equilibrium unemployment

Measuring employment and unemployment

The employment rate

Figure 16.3 shows changes in the UK employment rate for those over the school-leaving age, covering the years from April 2008 until April 2013. The employment rate is strongly correlated with the economic cycle, rising in the recovery and boom phases of the cycle, but falling when growth slows down or becomes negative. However, the employment and unemployment cycles usually lag a few months behind the output cycle. Employers hang on to their best workers at the beginning of a downturn, until they are sure that demand for their output is actually falling. Likewise, employers tend to wait and see at the beginning of a recovery period, offering overtime to their current employees before deciding to recruit new workers.

The employment rate measures the number of people in employment (working for at least 1 hour a week) as a percentage of the total population aged from 16 to 64. As Figure 16.3 shows, UK employment fell from a peak 73% in 2008 to less than 70.5% in the spring of 2010 and again in late 2011. The employment rate climbed back to 71.5% early in 2013. Be careful in interpreting this figure, which does not imply that the unemployment rate was 28.5%. The Labour Force Survey unemployment rate was in fact 7.8%. The employment and unemployment rates (i.e. the rates for the economically *active*) are measured as percentages of the total population aged 16 to 64, which in January 2013 included 22.4% who were economically *inactive*.) **Economically inactive** people are not in work and do not meet the internationally agreed definition of unemployment. They are people without a job who have not actively sought work in the last 4 weeks and/or are not available to start work in the next 2 weeks. In January 2013, there were 29.76 million people in employment aged 16 and over, 2.51 million unemployed and 8.99 million economically inactive.

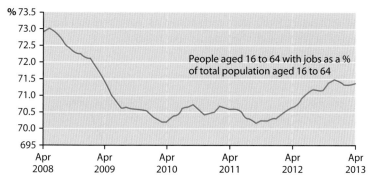

Figure 16.3 Changes in the UK employment rate, April 2008 to April 2013

Source: Labour Force Survey, ONS, June 2013

The unemployment rate

The Labour Force Survey

Two methods are used to calculate UK unemployment, but the one favoured by the government is the **Labour Force Survey (LFS)** method. The LFS, which uses internationally recognised definitions recommended by the International Labour Organisation (ILO), is a quarterly survey of 60,000 households. People are counted as unemployed if they are actively seeking work (that is, if they have been looking for a job in the last 4 weeks) and have not had a job in the week in question.

> **KEY TERM**
>
> **Labour Force Survey (LFS):** estimates unemployment by surveying 60,000 households to see if people are looking for work.

The claimant count

Before the switch to the LFS method of measurement, the government gave more attention to the monthly **claimant count**. This is a by-product of the administrative system for paying out unemployment-related benefits. The main benefit is the **jobseeker's allowance**, which in 2013 was merged into a new broader benefit, universal credit. Many economists believe that the claimant count provides an inaccurate measure of true unemployment. Free-market economists argue that the claimant count overstates true unemployment because many claimants are either not genuinely looking for work or not genuinely unemployed because they already have undeclared jobs in the informal economy.

> **KEY TERM**
>
> **claimant count:** measures the number of people claiming unemployment-related benefits.

But in other ways, the claimant count understates true unemployment. The toughening up of eligibility requirements in the 1980s and early 1990s reduced the claimant count without actually reducing unemployment. In addition, various groups of unemployed, such as young workers on government training schemes and unemployed workers approaching retirement (who were reclassified as 'early retired') have been removed from the register even though they would like full-time jobs.

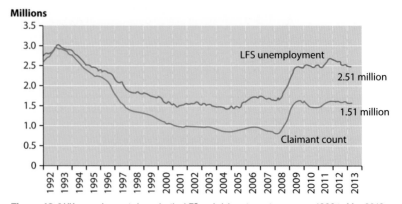

Figure 16.4 UK unemployment shown by the LFS and claimant count measures, 1992 to May 2013

Source: Office for National Statistics

Interpreting the data

The data in Figure 16.4 show LFS unemployment peaking at 3.02 million in January 1993, just after GDP began to recover from recession. There was then a more or less continuous fall over an 11-year period from 1993 to 2004. By 2001, unemployment had fallen below the psychologically important level of 1 million, at least when measured by the claimant count. The fall in unemployment is explained by the performance of the UK economy over most of the 1990s and early 2000s. Indeed, some economists believe that the economy was experiencing a second golden era (the first one having been in the golden age of Keynesian economics in the 1950s and 1960s). By the early 2000s, many communities in the UK, particularly in southeast England, were fully employed. However, much of the growth in employment was in the public sector. Relatively few new private sector jobs were created.

LFS unemployment fell to its lowest level of 1.4 million in September 2004 and then began to rise. However, the main increase in unemployment occurred when recession hit the UK economy in mid-2008. Compared to previous downturns, the 2008 recession led to job cuts right across the private sector. Even before the recession began, manufacturing had ceased to be a major employer of UK labour. Major manufacturing employers had gone to the wall and shed their labour forces, either in previous recessions, or, as in the case of MG Rover, when the economy as a whole was doing well. Unlike previous recessions, it was the previously resilient sectors such as banking and finance, and retailing, that were experiencing the greatest number of closures and mass redundancies.

But while private sector employment performed less well than public sector employment in the early 2000s, change of government from Labour to the Conservative-led Coalition in 2010 produced the opposite result. Swingeing public sector cuts reduced public sector employment, but private sector employment has grown. Critics have argued that many of the newly created jobs are not 'proper' jobs, in the sense that workers who would prefer to work full time have had to accept part-time employment at much lower rates of pay.

Causes or types of unemployment

As I mentioned at the beginning of the chapter, you first came across frictional, seasonal, structural and cyclical unemployment last year at AS. Before explaining the other causes or types of unemployment you must now learn, I shall remind you of what you should already know.

Frictional unemployment

Frictional unemployment, which is also known as **transitional unemployment**, is unemployment that occurs as people are between jobs. As its name suggests, this type of unemployment results from frictions in the labour market that create a delay or time-lag during which a worker is unemployed when moving from one job to another. Note that the definition of frictional unemployment assumes that a job vacancy exists and that frictions in the job market prevent

> **KEY TERM**
>
> **frictional unemployment:** unemployment that occurs while people are between jobs.

unemployed workers from filling vacancies. It follows that the number of unfilled job vacancies is a measure of the level of frictional unemployment in the economy.

Among the causes of frictional unemployment are geographical and occupational immobilities of labour, which prevent laid-off workers from filling job vacancies immediately. Family ties, ignorance about vacancies in other parts of the country and, above all, the cost of moving and obtaining housing are responsible for the *geographical* immobility of labour. The need for training and the effects of restrictive practices and discrimination in labour markets are among the causes of *occupational* immobility.

The **search theory of unemployment** provides a further explanation of frictional unemployment. Consider the situation illustrated in Figure 16.5, in which a worker earning £1,000 a week in a skilled professional occupation loses his job. While there appear to be no vacancies in his current line of work, there are vacancies for low-skilled office workers earning around £300 a week. Suppose now that the newly unemployed worker sets his *aspirational wage* at £1,000. This means that he will choose to remain unemployed, at least to start with, rather than to fill the lower-paid vacancy. The lower weekly wage on offer, and perhaps also poorer conditions of work and status associated with the lower-paid job, render the vacancy unattractive. He also lacks accurate information about the state of the job market. All this means that he needs to search the labour market to find out whether better-paid and higher-status vacancies exist.

Under this interpretation, frictional unemployment is a voluntary search period in which newly unemployed workers scan the labour market, searching for vacancies that are likely to meet their aspirations. There are a number of ways in which this voluntary search period can end. First, the job searcher eventually learns of a vacancy that meets his initial aspiration and for which he is qualified. Indeed, the vacancy may have been there all the time but, until he searched the job market, the worker did not know about it. Second, the vacancy may have arisen during his search period, perhaps resulting from a general improvement in the labour market. Third, he may end his voluntary unemployment as soon as he realises that his initial aspirations were unrealistically high, meaning he decides to settle for a lower-paid, less attractive job.

Figure 16.5 Search theory and frictional unemployment

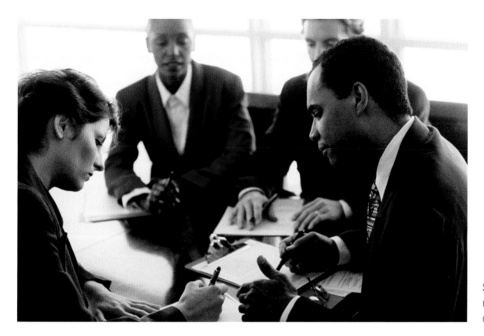

Skilled professionals are
unlikely to want low-paid
office jobs

Long search periods, which increase the amount of frictional unemployment in the economy, can be caused by the welfare benefit system. Without welfare benefits, search periods must be financed by running down stocks of savings, or through the charity of family and friends. In this situation, the threat of poverty creates incentives to search the job market more vigorously and to reduce aspirational wage levels. However, the availability of a **state safety net** of unemployment and other income-related welfare benefits, together in some cases with redundancy payments, permits unemployed workers to finance longer voluntary search periods. Because of this, free-market economists support a reduction in the real value of unemployment benefits relative to take-home pay in work, together with restricting the benefits to those who can prove they are genuinely looking for work. They believe that these policies create incentives for the unemployed to reduce aspirations quickly, which in turn shortens search periods.

The **replacement ratio** is a useful concept to use when analysing unemployment. For a relatively low-paid worker losing a job, the replacement ratio is a factor influencing the length of time searching for work while unemployed. It is given by the following formula:

$$\text{replacement ratio} = \frac{\text{disposable income out of work}}{\text{disposable income in work}} \times 100$$

The size of the replacement ratio is determined largely by the level of welfare benefits claimable when unemployed, relative to income after taxation and receipt of benefits when in work. A replacement ratio of 100% means that a worker is no better off in work than out of work, living off the state.

Even for low-paid workers, replacement ratios are seldom as high as 100%. Nonetheless, high replacement ratios approaching 100% destroy the incentive to work, at least in the formal economy. For people whose job prospects are poor, a high replacement ratio leads to the **unemployment trap**, which I briefly mentioned in Chapter 13. For the worker shown in Figure 16.5, the replacement ratio equals *B/A*. Point *B* shows the level of welfare benefit claimable out of work, while point *A* shows disposable income in work.

Casual and seasonal unemployment

Casual unemployment is a special case of frictional unemployment, occurring when workers are laid off on a short-term basis in trades such as tourism, agriculture, catering and building. **Seasonal unemployment** is casual unemployment resulting from seasonal fluctuations in demand: for example, building workers laid off during cold winter months.

> **KEY TERMS**
>
> **seasonal unemployment:** results from seasonal fluctuations in the demand for labour.
>
> **structural unemployment:** results from the structural decline of industries and the inability or difficulty of workers switching to new industries.

Structural unemployment

Structural unemployment results from the structural decline of industries, unable to compete or adapt in the face of either changing demand and new products or the emergence of more efficient competitors in other countries. Structural unemployment is also caused by changing skill requirements as industries change ways of producing their products.

Technological unemployment is a special case of structural unemployment, resulting from the successful growth of new industries using labour-saving technology. In contrast to **mechanisation** (workers operating machines), which has usually increased the overall demand for labour, **automation** (machines operating other machines) reduces the demand for labour. Whereas the growth of mechanised industry increases employment, automation of production can lead to the shedding of labour, even when industry output is expanding.

The growth of international competition in an increasingly globalised economy is an important cause of structural unemployment. During the Keynesian era from the 1950s to the 1970s, structural unemployment in the UK was concentrated in regions where nineteenth-century staple industries such as textiles and shipbuilding were suffering structural decline. Regional unemployment caused by the decline of **sunset industries** was more than offset by the growth of employment elsewhere in the UK in the **sunrise industries** that replaced them. However, in the severe recessions of the early 1980s and the early 1990s, structural unemployment affected almost all regions in the UK, as **deindustrialisation** spread across the manufacturing base. In the 2008 recession, deindustrialisation spread to service sector industries.

It is not easy to separate changes in structural unemployment from other causes of unemployment, particularly changes in aggregate demand. Manufacturing output grew in many of the years between 1993 and 2008, but manufacturing employment fell. However, during these years, there was a danger of exaggerating the growth of unemployment in manufacturing industries because many activities, ranging from cleaning to information technology maintenance, previously undertaken in-house by manufacturing firms, were out-sourced to external service-sector providers.

Structural unemployment has occured within the service sector, partly due to the increasing use of information and communication technology (ICT) and automated services. Call centre employment has grown significantly in the service sector in recent years. However, a decline has been forecast, partly due to call centres moving overseas, but also because companies employ automated communication software rather than humans to provide customer services.

Disequilibrium unemployment

As I explained earlier in the chapter, equilibrium unemployment, which is illustrated in Figure 16.2, comprises the frictional and structural unemployment occurring when the labour market is in equilibrium. By contrast, as the name indicates, disequilibrium unemployment results from the labour market being out of equilibrium. This occurs when:

- the aggregate supply of labour exceeds the aggregate demand for labour
- labour market imperfections prevent the real wage rate falling to restore labour market equilibrium (**wage stickiness**)

There are two main types of disequilibrium unemployment. These are:

- classical unemployment or real-wage unemployment
- Keynesian, cyclical or demand-deficient unemployment

Classical unemployment or real-wage unemployment

In the 1920s, large-scale persistent unemployment occurred in the United Kingdom, preceding the spread of unemployment worldwide in the Great Depression of the 1930s. Much of British unemployment in the 1920s probably resulted from the lack of competitiveness and decline of nineteenth-century staple industries such as shipbuilding and textiles. This problem was made worse by an overvalued exchange rate. However, the pre-Keynesians blamed a substantial part of the unemployment on excessively high wages.

Unemployment caused by excessively high wage rates is called **classical unemployment** or **real-wage unemployment**. This type of disequilibrium unemployment is illustrated in Figure 16.6. In the diagram, full employment is determined where the aggregate demand for labour equals the aggregate supply of labour, at the real wage rate w_{FE}. However, suppose wages are fixed at a higher real rate, at w_1 rather than w_{FE}. At this real wage rate, employers wish to hire E_1 workers, but E_2 workers wish to supply their labour. There is excess supply of labour in the labour market.

> **KEY TERM**
>
> **classical** or **real-wage unemployment:** a form of disequilibrium unemployment that occurs when the aggregate labour market fails to clear. This is caused by real wage rates being too high.

As I have mentioned, the pre-Keynesians believed that, as long as the labour market remained competitive, the resulting classical or real-wage unemployment would be temporary. Competitive forces in the labour market would cure the problem, bidding down the real wage rate to w_{FE}, thereby eliminating the excess supply of labour. Full employment would quickly be restored when the number of workers willing to work equalled the number that firms wished to hire.

But suppose labour market rigidity, perhaps caused by trade unions, prevents the real wage rate falling below w_1. In this situation, the market mechanism fails to work properly, the excess supply of labour persists, and real-wage or classical unemployment occurs. Pre-Keynesian free-market economists blamed trade unions and other causes of labour market imperfection for the resulting mass

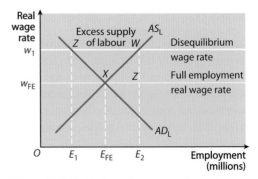

Figure 16.6 Classical or real-wage unemployment

unemployment. In their view, responsibility for unemployment lay with the workers in work and their trade unions who, by refusing to accept lower wages, prevented the unemployed from pricing themselves into jobs.

Cyclical, Keynesian or demand-deficient unemployment

In the inter-war years in the 1920s and 1930s, John Maynard Keynes argued that deficient aggregate demand was the main cause of persistent mass unemployment in the UK economy. Pre-Keynesian economists did not accept this explanation. They believed that although deficient demand can occur in the economy, the resulting **cyclical unemployment** (as they called it) would quickly be eliminated by the self-regulating nature of market forces.

To explain the difference between the pre-Keynesian (free-market) and Keynesian views on the existence of deficient demand in the economy, I must introduce **Say's Law**, named after an early nineteenth-century French economist, Jean-Baptiste Say. In popular form, Say's Law states that supply creates its own demand. Whenever an output, or supply, is produced, factor incomes such as wages and profits are generated that are just sufficient, *if spent*, to purchase the output at the existing price level, thereby creating a demand for the output produced. Stated thus, there is nothing controversial about Say's Law; it is really a statement that is true by definition.

The controversial and critical issue concerns whether the *potential* demand or incomes generated are *actually* spent on the output produced. The pre-Keynesians believed that the incomes are spent and that Say's Law holds. Keynes argued that under some circumstances incomes are saved and not spent and that Say's Law breaks down and the resulting deficient demand causes unemployment.

Figure 16.7 shows how **demand-deficient unemployment** occurs. In panel (a) of the diagram, macroeconomic equilibrium is initially at point X at the full-employment

KEY TERM

demand-deficient unemployment: also known as **cyclical** and **Keynesian unemployment,** this is unemployment caused by deficient aggregate demand in the economy.

level of output y_{FE}. However, a significant fall in aggregate demand, caused for example by a collapse of consumer and business confidence, shifts the AD curve inward from AD_1 to AD_2. Real output falls to y_2, which is considerably below y_{FE}.

Panel (b) of Figure 16.7 shows what happens in the economy's aggregate labour market following the fall in the aggregate demand for output. Producing the level of output y_2 requires fewer workers than level of output y_{FE}. As a result, the curve showing employers' aggregate demand for labour shifts inward from AD_{L1} to AD_{L2}. What happens next depends on whether real wage rates are flexible and adjust to the new situation, or are 'sticky' and inflexible downward. Given wage flexibility (as assumed by free-market economists), the real wage falls from w_{FE} to w_2. Employment also falls, but only to E_2. However, if wage rates are sticky, as Keynesians assume, the real wage rate may remain at w_{FE}. Given this outcome, demand-deficient unemployment is higher, with employment at E_3.

(a) A leftward shift of the AD curve leads to deficient aggregate demand

(b) The result is a shift in the employers' aggregate demand for labour curve

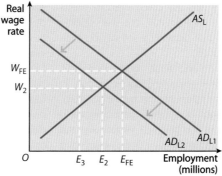

Figure 16.7 Demand-deficient or cyclical unemployment

The costs and consequences of unemployment

Unemployment is a waste of human capital. By definition, when unemployment occurs, the economy produces inside its production possibility frontier. Nevertheless, free-market economists believe that a certain amount of unemployment is necessary to make the economy function better. They believe that, by providing downward pressure on wage rates, unemployment reduces inflationary pressures. However, unemployment widens income differentials and increases absolute and relative poverty. Higher unemployment also means greater spending on unemployment and poverty-related benefits, the opportunity cost of which is less spending on the provision of hospitals, schools and other useful resources.

Unemployment is obviously bad for the unemployed themselves and for their families, largely through the way in which the low incomes that accompany unemployment lead to low standards of living. However, the costs of unemployment for the unemployed go further than this. Apart from situations in which the unemployed enjoy having 24 hours of leisure time each day and every day, or when the 'unemployed' are engaged in the black economy, unemployment destroys hope in the future. The unemployed become marginalised from normal economic and human activity and their self-esteem is reduced and sometimes shattered. Families suffer increased health risks, greater stress, a reduction in the quality of diet, an increased risk of marital break-up, and social exclusion caused by the loss of work and income. The longer the duration of unemployment, the greater is the loss of marketable skills in the labour market. Labour market hysteresis occurs.

CASE STUDY 16.1

The credit crunch and aggregate demand

By late 2008, the view that modern unemployment is caused primarily by supply-side factors had been overtaken by events. There is no doubt that the main cause of the massive increase in unemployment in the recession that hit the world economy was a collapse of aggregate demand on a global scale. The key event that triggered the collapse of demand was the credit crunch, which originated in the USA in August 2007, but then quickly spread to reduce aggregate demand in other countries including the United Kingdom.

Virtually all firms, large and small, require a reliable supply of credit or bank lending in order to remain in business. In normal circumstances, the banking system provides this liquidity, which businesses, consumers and governments usually take for granted. Historically, the source of this liquidity stemmed from banks borrowing household savings, which the banks then lent on for others to spend.

However, by 2007, banks throughout the world, but particularly in America, were raising the funds they lent to customers by borrowing from each other rather than from households. The funds were borrowed on the inter-bank market. In the USA, much of the borrowed funds were lent in the form of mortgages to low-income customers who

were bad credit risks. These loans became known as *sub-prime* mortgages (in contrast to *prime* mortgages, which are secured loans granted to low-risk home owners).

From a bank's point of view, a mortgage granted to a customer is an *asset*. For the borrower, it is a *liability*, since the house owner must eventually pay back the loan and pay interest in the intervening months and years. By definition, a sub-prime mortgage is a risky asset since there is a danger of the loan turning into a bad debt, which the bank owning the loan cannot recover. In 2007, the credit crunch developed because the banks that had created sub-prime mortgages repackaged the risky assets and sold them on to other banks as if they were prime mortgages. In essence, banks were buying 'toxic debt' from each other, without realising the repackaged assets were extremely risky. As banks realised that many of their so-called 'assets' were more or less worthless, the situation quickly deteriorated and the supply of liquidity began to freeze. Banks became unwilling to lend to each other because they distrusted each other's credit-worthiness. At the next stage, the credit crunch triggered a financial meltdown when banks either collapsed (Lehman Brothers in the USA) or were nationalised by governments (Northern Rock in the UK).

Follow-up questions

1 Why is a supply of liquidity so important for an economy to function properly?
2 How did the credit crunch affect business and consumer confidence and thence aggregate demand?

Appropriate government policies to reduce unemployment

Governments generally implement policies to try to reduce unemployment, but the appropriate policy obviously depends on identifying correctly the underlying cause of unemployment. For example, if unemployment is diagnosed incorrectly in terms of demand deficiency, when the true cause is structural, a policy of fiscal or monetary expansion to stimulate aggregate demand will be ineffective and inappropriate. Indeed, in such circumstances reflation of demand would create excess demand, which raises the price level through demand-pull inflation, with no lasting beneficial effects upon employment.

In the late 1990s and early 2000s, it was generally agreed, by Keynesians as well as by free-market economists, that the dominant cause of unemployment in countries such as the UK lay on the supply side of the economy rather than on the demand side. There was no evidence in these years of deficient aggregate demand. However, there was disagreement on the appropriate policies to improve supply-side performance. Free-market economists argue that poor supply-side performance was the legacy of the three decades of Keynesian interventionism from the 1950s to 1970s. In the free-market view, the economic role of the state should be reduced to cut frictional, structural and real-wage unemployment.

Free-market economists argue that by setting markets free, encouraging competition and fostering private enterprise and the entrepreneurial spirit, an enterprise culture can be created in which the price mechanism, and not the government, delivers economic growth and reduces unemployment. Free-market economists believe that the correct role of government is to create the conditions in which the market mechanism and private enterprise function properly. This is done by controlling inflation, promoting competitive markets and maintaining the rule of law and social order. Keynesian economists disagree, believing that unemployment results from a massive market failure that can be cured only by interventionist policies to modify markets and make them function better.

SUMMARY

- Full employment, or low unemployment, is a major macroeconomic objective.
- There is no single accepted definition of full employment, though full employment is most usually defined as occurring when the number of workers wishing to work equals the number of workers that employers wish to hire.
- There is still some unemployment, known as the equilibrium level of unemployment, when the economy is 'fully employed'.
- Equilibrium unemployment, which is also known as the natural level of unemployment, comprises frictional, seasonal and structural unemployment.
- Disequilibrium unemployment occurs when the economy's aggregate labour market fails to clear.
- There are two main types of disequilibrium unemployment: classical or real-wage unemployment and demand-deficient, cyclical or Keynesian unemployment.
- Classical unemployment is caused by real wage rates being too high. The policy solution is wage cuts.
- Cyclical or Keynesian unemployment is caused by deficient aggregate demand. The policy solution is to use fiscal and/or monetary policy to increase aggregate demand.
- To reduce unemployment without undesirable side-effects it is important to diagnose the cause or causes of unemployment and then to implement appropriate policies.
- Unemployment imposes significant costs on the economy and on the unemployed themselves and their families.

Exam-style questions

1 Explain the main causes of unemployment. **(15 marks)**

2 Explain different ways in which frictional and structural unemployment can be produced. **(15 marks)**

3 Assess the costs and benefits of unemployment. **(25 marks)**

4 Do you agree that it is supply-side, rather than demand-side, factors which have been the more important cause of UK unemployment in recent years? Justify your answer. **(25 marks)**

Extra resources to help you revise are available online at www.hodderplus.co.uk/philipallan

Inflation and the Phillips curve

Chapter 17

Forty or so years ago in the 1970s, accelerating and highly variable rates of inflation caused acute problems in the UK economy. As a result, in the monetarist decade of the 1980s, the control of inflation was elevated to pole position in the league table of government macroeconomic policy objectives. Eventually, the policy became remarkably successful. From 1993 until 2007, the UK inflation rate remained within 1% above or below the 2% inflation rate target set by the government, apart from on one occasion when it nudged over the 3% upper limit.

Until 2008, control of inflation was accompanied by arguably the longest period of continuous economic growth the UK has ever experienced, at least in modern times. However, in 2007 things started to go wrong. Along with other economies, the UK was hit by a sudden burst of cost-push inflation, mostly imported from the rest of the world via escalating oil, gas, commodity and food prices. Together with the credit crunch that began in the USA, severe cost-push inflation undermined business and consumer confidence. Then, in 2008, aggregate demand collapsed and the UK economy entered recession. The rate of inflation began to fall and many economists believed that deflation would replace inflation. However, except for in a very short period, deflation did not occur and at the time of writing (July 2013) the rate of inflation remains stubbornly above the government's 2% target.

LEARNING OUTCOMES

This chapter will:
- remind you of the meaning of inflation, deflation and reflation
- show how the UK rate of inflation has changed in recent decades
- describe how a price index is constructed to measure the average price level
- summarise how theories of the causes of inflation have changed over the years
- recap on the theories of demand-pull and cost-push inflation you learnt at AS
- introduce Phillips curve analysis
- use the concept of the long-run Phillips curve to develop the monetarist theory of inflation
- link the long-run Phillips curve to the natural rate of unemployment (NRU)
- explain how expectations of future inflation may affect current inflation
- assess the costs and benefits of inflation

WHAT YOU SHOULD ALREADY KNOW

At AS, you learnt how, along with other objectives such as economic growth and full employment, control of inflation is one of the government's major macroeconomic policy objectives. You also learnt about policy conflicts and policy trade-offs, for example the conflict between controlling inflation and achieving full employment. You should also understand how price indices, such as the CPI and the RPI, are used to measure the price level and the rate of inflation. The AS specification required knowledge and understanding of the basic differences between demand-pull and cost-push price inflation and of the difference between price inflation and price deflation. You also studied control of inflation as the main UK monetary policy objective.

Inflation, deflation and reflation

Inflation is best defined as a persistent or continuous rise in the price level, or as a continuing fall in the value of money. Deflation is the opposite, namely a persistent tendency for the price level to fall or for the value of money to rise. However, the overall price level has seldom fallen in western industrialised countries since the 1930s, though as I have stated, in 2009, many economists feared that a deepening recession might lead to a falling average price level. The term 'deflation' is therefore usually applied in a rather looser way to describe a reduction in aggregate demand and levels of economic activity, output and employment. A deflationary policy uses fiscal or monetary policy to reduce aggregate demand, in order to take excess demand out of the system. Likewise, reflation refers to an increase in economic activity and output, and a reflationary policy stimulates aggregate demand. Often, inflation is 'reflation gone wrong', stimulating the price level rather than real output and employment.

> **KEY TERMS**
>
> **inflation:** a continuous and persistent rise in the price level and fall in the value of money.
>
> **deflation:** a continuous and persistent fall in the price level and increase in the value of money.
>
> **reflation:** an increase in real output and employment following an increase in aggregate demand.

Changes in the UK inflation rate

Until 2003, the UK government measured changes in the rate of inflation through changes in the RPIX. The **retail prices index (RPI)** measures the headline rate of inflation, whereas **RPIX** measures the underlying rate of inflation: that is, the headline rate minus mortgage interest rates. Until recently, the government continued to use the RPI for deciding the level at which welfare benefits such as the state pension and the jobseeker's allowance should be set, but it now uses the CPI rather than the RPI.

Since 2003 the consumer prices index (CPI) has also been central to monetary policy. Currently, the Bank of England aims to hit a CPI target rate of inflation of 2%. The government justifies this on the ground that the CPI is based on the method of measuring the price level in the European Union. Handily for the

> **KEY TERMS**
>
> **consumer prices index (CPI):** the UK price index most central to UK monetary policy.
>
> **price index:** an index number that measures the average price level.

government, the CPI inflation rate is almost always lower than the RPI inflation rate, which should make it easier both to hit the 2% target and to slow down increases in index-linked benefits and public sector pay.

Figure 17.1, which shows how the rates of CPI and RPI inflation changed in the UK between 2000 and 2013, divides into five distinct data periods. These were:

- **2000–2006.** The so-called **nice** (non-inflationary, consistently expansionary) years, when the UK inflation rate was almost always close to the central target of 2%.
- **2007–mid-2008.** The UK economy suffered a severe bout of cost-push inflation, as rising prices of imported oil, gas and food pushed up the inflation rate to 5.2%, well above the upper 3% target ceiling. *Nice-ness* had come to an end and some economists gloomily predicted a return to 1970s-style **stagflation** of low or non-existent growth combined with unacceptably high inflation.
- **Mid-2008–late 2009.** The inflation rate began to fall, with the previous bout of cost inflation having passed through the system. The UK and other economies had now entered a severe recession, and many economists and politicians feared that deflation (falling prices) would replace inflation. The RPI inflation rate, but not the CPI inflation rate, did indeed become negative for a few months.
- **Late 2009–late 2011.** Both the CPI and the RPI inflation rates rose steeply, with both rates peaking above 5% in September 2011. Once again, rising inflation was fuelled by the rising prices of imported energy, food and commodities, and also by China increasing the prices of many of its exports of manufactured goods.
- **Late 2011 onward.** The end of this bout of imported cost-push inflation contributed to a fall, and then to a stabilisation, in the UK inflation rate, which nevertheless (at the time of writing in July 2013) remains above the government's target of 2% CPI inflation.

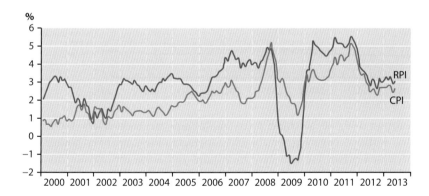

Figure 17.1 The annual UK inflation rate, measured by changes in the retail prices index and the consumer prices index, 2000–2013

Source: Office for National Statistics

Constructing a price index to measure inflation

Two main tasks are undertaken in the construction of the CPI and the RPI. These are the choice of a representative sample of goods, and the *weighting* of each good in the sample.

Choice of sample

According to the **Office for National Statistics (ONS)**, the most useful way to think about both the CPI and RPI is to imagine a shopping basket containing those goods and services on which people typically spend their money. As the prices of the various items in the basket change over time, so does the total cost of the basket. Movements in the CPI and RPI indices represent the changing cost of this representative shopping basket (see Figure 17.2).

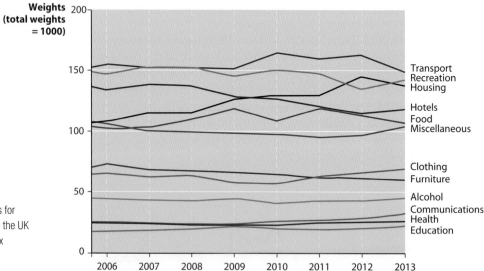

Figure 17.2 Weights for goods and services in the UK consumer prices index

Source: Office for National Statistics

Currently, around 180,000 separate price quotations are used every month in compiling the indices, covering nearly 700 representative consumer goods and services, for which prices are collected in around 150 areas throughout the UK. The goods and services that figure in the representative sample are derived from the annual **Living Costs and Food Survey (LCFS)**, in which 7,000 households throughout the country are asked to record what they spent in a given fortnight and to give details of big purchases over a longer period. Every year the contents of the sample are revised to reflect changes in how the average family spends its income.

There are some specific differences in the commodity coverage of the CPI and RPI indices. For example, the RPI basket includes a number of items chosen to represent owner-occupier housing costs, including mortgage interest payments and depreciation costs, all of which are excluded from the CPI. Otherwise, the contents of the CPI and RPI baskets are very similar, although the precise weights attached to the individual items in each index do differ.

Weighting the goods in the sample

Each item in the sample is given a *weight* to reflect its relative importance in the expenditure pattern of a typical family.

The contents of the RPI and CPI baskets of goods and services and their expenditure weights are updated each year.

CASE STUDY 17.1

Changes in the national shopping basket

Every March since 1947 the Office for National Statistics has revised the items in the national shopping baskets from which the CPI and the RPI are constructed. However, because of a lag effect, the annual review has gained a reputation for including an item just as it has gone out of fashion. Here are some of the details of the changes to the CPI shopping basket made in 2013.

Champagne, symbol of the banker's bonus culture and the pre-recession consumer boom, has fallen out of the national shopping basket. Falling sales at restaurants, pubs and other outlets have left 'bubbly' unrepresentative of modern shopping habits. The ONS is replacing champagne with white rum, which is cheaper and popular with young people. In other changes, e-books read on digital readers such as Kindles are in, while digital television recorders have replaced Freeview set-top boxes. As consumers abandon traditional photography in favour of digital cameras, charges for developing and printing colour film have been ejected from the basket.

E-readers are now in the national shopping basket

Follow-up question

Why is it necessary to change each year the items in the national shopping baskets used to construct the CPI and the RPI, and the weights attached to the different items?

How theories of the causes of inflation have changed over the years

Table 17.1 provides a summary of how theories of inflation have developed over the years, together with some key events in the recent history of inflation. The following sections then explain in some detail the main theories of the causes of inflation.

Theories on the causes of inflation

Table 17.1 A summary of how the main theories of inflation have changed over the years and recent inflation events

Eighteenth century to the 1930s	The old quantity theory of money is dominant.
1930s	The problem of inflation disappears. Keynes's *General Theory* explains deflation in terms of deficient aggregate demand.
1940s	Keynes develops his *General Theory* to explain how, in conditions of full employment, excess demand can pull up the price level through demand-pull inflation.
1950s	The early monetarist theory of inflation begins to develop when Milton Friedman revives the quantity theory of money (the modern quantity theory).
1950s–1960s	Many Keynesians switch away from demand-pull to the cost-push theory of inflation.
1960s	The Keynesian demand-pull versus cost-push debate is conducted with the aid of the Phillips curve.
1968	The role of expectations in the inflationary process is incorporated into the monetarist theory of inflation. The theory of adaptive expectations is built into Milton Friedman's theory of the expectations-augmented Phillips curve (or long-run Phillips curve).
1970s	The short-run Phillips curve relationship breaks down.
1980s onward	There is controversy once again between cost-push and demand-pull explanations of inflation with New-Keynesian explanations versus monetarist and new-classical (rational expectations) explanations.
2008–2009	For a short period the problem of inflation largely disappears, being replaced by the fear of deflation or falling prices. However, fears of the return of accelerating inflation remain.
2010 onward	Inflation returns, fuelled by periods of rapidly rising prices of imported energy, food, commodities and Chinese manufactured goods. The rate of inflation exceeds the UK government's 2% CPI target.

EXAM TIP

As at AS, you must continue to understand the difference between demand-pull and cost-push inflation and be able to use *AD/AS* diagrams to illustrate both causes of inflation. Questions set at A2 require more understanding of the theories of inflation than those at AS.

The old quantity theory of money

The **quantity theory of money** is the oldest theory of inflation, dating back at least to the eighteenth century. For two centuries until the 1930s, when it went out of fashion with the Keynesian revolution, the quantity theory was *the* theory of inflation. However, Milton Friedman's revival of the quantity

KEY TERM

quantity theory of money: the theory that assumes inflation is caused by a prior increase in the money supply.

theory in modern form in the 1950s is usually regarded as marking the beginning of the monetarist counter-revolution. In recent years, the quantity theory has once again occupied a central place in debate and controversy about the causes of both inflation and deflation.

All versions of the quantity theory, old and new, are based on a special case of **demand-pull inflation**, in which rising prices are caused by excess demand. In the quantity theory, the source of excess demand is located in *monetary* rather than *real* forces, in an excess supply of money created or condoned by the government. At its simplest, the quantity theory is sometimes described as too much money chasing too few goods. The starting point for developing the theory is the **Fisher equation of exchange**, devised by an American economist, Irving Fisher, early in the twentieth century:

$$\text{money supply (stock of money)} \times \text{velocity of circulation of money} = \text{price level} \times \text{total transactions}$$

or:

$$MV = PT$$

In the Fisher equation, for a particular time period, say a year, the stock of money in the economy (M) multiplied by the velocity of circulation of money (V) equals the price level (P) multiplied by the total number of transactions (T). A transaction occurs when a good or service is bought. T measures all the purchases of goods and services in the economy. (These days, the equation is usually written as $MV = Py$, where y is real output.)

To convert the equation of exchange ($MV = PT$) into a theory of inflation, it is necessary to make three assumptions. The first two are:
- The velocity of circulation or speed at which money is spent and total transactions (which are determined by the level of real national output in the economy) are both fixed, or at least stable.
- In the quantity theory, money is a *medium of exchange* (means of payment), but *not* a store of value. This means that people quickly spend any money they receive.

Suppose the government allows the money supply to expand faster than the rate at which real national output increases. As a result, households and firms possess money balances that are greater than those they wish to hold. According to the quantity theory, these excess money balances will quickly be spent. This brings us to the third assumption in the quantity theory: changes in the money supply are assumed to bring about changes in the price level (rather than vice versa).

In summary, the main elements of the quantity theory that you need to know are:
- Initially the government creates or condones an expansion of the money supply greater than the increase in real national output.
- As a result, households and firms hold excess money balances which, when spent, pull up the price level. It is assumed that real output cannot expand in line with the increase in spending power.

Keynesian rejection of the quantity theory

Keynesians generally reject the quantity theory of money as an explanation of inflation, or claim that it only provides an explanation of rising prices when a number of highly restrictive assumptions hold. There are three ways in which Keynesians have attacked the quantity theory.

- Much of the debate between Keynesians and monetarists about the quantity theory has centred on the issue of whether the velocity of circulation of money (V) is constant. In ordinary language, V represents how often money is spent. Monetarists believe that, because money earns little or no interest, it is rational to spend quickly any extra money holdings, either on goods or on non-money financial assets such as shares. For a monetarist, it is irrational to hold idle money balances for any length of time. By contrast, Keynesians take the opposite view, arguing that under certain circumstances (particularly when share and bond prices are expected to fall), it is perfectly sensible to hold idle money balances. In this situation, to avoid capital losses they expect to suffer from falling financial asset prices, people decide to hold money instead as an idle wealth asset. They hang on to, rather than spend, their extra money holdings.

- Keynesians also attack the quantity theory by arguing that if there is spare capacity and unemployment in the economy, an increase of the money supply may increase real income and output (y and q) rather than the price level P.

- The two Keynesian attacks on the quantity theory I have so far examined accept the monetarist argument that changes in MV can cause changes in Py, but they argue that an increase in the money supply (M) does not *necessarily* result in inflation (an increase in P). Instead an increase in the money supply may be absorbed in a slowing down of the velocity of circulation of money (V), or in a reflation of real income or output, which is a good thing. The third Keynesian attack on the quantity theory is more deep seated, since it is based on the idea of *reverse causation*. Reverse causation means that, instead of changes in the money supply causing changes in the price level, the true relationship is the opposite, i.e. changes in the price level cause the money supply to change. In this interpretation, inflation is caused by cost-push institutional factors in the real economy. The money supply then passively adapts, expanding to the level required to finance the level of desired transactions that the general public undertake at the new higher price level. In essence, the money supply accommodates itself to (rather than determines) the price level. Keynesians agree with the monetarists over what they consider to be the rather trivial point that an increase in the money supply is needed to finance a higher price level and allow inflation to continue. However, the reverse causation argument rejects the view that an increase in the money supply is the cause of inflation.

Keynesians argue that if a government tightly restricts the growth of money to try to stem inflation, the main effects might be that the current level of transactions cannot be financed, so real activity will fall, resulting in higher unemployment. This effect occurred in the credit crunch that started in 2007, though the cause of the credit crunch lay not in tight control of the money supply by the government, but in a sudden collapse in the supply of money or liquidity emanating from the banking system itself.

The Keynesian demand-pull theory of inflation

The quantity theory of money and the Keynesian demand-pull theory are both demand theories of inflation, which locate the cause of inflation in excess demand for goods and services. After 1945, Keynesian economists accepted the argument that inflation results from excess demand pulling up the price level, but they rejected the quantity theory view that the source of the excess demand lies solely in excess monetary growth. Instead, Keynesians located the cause of inflation firmly in the real economy, in behavioural factors that cause the planned expenditure of economic agents (households, firms, the government and the overseas sectors) to exceed the quantity of output that the economy was capable of producing. In Keynesian theory, inflation is explained by real forces determining how people behave and not by money.

In the Keynesian era, from the 1950s to the 1970s, governments were committed to achieving full employment. Arguably, this caused people to behave in an inflationary way, both as workers and as voters. Workers and their unions bargained for money wage increases in excess of any productivity increase without fear of unemployment. At the same time in the political arena, the electorate added to the pressure of demand by voting for increased public spending and budget deficits. As a result of these pressures, excess demand for output emerged.

Nonetheless, the Keynesian demand-pull theory and the quantity theory of inflation may not really be very different. In both theories, the ultimate cause of inflation may lie with the government. In the quantity theory of money, the government's budget deficit and borrowing requirement cause monetary expansion, which first triggers and then sustains **demand-pull inflation**. In the Keynesian demand-pull theory, a budget deficit leads to an injection of spending into the circular flow of income that, with full or near-full capacity, results in excess demand.

> **KEY TERM**
>
> **demand-pull inflation:** caused by excess aggregate demand for output.

> **EXAM TIP**
>
> Students often fail to appreciate that the quantity theory of money and the monetarist theory of inflation assume that the price level is pulled up by excess demand. The main difference between monetarist and Keynesian demand-pull theories lies in their assumptions about the underlying cause of excess demand.

At A2, you can use exactly the same *AD/AS* diagrams to illustrate inflation as you used last year at AS. Figure 17.3 illustrates demand-pull inflation. Suppose aggregate demand and supply are initially represented by the curves AD_1 and *SRAS*, with macroeconomic equilibrium at point *X*. Real national output is y_1 and the price level is P_1. There is spare capacity in the economy, which means that demand-deficient unemployment is also present.

If aggregate demand increases to AD_2, real output and the price level both increase respectively to y_{FE} and P_2. Demand-deficient unemployment is eliminated, though at the expense of some inflation.

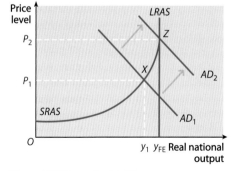

Figure 17.3 Demand-pull inflation

But once full employment arrives, real output cannot increase any more, at least in the short run. The economy is now producing at its production potential on the *LRAS* curve. Since there is no spare capacity, a further shift to the right of the aggregate demand curve would lead only to inflation, with no increase in output.

The Keynesian cost-push theory of inflation

During the Keynesian era, creeping inflation continued even when there was no evidence of excess demand in the economy.

Towards the end of the 1950s and during the 1960s and 1970s, this caused many Keynesians to switch away from the demand-pull theory of inflation to a new theory: the theory of **cost-push inflation**.

Cost theories of inflation locate the cause of inflation in structural and institutional conditions on the supply side of the economy, particularly in the labour market and the wage-bargaining process. Most cost-push theories are essentially **wage-push theories**, although other variants include **profits-push** and **import cost-push theories**. The rapid cost-push inflation that occurred in the UK in 2008 and in 2011 was caused by rises in the price of imported oil, gas, commodities such as copper, and food.

Wage-push theories generally argue that the growth of monopoly power in both the labour market and the goods market is responsible for inflation. They usually assume that wages are determined in the labour market through the process of **collective bargaining**, while in the goods market, prices are formed by a *cost-plus pricing rule* in which imperfectly competitive firms add a standard profit margin to average cost when setting prices. In labour markets, growing trade union strength in the Keynesian era enabled trade unions to bargain for money wage increases in excess of any rise in labour productivity. Monopoly firms were prepared to pay these wage increases, partly because of the costs of disrupting production and partly because they believed that they could pass cost increases on to consumers through higher prices when output was sold.

The question then arises as to why trade union militancy and power grew in the Keynesian era. The guarantee of full employment by the state and the provision of a safety net of labour protection legislation and welfare benefits may have sustained the inflationary process. In the cost-push theory this created the conditions in which trade unions could successfully be more militant.

Cost-push inflation is illustrated on an aggregate demand and supply diagram in Figure 17.4. Initially, macroeconomic equilibrium is at point X, with real output and the price level respectively at y_1 and P_1. Firms' money costs of production rise, for example, because money wages or the price of imported raw materials increases. This causes the $SRAS$ curve to move upward and to the left from $SRAS_1$ to $SRAS_2$. The cost-push inflationary process increases the price level to P_2, but higher production costs have reduced the equilibrium level of output that firms are willing to produce to y_2. The new macroeconomic equilibrium is at point Z.

Figure 17.4 Cost-push inflation

The rise of the Phillips curve

Fifty years or so ago, Keynesians could be divided into demand-pull and cost-push schools in terms of the views held by members of each school on the causes of inflation. After 1958, the debate between demand-pull and cost-push Keynesians was conducted with the aid of a statistical relationship, the **Phillips curve**, which is illustrated in Figure 17.5.

When developing the Phillips curve from his analysis of the role of aggregate demand in the economy, Phillips argued that a stable inverse statistical relationship existed between the rate of change of wages (the rate of *wage* inflation) and the percentage of the labour force unemployed. Later versions of the Phillips curve, such as the one illustrated in Figure 17.5, measure the inverse relationship between unemployment and the rate of *price* inflation.

The Phillips curve is *not* a theory of inflation, but it does give support to both Keynesian theories of inflation. In the demand-pull theory, falling unemployment is associated with excess demand, which pulls up money wages in the labour market. In the cost-push theory, falling unemployment means that trade union power increases, enabling unions to use their monopoly power to push for higher wages.

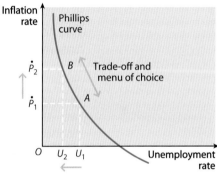

> **KEY TERM**
>
> **Phillips curve:** based on evidence from the economy, showing the relationship between the rate of inflation and the level of unemployment.

Figure 17.5 The Phillips curve

Although the Phillips curve illustrates the conflict between full employment and control of inflation as policy objectives, it also suggests how the conflict can be dealt with. Suppose unemployment initially is U_1 and the rate of inflation is $\dot{P}_1$ with the economy at point A on the Phillips curve. (Note, I am using the symbol $\dot{P}$ to show the rate of price inflation.) By increasing aggregate demand, the government can move the economy to point B. Unemployment falls to U_2, but at the cost of a higher rate of inflation at $\dot{P}_2$. By using demand management policies, it appears possible for governments to trade off between increasing the number of jobs in the economy and reducing inflation. Points such as A and B on the Phillips curve represent a menu of choice for governments when deciding an acceptable combination of unemployment and inflation.

The monetarist theory of inflation

To understand the monetarist theory of inflation, it is useful to divide its development into three stages:

- the revival in 1956 by Milton Friedman of the **quantity theory of money**
- the development, also by Milton Friedman, of the theory of the **expectations-augmented Phillips curve**, which gave rise to gradualist monetarism
- the incorporation of the theory of **rational expectations** into the explanation of the inflationary process, which became known as new-classical monetarism

In order to understand how the monetarist theory of inflation has developed through these three stages, I need first to take a look at the breakdown of the Phillips curve relationship that occurred in the 1970s.

The breakdown of the Phillips relationship

In the 1970s, the Phillips relationship broke down when accelerating inflation and growing unemployment occurred together. The nicknames **stagflation** and **slumpflation** were given to the combination of these two evils. Out of stagflation and the breakdown of the Phillips relationship developed the second and third stages in the monetarist explanation of inflation, in which theories on the role of expectations in the inflationary process were tacked on to the quantity theory of money. In the second stage in 1968 Milton Friedman developed the theory of the expectations-augmented Phillips curve. Then, in the third stage in the 1970s and 1980s, the new-classical school of monetarists explained inflation in terms of the theory of rational expectations.

The theory of the expectations-augmented Phillips curve and the natural rate of unemployment (NRU)

The word *augment* means *to add*. The rather clumsy term 'expectations-augmented Phillips curve' reflects the fact that expectations of future inflation came to be viewed as a determinant of current inflation.

Economists now generally recognise that the Phillips curve in Figure 17.5 is a **short-run Phillips curve** (*SRPC*), representing the short-run relationship between inflation and unemployment. In Figure 17.6, a vertical **long-run Phillips curve** (*LRPC*) has been added to the diagram, intersecting the short-run Phillips curve where the rate of inflation is zero. The rate of unemployment at this point is called the **natural rate of unemployment** (**NRU**), depicted by the symbol U_N. (As I explained in Chapter 16, when expressed as the number of workers unemployed, it is called the natural *level* of unemployment.)

Free-market economists argue that it is impossible to reduce unemployment below the NRU, except at the cost of suffering an ever-accelerating unanticipated inflation. This is likely to accelerate into a hyperinflation, which in any case eventually destroys the economy. The explanation for this lies in the fact that the original

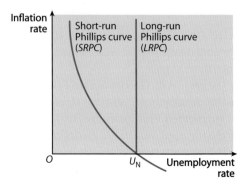

Figure 17.6 The long-run Phillips curve and the natural rate of unemployment

Keynesian explanation of the (short-run) Phillips curve wrongly took into account only the *current* rate of inflation and ignored the important influence of the *expected* rate of inflation.

The theory of the expectations-augmented Phillips curve brings together two important theories supported by modern free-market economists:
- the free-market theory of the labour market
- the theory of the role of expectations in the inflationary process

The free-market theory of the labour market assumes that the natural levels of employment and unemployment are determined at the equilibrium real wage at which workers voluntarily supply exactly the amount of labour that firms voluntarily employ.

I shall now use Figure 17.7 to introduce the role of expectations into the inflationary process. As a simplification, I shall assume that the rate of growth of labour productivity is zero and that the rate of increase of prices (price inflation) equals the rate of increase of wages (wage inflation). The economy is initially at point A, with unemployment at the natural rate U_N. At point A, the rate of inflation is zero, as is the rate of increase of money wages. I shall also assume that people form expectations of future inflation in the next time period solely on the basis of the current rate of inflation. Thus at point A, current inflation is zero, so workers expect the future rate of inflation also to be zero.

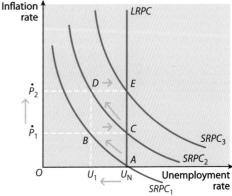

Figure 17.7 Long-run and short-run Phillips curves

Suppose the government increases aggregate demand, to trade off along Phillips curve $SRPC_1$ to a point such as B, where unemployment at U_1 is below the natural rate, U_N. Inflation initially rises to $\dot{P}_1$ (let's say 5%). But a point such as B is unsustainable. For workers to supply more labour, the real wage must rise, yet a rising real wage causes employers to demand less labour. In the short run, more workers may indeed enter the labour market in the false belief that a 5% increase in money wages is also a real wage increase. (This false belief is an example of **money illusion**.) Similarly, firms may be willing to employ more labour if they also suffer money illusion, falsely believing that rising prices mean that sales revenues are rising faster than labour costs.

This means that, to sustain an increase in employment above the natural rate, workers and employers must suffer money illusion in equal but opposite directions, thereby keeping expectations of inflation, formed in the previous time period, consistently below the actual rate to which inflation has risen. However, as workers continuously adjust their expectations of future inflation to the rising actual rate and bargain for ever-higher money wages to restore the real wage to the level necessary to reduce unemployment below U_N, the short-run Phillips curve shifts outward from $SRPC_1$ to $SRPC_2$ and so on. There is indeed a separate short-run Phillips curve for each expected rate of inflation. Further out short-run Phillips curves such as $SRPC_2$ and $SRPC_3$ are associated with higher expected rates of future inflation. Conversely, the short-run Phillips curve shifts inward when the expected rate of inflation falls.

Free-market economists argue that, in the long run, the only way to keep unemployment below the NRU is to permit the money supply to expand and finance an ever-accelerating inflation. Actual inflation always has to be above the expected rate for workers and firms to be willing respectively to supply and to demand more labour. But, as I noted earlier, accelerating inflation will eventually create a hyperinflation, which, in the resulting breakdown of economic activity, is likely to increase the NRU. Any attempt to reduce unemployment below the NRU is therefore foolhardy and irresponsible. In the short run it accelerates inflation, while in the long run it perversely increases the NRU to an unnecessarily high level.

If the government realises it made a mistake when expanding the economy to point B, it can stabilise the rate of inflation at 5%. Workers and employers 'see through' their money illusion and realise that they have confused money quantities with real quantities. As soon as this happens, they refuse respectively to supply and to demand the labour necessary to keep unemployment below the NRU. The economy now moves to point C. Once point C is reached, any further increase in aggregate demand moves the economy to point D and an inflation rate of P_2 and to a repeat of the process just described, but starting from a higher initial rate of inflation.

Rational expectations

The theory I have just described is based on the theory of adaptive expectations, in which workers and firms form expectations of what will happen in the future only on the basis of what is happening currently and upon what has happened in the recent past. However, new-classical economists favour an alternative theory of how expectations are formed, called the theory of rational expectations. According to this theory, it is unrealistic to assume that workers and firms, acting rationally in their self-interest, form expectations of future inflation solely on the basis of current or recent inflation.

KEY TERMS

adaptive expectations: describe how economic agents adapt their expectations of what is likely to happen in the future on the basis of what has happened in the recent past.

rational expectations: explain how economic agents form expectations of what is likely to happen in the future on the basis of the most up-to-date and relevant information that is available.

EXTENSION MATERIAL

The difference between adaptive expectations and rational expectations

To understand the difference between the theories of adaptive and rational expectations, consider the situation of a gambler deciding whether to place a bet on a particular horse winning a race. Three races ago, the horse ended the race in fourth position, improving to third place two races ago and to second place recently. Forming his expectations adaptively, the gambler decides to bet on the horse, expecting it now to win. But gambling on the basis of recent form alone could be less successful than a strategy that makes use of all the information available, including past form. Information about the quality of the jockey, and about other matters such as the qualities of the other horses and their jockeys, the length of the race, the state of the track, and perhaps 'inside information' provided by a stable boy, might lead to a more rational gambling decision.

This story does not mean that a gambler, forming expectations rationally, always wins his bets. He may win or lose, just as bets made on decisions formed adaptively or by picking a name out of a hat may be right or wrong. However, over a long sequence of races, it is likely that gambling decisions formed on the basis of rational expectations produce better outcomes than decisions formed adaptively or randomly. The more 'perfect' the information on which rational expectations are formed, the more likely it is that the expectations prove correct. It is less sensible to gamble on the basis of limited information when more up-to-date and relevant information is available.

Returning to the causes of inflation, new-classical economists argue that it is unrealistic to assume that a rational economic agent, acting on self-interest, forms expectations of future inflation solely on the basis of past or experienced inflation. Self-interest requires quick modification of economic behaviour in line with expectations formed on the basis of the most up-to-date information available. This means that it is *not* in people's interests to suffer money illusion.

As a result, new-classical economists reject the idea that economic agents suffer money illusion for quite long periods. If expectations are formed rationally rather than adaptively, people don't suffer from money illusion and any attempt by a government to reduce unemployment below its natural rate fails, leading solely to accelerating inflation. The correct way to reduce unemployment is to reduce the natural rate itself, rather than to increase demand to try to reduce unemployment below the NRU. To do this, the government should use appropriate free-market supply-side policies.

The incorporation of the theory of rational expectations into the explanation of the inflationary process represents the third stage in the development of monetarist and free-market theories of inflation. New-classical economists continue to accept the Friedmanite concept of the natural rate of unemployment. But whereas Milton Friedman believed that, in the short run at least, governments can trade off along a short-run Phillips curve and reduce unemployment below the natural rate, the theory of rational expectations rejects this possibility.

In new-classical thinking, it is in workers' and employers' interests to realise instantly any mistakes made when forming expectations, and to see through any attempt by an 'irresponsible' government to reflate the economy beyond the full-employment level. New-classical economists believe that in this situation, attempts by government to increase aggregate demand to stimulate output and employment are anticipated fully by private economic agents. Workers and firms modify their behaviour to offset or neutralise the effects intended by the government, so the increase in aggregate demand has no effect upon real activity and employment. In extreme new-classical economics this is the case in both the short run and the long run because output and employment are always assumed to be at their natural or equilibrium levels.

An important difference separating the adaptive and rational expectations of free-market economics is the length of time unemployment must remain above its natural rate as the cost or penalty of an attempt to reduce unemployment below the natural rate. In Friedmanite theory, the economy experiences a lengthy period of unemployment above its natural rate, to 'bleed' the system of inflationary expectations built up during the period of fiscal or monetary expansion.

In contrast to this gradualist theory, new-classical theory assumes that economic agents immediately reduce expectations of future inflation, providing they believe in the credibility of a tough free-market government's commitment to reducing inflation. Believing that the government means business in pursuing tight fiscal and monetary policies to control inflation, workers and firms immediately build a lower expected rate of inflation into their wage-bargaining and price-setting behaviour. Inflation falls quickly and painlessly, without the need for a lengthy period of unemployment above its natural level. In effect, a firmly free-market government reduces inflation by 'talking down' inflation. However, if credibility in government policy were to disappear, its ability to control inflation would also be lost. People would now expect higher prices, and would alter behaviour accordingly. Expectations of higher prices would become self-fulfilling.

Inflation psychology

It is now widely agreed by Keynesians as well as by free-market economists that what has made inflation particularly difficult to control in the UK has been the existence, built up over decades, of an **inflation psychology**. Over the years, many groups in UK society, including house owners and wage earners in strong bargaining positions, did extremely well out of inflation. For example, house owners with large mortgages had a vested interest in allowing inflation to continue, in order to reduce the real value of their personal debt. Indeed, house owners did even better when house price inflation exceeded the general rate of inflation. In this situation, the real value of houses increased while the real value of mortgages fell.

Between the late 1990s and 2007, the UK government and the Bank of England succeeded in reducing people's expectations of inflation (except with regard to house price inflation). Therefore, because of the benign effect on people's behaviour, it became much easier to control inflation. The authorities had successfully 'talked down' the rate of inflation. However, as recent bursts of cost-push inflation have shown, circumstances can quickly change for the worse and while inflation can be dormant, it is never dead.

The possible problem of price deflation

In the late 1990s and early 2000s, when the UK inflation rate fell toward 1%, some economists argued that inflation would soon be replaced with deflation (i.e. a continuously falling price level). The fear of deflation resurfaced in 2008 and 2009. For a few months the inflation rate, measured by changes in the RPI, was negative. This was really too short a period for the supposed disadvantages of falling prices to emerge. Extended price deflation may bring its own problems. When people believe prices are going to fall, they postpone big ticket consumption decisions, for example replacing their cars. This may erode business confidence and trigger recession or deepen and lengthen an already existing recession. However, this assumes that falling prices are the result of a *bad* deflation rather than a *good* deflation.

The difference between the two is illustrated in Figure 17.8. A good or 'benign' deflation, shown in panel (a) of Figure 17.8, results from improvements in the economy's supply side, which reduces business costs of production. Both the *SRAS* curve and the *LRAS* curve shift to the right and assuming the *AD* curve does not itself shift, the price level falls, but output and employment rise. However, in the recessionary conditions existent in the UK economy in 2009, it was much more likely that a falling price level would signal a bad deflation. A bad or 'malign' deflation, shown in panel (b) of the diagram, is caused by a collapse of aggregate demand, negative multiplier effects, and possibly a credit crunch.

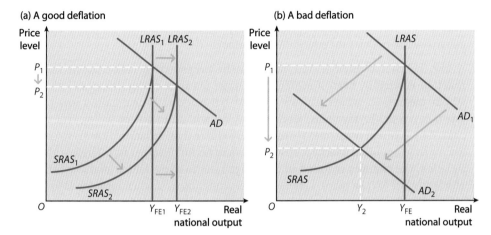

Figure 17.8 Good and bad deflations

CASE STUDY 17.2

Are lower prices are a good thing? Not really

Deflation — if it gets out of control — can be just as bad as inflation. Like inflation, deflation is a form of monetary instability. It disrupts the price mechanism, so people become confused about the true value of things. Consumers see prices are going to fall, so they defer purchases and even procrastinate on other decisions, such as getting married, in the expectation it will be cheaper later. Pay rises are few and far between. Economic growth is almost non-existent.

In a deflation interest rates may appear to be low, but may actually be high. This is explained by the difference between nominal interest rates and real ones. For example,

if the Bank of England's base rate is 2%, and prices are falling at 3%, real interest rates are actually 5%. The cost of borrowing is, therefore, actually higher than people think. Owing £10 is a heavier burden at the end of the year than it was at the beginning. A factory must sell more widgets, a farmer more milk and a shop more goods to meet those monthly interest payments.

When people wake up to this, they might take steps to remedy the situation quickly. For individuals, the key is the housing market. If it cracks and those with huge mortgages — secured on a dwindling asset — suddenly put their homes up for sale, a deflationary spiral could erupt.

Follow-up questions

1 Who may benefit from deflation in an economy?
2 What is a 'deflationary spiral'?

The costs and benefits of inflation

Everybody agrees that inflation can have serious adverse effects or costs. However, the seriousness of the adverse effects depends on whether inflation is anticipated or unanticipated. If inflation could be anticipated with complete certainty, it would pose few problems. Households and firms would simply build the expected rate of inflation into their economic decisions, which would not be distorted by wrong guesses.

When inflation is relatively low, with little variation from year to year, it is relatively easy to anticipate next year's inflation rate. Indeed, **creeping inflation**, which is associated with growing markets, healthy profits and a general climate of business optimism, greases the wheels of the economy. Viewed in this way, a low rate of inflation — but not absolute price stability — may be a necessary side-effect of expansionary policies to reduce unemployment.

A low, but stable inflation rate may also be necessary to make labour markets function efficiently. Even if average real wage rates are rising, there will be some labour markets in which real wages must fall in order to maintain a low rate of unemployment. To save jobs, workers may be willing to accept falling real wages caused by nominal wage rates rising at a slower rate than inflation. However, workers are much less willing to accept absolute cuts in nominal wage rates. Thus, with zero inflation, the changes required in real wage rates to make labour markets function efficiently fail to take place. Labour markets function best when inflation is low, but also stable. By contrast, absolute price stability produces real wage stickiness, which then results in unnecessarily high unemployment.

However, the adverse effects of inflation begin to exceed the benefits as soon as inflation becomes difficult to anticipate. An inflation rate that varies unpredictably from year to year is difficult for people to anticipate fully. Additionally, an inflation rate that is both high and difficult to anticipate creates distortions, which increasingly destabilise normal economic activity. Free-market economists generally argue that when inflation creeps upward, all too soon it acts as sand thrown in the wheels of the economy, making markets less efficient and competitive. When the *sand in the wheels* effect becomes stronger than the *greasing the wheels* effect, the costs of inflation exceed the benefits. The costs of inflation are described below.

Distributional effects

One cost of inflation is that weaker social groups in society, such as pensioners on fixed incomes, lose while others in strong bargaining positions gain. Moreover, in times of rapid inflation, real rates of interest are often negative. In this situation, lenders are really paying borrowers for the doubtful privilege of lending to them and inflation acts as a hidden tax, redistributing wealth from creditors to debtors.

Distortion of normal economic behaviour

Inflation actually distorts consumer behaviour by causing households to bring forward purchases and hoard the goods they buy if they expect the rate of inflation to accelerate. Similarly, firms may divert funds out of productive investment in fixed investment projects into unproductive commodity hoarding and speculation. People are affected by **inflationary noise**, which occurs when changes in relative prices are confused with a change in the general price level.

Breakdown in the functions of money

In a time of severe inflation, money becomes less useful and efficient as a medium of exchange and a store of value. Rapidly changing prices also erode money's functions as a unit of account and standard of deferred payment. In a **hyperinflation**, in which the inflation rate may accelerate to several hundred per cent a year or even higher, less efficient bartering replaces money and imposes extra costs on most transactions.

Stacks of worthless banknotes during the German hyperinflation of 1923

International uncompetitiveness

When the inflation rate is higher than in competitor countries, exports increase in price, making them uncompetitive. This puts pressure on a fixed exchange rate. With a floating exchange rate, the rate falls to restore competitiveness, but rising import prices may fuel a further bout of inflation.

Shoe leather and menu costs

With rapid inflation, consumers incur **shoe leather costs**, spending time and effort shopping around to check which prices have or have not risen. By contrast, **menu costs** are incurred by firms having to adjust price lists and vending machines more often.

- Control of inflation is a major macroeconomic objective.
- Inflation can be defined as a persistent or continuous rise in the price level or as a continuing fall in the value of money.
- Deflation can be described a persistent or continuous fall in the price level or as a continuing increase in the value of money.
- The price level is measured by a price index and the rate of inflation is measured by annual changes in the level of the index.
- The consumer prices index (CPI) and the retail prices index (RPI) measure consumer price inflation in the UK.
- The construction of a price index requires choice of a sample (the national shopping basket) and the weighting of all items in the sample.
- Theories of inflation can be divided into demand-pull and cost-push theories.
- The quantity theory of money, which is the oldest theory of inflation, is a demand theory of inflation.
- Cost-push theories came into fashion in the Keynesian era in the 1960s and 1970s.
- A short-run Phillips curve illustrates the conflict between controlling inflation and reducing unemployment, but is not itself a theory of inflation.
- The monetarist theory of inflation stems from the modern quantity theory of money, but also incorporates the role of expectations in the inflationary process.
- Monetarist and free-market economists argue that the long-run Phillips curve is vertical, located at the economy's natural level of unemployment.
- Around 2009 many economists feared that the problems of deflation might replace the problems of inflation.
- At low and stable inflation rates the benefits of inflation may exceed the costs, but at higher and more variable inflation rates the reverse is true.

Exam-style questions

1 Explain the differences between inflation, deflation and reflation.   (15 marks)

2 Explain the Phillips curve relationship.   (15 marks)

3 Do you agree that as the economy approaches full employment, inflation inevitably results? Justify your answer.   (25 marks)

4 Evaluate the view that the avoidance of inflation should always be the major macroeconomic objective.   (25 marks)

Extra resources to help you revise are available online at www.hodderplus.co.uk/philipallan

Money, banks and monetary policy

Chapter 18

Besides being a mixed economy, the economy we live in is a monetary economy, in which most of the goods and services produced are traded or exchanged via the intermediary of money. This chapter describes the nature and functions of money in a modern economy, before explaining how bank deposits, which are created by the private enterprise and commercial banking system, form the largest part of modern money. The second half of the chapter surveys the changes that have taken place in monetary policy in the UK, showing how the main features of current monetary policy developed out of the monetary policies implemented by UK governments and the Bank of England over the last 20–30 years. The chapter concludes by explaining how a significant sea change may be taking place in the nature of monetary policy, in response to recent recessionary conditions and subsequent difficulties in bringing about economic recovery and faster growth.

LEARNING OUTCOMES

This chapter will:
- describe the nature and functions of money
- emphasise how the private enterprise banking system creates the lion's share of modern money
- develop your understanding of monetary policy, focusing on the use of interest rates to try to control inflation
- evaluate the success of monetary policy before 2008
- discuss whether, with the introduction of quantitative easing, the nature of monetary policy has changed since the 2008 recession

WHAT YOU SHOULD ALREADY KNOW

At AS you learnt that in the UK monetary policy is implemented by the Monetary Policy Committee (MPC) of the Bank of England, which raises or lowers Bank Rate to try to achieve the government's target rate of inflation. You also learnt how monetary policy can involve the use of the money supply and exchange rates. However, Bank Rate set by the Bank of England has been the main instrument of monetary policy affecting other interest rates and thence the level of aggregate demand in the economy. Essentially, monetary policy is a demand-side policy, which shifts the aggregate demand curve in the *AD/AS* macroeconomic model.

The nature and functions of money

Money is best defined by focusing on the two principal functions money performs in the economy. Money functions as:

- **A medium of exchange (means of payment).** The economy we live in is a monetary economy in which most of the goods and services produced are traded or exchanged via the intermediary of money, rather than through **barter** (i.e. swapping goods). Whenever money is used to pay for goods or services, or for the purpose of settling transactions and the payment of debts, it performs this function.
- **A store of value (wealth).** Instead of being spent, money may be stored as a **wealth asset**, in preference to holding other *financial* assets, such as stocks and shares. When stored rather than spent, money's purchasing power is transferred to the future, although inflation may erode money's future purchasing power.

CASE STUDY 18.1

The development of modern money

Barter

Before the development of money, exchange and trade took place in simple and primitive village economies, based on barter: the swapping of goods and services. However, barter is inefficient and impractical in a more complex economic system. Successful barter requires a **double coincidence of wants**, which means that a person wishing to trade a television set for a refrigerator must not only establish contact with someone with equal but opposite wants (that is, an individual possessing a refrigerator who wishes to exchange it for a television set); they must also agree that the television set and refrigerator are of equal value.

Barter is inefficient because the time and energy spent searching the market to establish the double coincidence of wants results in unnecessary search costs, shoe-leather costs and transaction costs. These, in turn, promote a much greater inefficiency: namely, preventing the development of specialisation, division of labour and large-scale production.

Commodity money

Figure 18.1 shows the three main forms of money that have developed since money replaced barter. The earliest form of money was **commodity money**. Commodities that functioned as money had an intrinsic value of their own:

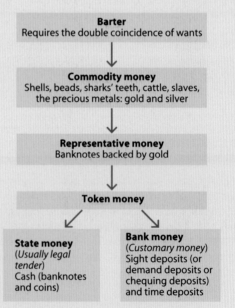

Figure 18.1 Barter and the different forms of money

they yielded utility and consumer services to their owners. Beads, shells, sharks' teeth and other commodities could be used for decorative purposes while being stored as

---

wealth. Some commodities used as money, such as cattle, could be slaughtered and eaten.

Representative money

As money evolved, gold and silver gradually replaced other forms of commodity money because they possessed, to a greater degree, the desirable characteristics necessary for a commodity to function as money: relative scarcity, uniformity, durability, portability and divisibility. All of these help to create confidence in money, which is necessary for its acceptability. Nevertheless, gold and silver are vulnerable to theft and are difficult to store safely. Eventually, wealthy individuals deposited the precious metals they owned with goldsmiths for safekeeping.

At the next stage, the goldsmiths developed into banks, and the receipts they issued in return for deposits of gold became the first banknotes or paper money. These notes were **representative money**, representing ownership of gold. Early banknotes were acceptable as a means of payment because they could be exchanged for gold on demand. They were issued by privately owned banks rather than by the state, although the state continued to issue gold and silver coinage. Although worthless in themselves, banknotes functioned as money because people were willing to accept them as long as there was confidence that notes could be changed into gold, which does have an intrinsic value.

Gold has long been considered a form of money

Token money

Modern money is almost all token money with no intrinsic value of its own. It takes two main forms: **cash** and **bank deposits**. In the UK, the state, or rather its agent, the Bank of England, has a monopoly over the issue of cash (although, Scottish and Northern Ireland banks also have a limited ability to issue banknotes). However, cash is literally the *small change* of the monetary system; bank deposits form by far the largest part of modern money. Most modern money takes the form of bank deposits created by the private enterprise banking system.

Follow-up questions

1 Why does money provide a more *efficient* means of payment than barter?
2 What are the advantages and disadvantages of using cash as the main form of personal wealth?

Banks and bank deposits

A **bank** is an institution that:

- accepts deposits from the general public that can be transferred by cheque or debit card
- creates deposits when it lends to the general public

Almost all banks in the UK are commercial companies. Most banks aim to make a profit for their owners. The Bank of England is an exception, since its aims are primarily to oversee the financial system and to implement the country's monetary policy. Commercial banks divide into retail banks such as HSBC and Barclays, whose main business is with the general public, and **wholesale banks**, which deal with each other and with other financial institutions largely located in the City of London. Wholesale banks are often called **investment banks**, although until recently they were generally known as merchant banks.

Barclays is a retail bank, though it has an investment arm

In contrast to cash, which is tangible and can be seen and touched, bank deposits are intangible. Customers only 'see' a bank deposit when reading the statement of a bank account, or when viewing the electronic display in a cash-dispensing machine. Bank deposits are the main form of money because banks possess the ability to create new deposits, almost out of thin air, where none previously existed. I explain the essential features of the deposit-creating process in the Extension material that follows.

EXTENSION MATERIAL

How banks create money

Bank deposits make up by far the largest part of modern money, between about two-thirds and 90% depending on how money is defined.

Many students are completely mystified as to how bank deposits are created. A good starting point for developing an understanding is provided by the following story:

Suppose I write my signature on a scrap of paper, together with the words 'I owe the bearer £100'. I then give you the scrap of paper and ask you to go to a shop and buy £100 worth of goods. Then, when the time comes to pay, you must give the scrap of paper to the shop assistant. In real life, we all know that shops refuse to accept such an 'I owe you'.

But just suppose the shop did accept my scrap of paper, believing it could then use the note to buy goods from its suppliers. My 'I owe you' note would have become money.

Now while ordinary individuals can't generally create money in the manner in which I have described, banks can. Bank deposits are the main form of money because banks possess the ability to create loans or **credit**. Every time a bank grants a new loan to a customer, new money is created. Banks wish to create new loans because loans are profitable. Think of a bank as an institution which makes much of its profit by borrowing from the general public and then lending a greater amount to other members of the general public. However, a bank's ability to create new loans is limited by the fact that it must possess sufficient liquid assets or reserve assets to 'back' the new credit it creates. Cash, or notes issued by the Bank of England, is a reserve asset. To make sure that the general public remains confident that it will not run out of cash and 'crash', a bank chooses to maintain a *prudential ratio* between the total deposits it creates and lends to customers, and the liquid or reserve assets it possesses. For example, a prudential ratio of 5 means that a bank can create total deposits which are five times the size of its reserve asset base. As a result, bank deposits form a much larger part of modern money than cash. Think of cash as the 'small change' of modern money.

CASE STUDY 18.2

A brief history of banking

To understand how a bank such as Barclays operates, it is useful to divide the bank's customers into two different groups: those in credit and those in debit. Members of the former group deposit cash in the bank, while members of the latter group borrow from the bank. The bank makes a profit by charging borrowers a higher interest rate than it pays to attract deposits.

Before the middle of the nineteenth century, banks printed their own banknotes. Some of these were given to customers depositing gold in the banks, but the rest were lent to customers borrowing from the banks. By printing and lending notes in this way, the banks' note issue grew to exceed the gold deposits held by the banks. Prudent banking requires a bank to keep sufficient reserve assets (in this case, gold) to meet all likely calls by customers on the bank's liabilities.

However, greedy or imprudent banks were often tempted, in pursuit of profit, to over-extend their note issue by printing and lending banknotes greatly in excess of the gold they owned. In these circumstances, the banks' holdings of gold might prove insufficient to meet the demand by customers to convert banknotes (the banks' liabilities) into gold. Imprudent over-extension of the note issue thus led to bank crashes, which occurred periodically when banks ran out of gold. The large number of bank crashes that occurred in the early nineteenth century led to the 1844 Bank Charter Act,

which largely removed the right of British banks to issue their own notes.

However, the 1844 Bank Charter Act encouraged a new monetary development, namely the creation of **deposit money**, which is now the main form of modern money. Apart from Scottish and Northern Irish banks (which have to deposit an equivalent amount of gold at the Bank of England), banks can no longer print and issue their own notes. However, banks get round this inconvenience by simply *crediting a deposit* to the account of a customer to whom a loan is given. Whenever loans are made, bank deposits are created.

Sight deposits or **demand deposits**, which in the UK are known as **current account deposits**, upon which cheques can be drawn, are money because they are both a store of value and a medium of exchange.

Note that the *deposit* is money and not the *cheque*. The cheque is just an instruction to make a cash withdrawal or to shift ownership of a bank deposit from one person to another. However, the fact that cheques are customarily acceptable as a means of payment turns bank deposits into money. These days, **debit cards** are increasingly used instead of cheques to make payments and to transfer ownership of bank deposits.

Cash became mere token money, rather than representative money, when the state withdrew the promise to convert its notes and coins into gold on demand: that is, when the currency came off the **gold standard**. Cash is also usually **legal tender** — *fiat money* made legal by government decree — which must be accepted as a medium of exchange and in settlement of debts. Like cash, bank deposits created by the private enterprise banking system are token money, but they are also **customary money** rather than legal tender. This means that bank deposits are generally accepted because of people's confidence in the banks and in the monetary system. However, people can refuse to accept payment by cheque or debit card, demanding instead payment in legal tender.

Follow-up questions

1 Explain the difference between a bank's customer being in credit or in debit.
2 What is the difference between legal tender and customary money?

EXAM TIP

You must understand the money supply as well as interest rates. However, detailed knowledge is not required of the financial assets that function as money, the money supply, or the structure of interest rates.

EXTENSION MATERIAL

The problem of defining the money supply

Before the advent of monetarism, few economists gave much attention to the precise definition of the money supply or stock of money in the economy. This reflected the Keynesian view that money did not matter in the macroeconomic management of the economy. However, when monetarism replaced Keynesianism as the new prevailing orthodoxy in the 1970s, money did begin to matter — particularly in the years before monetarism itself drifted from favour around 1985. For a few years from the mid-1970s to the mid-1980s, during the 'monetarist era', control of the money supply became an important part of monetarist economic management in general and monetary policy in particular. During this period, monetarist economists devoted considerable attention to the problem of deciding which assets to include and exclude when defining the money supply.

A significant problem that faced the monetarists stemmed from what has become known as **Goodhart's Law**. This is named after Charles Goodhart, formerly a professor at the London School of Economics and a member of the Bank of England's Monetary Policy Committee (MPC). Goodhart argued that, as soon as a government tries to control the growth of a particular measure of the money supply, any previously stable relationship between the targeted measure of money and the economy breaks down. The more successful the Bank of England appears to be in controlling the rate of growth of the financial assets defined as the money supply, the more likely it is that other financial assets, regarded previously as 'near money' outside the existing definition and system of control, will take on the function of a medium of exchange and become money.

In this way, attempting to control the money supply is rather like a man trying to catch his own shadow. As soon as he moves, his shadow also moves. Although what is defined as money may be controlled, when other financial assets become money, this becomes irrelevant. The difficulties of first defining the money supply, and second, exerting control over its rate of growth, contributed to the downfall of monetarism after 1985.

Over the years, the Bank of England has used more than one definition of the money supply. These divide into measures of narrow money and broad money. **Narrow money**, which restricts the measure of money to cash and bank and building society sight deposits, reflects the medium of exchange function of money, namely money functioning as a means of payment. **Broad money** also measures time deposits, which are a store of value rather than a medium of exchange.

The Bank of England and monetary policy

As already noted, most banks are commercial banks, whose main aim is to make a profit for their owners. Although it makes a considerable profit, the most significant exception is the Bank of England, which is the UK's **central bank**. For most of the period since its formation in 1694, the Bank of England was a private enterprise company. The Bank is now a nationalised industry and its surplus profit goes to the state. The Bank of England's principal function (besides overseeing and trying to maintain confidence in the whole of the financial system) is to implement **monetary policy** on behalf of the UK government.

Monetary policy is the part of economic policy that attempts to achieve the government's macroeconomic objectives using monetary instruments, such as controls over bank lending and the rate of interest. Before 1997, monetary policy was implemented more or less jointly by the Treasury (a part of central government) and the Bank of England, which were known as the *monetary authorities*. But the Treasury abandoned its hands-on role in implementing monetary policy in 1997 when the government made the Bank of England operationally independent. Unless the Bank is put under pressure by the Treasury, there is now only one monetary authority: the Bank of England.

Objectives and instruments of monetary policy

To understand monetary policy, it is useful to distinguish between policy *objectives* and policy *instruments*. A policy objective is the target that the Bank of England aims to hit. By contrast, a policy instrument is the tool of control used to try to achieve the objective.

Monetary policy objectives and instruments can be classified in different ways. Policy objectives can be divided into *ultimate* and *intermediate* objectives. Policy instruments separate into those that affect the supply of new deposits that the commercial banks can create and those that affect the demand for loans or credit.

Monetary policy objectives

For over 30 years, *control of inflation* has been the main objective of UK monetary policy. The government needs to control inflation in order to create conditions in which the ultimate policy objective of *improved economic welfare* can be attained. However, at various times, the Bank of England has tried to control inflation by first meeting an *intermediate* monetary policy objective. In the monetarist years of the early 1980s, this was the *money supply* and from the mid-1980s until 1992, when intermediate policy objectives were abandoned, it was the *exchange rate*. Since 1992, monetary policy has targeted the control of inflation directly, without the use of any intermediate policy objectives.

EXTENSION MATERIAL

Monetarism and monetary policy

Monetarist economists believe that inflation is caused by a prior increase in the quantity of money in the economy. The quantity theory predicts that if the quantity of money increases and people end up holding money balances larger than those they wish to hold, the excess money holdings will be spent. This creates excess demand for real goods and services in the economy, which in turn pulls up the price level in a demand-pull inflation.

From the late 1970s until the mid-1980s, monetary policy was based on announcing, first, a target rate of growth of the money supply, and second, that policy would then be implemented to achieve the announced target. Suppose, for example, growth of real GDP is 2% and the government aims for a maximum inflation rate of 3%. Under these conditions, the target rate of growth of the money supply should be set at a maximum rate of 5%, to enable goods and services to be purchased at prices up to 3% higher than last year's prices.

The monetarist period in UK monetary policy ended in 1985 when Thatcher's Conservative government abandoned setting formal money supply targets. There were two main reasons for the collapse of monetarism, both suggested by Goodhart's Law. First, the growth of the money supply proved difficult if not impossible to control. Second, the relationship between the growth of the money supply and the rate of inflation, which had seemed stable *before* monetarist policies were implemented, broke down *after* the attempt was made to control the growth of the money supply.

Monetary policy instruments

As you learnt at AS, policy instruments are the tools used to achieve policy objectives. There are two categories of monetary policy instrument: those that affect the general public's *demand* for bank loans and those that affect the retail banks' ability to *supply* credit and to create bank deposits. Before 2009, UK monetary policy relied almost exclusively on the use of **Bank Rate**, which is the Bank of England's key interest rate, to *manage the demand* for bank loans. In 2009, however, the Bank of England began to use **quantitative easing (QE)** to influence commercial bank's ability to *supply* new loans to their customers. I shall now look at each of these in turn.

Managing the demand for credit through the use of Bank Rate

As mentioned, Bank Rate is a key interest rate used by the Bank of England in the operation of monetary policy. Bank Rate is the rate of interest charged when the Bank of England lends money to the commercial banks to enable the banks to maintain their liquidity or reserve assets ratios. An increase in Bank Rate makes it more expensive for banks to borrow from the Bank of England and, in theory at least, the banks then have to increase the interest rates they charge when lending these funds on to the general public. Likewise, a cut in Bank Rate leads to a fall in the interest rates charged by the banks. In this way, changes in Bank rate cause changes in other *short-term* interest rates (though less so in *long-term* interest rates such as the yield on government bonds or gilts).

Two factors affecting interest rates are time and risk. As a general rule, long-term interest rates are higher than short-term interest rates, because lenders are sacrificing for longer periods their ability to spend their own money. However, there are exceptions to this rule, partly explained by the second factor: risk. The riskier the loan, the higher the rate of interest. Thus short-term risky and *unsecured* credit card loans carry much higher rates than long-term mortgage loans, *secured* by the value of the house being purchased.

For several decades before 2009, modern UK monetary policy operated almost solely through changes in Bank Rate (i.e. through interest rate policy). To influence the quantity of bank deposits being created (and also the level of aggregate demand in the economy), the Bank of England rationed demand for credit by raising or lowering Bank Rate. To explain how this was done, a good starting point is the aggregate demand equation I explained in Chapter 15, and which you learnt at AS:

$$AD = C + I + G + (X - M)$$

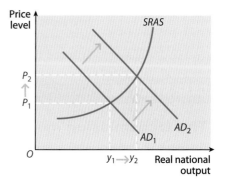

Figure 18.2 How a decrease in interest rates causes the *AD* curve to shift to the right

Whereas fiscal policy can affect aggregate demand by changing the level of government spending (G), monetary policy affects the other components of aggregate demand, C, I and ($X - M$). A cut in interest rates causes the *AD* curve illustrated in Figure 18.2 to shift to the right from AD_1 to AD_2.

There are three main ways in which a cut in interest rates, brought about by a change in Bank Rate, increases aggregate demand. These are:

■ **Lower interest rates increase household consumption (C).** First, lower interest rates discourage saving, which means that more income is available for consumption. Second, the cost of household borrowing falls, which cuts the cost of servicing a mortgage and credit-card debt. Borrowers have more money to spend on consumption because less of their income is used for interest payments. Third, lower interest rates may cause asset prices to increase, e.g. the prices of houses and shares. Higher house and share prices increase personal wealth, which in turn increases consumption. Fourth, rising house and share prices lead to an increase in consumer confidence, which further boosts consumption.

■ **Lower interest rates increase business investment (I).** Business investment means the purchase of capital goods such as machines by firms. Businesses bring forward investment projects they would have cancelled or postponed at a higher cost of borrowing, believing that new capital goods can now be profitably used. A rise in business confidence is also likely to boost investment.

■ **Lower interest rates have an effect on net export demand ($X - M$).** Lower UK interest rates lead to the selling of pounds or sterling, as owners of international capital decide to hold other currencies instead. This causes the pound's exchange rate to fall, which increases the price competitiveness of UK exports in world markets. At the same time, the prices of imports rise and they become less competitive in the UK market. The UK's balance of payments on current account improves, with the increase in net export demand shifting the *AD* curve to the right.

By contrast, a rise in interest rates triggers a capital inflow in the balance of payments, which increases the exchange rate. Exports lose their competitiveness, and the current account of the balance of payments deteriorates. Aggregate demand falls and the *AD* curve shifts to the left.

CASE STUDY 18.3

The transmission mechanism of interest rate policy

The Bank of England believes that interest rate policy affects aggregate demand and inflation through a number of channels, which form the transmission mechanism of monetary policy. The flow chart in Figure 18.3 shows the routes through which changes in Bank Rate (the instrument of monetary policy), shown at point 1 in the diagram, eventually affect inflation (the objective of monetary policy), shown at point 11.

Official Bank Rate decisions (point 1 in Figure 18.3) affect **market interest rates** (point 2), such as mortgage rates and bank deposit rates set by commercial banks and financial institutions. At the same time, policy actions and announcements affect **expectations** about the future course of the economy and the **confidence** with which these expectations are held (point 4). They also affect **asset prices** (point 3) and the **exchange rate** (point 5). These changes in turn affect **aggregate demand**

in the economy (point 8). This comprises **domestically generated demand** (point 6) and **net external demand** (point 7), which is determined by export and import demand.

Domestic demand results from the spending, saving and investment behaviour of individuals and firms within the economy. Lower market interest rates increase domestic demand by encouraging consumption rather than saving by households and investment spending by firms. Conversely, higher market interest rates depress domestic spending. If the official interest rate falls, asset prices rise and people feel wealthier and generally more confident about the future. As a result, consumption increases. A lower official interest rate causes financial capital to flow out of the pound and into other currencies, which in turn causes the exchange rate to fall. A falling exchange rate reduces UK export prices, while raising the price of imports. Demand for UK-produced goods increases.

Figure 18.3 The transmission mechanism of interest rate policy

Changes in aggregate demand (relative to the economy's ability to supply output) affect **domestic inflationary pressures** in the economy (point 9). Changes in aggregate demand affect demand-pull inflationary pressures. However, there are also cost-push pressures from the effects of changes in aggregate demand on domestic wage rates. Changes in **import prices** (point 10) brought about by changes in the exchange rate affect inflation in two ways. Changes in the prices of imported food and consumer goods affect inflation directly, while changes in the prices of imported raw materials affect cost-push inflationary pressures.

The Bank of England estimates a time lag of up to 2 years between an initial change in the Bank's official rate of interest (point 1) and the resulting change in the rate of inflation (point 11). Output is affected within 1 year, but the fullest effect on inflation occurs after a lag of 2 years. In terms of the size of the effect, the Bank believes a 1% change in its official interest rate affects output by about 0.2–0.35% after about a year and inflation by around 0.2–0.4% per year after 2 years.

Follow-up questions

1 What is meant by an 'asset price'? Explain how an increase in interest rates affects asset prices.
2 How does a fall in interest rates affect import prices in the UK?

CASE STUDY 18.4

Libor and Bank Rate

Until quite recently, high-street banking was a boring form of business. For each borrower, a bank had to have around ten savers to provide the funds being lent. The need to attract savers was a significant constraint on the banks' ability to provide new loans or credit.

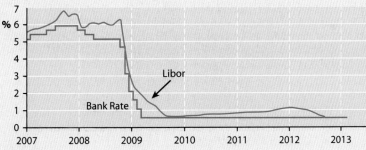

Figure 18.4 Libor and Bank Rate, 2007 to 2013

Source: Bank of England

All this changed in the deregulated and liberalised financial world created in the 1980s and 1990s. The traditional business of 'boring' banking went out of the window as high-street banks moved onto a much more interesting business plan. Out went household savings as the banks' principal source of liquidity and in came the borrowing of funds on the London interbank wholesale money market.

The rate of interest at which banks lend to each other is called the **Libor**, which is the acronym for the London interbank offered rate of interest. Unlike **Bank Rate**, which is set monthly by the Bank of England, the Libor rate is determined on a daily basis by the demand and supply for funds as banks lend to each other to balance their books.

In normal times, the 3-month Libor rate trades at a small premium of around 0.15% above where the market thinks Bank Rate will be in 3 months' time. However, when the credit crunch spread from America in 2007, Libor shot up to around 1.5% above Bank Rate. As Figure 18.4 shows, for most of the time, Libor remained well above Bank Rate during the period from 2007 to 2012, especially in 2008.

In 2013 the two rates were converging at the 0.5% Bank Rate set by the Bank of England. The convergence was partly the result of the break-up of a 'Libor-fixing' scam operated by the banks to keep Libor above Bank Rate.

Divergence between Bank Rate and Libor makes it difficult for the Bank of England to operate monetary policy effectively. When Libor is significantly above Bank Rate, a cut in Bank Rate aimed at reducing the interest rates that the general public have to pay when borrowing from high-street banks is ineffective if the rates the banks charge is determined by Libor rather than by Bank Rate.

Follow-up questions

1 How are changes in Bank Rate expected to affect mortgage interest rates?
2 What has happened to Bank Rate and Libor in the months or years since 2013?

CASE STUDY 18.5

The 2007 credit crunch and the 2008 recession

Over 80 years ago, the 1929 Wall Street Crash led into the Great Depression which devastated many of the world's economies. Several generations later a rather similar financial crisis, the 2007 credit crunch, became the precursor of the 2008 recession. In both cases, the financial crisis destroyed personal wealth and consumer and business confidence, thereby creating the conditions for a massive collapse of aggregate demand.

A credit crunch is defined as a severe shortage of money or credit. The crunch followed on from the sub-prime mortgage crisis in the USA. In America, interest rates had risen between 2004 and 2006 from 1% to 5.35%, which triggered a slowdown in US housing markets. House buyers, many of whom could only barely afford their mortgage payments when interest rates were low, began to default on their mortgages. The mortgages granted by American banks to these customers became known as sub-prime mortgages. They were high-risk loans to clients with poor or no credit histories.

The impact of these defaults was felt across financial systems, not only in the USA but also in Europe, as many of the mortgages had been bundled up and sold on to banks and investors. These bundled-up mortgages became known as 'toxic debt'. In the USA, New Century Financial, which specialised in sub-prime mortgages, collapsed. As New Century Financial had sold much of its toxic debt to other banks, the sub-prime mortgage market began to unravel. Banks refused to trade with each other because they didn't know whether other banks were in danger of collapsing. On 1 October 2007, Swiss bank UBS became the world's first top bank to announce losses caused by sub-prime related investments. Banking giant Citigroup then unveiled a sub-prime related loss of $3.1 billion, rising within six months to $40 billion.

During the following year, a succession of banks announced massive sub-prime related losses, culminating in Lehman Brothers becoming the first major bank to go bust since the start of the credit crisis. Aggregate demand collapsed and on 24 October 2008, the UK was said to be in recession. The Office for National Statistics stated that the economy had shrunk for the first time in 16 years between July and September 2008. In a later revision, the recession was said to have started rather earlier in the second quarter of 2008.

Follow-up questions

1 Explain the difference between a 'prime' mortgage and a 'sub-prime' mortgage.
2 Name a British bank which collapsed during the credit crunch.

Quantitative easing (QE)

Background to the introduction of QE

Between 1992 and 2009, UK monetary policy was directed explicitly at a published inflation rate target and, as previously noted, Bank Rate was almost the sole monetary policy instrument. At the time, monetary policy was *pre-emptive*. This means that the Bank of England was prepared to raise Bank Rate even when there was no immediate sign of accelerating inflation, in order to anticipate and head off a rise in the inflation rate that might otherwise occur many months in the future. The Bank estimated what the inflation rate would be 18 months to 2 years ahead (the medium term), if policy (that is, Bank Rate) remained unchanged. If the forecast rate of inflation was different from the target rate set by the government, the Bank was prepared to change Bank Rate to prevent the forecast inflation rate becoming a reality in the future. Bank Rate was also raised or lowered to pre-empt any likely adverse effect upon the inflation rate of an adverse outside shock hitting the economy.

In 1997 the inflation rate target was made *symmetrical*. This means that the Bank of England must stimulate aggregate demand, which will generally raise the rate of inflation, whenever actual inflation is below the target rate, just as the Bank must try to reduce the rate of inflation whenever actual inflation is above the target rate. The Labour government in power at the time stated that although the primary objective of monetary policy is price stability, the Bank of England must also support the government's economic policy objectives, including those for growth and employment.

The fact that the Bank of England now has a duty to use monetary policy to protect economic growth and employment helps to explain why UK monetary policy changed so radically in 2009, when the Bank of England added **quantitative easing (QE)** to Bank Rate as a monetary policy instrument.

The introduction of QE was a response to recession. To try to end the recession, as Figure 18.4 shows, the Bank of England slashed Bank Rate from 5% to 0.5%, where it has remained ever since (at least until the time of writing this book in July 2013). The policy was ineffective, partly because as Bank Rate gets closer and closer to zero (the so-called zero-bound), the possibility diminishes of stimulating the economy by further cuts in Bank Rate. With the inflation rate also close to zero in 2009, recession rather than inflation was the problem of the day. QE was introduced as a new monetary policy instrument to stimulate economic growth.

> **KEY TERM**
>
> **quantitative easing (QE):** the introduction of new money into the money supply by a central bank such as the Bank of England. The opposite policy of **quantitative tightening** (which might be used in the future) involves 'clawing back' new money previously released into the money supply.

So what is quantitative easing?

As I stated earlier, monetary policy can operate in two contrasting ways: on the **demand for money**, or on the **supply of money**. Unlike Bank Rate, which attempts to influence the demand for money and thence aggregate demand, QE is a method of increasing the money supply. At the time QE was started in 2009, the Bank of England hoped that the general public would spend the new money pumped into the economy, which would revive consumer spending and economic growth.

People often think that QE involves increasing the money supply by printing new banknotes. Indeed, when QE started in 2009, the metaphor was used of a central bank filling a helicopter with newly printed banknotes, before dropping the 'helicopter money' on the general public. However, QE was not as simple as this. To understand why, you must remember that bank deposits, and not cash, make up the lion's share of the money supply. QE increased the deposits commercial banks held at the Bank of England. This increased the banks' ability to lend to the general public. If the general public took up these newly available loans, their desire to hold cash would probably have increased. Since the Bank of England operates what is called an 'accommodating monetary policy', it is always willing to supply more cash to meet the general public's wish to hold more banknotes. In this way, increased note issue was a *result* of QE, but it was not its *cause*. Nevertheless, QE had the same effect as printing more money.

QE is formally known as the Bank of England's **asset purchase scheme**. The Bank buys financial assets, mostly long-dated government bonds (gilts), previously held by commercial banks and other financial institutions such as insurance companies. The Bank purchased bonds using electronic money it had simply created out of thin air (i.e. by crediting its own account at the Bank of England with a new deposit which it then used to purchase bonds). The institutions selling those bonds to the Bank then had 'new' money in their accounts, which increased the money supply.

The purchase by the Bank of government bonds pushed up bond values, thereby making the bonds more expensive to buy. As a result, bonds became a less attractive investment for commercial banks and other financial institutions. Instead of buying more bonds to replenish those they had sold to the Bank of England, commercial banks used the deposits they now held to invest in other companies or to lend to individuals. The Bank of England hoped that the interest rates banks charge their customers would fall, thereby boosting the economy.

Has QE been successful?

You may notice that the last two paragraphs were written in the past tense. This is because, at the time of writing in July 2013, QE is no longer being actively used, at least in the UK. Between 2009 and 2012, there were three bouts of quantitative easing: first in March 2009 (QE1), then in October 2011 (QE2) and finally in February 2012 (QE3). In the three bouts, first £200 billion, then £75 billion and finally £100 billion of 'new money' was unleashed into the banking system, making a total of £375 billion.

QE may be used again in the future. The main argument that has been put forward in favour of QE is that in 2009 it stopped economies such as the UK from falling into a deep recession. But the arguments against QE include:

- QE has been not been effective in stimulating recovery from recession and economic growth. In a sense, QE has suffered from diminishing returns: QE1 was quite successful, but less so QE2 and QE3. However, continuing quantitative easing in the USA has been successful in promoting economic recovery.
- By pumping 'new money' into the economy, QE is potentially inflationary. So far, QE has not been responsible for accelerating inflation, but the fact that the inflation rate remains stubbornly above the government's 2% target rate may be largely the result of quantitative easing.
- Combined with very low interest rates, QE is blamed for serious adverse effects on the distribution of income. Savers, who are mostly the elderly, have seen the value of their pensions fall, while borrowers, who include the government and people with mortgages, have benefited from negative or very low real interest rates.
- Whereas the Bank of England hoped that the 'new money' created by QE would be directed into productive investment, much has actually gone into unproductive speculation. Share, bond and house prices have risen rapidly, prompting fears of speculative bubbles similar to those before the 2008 recession. The eventual 'pricking' of such bubbles, possibly because of rising interest rates and quantitative 'tightening' replacing quantitative 'easing', may lead again into another recession.

Recent changes in monetary policy

Forward guidance

In August 2013, Mark Carney, the new governor of the Bank of England, introduced a new policy of **forward guidance**. Forward guidance is used to send signals to financial markets, businesses and individuals about the Bank's interest rate policy in the months and years ahead. At the time of the policy's launch, Carney said that the Bank would not consider raising Bank Rate from its low of 0.5% until the unemployment rate falls to 7% or below, which in the Bank's view could be in 2016.

If financial markets believe what Carney and the MPC say, the hope is that markets remain calm and orderly, and behave in a way that is consistent with the forward guidance strategy. There are, however, two dangers. First, the strategy may be knocked off course by an event such as a house price bubble hitting the UK economy. Second, and related to this, financial markets may form their own expectations of what is going to happen in the future. If markets believe that a bubble is going to occur, then, whatever the Bank's official policy, market operators may ignore the forward guidance strategy and raise interest rates anyway.

In late 2013, the jury is thus out on the issue of whether forward guidance will work. Forward guidance should be seen as a policy which tries increase the credibility of monetary policy. However, if market operators perceive the strategy to be 'wishful thinking', forward guidance could destroy rather than increase the credibility of the Bank of England in its management of the UK economy.

Mark Carney, who replaced Mervyn King as governor of the Bank of England in July 2013

Funding for Lending

Launched in 2012, the **Funding for Lending Scheme (FLS)** allows banks and other lenders to borrow money cheaply from the Bank of England. The FLS is designed to make it easier for banks to pass money on to borrowers at a time when the banks might otherwise be reducing lending because of their need to shore up battered balance sheets. By helping to cut mortgage rates for house buyers, the FLS has promoted recovery in UK housing markets. However, the FLS has generally failed to increase lending to UK businesses, particularly to small- and medium-size companies.

SUMMARY

- Money is best defined by its two principal functions, as a medium of exchange and a store of value or wealth.
- Virtually all modern money is token money with no intrinsic value.
- Cash (notes and coins) is fiat money, issued by the state.
- Cash is the 'small change' of the system and bank deposits are by far the largest part of modern money.
- Banks can create deposits, which in total form a multiple of the cash or monetary base the banks possess.
- The main function of the Bank of England is to implement the government's monetary policy.
- Under monetarism, monetary policy aimed to control the rate of growth of the money supply.
- In recent decades, the rate of interest has been the main monetary policy instrument, aimed at targeting the rate of inflation.
- In an *AD/AS* diagram, monetary policy is illustrated by shifts of the *AD* curve to the right (expansionary monetary policy) and to the left (contractionary monetary policy).
- UK monetary policy was successful in controlling inflation from 1992 until 2008.
- Monetary policy became much less successful with the onset of recession in 2008. First, there was a fear of deflation, followed by the rate of inflation remaining persistently above the government's target rate of 2%.
- In 2009, monetary policy switched away from relying solely on interest rate changes to a policy of quantitative easing, through which the Bank of England creates more money for people to spend.
- The jury is out on whether quantitative easing has been successful.
- Forward Guidance is a policy introduced in 2013 to try to influence long-term interest rates.

Exam-style questions

1 Explain how changes in Bank Rate affect bank lending and the economy. **(15 marks)**

2 Explain how quantitative easing operates. **(15 marks)**

3 Evaluate the effectiveness of monetary policy in controlling the rate of inflation in the UK in recent years. **(25 marks)**

4 Do you agree that, in recent years, UK monetary policy has been used solely to stimulate economic growth, and not to control inflation? Justify your answer. **(25 marks)**

Extra resources to help you revise are available online at www.hodderplus.co.uk/philipallan

Fiscal policy and supply-side policy

Fiscal policy is the part of economic policy in which the government attempts to achieve policy objectives using the fiscal instruments of government spending, taxation and the government's budgetary position (balanced budget, budget deficit or budget surplus).

In this chapter I explain how the main thrust of UK fiscal policy changed over the years from 'sound finance' and balanced budgets to the management of aggregate demand in the Keynesian era running from the 1950s to the 1970s.

Then, in the 1980s and 1990s, fiscal policy became an important part of supply-side economic policy, which itself was part of the anti-Keynesian free-market revival. Supply-side economics encompasses more than just fiscal policy, but tax cuts and reductions in public spending, which aim to increase personal incentives and to free resources for the private sector to use, lie at the heart of supply-side economic policies.

Very recently, between 2008 and 2010, and in response to recession, fiscal policy switched back to the Keynesian-style management of aggregate demand. This was the short-lived 'fiscal stimulus', which ended in 2010 when replaced by the current policy of 'fiscal austerity'.

LEARNING OUTCOMES

This chapter will:
- provide a brief history of UK fiscal policy
- describe the structure of public finance in the UK
- outline the main features of Keynesian or demand-side fiscal policy
- explain automatic stabilisers, crowding out and the structural and cyclical components of a budget deficit
- use *AD/AS* diagrams to analyse different types of fiscal policy
- explain supply-side fiscal policy and relate it to the current programme of fiscal austerity
- remind you of the wider meaning of supply-side economics
- introduce you to European Union fiscal policy

WHAT YOU SHOULD ALREADY KNOW

At AS, you learnt the meaning of fiscal policy and about how fiscal policy is both similar to, and different from, monetary policy. At the start of the A2 course, you should understand how fiscal policy has both macroeconomic and microeconomic functions, influencing both aggregate demand and aggregate supply, and how, through the fiscal instruments of government spending and taxation, fiscal policy affects the pattern of economic activity.

A brief history of UK fiscal policy

From the 1850s onward, until the birth of Keynesian economics just before the Second World War, UK governments generally followed the principles of 'sound finance' (fiscal orthodoxy). This tradition is associated with the nineteenth-century prime minister William Gladstone, who in his earlier role as chancellor of the exchequer aimed to balance the government's budget and to keep both government spending and taxation as low as possible.

For three decades from the 1950s to the end of the 1970s, Keynesian economics fundamentally changed the nature of UK fiscal policy. In his *General Theory*, published in 1936, Maynard Keynes legitimised the use of fiscal policy as a means of managing the level of aggregate demand in the economy. In the Keynesian era, deficit financing became respectable and part of the new Keynesian orthodoxy.

However, under Margaret Thatcher in the 1980s, demand management was rejected and there was a return to the principles of 'sound finance', though balanced budgets were seldom achieved. During the free-market revival and the relatively short-lived monetarist years of the early 1980s, there was of course still a fiscal policy, but now used in a supply-side way to improve the economy's ability to produce. In these years, income tax rates were cut, not to stimulate aggregate demand, but to improve personal incentives to work harder, save, invest, and be entrepreneurial.

In the 1990s, although demand management policies were reintroduced, monetary policy and *not* fiscal policy was used to influence demand, with control of inflation as the policy objective. Fiscal policy continued to be used in a supply-side way and also to promote macroeconomic stability.

EXAM TIP

Exam questions may ask you to describe the main UK taxes and/or forms of public spending, or to describe the pattern of public spending.

In 2008, there was again a significant U-turn in UK fiscal policy. To try to prevent the collapse of aggregate demand from turning the *recession* into a deep *depression*, the Labour government introduced a **fiscal stimulus** to manage aggregate demand. The fiscal stimulus, which contributed to the growth of a huge budget deficit, was abandoned in 2010. This was partly due to the election of the Conservative-dominated Coalition government, but also partly due to the emergence of a completely new problem: the **sovereign debt problem**. **Fiscal austerity (fiscal restraint** or **fiscal consolidation)** replaced the fiscal stimulus. In 2013 fiscal policy is no longer used to manage aggregate demand. The supply-side elements of fiscal policy have once again become dominant and chancellor George Osborne now aims for a budget surplus in the next parliament.

The structure of public finance in the UK

Taxation and other sources of government revenue

A tax is a compulsory levy charged by government or by a public authority to pay for its expenditure. Taxation is the principal source of government revenue for most economies.

KEY TERM

taxation: compulsory levies charged by the government to raise revenue, primarily to finance government spending.

In the UK about 89% of total taxation is levied by central government, with local government taxation (currently the council tax and business rates) accounting for the remaining 11% of taxation levied by government.

Progressive, proportionate and regressive taxation

In a **progressive tax** system, the proportion of a person's income paid in tax *increases* as income rises, while in a **regressive tax** system, the proportion paid in tax *falls* as income increases. A tax is **proportionate** (a **flat tax**) if exactly the same proportion of income is paid in tax at all levels of income. Progressivity can be defined for a single tax or for the tax system as a whole.

The word *progressive* is value-neutral, implying nothing about how the revenue raised by the government is spent. Nevertheless, progressive taxation has been used by governments, particularly during the Keynesian era, to achieve the social aim of a 'fairer' distribution of income. But progressive taxation cannot by itself redistribute income — a policy of transfers in the government's public expenditure programme is required for this. Progressive taxation used on its own merely reduces post-tax income differentials compared to pre-tax differentials.

Average and marginal rates of income tax

For particular taxes such as income tax or inheritance tax, we can identify whether the tax is progressive, regressive or proportionate by examining the relationship between the average rate at which the tax is levied and the marginal rate. In a progressive income tax system, the **marginal tax rate** is higher than the **average tax rate**, although the average rate, which measures the proportion of income paid in tax, rises as income increases. Conversely, in a regressive income tax system, the marginal tax is less than the average rate, while the two are equal in the case of a proportionate tax or flat tax.

For income tax, the average tax rate is calculated as total tax paid divided by total income. By contrast, the marginal tax rate is calculated as the *change* in total tax paid divided by the *change* in total income.

$$\text{average tax rate} = \frac{\text{total tax paid}}{\text{total income}} \qquad \text{or:} \quad \frac{T}{Y}$$

$$\text{marginal tax rate} = \frac{\text{change in total tax paid}}{\text{change in total income}} \qquad \text{or:} \quad \frac{\Delta T}{\Delta Y}$$

As a general rule, the *average* tax rate indicates the overall burden of the tax upon the taxpayer, but the *marginal* rate may significantly affect economic choice and decision making. In the case of an income tax, it influences the choice between work and leisure when deciding how much labour to supply. The marginal rate of income tax also influences decisions on whether to spend income on consumption or to save.

The principles of taxation

Taxpayers commonly view all taxes as 'bad', in the sense that they do not enjoy paying them, although most realise that taxation is necessary in order to provide for the useful goods and services provided by the government. A starting point for analysing and evaluating whether a tax is 'good' or 'bad' is Adam Smith's four **principles** (or **canons**) **of taxation**. Adam Smith suggested that taxation should be equitable, economical, convenient and certain, and to these I may add the canons of efficiency and flexibility. A 'good' tax

KEY TERM

principle (or **canon**) **of taxation:** a criterion for judging whether a tax is a good tax or a bad tax.

meets as many of these canons as possible, although because of conflicts and trade-offs, it is usually impossible for a tax to meet them all at the same time. A 'bad' tax meets few if any of the guiding principles of taxation. **Economy** means a tax should be cheap to collect in relation to the revenue it yields. **Equity** means a tax system should be fair, although there may be different and possibly conflicting interpretations of what is fair or equitable. Specifically, a particular tax should be based on the taxpayer's *ability to pay*. This principle is one of the justifications of progressive taxation, since the rich have a greater ability to pay than the poor. A tax is **efficient** if it achieves its desired objective(s) with minimum undesired side effects or unintended consequences. A tax is **flexible** if it can easily be changed to meet new circumstances. People must be reasonably certain of the amount of tax they must pay and the method of payment should be convenient to the taxpayer.

Public expenditure

The measurement of **public expenditure** is usually restricted to spending by central government and local government. Taken together this is called **general government expenditure**.

The measurement of public spending can also include spending on net investment in new capital by nationalised industries. However, most spending by nationalised industries is excluded on the grounds that it is financed by revenue raised from the sale of the industries' output and is not dependent on finance from the taxpayer. In any case, privatisation of most of the former nationalised industries means that spending by the few enterprises that remain in the state sector is very small, though recent bank nationalisations have changed this.

Perhaps more significant than the *absolute* totals of public expenditure is the **ratio of public expenditure to national income**, which indicates the share of the nation's resources taken by the government. Apart from the periods 1914–18 and 1939–45, which saw rapid, but temporary, increases in government spending to pay for the First and Second World Wars, the twentieth century witnessed a steady but relatively slow increase in government expenditure from around 10% to over 40% of GDP, reaching 46.75% in 1982/83. The ratio falls in a period of national prosperity but rises rapidly in times of recession, being closely related to what is happening to employment and unemployment. In the 2008 recession the ratio peaked at 47.7% in the financial year 2009/10, falling to 44.4% in 2013/14. The Coalition government hopes to reduce the ratio to less than 40% in 2017/18.

Spending on social security, which includes unemployment-related benefits, is by far the largest single category of public spending. Before the 2008 recession, the main unemployment benefit, the **jobseeker's allowance** (now being merged into universal credit), only amounted to about 5% of total welfare benefits. The **income-support benefit** (also being merged into universal credit) claimed by poor families and the **state pension** were much more important. When the economy booms, unemployment falls, so spending on social security also falls. The reverse is true in a recession. I revisit this issue later in the chapter when explaining the cyclical and structural components of the government's budget deficit and borrowing requirement, and the role of automatic stabilisers in the economy.

The ratio of public spending to GDP is an accurate measure of the share of the nation's total financial resources under the command of the government. However, because a large part of government expenditure is on **transfers**, such as the unemployment-related benefits just described, it is a misleading indicator of the share of national output produced by the government itself. Transfers do not involve a claim by the government on national output, or a diversion of resources by the government away from the private sector. Rather, spending on transfers merely redistributes income and spending power from one part of the private sector to another: from taxpayers to recipients of state benefits and pensions.

When transfers are excluded, government spending falls from over 40% or more of GDP to between only 20 and 30%. This figure is a more accurate measure of the share of national output directly commanded by the state (and thus unavailable for use in the private sector) to produce the hospitals, roads and other goods and services that the government collectively provides and finances, mostly out of taxation.

In 2013/14, interest payments on the **national debt** were expected to be £51 billion, or nearly 14% of public spending. For an obvious reason, this item of public spending increases when interest rates rise. However, *total* interest payments are also affected by the government's budgetary position. A budget deficit generally increases interest payments because it increases the total *stock* of government debt. Conversely, a budget surplus allows the government to reduce the national debt by paying back past borrowing. As a result total interest payments fall. In the early 2000s, low interest rates and a budget surplus both reduced debt repayments as a proportion of public spending and of GDP. By 2005, however, a budget deficit was once again increasing debt repayments, although to some extent this was offset by interest rates remaining low. From 2008 until 2013, the government's budget deficit grew even larger. (For more information, read Case Study 19.2 later in this chapter on the sovereign debt problem.)

The aims of taxation and public spending
An obvious aim of taxation is to raise the revenue required to finance government spending. In addition, you learnt when studying microeconomics at AS that, taxes and subsidies can be used to alter the relative prices of goods and services in order to change consumption patterns.

Ultimately, the aims of both taxation and public spending depend on the underlying philosophy and ideology of the government in power. They differ significantly, for example, between Keynesian and free-market or supply-side inspired governments.

I shall divide the aims or objectives of public spending and taxation into three main categories: allocation, distribution and economic management.

> **EXAM TIP**
>
> The aims of taxation should not be confused with the principles of taxation, though an aim might be to organise the tax system in accordance with the principles of taxation as much as possible.

Allocation

As I have just noted, taxes are used to alter relative prices and patterns of consumption. Demerit goods, such as alcohol and tobacco, are taxed in order to discourage consumption, while merit goods, such as museums, are untaxed and subsidised and sometimes directly provided by the state. Taxes are also used to finance the provision of public goods, such as defence, police and roads. Also, under the 'polluter must pay' principle, taxes are used to discourage and reduce the production and consumption of negative externalities, such as pollution and congestion. Likewise, subsidies are used to encourage the production or provision of external benefits or positive externalities. Taxation can be used to deter monopoly by taxing monopoly profit through removing the windfall gain accruing to a monopolist as a result of barriers to entry and inelastic supply.

Taxes are used to finance the provision of public goods, such as defence, police and roads

Distribution

The price mechanism is value-neutral with regard to the equity or social fairness of the distributions of income and wealth resulting from market forces in the economy.

If the government decides that the distributions of income and wealth produced by free-market forces are undesirable, taxation and transfers in its public spending programme can be used to modify these distributions and reduce the alleged market failure resulting from inequity.

Before 1979, UK governments of all political complexions used progressive taxation and a policy of transfers of income to the less well off in a deliberate attempt — albeit with limited success — to reduce inequalities in the distribution of income. Governments also extended the provision of merit goods such as free state education and healthcare, in order to improve the **social wage** of lower-income groups. The social wage is the part of a worker's standard of living received as goods and services provided at zero price or as income in kind by the state, being financed collectively out of taxation.

Between 1979 and 1997, Conservative governments changed the structure of both taxation and public spending to *widen* rather than *reduce* inequalities in the distributions of income and wealth. The reason for this change relates to the conflict between two of the principles or canons of taxation I mentioned earlier: equity and efficiency. The Conservatives believed that greater incentives for work and enterprise were necessary in order to increase the UK's growth rate. For free-market economists and politicians, progressive taxation and transfers to the poor meant that people had less incentive to work hard and to engage in entrepreneurial risk. Moreover, the ease with which the poor could claim welfare benefits and the level at which they were available created a situation in which the poor rationally chose unemployment and state benefits in preference to low wages and work. In this so-called **dependency culture**, the unwaged were effectively 'married to the state', but some of the poor, obviously not enjoying this marriage, drifted into antisocial behaviour, attacking bus shelters and other public property, as well as privately owned property.

The Conservatives argued that income tax rates and benefit rates should *both* be reduced. They believed that tax and benefit cuts would alter the labour/leisure choice in favour of supplying labour, particularly for benefit claimants who lack the skills necessary for high-paid jobs. They also believed that to make everyone eventually better off, the poor must first be made worse off. Increased inequality was necessary to facilitate economic growth from which all would eventually benefit. Through a *trickle down* effect, the poor would end up better off in absolute terms, but because inequalities had widened, they would still be relatively worse off compared to the rich.

After 1997, policy was again reversed, particularly in the late 1990s. Using initiatives such as the New Deal, New Labour governments tried to reduce income inequalities. But although the real incomes of most of the poor increased, income inequalities continue to grow, largely because high incomes have grown at a much faster rate than low incomes. However, recent Coalition government fiscal policy has one again widened income inequalities, though fewer low-income families now have to pay income tax.

EXAM TIP

Make sure you don't confuse fiscal and monetary policy, but understand the links between the two.

Economic management and fiscal policy

Everything I have written when discussing the allocative and distributional aims of taxation and government spending broadly relates to fiscal policy. However, the term 'fiscal policy' is normally used in relation to the economic management of the economy, usually, though not always, at a macro level.

Before proceeding further, I shall remind you of the definition of fiscal policy previously learnt at AS. **Fiscal policy** is used to achieve the government's economic objectives through the use of the fiscal instruments of taxation, public spending and the government's budgetary position. As an economic term, fiscal policy is often associated with Keynesian economic theory and policy. I noted earlier how, in the 1950s and 1960s, Keynesian governments abandoned the fiscal neutrality of sound finance and balanced budgets, preferring an active fiscal policy based on managing the level of aggregate demand.

However, it is misleading to associate fiscal policy exclusively with Keynesianism. Until recently, the Keynesian fiscal policy implemented in the UK in the three decades before 1979 was replaced by a very different supply-side fiscal policy. I shall now explain first **Keynesian fiscal policy** and then **supply-side fiscal policy**.

> **KEY TERMS**
>
> **fiscal policy:** the use of government spending, taxation and the government's budgetary position to achieve the government's policy objectives.
>
> **Keynesian fiscal policy:** policy used to manage aggregate demand, named after John Maynard Keynes.
>
> **supply-side fiscal policy:** policy used to increase personal incentives, favoured by free-market economists.

Keynesian fiscal policy

During the Keynesian era, fiscal policy took on a meaning more narrow and specific than the rather general definition I gave earlier. In the Keynesian era, fiscal policy came to mean the use of the overall levels of public spending, taxation and the budget deficit to manage the level of aggregate demand in the economy. The aim was to achieve full employment and to stabilise the economic cycle, without at the same time creating excessive inflationary pressures. Keynesian fiscal policy was implemented with varying degrees of success in the decades before 1979. Some of the Keynesian views which strongly influenced fiscal policy at the time were:

- Left to itself, an unregulated market economy results in unnecessarily low economic growth, high unemployment and volatile business cycles.
- A lack of aggregate demand, caused by a tendency for the private sector to save too much and invest too little, can mean that the economy settles into an under-full employment equilibrium characterised by demand-deficient unemployment.
- By deliberate deficit financing, the government can, using fiscal policy as a demand management instrument, inject demand and spending power into the economy to eliminate deficient demand and achieve full employment.
- Having achieved full employment, the government can then use fiscal policy in a discretionary way (that is, changing tax rates and levels of public spending to

meet new circumstances) to fine-tune the level of aggregate demand. For much of the Keynesian era, governments believed that fiscal policy could achieve full employment and stabilise the economic cycle, while avoiding an unacceptable increase in the rate of inflation.

- The overall stance of fiscal policy and, indeed, of economic policy in general, was orientated towards the demand side of the economy. The more microeconomic elements of fiscal policy, such as transfers to industry, were aimed at improving economic performance on the supply side. But on the whole, supply-side fiscal policy was treated as subordinate to the macroeconomic management of aggregate demand and to the assumption that output would respond to demand stimulation. In any case, the microeconomic elements of Keynesian fiscal policy were generally interventionist rather than non-interventionist, extending rather than reducing the state's role in the mixed economy.

- Central to Keynesian fiscal policy was the assumption that the government spending multiplier has a high value. At this stage you should refer back to Chapter 15 and refresh your knowledge of the national income multiplier in the context of shifts of the economy's aggregate demand curve. If the national income multiplier is large with respect to real output, for example 8, an increase in government spending of £10 billion increases aggregate demand and money national income by £80 billion. A large multiplier means that changing the levels of government spending, taxation and the budget deficit (or surplus) can be extremely effective in managing aggregate demand. However, for the reasons explained in Chapter 15, real-world government spending multipliers are small, not significantly different from unity (1).

> **EXAM TIP**
>
> Students often define fiscal policy too narrowly, simply in terms of Keynesian fiscal policy and demand management.

The government's budgetary position

Using the symbols G for government spending and T for taxation and other sources of revenue, the three possible budgetary positions of the government (and of the whole of the public sector) are:

$G = T$ (**balanced budget**)

$G > T$ (**budget deficit**)

$G < T$ (**budget surplus**)

A **government budget** deficit occurs when public spending exceeds revenue from taxation and other sources of revenue. A budget deficit can be eliminated by cutting public spending or raising taxation, both of which can balance the budget or move the budget into surplus. However, assuming that a deficit persists, the extent to which spending exceeds revenue must be financed by public sector borrowing. The Treasury has used various official terms for public sector borrowing, including the **public sector net cash requirement** (PSNCR) and **public sector net borrowing** (PSNB). However, because the Treasury frequently changes its official terminology, the most important thing to learn is that public sector borrowing represents 'the other side of the coin' to the budget deficit. Whenever there is a

> **KEY TERMS**
>
> **balanced budget:** total government spending equals total government revenue in a particular time period.
>
> **budget deficit:** total government spending exceeds total government revenue in a particular time period.
>
> **budget surplus:** total government spending is less than total government revenue in a particular time period.
>
> **government budget:** total government spending minus total government revenue in a particular time period, e.g. a year.

budget deficit there is a positive **borrowing requirement**. Conversely, a budget surplus means that the government can use the tax revenues that it is not spending to repay previous borrowing. In this case, the borrowing requirement is negative.

CASE STUDY 19.1

Sound finance and balanced budgets

The passage below is an extract from a budget speech delivered by Conservative chancellor Nigel Lawson during a period known as the 'Lawson boom'. The budget followed nearly 6 years of economic growth. During these years the public finances moved from deficit into surplus. Margaret Thatcher, the prime minister, hoped that the budget would remain in balance or in surplus and that budget deficits were a thing of the past. This was not to be. The severe recession that followed the Lawson boom in the early 1990s led to the return of a budget deficit. Thatcher probably hadn't understood the cyclical nature of budget surpluses and deficits.

At one time, it was regarded as the hallmark of good government to maintain a balanced budget; to ensure that government spending was fully financed by revenues from taxation, with no need for government borrowing.

Over the years, this simple and beneficent rule was increasingly disregarded. Profligacy not only brought economic disaster and the national humiliation of a bail out by the IMF; it also added massively to the burden of debt interest, not merely now but for a generation to come.

Thus, one of our main objectives, when we first took office in 1979, was to bring down government borrowing.

In 1987–88, the year now ending, we are set to secure something previously achieved only on one isolated occasion since the beginning of the 1950s: a balanced budget.

Indeed, we have gone even further. It looks as if the final outturn for 1987–88 will be a budget surplus of £3 billion. Instead of a PSBR, a PSDR: not a public sector borrowing requirement, but a public sector debt repayment.

Some two thirds of this substantial undershoot of the PSBR I set at the time of last year's Budget is the result of the increased tax revenues that have flowed from a buoyant economy; while the remaining third is due to lower than expected public expenditure, again the outcome of a buoyant economy: less in benefits for the unemployed.

A balanced budget is a valuable discipline for the medium term. It represents security for the present and an investment for the future. Having achieved it, I intend to stick to it. In other words, henceforth a zero PSBR will be the norm. This provides a clear and simple rule, with a good historical pedigree.

Source: Nigel Lawson's budget speech, 15 March 1988

Follow-up questions
1 Explain the meaning of a *balanced budget*.
2 Relate the two terms *PSBR* and *PSDR* to the state of the public finances.
3 Research the changes that have taken place in the state of the public finances from 1988 to the present day. In which years was there a budget surplus? How has the 2008 recession and subsequent recovery affected the public finances?

Automatic stabilisers

The previous sections might indicate that the fiscal policy choice facing a government lies between Keynesian-style discretionary demand management and balancing the budget as advocated by many supply-side economists. But in reality, there is an alternative approach that lies between these extremes, in which a government bases fiscal policy on the operation of automatic stabilisers. These dampen or reduce the multiplier effects resulting from any change in aggregate demand within the economy.

Suppose, for example, that a collapse of confidence or export orders causes aggregate demand to fall. National income then also begins to fall, declining by the initial fall in demand. But as national income falls and unemployment rises, *demand-led* public spending on unemployment pay and welfare benefits also rises. If the income tax system is progressive, the government's tax revenues fall faster than national income. In this way, increased public spending on transfers and declining tax revenues inject demand back into the economy, thereby stabilising and dampening the deflationary impact of the initial fall in aggregate demand, and reducing the overall size of the contractionary multiplier effect.

Automatic stabilisers also operate in the opposite direction to dampen the expansionary effect of an increase in aggregate demand. As incomes and employment rise, the take-up of means-tested welfare benefits and unemployment-related benefits automatically falls, while at the same time tax revenues rise faster than income. By taking demand out of the economy and reducing the size of the expansionary multiplier, automatic stabilisers reduce **overheating** in the boom phase of the economic cycle.

It is now widely agreed that automatic stabilisers such as progressive taxation and income-related transfers contributed to milder economic cycles experienced by the UK, prior to 1979 at least. Before the Second World War, economic cycles — or trade cycles, as they were then known — were much more volatile, displaying greater fluctuations between boom and slump than in the years between the Second World War and 1979. Keynesians claimed that recent relatively mild economic cycles prior to 1979 were evidence of the success of Keynesian demand management policies in stabilising cyclical fluctuations.

However, the economic cycle was relatively mild both in the UK and in countries such as Germany, which did not use fiscal policy to manage aggregate demand in a discretionary way. This suggests that the automatic stabilisers of progressive taxation and the safety net provided by welfare benefits for the poor — both of which were introduced widely in western industrialised economies after 1945 — were more significant than discretionary fiscal policy in reducing fluctuations in the economic cycle. Either way, economists now generally agree that a deficit should grow in the downswing of the economic cycle, provided the deficit is matched by a surplus in the subsequent upswing. There is some doubt, however, as to whether the chancellor George Osborne accepted this view when taking drastic action to cut the budget deficit in the depressed UK economy in 2010 and 2011.

> **KEY TERM**
>
> **automatic stabiliser:** a factor that changes in such a way as to automatically stabilise aggregate demand and the economic cycle. Examples are progressive taxation and unemployment benefits.

The cyclical and the structural budget deficit and borrowing requirement

To understand fully the links between the government's budgetary position and the wider economy, it is useful to distinguish between the cyclical and the structural components of the budget deficit and borrowing requirement. As the previous paragraphs indicate, the **cyclical budget deficit** is the part of the overall budget deficit that rises and falls with the downswings and upswings of the economic cycle as automatic stabilisers kick in. In the downswing of the economic cycle, tax revenues fall but public spending on unemployment and poverty-related welfare benefits increases. As a result, the government's finances deteriorate. Conversely, in the recovery and boom periods, tax revenues rise and spending on benefits falls.

If all the growth of the budget deficit and the related borrowing requirement were cyclical, the problem of a growing budget deficit would disappear when economic growth occurred, providing growth was sufficiently buoyant and sustained. But this does not happen if the cyclical changes are overridden by more powerful structural changes operating in the reverse direction. As the name suggests, growth in the *structural* component of the budget deficit and borrowing requirement relates to the changing structure of the UK economy. In recent years, a number of factors and trends, ranging from **deindustrialisation** and **globalisation** eroding the tax base via the movement of industries to eastern Europe and Asia, through to an ageing population and the growth of single-parent families dependent on welfare benefits, have contributed to the growth of the **structural budget deficit**.

The growing structural deficit carries the rather dispiriting message that a government that seriously wishes to improve public sector finances will need to introduce significant tax increases or public spending cuts, or possibly both.

Using *AD/AS* diagrams to illustrate Keynesian and supply-side fiscal policy

I shall first remind you of the aggregate demand equation or identity you learnt when studying Unit 2 last year:

$$AD = C + I + G + (X - M)$$

Government spending (G) is one of the components of aggregate demand. An increase in government spending and/or a cut in taxation increases the size of the budget deficit (or reduces the size of the budget surplus). Either way, an injection into the circular flow of income occurs and the effect on aggregate demand is expansionary.

Figure 19.1 illustrates the effect of such an expansionary or reflationary fiscal policy.

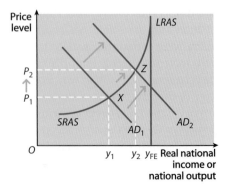

Figure 19.1 Keynesian or demand-side fiscal policy

Initially, with the aggregate demand curve in position AD_1, macroeconomic equilibrium occurs at point X. Real income or output is y_1, and the price level is P_1.

To eliminate the demand-deficient unemployment, the government increases the budget deficit by raising the level of government spending and/or by cutting taxes. The **expansionary fiscal policy** shifts the AD curve to the right from AD_1 to AD_2, and the economy moves to a new macroeconomic equilibrium at point Z.

However, the extent to which expansionary fiscal policy *reflates* real output (in this case from y_1 to y_2), or creates excess demand that leads to demand-pull inflation (in this case an increase in the price level from P_1 to P_2), depends on the shape of the AS curve, which in turn depends on how close the economy was to full employment. The nearer the economy gets to full employment, the greater the inflationary effect of expansionary fiscal policy and the smaller the reflationary effect. Once the full-employment level of real income is reached on the long-run aggregate supply curve at y_{FE}, a further increase in government spending or a tax cut inflates the price level. In this situation, real output cannot grow (except possibly temporarily), because there is no spare capacity. The economy is producing on its production possibility frontier.

Figure 19.1 can be adapted to illustrate the effect of a **contractionary** (deflationary) **fiscal policy**. In this case a cut in government spending and/or an increase in taxation shifts the AD curve to the left. The extent to which the demand deflation results in the price level or real income falling once again depends on the shape and slope of the $SRAS$ curve.

Along with other supply-side policies, which I mention briefly later in this chapter, supply-side fiscal policy is used to try and shift the economy's long-run aggregate supply ($LRAS$) curve to the right, thereby increasing the economy's potential level of output. The effect of successful supply-side fiscal policy on the $LRAS$ curve is shown in Figure 19.2. (Note that an outward movement of the economy's production possibility frontier can also illustrate the intended effect of supply-side policies.)

Crowding out

Many supply-side economists believe that government spending and taxation *crowds out* private sector spending and output. There are two forms of **crowding out**: resource crowding out and financial crowding out.

Resource crowding out is associated with two basic economic concepts: scarcity and opportunity cost. Because it is impossible to employ real resources simultaneously in both the private and public sectors, the opportunity cost of employing more capital and labour in the public sector inevitably involves sacrificing the opportunity to use the same resources in private employment.

KEY TERMS

expansionary fiscal policy: uses fiscal policy to increase aggregate demand and to shift the *AD* curve to the right.

contractionary fiscal policy: uses fiscal policy to decrease aggregate demand and to shift the *AD* curve to the left.

crowding out: a process through which private sector spending and output is displaced by the growth of public sector spending and output.

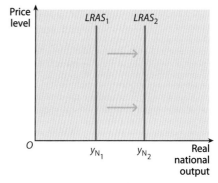

Figure 19.2 The intended effect of supply-side fiscal policy

Financial crowding out results from the method of financing an increase in public spending. As I have explained, public spending can be financed by taxation or borrowing. Taxation obviously reduces the spending power of the private individuals and firms paying the taxes. Note, however, that if extra tax revenues paid by high income earners with a relatively low marginal propensity to consume are transferred as welfare benefits to poorer people with higher marginal propensities to consume, higher taxation may *increase* private sector spending, although at the probable cost of reduced personal incentives.

However, suppose, for example, that the government increases public spending by £40 billion, financing the resulting budget deficit with a sale of new gilt-edged securities (gilts) on the capital market. In order to persuade insurance companies, pension funds and the other financial institutions in the market for gilts to buy the extra debt, the guaranteed annual interest rate offered on new gilt issues must increase. But the resulting general rise in interest rates makes it more expensive for firms to borrow and to raise capital. Private sector investment thus falls.

Resource crowding out versus Keynesian crowding in

Resource crowding out assumes full employment of all resources, including labour. But when spare capacity and unemployed labour exist in the economy, increased public spending does not necessarily reduce the private sector's use of resources. Instead, by using previously idle resources, increased government spending merely takes up the slack in the economy. Indeed, with unemployed resources, increased public spending financed by a budget deficit may, via the multiplier process I explained in Chapter 15, stimulate or *crowd in* the private sector. For example, increased spending on a public works road-building programme creates orders for private sector construction firms that, through their own spending in the subsequent stages of the multiplier process, generate further business for the private sector.

Resource crowding out and Keynesian crowding in are illustrated in panel (a) of Figure 19.3. The production possibility frontier drawn in the diagram shows maximum levels of output that can be produced with various combinations of public sector and private sector spending and output. Assuming there is full employment and the economy is initially at point A, an increase in public sector spending from Pu_1 to Pu_2 crowds out or displaces private sector spending, which falls from Pr_1 to Pr_2, shown at point B. The size of the multiplier with respect to real output is therefore zero. Indeed, extreme free-market economists go further, arguing that the multiplier may be negative because in their view, 'wealth-consuming' public sector spending displaces 'wealth-creating' private sector spending, thereby shifting inward the economy's production possibility frontier. In the extreme, this argument is rather silly, since it implies that *all* private sector spending, such as gambling, is 'wealth-producing', while *all* public sector spending, for example on roads or hospitals, is 'wealth-consuming' or unproductive.

Keynesians agree that crowding out occurs if the economy is initially fully employed with no spare capacity. But suppose that to begin with the economy is producing *inside* the frontier, at a point such as C in panel (a) of Figure 19.3. In this situation, crowding in rather than crowding out may occur. An increase in public spending from C to D stimulates private sector output, which is shown by the movement along the horizontal arrow from D to point E on the production possibility frontier. If the size of the multiplier exceeds unity (1) most of the increase in output takes place in the private sector rather than in the public sector. The initial increase in government spending stimulates rather than displaces the private sector.

Whether an increase in public sector spending crowds out or crowds in the private sector should depend on whether the economy is initially on its production possibility frontier, at a position such as A, or inside the frontier, such as at C. Keynesians argue that the size of unemployment indicates whether or not the economy is *on* or inside the production possibility frontier, and that, in periods of recession, the economy is definitely inside its frontier. Free-market economists respond by arguing that unemployment figures provide a misleading indicator of whether the economy is on its production possibility frontier. The correct indicator is the existence of spare and competitive capacity capable of producing goods and services of a quality that people actually want. According to this view, increased public spending can crowd out the private sector even when unemployment is high. If the required supply-side production capacity is not in place to respond to the stimulus of extra government spending, the economy behaves *'as if'* it is fully employed.

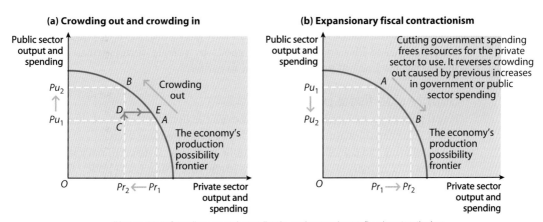

Figure 19.3 Crowding out and crowding in, and expansionary fiscal contractionism

Expansionary fiscal contractionism

Panel (b) of Figure 19.3 illustrates how chancellor George Osborne implemented fiscal policy after May 2010. Osborne believed that severe cuts in government spending would free resources for the private sector to use, and that the private sector would make better use of these resources than the government. If this is the case, workers who lose their jobs in the public sector immediately become employed more productively in the private sector. This view of how fiscal policy should operate has been called **expansionary fiscal contractionism**. Needless to say, many economists don't accept Osborne's idea of how the economy works. Christina Romer at the University of California commented:

> Despite what I feel is overwhelming and compelling evidence that fiscal stimulus is expansionary, and fiscal contraction is, well, contractionary, many politicians claim the opposite is true. …But even more striking are the number who assert forcefully that fiscal austerity — getting the budget deficit down immediately — would be good for unemployment and growth.

The link between fiscal policy and monetary policy

Recent UK governments (and the Bank of England) have realised that, because monetary and fiscal policy are *interdependent* rather than *independent* of each other, the success of monetary policy depends on the fiscal policy implemented by the Treasury. As I have explained, whenever the Treasury runs a budget deficit, the government has to borrow to finance the difference between spending and revenue. Conversely, a budget surplus enables repayment of past borrowing and a fall in the national debt.

The government borrows in two main ways: by selling short-dated debt or **Treasury bills** and by borrowing long term by selling **government bonds** or **gilt-edged securities**, commonly known as **gilts**. New issues of gilts are largely sold to non-bank financial institutions such as pension funds and insurance companies. To persuade these institutions to finance a growing budget deficit, the government may have to raise the rate of interest offered on new gilt issues. However, higher interest rates discourage investment in capital goods by private sector firms. This is the financial crowding out process I referred to earlier.

Supply-side fiscal policy

Fiscal policy is a major element, perhaps even the dominant element, of supply-side policy. Three main features of supply-side fiscal policy have been:

- Abandoning the use of taxation and public spending as discretionary instruments of demand management. Supply-siders argue that using fiscal policy to stimulate or reflate aggregate demand to achieve growth and full employment is, in the long run, at best ineffective and at worst damaging. They argue that any growth of output and employment resulting from an expansionary fiscal policy is at best short-lived and that in the long term the main effect of such a policy is inflation, which quickly destroys the conditions necessary for satisfactory market performance and wealth creation.
- Adopting **medium-term policy 'rules'** (in place of demand management) to reduce public spending, taxation and government borrowing as proportions of national

output. In 2010, chancellor George Osborne introduced two medium-term fiscal rules. These were the **deficit rule** and the **debt rule**, which I explain later in this chapter.

- Using fiscal policy in a microeconomic way to create supply-side incentives in the economy. Supply-side influenced governments subordinated the more macroeconomic elements of fiscal policy, which were dominant during the Keynesian era, to a much more microeconomic fiscal policy, intended to combine an overall reduction in the levels of taxation and public spending with the creation of incentives aimed at improving economic performance on the supply side of the economy.

Furthermore, the macroeconomic elements of fiscal policy became subservient to the needs of *monetary* policy. Control over public spending and borrowing was seen as a precondition for successful control of monetary growth and inflation. Again, I explain this later in the chapter.

CASE STUDY 19.2

The sovereign debt problem

While exam questions will not require you to know about sovereign debt, your understanding of current economic problems will be weak and superficial if you don't know what sovereign debt is, and its implications for economic policy. Sovereign debt does *not* refer to the amount of money the Queen has borrowed (though when the Queen Mother died at the age of 101 in 2002, she allegedly left debts of £7 million for UK taxpayers to pay). Instead, sovereign debt is the part of the **national debt** that is the debt of UK central government. (Strictly, sovereign debt is the part of the national debt owned outside the UK.) In contrast to the annual central government borrowing requirement, which is the *flow* of net new borrowing which finances the government's budget deficit, the national debt is the accumulated *stock* of past borrowing which the government has not paid back. In 2013, the national debt stock was estimated to be around £1.6 trillion, while the flow of central government borrowing in financial year 2012/13 was approximately £120 billion (ignoring the effect of revenue received from one-off events).

So why does the size of sovereign debt create problems for UK economic policy? Several decades ago, UK governments financed budget deficits largely by borrowing from their own citizens. This is no longer the case. These days, much UK government borrowing takes place on international financial markets. Large UK budget deficits and borrowing requirements, together with the additional borrowing that has to take place to renew or 'roll over' the national debt, require the rest of the world to lend huge amounts of money to the UK government. In this situation, international financiers may be reluctant to lend to Britain, except at ever-higher interest rates which the country cannot afford.

Overseas lenders are also influenced by the credit rating granted to UK government borrowing by credit-rating agencies such as Standard and Poor's and Moody's. Before 2013, the UK government enjoyed a 'Triple A' rating, which indicated that overseas investors had a high degree of confidence in the government's ability to repay its debt. However, in February 2013, Moody's cut the UK's rating from AAA to Aa1 on the ground that UK growth would 'remain sluggish over the next few years'.

Follow-up questions

1 To what extent, if any, has the removal of the UK's 'Triple A' rating affected the UK government's ability to borrow?
2 Do you agree that the emergence of the sovereign debt problem has been the sole cause of chancellor George Osborne's fiscal austerity programme? Justify your answer.

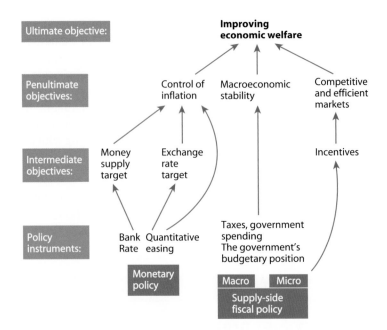

Figure 19.4 Comparing monetary policy and supply-side fiscal policy on a flow-line diagram

The flow chart I have set out in Figure 19.4 allows us to compare important aspects of monetary policy and supply-side fiscal policy.

The left-hand side of the flow chart shows the instruments and objectives of monetary policy. The monetary policy flow-lines assume that control of inflation is the principal monetary policy objective. However, even if this is true, control of inflation is best viewed as a penultimate policy objective, since improving economic welfare (shown at the top of the flow chart) should be regarded as the true ultimate policy objective. The two monetary policy instruments on the flow chart are Bank Rate and quantitative easing. At this stage, you might refer back to Chapter 18 to remind yourself of how monetary policy works and of the fact that recent monetary policy has focused more on stimulating recovery from recession rather than on controlling inflation. Remember also that monetary policy and not fiscal policy is used to manage aggregate demand, though as I have noted, fiscal policy was used to manage demand in the 2008–10 fiscal stimulus.

The macroeconomic element of supply-side fiscal policy focuses, not on demand management, but on creating conditions of macroeconomic stability. Macroeconomic stability, which is a rather vague term, can be taken to mean a national economy in which the macroeconomic environment is conducive to sustained growth and attaining other objectives such as a stable price level and low unemployment. Supply-side economists believe that a prerequisite for macroeconomic stability is a reduction in the size of the public sector so as to free resources for the private sector to use. (See my earlier description of *expansionary fiscal contractionism*.) By contrast, the microeconomic element of fiscal policy aims at creating the personal incentives deemed necessary to create competitive and efficient markets.

The Laffer curve

Supply-side economists believe that high rates of income tax and the overall burden on taxpayers create disincentives that, by reducing national income as taxation increases, also reduce the government's total tax revenue. This effect is illustrated by the **Laffer curve** in Figure 19.5.

The Laffer curve is named after the leading supply-side economist, Arthur Laffer. Laffer's curve shows how the government's total tax revenue changes as the average tax rate increases from 0% to 100%. Tax revenue must be zero when the average tax rate is 0%, but the diagram also shows that total tax revenue is again zero when the tax rate is 100%. With the average tax rate set at 100%, all income must be paid as tax to the government. In this situation, there is no incentive to produce output other than for subsistence, so with no output produced, the government ends up collecting no tax revenue.

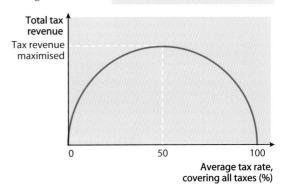

Figure 19.5 The Laffer curve

Between the limiting tax rates of 0% and 100%, the Laffer curve shows tax revenue first rising and then falling as the average rate of taxation increases. Tax revenue is maximised at the highest point on the Laffer curve, which in Figure 19.5 occurs at an average tax rate (for all taxes) of 50%. Beyond this point, any further increase in the average tax rate becomes counter-productive, causing total tax revenue to fall.

Supply-side economists argue that the increase in the tax burden in the Keynesian era, needed to finance the growing size of the government and public sectors, raised the average tax rate towards or beyond the critical point on the Laffer curve at which tax revenue is maximised. As noted, in this situation any further tax increase has the perverse effect of reducing the government's total tax revenue. This means that if the government wishes to increase total tax revenue, it must cut tax rates rather than increase them. A reduction in tax rates creates the incentives needed to stimulate economic growth. Faster growth means that *total tax revenue* increases despite the fact that *tax rates* are lower. Arguably, the effect is reinforced by a decline in tax evasion and avoidance, as the incentive to engage in these activities reduces at lower marginal tax rates.

The Office for Budgetary Responsibility (OBR)

On coming into office in 1997, the then Labour government made the Bank of England operationally independent from the Treasury. Over the next few years, many politicians and economists argued that fiscal policy should be treated in a similar way. Although this has not happened (the Treasury remains firmly in control of fiscal policy), in 2010 George Osborne, the incoming Conservative chancellor, created the **Office for Budget Responsibility (OBR)** to provide independent analysis of the UK's public sector finances. The OBR produces forecasts for the economy and public finances. The Treasury still produces the bulk of the forecasting. But, instead of the chancellor making judgements based on these data, the OBR rules on whether the government's policy has a better than 50% chance of meeting fiscal targets. (Cynics say that the OBR's main function is to act as a panel of expert economists whom the chancellor can blame 'when things go wrong').

Amongst its other functions, the OBR judges progress being made toward achieving the two fiscal rules which the government aims to meet in the medium term, i.e. up to about 5 years ahead. These are explained in the next section.

George Osborne's two fiscal rules

As already mentioned, since 2010 chancellor George Osborne has abandoned demand-side fiscal policy and reverted to supply-side fiscal policy. Instead of using fiscal policy to manage or 'tweak' aggregate demand, Osborne's macro policy is 'rule-based'. The chancellor has set out two **fiscal rules** which he aims to meet and which are meant to constrain fiscal policy at the macro level. These are the **deficit rule** and the **debt rule**.

- **The deficit rule.** According to the OBR, the deficit rule is to: *'Balance the cyclically adjusted current budget (CACB) by the end of a rolling, five-year period.'* Cutting through this gobbledygook, this means taking action to get rid of the structural part of the budget deficit within 5 years, but not stating when the 5 years begin. Osborne's opponents have interpreted this as meaning eliminating the structural deficit before the end of the 2010 parliament, i.e. by May 2015, but this is not the case. The definition of the deficit rule is in fact so woolly that it is impossible for Osborne to break the rule. But by the same token, as it does not bind the chancellor to a definite deficit-reduction programme, this largely reduces the rule's usefulness.
- **The debt rule.** This is more straightforward than the deficit rule, since the debt rule doesn't involve rolling forecast horizons and tricky definitions. The debt rule (relating to the national debt or debt of central government) is to *'Ensure that debt is falling as a share of GDP by 2015–16'.*

CASE STUDY 19.3

'We're paying down Britain's debts.' David Cameron, 24 January 2013

It's not just the politicians who are in a muddle about the economy. Only a tiny proportion of Britons understand the difference between debt and deficit — or know which one the government is trying to reduce. According to a Centre for Policy Studies (CPS) report 'A Distorted Debate', only 10% of Britons know that the government's cuts package is projected to increase the national debt by around £600 billion by 2015. Many more (47%) assume — incorrectly — that the government wants to reduce the debt by this amount. The think-tank report shows that the prime minister, his deputy and the chancellor have all fed this confusion by making 'misleading' claims about their financial plans.

The confusion stems from 'debt' and 'deficit' being used interchangeably. In fact, the UK's debt is the total amount the country owes historically, while the deficit is what is added to that debt each year.

According to the CPS report 'The Government has often said that it wants to pay off the nation's credit card. But if it wants to use that analogy correctly, it should be saying that it wants to reduce the amount that is added to the credit card debt each year — that is, reduce new borrowing.'

Follow-up questions

1 Explain why the national debt must always rise when there is a budget deficit.
2 Find out what has happened to the budget deficit and the national debt since 2013. Has the government met its fiscal rules?

The wider meaning of supply-side economic policy

Supply-side economic policy now encompasses more than just fiscal policy. In a rather broader interpretation, supply-side economic policy can be defined as the set of government initiatives that aim to change the underlying structure of the economy and improve the economic performance of markets and industries and of individual firms and workers within markets. For the most part, **supply-side policies** are also microeconomic rather than simply macroeconomic, since they act on the motivation and efficiency of individual economic agents within the economy to improve general economic performance.

> **KEY TERM**
>
> **supply-side policies:** aim to make markets more competitive and efficient, increase production potential, and shift the *LRAS* curve to the right. Supply-side fiscal policy is arguably the most important type of supply-side policy.

Supply-siders, along with other members of the free-market revival, believe that the economy is usually close to its natural levels of output and employment. However, due to distortions and inefficiencies resulting from Keynesian neglect of the supply side, towards the end of the Keynesian era the natural levels of output and employment became unnecessarily low, which meant that the natural rate of unemployment (NRU) became unnecessarily high. To increase the natural levels of output and employment and to reduce NRU, supply-side economists recommend the use of appropriate microeconomic policies to remove distortions, improve incentives and generally make markets more competitive.

During the Keynesian era of the 1960s and 1970s, government microeconomic policy in the UK was generally interventionist, extending the roles of the state and of the planning mechanism. The policy became known as industrial policy. Aspects of industrial policy, such as regional policy, competition policy and industrial relations policy, generally increased the role of the state and limited the role of markets. By contrast, supply-side microeconomic policy is anti-interventionist, attempting to roll back government interference in the activities of markets and of private economic agents and to change the economic function of government from *provider* to *enabler*. The fiscal policy elements of supply-side economic policy include: tax cuts to create incentives to work, save and invest, and cuts in welfare benefits to reduce the incentive to choose unemployment rather than a low-paid work alternative. There are many other supply-side policies in addition to fiscal policies. These include policies of privatisation, marketisation (commercialisation) and deregulation, which I described in Chapter 9.

In essence, the supply-siders, together with the other free-market economists, wish to create an **enterprise economy.** In this broad interpretation, supply-side policies aim to promote entrepreneurship and popular capitalism and to replace the dependency culture and statism. Indeed, for free-market economists in general, the Keynesian *mixed economy* could perhaps best be described as a *mixed-up economy.*

The European Union fiscal policy

The European Union (EU) does not as yet have a common fiscal policy. However, if the EU ever achieves full economic union, member countries will have to dispense with large elements of national fiscal policies. They would have to have similar tax structures and tax rates and would lose the freedom to use budget deficits and surpluses to manage demand within their countries. But, so far, this has not happened, and many argue it never will, at least in the foreseeable future.

The EU's **common monetary policy** and the **single currency** (the euro) within the eurozone mean that countries such as Ireland and Greece can no longer use monetary policy to manage demand within their borders. As a result, member states try to use fiscal policy for this purpose. This freedom is limited because, in an increasingly globalised economy, financial markets exert discipline over any government that implements an irresponsible national fiscal policy. Financial markets simply refuse to supply the funds to finance the government's budget deficit, except at a much higher interest rate than before.

EU tax harmonisation

Currently, the EU imposes two main limits on a member state's fiscal freedom. These result from **tax harmonisation** and the Stability and Growth Pact. The logic behind tax harmonisation is as follows. Although trade barriers have been eliminated in the EU's single market, the common market is incomplete. A genuine common market also requires that indirect taxes among the member countries are brought closely into line or harmonised. For eventual economic union to occur, tax harmonisation is indispensable, though this does not necessarily imply the complete equalisation of tax rates.

The European Union requires all new member states to introduce **value added tax (VAT).** However, the rate at which VAT is levied varies between states. Although some progress has been made in harmonising VAT rates by agreeing maximum and minimum rates, it has been harder to persuade member states to end zero-rating of certain items (e.g. newspapers and books within the UK). Harmonisation of excise duties has been even less successful and the big difference in duties between member states leads to phenomena such as the 'booze-cruises' that transport alcoholic drink and cigarettes between France and Britain.

The Stability and Growth Pact

In the 1990s, the **Stability and Growth Pact** (SGP) was established as an agreement to limit budget deficits in countries that are members of the eurozone. Establishing the eurozone meant that control of interest rates passed from member state governments to the European Central Bank, whose task is to keep inflation under control. At the time, Germany and France feared that so-called 'club-med' countries in southern Europe would try to escape the deflationary impact of the ECB's tough monetary policy by increasing public spending and by running large budget deficits. The eurozone's northern member states therefore insisted that *all* member countries agreed to limit their budget deficits as a proportion of GDP.

> **KEY TERM**
>
> **Stability and Growth Pact:** an agreement by EU countries to limit budget deficits in order to promote economic convergence among the member states of the European Union.

The basic principle of the SGP was simple. In normal times all members of the European Union (and not only the eurozone members) were meant to aim for government budgets that are 'close to balance or in surplus'. Governments that run fiscal deficits bigger than 3% of GDP had to take swift corrective action.

In the outcome, the recession suffered by almost all eurozone countries since 2008, and the accompanying financial and fiscal crises, have meant that the 'club-med' countries, along with Ireland, have far exceeded the 3% budget deficit rule. In the crisis, the average deficit increased by more than 5 percentage points, reaching 6% of GDP in 2010. Ireland's record deficit of 32.4% (which included one-off support for the banking sector) dwarfed the next three largest deficits, which stood at around 10% of GDP. In 2010, average national debts reached 85% of GDP in the euro area, almost 20 percentage points above the pre-crisis level. Five countries had debt ratios approaching or exceeding 100%. These countries were forced to seek financial support. In order to establish an institutional framework for such operations, the European Financial Stability Facility (EFSF) was set up in 2010 and tasked with providing emergency financing until 2013. Thereafter, the European Stability Mechanism (ESM) takes over this role. The agreed increase in deficits above the 3% limit meant that the requirements laid down in the Stability and Growth Pact had become meaningless.

Many economists now believe that for the eurozone to survive, member countries must adopt a common fiscal policy that goes far beyond the requirements of the Stability and Growth Pact. Achieving this will be difficult, but what is certain is that the UK will never decide to adopt the euro and join the eurozone, given the loss of fiscal sovereignty this would inevitably involve.

- Over more than a century, UK fiscal policy developed from balanced budgets and 'sound finance' to Keynesian demand management, to supply-side fiscal policy, and in 2008 back to Keynesian demand management.
- Taxes can be progressive, regressive or proportionate.
- The principles or canons of taxation are used to judge whether a tax is good or bad.
- Public spending is used to provide economic services, to transfer income from rich to poor and to pay interest on past government borrowing.
- Taxation and public spending have allocative, distributional and economic management aims.
- Keynesian fiscal policy centres on using the budget deficit to manage aggregate demand, through shifts of the aggregate demand (AD) curve.
- Supply-side fiscal policy focuses on shifting the long-run aggregate supply (LRAS) curve to the right via increases in personal incentives.
- Progressive taxation and means-tested welfare benefits function as automatic stabilisers.
- Supply-side economists believe that increased public spending crowds out the private sector, whereas Keynesians believe it crowds in or stimulates private spending.
- The Laffer curve is used to justify supply-side tax cuts.
- Current UK fiscal policy aims to meet two fiscal rules: the deficit rule and the debt rule.
- Financial and fiscal crisis in the European Union has made the European Union's Stability and Growth Pact more or less meaningless.

Exam-style questions

1 Explain the difference between the cyclical and the structural components of a budget deficit. **(15 marks)**

2 Explain how automatic stabilisers operate. **(15 marks)**

3 Evaluate the view that budget deficits and government borrowing are a cause for concern. **(25 marks)**

4 Do you agree that supply-side policies on their own are sufficient to help the economy achieve a sustainable and satisfactory rate of economic growth? Justify your answer. **(25 marks)**

Extra resources to help you revise are available online at www.hodderplus.co.uk/philipallan

International trade and globalisation

Chapter 20

This chapter explains the case for international specialisation and trade, the benefits of the international division of labour and the principle of comparative advantage, and weighs up counter-arguments to justify import controls or protectionism. This section of the chapter is followed by an analysis of the welfare gains resulting from free trade and of the welfare losses caused by tariffs.

The chapter goes on to explain changes in the patterns of world trade and UK trade. The main changes have been a switch from a North–South pattern to a North–North pattern of trade and the growth of exports of manufactured goods produced in newly industrialising countries (NICs), particularly China. I develop the chapter by linking trade theory, in part via the role of the World Trade Organization (WTO), to globalisation. However, globalisation covers much more than just trade liberalisation, including the effects of increased capital and labour mobility and the growing ability of multinational corporations (MNCs) to exert power over the national economies in which they operate. I survey these and other features of globalisation in the concluding sections of the chapter.

LEARNING OUTCOMES

This chapter will:
- explain the case for free trade
- describe different forms of protectionism
- survey patterns of trade, both for global trade and for the UK
- discuss the meaning of globalisation
- examine the main elements of globalisation
- describe the role of the World Trade Organization (WTO)

WHAT YOU SHOULD ALREADY KNOW

At AS you came across the concepts of specialisation and the division of labour and exchange, but you learnt little about international trade. What you did learn was in the context of the current account of the balance of payments and exchange rates. For example, you learnt about the meaning of the balance of trade in goods and the balance of trade in services and how changes in exchange rates can affect these balances. International trade is best regarded as a completely new topic at A2, which you must learn from scratch.

The case for international trade

Widening choice

Imagine a small country such as Iceland in a world without international trade. As a **closed economy**, Iceland's production possibilities are limited to the goods and services that its narrow resource base can produce. This means that Iceland's average costs of production are likely to be high because the small population and the absence of export markets mean that economies of scale and long production runs cannot be achieved. At the same time, the consumption possibilities of Iceland's inhabitants are restricted to the goods that the country can produce.

Compare this with Iceland's position in a world completely open to international trade. In an **open economy**, imports of raw materials and energy greatly boost Iceland's production possibilities. In theory at least, Iceland can now produce a much wider range of goods. In practice, however, Iceland produces the relatively few goods and services that it is good at producing, and imports all the rest. By gaining access to the much larger world market, Iceland's industries benefit from economies of scale and long production runs. Likewise, imports of food and other consumer goods present Iceland's inhabitants with a vast array of choice and the possibility of a much higher living standard and level of economic welfare than are possible in a world without trade.

International trade improves consumer choice

CASE STUDY 20.1

The collapse of Iceland's economy

Since first writing the above section about Iceland's economy several years ago, the country has become a case study, first of the benefits of opening up its economy to free trade, but more recently of the disadvantages of such openness. However, since 2010 Iceland has been praised for its handling of the financial crisis. Unlike in eurozone countries such as Greece, a newly elected government allowed banks to fail, rather than bailing them out. (In 2013 the 'rescue-government' was voted out of office and replaced by the politicians responsible for the crisis in the first place!)

Iceland has a population just larger than 300,000, which is roughly equal to the population of Cardiff. Following the deregulation of the country's financial system in 2000, Iceland's banks grew to become the nation's largest industry. Because of the small size of Iceland's economy, this growth could only happen if the banks expanded overseas, particularly in Britain. Iceland began to 'export' financial services and accumulated assets in the rest of the world equal to about ten times the country's GDP. In return, it imported luxury goods to maintain the lifestyles of Iceland's newly rich population. Before the crash of 2008, Iceland was ranked first in the United Nation's Human Development Index.

But it all ended in tears. Iceland's banks had grown to be far larger than the domestic economy could sustain. They owned 'toxic' assets and were allegedly riddled with fraud. The financial system collapsed in 2008, the economy shrank, the exchange rate lost most of its value and unemployment grew very rapidly. Although other factors were involved, much of this debacle resulted from over-exposure to free trade and to the free movement of capital in little-regulated and increasingly globalised financial markets.

Follow-up questions

1 For Iceland, financial services have been an invisible export. What does this mean?

2 What is meant by financial deregulation?

Specialisation and the division of labour

Before explaining the benefits of international trade, I must first introduce you to two important economic principles: the **division of labour** and the **principle of comparative advantage**.

Over 200 years ago, the great classical economist, Adam Smith, first explained how, within a single production unit or firm (he took the example of a pin factory), output can increase if workers specialise in different tasks in a manufacturing process. Smith established one of the most fundamental of all economic principles: the benefits of **specialisation** and the division of labour. According to Adam Smith, there are three main reasons why specialisation increases total output:

> **EXAM TIP**
>
> You must appreciate the different contexts in which the division of labour occurs: locally, regionally and internationally.

- Workers don't need to switch between tasks, so time is saved.
- More and better machinery or capital is employed. Increasing capital at the same rate at which the labour force is increasing is called capital widening. Increasing the amount of capital per worker is called capital deepening.
- Practice makes workers more efficient and productive when performing specialised tasks (although because of 'deskilling', boredom and the creation of alienation towards employers, this can easily become a disadvantage).

The principle of the division of labour not only explains specialisation *between* workers *within* a factory: it can also be extended to explain the specialisation between plants or factories within a firm; specialisation between separate firms; and, lastly, geographical or spatial specialisation both internally within a country and externally between countries. Such *international* specialisation is the main subject of this chapter.

Absolute advantage

The benefits of the **international division of labour** suggest that if each of the world's countries, with its own endowment of natural resources such as soil, climate and minerals, and of man-made resources such as capital, know-how and labour skills, specialises in what it does best, total world output or production can increase compared to the outcome without specialisation. Being 'better at' producing a good or service means that a country can produce the good at the lowest cost

> **KEY TERMS**
>
> **international division of labour:** describes different countries specialising in producing different goods.
>
> **absolute advantage:** occurs when a country is absolutely best (or more technically efficient) than other countries in a particular industry.

in terms of resources used. Using microeconomic terminology, the country is technically and productively efficient in producing the good. We can also say that a country that is absolutely 'best at', or most technically efficient at, producing a good or service possesses an **absolute advantage** in the good's production. Conversely, if it is not the best, the country suffers an absolute disadvantage compared to other more technically efficient producers.

To explain absolute advantage, I shall assume just two countries in the world economy, Atlantis and Pacifica. Each country has only 2 units of resource. Only two goods can be produced: guns and butter. Each unit of resource, or indeed a fraction of each unit (because I shall assume that resources or inputs are divisible), can be switched from one industry to another, if so desired, in each country. In each country the production possibilities are such that 1 unit of resource can produce:

- in Atlantis: 4 guns or 2 tonnes of butter
- in Pacifica: 1 gun or 6 tonnes of butter

Quite clearly, in terms of technical efficiency, Atlantis is 'best at' — or has an absolute advantage in — producing guns. It is four times more technically efficient in gun production than Pacifica. However, this is not the case for butter production. Pacifica is three times more technically efficient in butter production and so possesses an absolute advantage in this good.

Suppose that both countries devote half their total resources to each activity (that is, 1 unit of resource out of the 2 units available for each country). Atlantis produces 4 guns and Pacifica produces 1 gun, which means that 5 guns are produced in total. Likewise, total butter production is 8 tonnes. Atlantis produces 2 tonnes and Pacifica produces 6 tonnes.

Now let's see what happens when each country produces only the good in which it has an absolute advantage. Atlantis devotes both its resource units to guns, producing 8 guns. Likewise, Pacifica completely specialises, producing 12 tonnes of butter with its 2 units of resource.

- Without specialisation, outputs are 5 guns and 8 tonnes of butter.
- With specialisation, outputs become 8 guns and 12 tonnes of butter.

In this example, specialisation produces a net output gain of 3 guns and 4 tonnes of butter.

But for output gains to translate into gains from trade, two further factors have to be taken into account. First, administration and transport costs occur whenever trade takes place. As a result, the output gains from trade are:

(3 guns + 4 tonnes of butter) – transport and administration costs

Clearly, specialisation and trade are not worthwhile if transport and administration costs exceed the output gains resulting from specialisation.

Second, assuming that only two countries trade with each other, for output gains to transfer into *welfare* gains for the inhabitants of both countries, the goods being traded must be in demand in the importing country. Given this assumption about demand, I shall further assume that each country exports its surplus to the other country once it has satisfied its own inhabitants' demand for the good in which it specialises. (This **double coincidence of wants** is not necessary when more than two countries trade together.)

But suppose Atlantis's inhabitants are vegans who refuse to eat animal products, while Pacifica's inhabitants are pacifists who hate guns. For Atlantis's inhabitants, butter is a *bad* rather than a *good*. Likewise, guns are a bad for Pacifica's residents. (A **good** yields **utility** or **economic welfare** to consumers, but a **bad** yields **disutility** or **negative welfare**.) Atlantis refuses to import butter, and Pacifica refuses to buy guns. Specialisation and trade do not take place. Without suitable demand conditions, the case for specialisation and trade disappears.

> **EXAM TIP**
>
> It is important to understand the difference between absolute and comparative advantage.

Comparative advantage

Absolute advantage must not be confused with the rather more subtle concept of **comparative advantage**. However, understanding *absolute* advantage is a stepping-stone to understanding *comparative* advantage. To introduce and illustrate this very important economic principle, I shall change the production possibilities of both countries so that Atlantis possesses the absolute advantage for *both* guns and butter (which means that Pacifica has an absolute disadvantage in both goods).

One unit of resource now produces:
- in Atlantis: 4 guns or 2 tonnes of butter
- in Pacifica: 1 gun or 1 tonne of butter

> **KEY TERM**
>
> **comparative advantage:** this is measured in terms of opportunity cost. The country with the least opportunity cost when producing a good possesses a comparative advantage in that good.

Although Atlantis is 'better at' — or has an absolute advantage in — producing *both* guns and butter, the country possesses a comparative advantage *only* in gun production. This is because comparative advantage is measured in terms of **opportunity cost**, or what a country gives up when it increases the output of an industry by 1 unit. The country that gives up *least* of the other commodity when increasing output of a particular commodity by 1 unit possesses the comparative advantage in that good. Ask yourself how many guns Atlantis has to give up in order to increase its butter output by 1 tonne. The answer is 2 guns. But Pacifica only has to give up 1 gun to produce an extra tonne of butter. Thus Pacifica possesses a *comparative* advantage in butter production even though it has an *absolute* disadvantage in both products.

When one country possesses an absolute advantage in both industries, as in the example above, its comparative advantage always lies in producing the good in which its absolute advantage is greatest. Similarly, the country that is absolutely worst at both activities possesses a comparative advantage in the industry in which its absolute disadvantage is least.

In this example, *complete* specialisation results in *more* guns but *less* butter being produced, compared to a situation in which each country devotes half its total resources to each activity. Without specialisation, the combined output of both countries is 5 guns and 3 tonnes of butter. With complete specialisation, this changes to 8 guns and 2 tonnes of butter. While production of guns has increased, production of butter has fallen.

When one country has an absolute advantage in both goods, *complete* specialisation in accordance with the principle of comparative advantage does not result in a net output gain. The output of one good rises, but the output of the other good falls.

Students often get puzzled by this, thinking (wrongly) that specialisation cannot lead to gains from trade. However, *partial* specialisation can produce a net output gain. For example, suppose Pacifica (which suffers an *absolute* disadvantage in *both* goods) completely specialises and produces 2 tonnes of butter. By contrast, Atlantis (which has the absolute advantage in both goods) devotes just enough resource (half a unit) to top up world production of butter to 3 tonnes. This means that Atlantis can still produce 6 guns using 1.5 units of resource. Total production in both countries is therefore 6 guns and 3 tonnes of butter. At least as much butter and more guns are now produced compared with the no-specialisation outcome. This example shows that specialisation can produce a net output gain, even though one country is absolutely better at both activities.

EXAM TIP

Think carefully before you introduce and explain a numerical example of comparative advantage. Unless an exam question asks for a numerical example, it may be best to limit your answer to defining the concept and then stating that if countries specialise in activities in which they possess a comparative advantage and then trade their surpluses, output and welfare gains can result. Candidates often make mistakes in numerical examples, waste time, and drift into irrelevancies.

The assumptions underlying the principle of comparative advantage

When arguing that definite benefits result when countries specialise and trade in accordance with the principle of comparative advantage, I made a number of rather strong but not necessarily realistic assumptions. Indeed, the case for trade — and hence the case *against* import controls and other forms of protectionism — is heavily dependent upon these assumptions. Likewise, some of the arguments in favour of import controls and against free trade, which I shall explain shortly, depend on showing that the assumptions necessary for the benefits of specialisation and trade to occur are simply not met in real life. These assumptions are as follows:

- Each country's endowment of factors of production, including capital and labour, is fixed and immobile between countries, although factors can be switched between industries within a country. In the course of international trade, *finished goods* rather than *factors of production* or inputs are assumed to be mobile between countries.
- The principle of comparative advantage assumes **constant returns to scale**. In my example, 1 unit of resource is assumed to produce 4 guns or 2 tonnes of butter in Atlantis, whether it is the first unit of resource employed or the millionth unit. But in the real world, increasing or decreasing returns to scale are both possible and indeed likely. In a world of **increasing returns to scale**, the more a country specialises in an activity in which it initially has an absolute advantage, the more its productive efficiency and advantage increases. Countries that are 'best' to start with become even 'better'. But if **decreasing returns to scale** occur, specialisation erodes efficiency and destroys a country's initial advantage. A good example occurs in agriculture, where over-specialisation can result in monoculture or the growing of a single cash crop for export. Monoculture often leads to soil erosion, vulnerability to pests and falling future agricultural yields.
- The principle of comparative advantage implicitly assumes relatively stable demand and cost conditions. Over-specialisation can cause a country to become particularly vulnerable to sudden changes in demand or to changes in the cost and availability of imported raw materials or energy. Changes in costs, and new inventions and technical progress, can quickly eliminate a country's earlier comparative advantage. The greater the uncertainty about the future, the weaker the case for complete specialisation. Indeed, if a country is self-sufficient in all important respects, it is neutralised against the danger of importing recession and unemployment from the rest of the world when international demand collapses.

Comparative advantage and competitive advantage

Comparative advantage must not be confused with *competitive* advantage. A country, or a firm within a country, enjoys a **competitive advantage** when it produces better-quality goods at lower costs and better prices than its rivals. Competitive advantage is more similar to *absolute* advantage than to comparative advantage.

Dynamic factors that promote the growth of firms can create competitive advantage. Successful investment undertaken over many years equips a country with modern, 'state-of-the-art' production capacity, capable of producing high-quality goods that people want to buy. Properly funded and organised research and development (R&D) contributes in a similar way, while the stock of human capital resulting from investment in education and training adds to competitive advantage.

Factors that create competitive advantage can trigger a **virtuous spiral** of larger profits, higher investment, better products and greater sales, which in turn leads to even higher profits, and so on. Conversely, countries and firms that are not competitive may enter a **vicious spiral** of decline. Inability to compete causes profits to fall, which in turn reduces investment. The quality of goods declines and sales are lost to more competitive countries or firms. Profits again fall (maybe disappearing altogether), and a further round in the vicious circle of decline is unleashed.

The case for import controls and protectionism

Import controls can be divided into quantity controls such as **import quotas**, which put a maximum limit on imports, and **tariffs** or **import duties** (and their opposite, **export subsidies**), which raise the price of imports (or reduce the price of exports).

> **KEY TERM**
>
> **import controls:** include tariffs or import duties, quotas, export subsidies and informal controls.

Supporters of free trade believe that import controls prevent countries from specialising in activities in which they have a comparative advantage and trading their surpluses. As a result, production takes place inefficiently and economic welfare is reduced. But as I have already noted, the case for free trade depends to a large extent upon some of the assumptions underlying the principle of comparative advantage. Destroy these assumptions and the case for free trade is weakened.

Below are some of the contexts in which import controls have been justified.

- **Infant industries.** As I have already explained, many economic activities benefit from increasing returns to scale, which mean that the more a country specialises in a particular industry, the more productively efficient it becomes. This increases its competitive advantage. Developing countries justify the use of import controls to protect infant industries from established rivals in advanced economies. Protectionism is needed while newly established industries develop full economies of scale.
- **Strategic trade theory.** The infant industry argument is closely related to strategic trade theory, a relatively new theory that has grown in influence in recent years. Strategic trade theory argues that comparative and competitive advantage are

often not 'natural'. Rather, governments try to create competitive advantage by nurturing strategically selected industries or economic sectors. This justifies protecting the industries while competitive advantage is being built up. The skills that are gained will then spill over to help other sectors in the economy. Strategic trade theory also argues that protectionism can prevent exploitation by a foreign-based monopoly.

■ **Agricultural efficiency.** As I noted earlier in the context of agriculture, monoculture erodes efficiency and destroys comparative advantage that existed before specialisation took place. Decreasing returns to scale weaken the case for complete specialisation.

■ **Changes in demand or cost conditions.** Over-specialisation may cause a country to become particularly vulnerable to sudden changes in demand or to changes in the cost and availability of imported raw materials or energy.

■ **Sunset industries.** A rather similar case to the infant industry argument is sometimes made in advanced industrial economies such as the UK to protect older industries from the competition of infant industries in developing countries. Keynesian economists have sometimes advocated the selective use of import controls as a potentially effective supply-side policy instrument to prevent unnecessary deindustrialisation and to allow orderly rather than disruptive structural change in the manufacturing base of the economy. According to this view, import controls are justified, at least on a temporary basis, to minimise the social and economic cost of the painful adjustment process, as the structure of an economy alters in response either to changing demand or to changing technology and comparative and competitive advantage.

■ **Anti-dumping.** When a country produces too much of a good for its own domestic market, the surplus may then be 'dumped' and sold at a price below cost in overseas markets. Import controls are sometimes justified as a means to prevent this supposedly 'unfair' competition.

■ **Demerit goods and 'bads'.** In the case of narcotic drugs and weapons, an *output* gain does not necessarily lead to a *welfare* gain. Governments argue they have a moral duty to ban imports of heroin, cocaine and handguns to protect the welfare of their citizens.

■ **Self-sufficiency.** Politically, it is often argued that protection is necessary for military and strategic reasons to ensure that a country is relatively self-sufficient in vital foodstuffs, energy and raw materials in a time of war.

■ **Employment.** Trade unions argue that import controls are necessary to prevent multinational firms shifting capital to low-wage developing countries and exporting their output back to the countries from which the capital was moved. They further argue the case for employing labour, however inefficiently, in protected industries rather than allowing labour to suffer the greatest inefficiency of all: mass unemployment. This is an example of **second-best theory**. The second-best argument stems from the fact that the 'first best' (free trade in a world of fully employed economies and perfect markets) is unattainable. Therefore, a country can settle legitimately for the second best. Employing resources inefficiently, protected by tariffs, is better than not employing resources at all. This justification for protecting domestic industries and maintaining employment came into prominence around the time that Barack Obama took over the US presidency in 2009.

EXAM TIP

When answering an exam question requiring evaluation of the case for free trade (or the case for import controls) it is best to avoid a 'shopping list' approach. Instead, select, develop, analyse and evaluate three or four arguments or counter-arguments.

CASE STUDY 20.2

Paul Krugman and strategic trade theory

In 2008, Paul Krugman, professor of economics at Princeton University, USA, was awarded the Nobel Prize in Economics, in part for his pioneering work in developing strategic trade theory in the 1980s and 1990s. In contrast to the orthodox free-market approach to international trade, firmly grounded in the principle of comparative advantage, strategic trade theory argues that import controls can sometimes be justified. Krugman argued that rich developed countries benefited from protectionism while they established their national wealth. However, they now put pressure on poor countries to abandon import controls and to allow overseas-based multinational corporations unlimited access to their economies. As I explain later in the chapter, opponents of globalisation argue that free trade theory is used to justify first-world economic imperialism. Below is an extract from the beginning of a paper Krugman wrote in 1987:

> If there were an Economist's Creed, it would surely contain the affirmations 'I understand the principle of comparative advantage' and 'I advocate free trade'. For 170 years, the appreciation that international trade benefits a country whether it is 'fair' or not has been one of the touchstones of professionalism in economics.

Yet the case for free trade is currently more in doubt than at any time since the 1817 publication of Ricardo's *Principles of Political Economy*. This is not because of the political pressures for protection, which have triumphed in the past without shaking the intellectual foundation of comparative advantage theory. Rather, it is because of the changes that have recently taken place in the theory of international trade itself.

In the last 10 years the traditional <u>constant returns</u>, <u>perfect competition</u> models of international trade have been supplemented and to some extent supplanted by a new breed of models that emphasise <u>increasing returns</u> and <u>imperfect competition</u>. These new models call into doubt the extent to which actual trade can be explained by comparative advantage.

Showing that free trade is better than no trade is not the same thing as showing that free trade is better than sophisticated government intervention. The view that free trade is the best of all possible policies is part of the general case for laissez-faire in a market economy and rests on the proposition that markets are efficient. If increasing returns and imperfect competition are necessary parts of the explanation of international trade, we are living in a <u>second-best</u> world where government intervention can in principle improve on market outcomes.

Source: 'Is free trade passé?' by Paul Krugman, published in the *Journal of Economic Perspectives*, 1987. The full article can be found online at: www.aeaweb.org.

Follow-up questions

1 Briefly define each of the underlined terms in the extract.
2 How do increasing returns to scale and imperfect competition weaken the case for unlimited free trade based on the principle of comparative advantage?

International trade

Welfare losses and welfare gains

In this and the next two sections of the chapter, I bypass the justifications for tariffs put forward by economists such as Paul Krugman and return to the free-market case for free trade. Analysis of the welfare gains from free trade and the welfare losses caused by import controls centres on the concepts of **consumer surplus** and **producer surplus** that you learn when studying Unit 3.

If a country does not enter into international trade, which means its economy is *closed*, domestic demand for a good within a country can only be met by domestic supply (that is, by firms producing *within* the country). Such a situation is shown in Figure 20.1, in which market equilibrium for the good occurs at point X. Consumers pay price P_1 for the good, and the quantity bought and sold is Q_1. Consumer surplus, which measures **consumer welfare**, is shown by the triangular area bounded by points XZP_1. Likewise, **producer welfare** (producer surplus) is the triangular area bounded by points XP_1U.

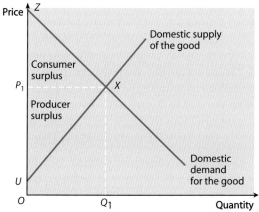

Figure 20.1 Consumer and producer surplus in a market closed to international trade

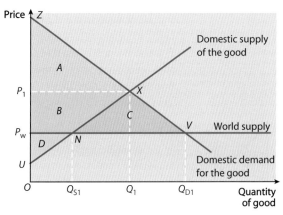

Figure 20.2 The welfare gains and losses resulting from the introduction of a tariff

But consider what happens in a world of completely free trade, in which domestically produced goods have to compete with cheaper imports. In the next diagram, Figure 20.2, imports are priced at the ruling world price of P_W, which is lower than P_1. In this situation, equilibrium now occurs in the domestic market at point V. Although domestic demand has increased to Q_{D1}, domestic supply (located where the domestic supply curve cuts the horizontal price line at P_W) falls to Q_{S1}. Imports (equal to $Q_{D1} - Q_{S1}$) fill the gap between domestic demand and supply.

> **EXAM TIP**
>
> You should practise drawing and explaining these diagrams to show the welfare gains and losses resulting from trade and import controls. Remember, however, the assumptions that underpin free-trade theory that I explained earlier. Question these assumptions and the case for free trade weakens.

To understand how imports affect economic welfare within the country, it is important to understand how consumer surplus and producer surplus change after the price of the good falls to the world price P_W. Consumer surplus increases by the wedge-shaped area bounded by the points $P_W VXP_1$. This divides into two parts, shown on the diagram by areas B and C. Look closely at the area B. This shows a welfare transfer away from domestic firms to domestic consumers. The fall in the price from P_1 to P_W, brought about by lower import prices, means that part of the producer surplus domestic firms previously enjoyed now becomes consumer surplus. The consumers 'win' and the domestic producers 'lose'.

But this is not the end of the story. Consumers enjoy a further increase in consumer surplus, which is brought about by receipt of the area C. As a result, the total increase in consumer surplus gain exceeds the size of the welfare transfer from producer surplus to consumer surplus. A **net welfare gain** thus results, equal to area C, which makes up part of the consumer surplus that households now enjoy.

How a tariff or import duty affects economic welfare

I shall now assume that domestic firms pressure the government to introduce a tariff to protect the home market. If the tariff equals the distance between P_1 and P_W, the domestic market for the good reverts to the original equilibrium position that existed before imports entered the country. But suppose the government imposes a smaller tariff, which is just sufficient to raise the price of imports (and also of domestically produced goods) to $P_W + t$ in Figure 20.3. At price $P_W + t$, domestic demand falls to Q_{D2}, while domestic supply rises to Q_{S2}. Imports fall from $Q_{D1} - Q_{S1}$ to $Q_{D2} - Q_{S2}$.

At the higher price, consumer surplus *falls* by the 'wedge' shaped area $P_W VY P_W + t$, which equals the areas $D + A + B + C$. The higher price increases producer surplus by the area D, and the government gains tariff revenue shown by the area B. The areas D and B are *transfers* of welfare away from consumers respectively to domestic producers and to the government. The *net* welfare *loss* resulting from the tariff, which is the sum of triangles A and C in the diagram, is:

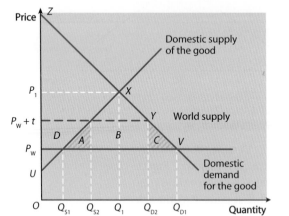

Figure 20.3 The effect of imposing a tariff

$(D + A + B + C) - (D + B)$, which equals $A + C$

Changing comparative advantage and the pattern of world trade

When, over two centuries ago, Adam Smith first explained the advantages of the division of labour, and a few years later in the early nineteenth century another distinguished classical economist, David Ricardo, developed Adam Smith's ideas into the principle of comparative advantage, they were not just interested in abstract theory. Instead, like most great economists, they wished to change society for the better by influencing the politicians of their day. Smith and Ricardo believed in the virtues of a competitive market economy and industrial capitalism. Ricardo, in particular, believed that a single country such as the UK, and indeed the whole world economy, can only reach their full productive potential, maximising output, welfare and living standards, if the market economy is truly international. He argued that each country should specialise in the activities in which it possesses a comparative advantage and trade the output that is surplus to its needs in a world free of tariffs and other forms of protectionism.

To many people living in industrial countries during the nineteenth century and the first half of the twentieth century, it must have seemed almost natural that the earliest countries to industrialise, such as the UK, had done so because they possessed a competitive and comparative advantage in manufacturing. It probably seemed equally natural that a pattern of world trade should have developed in which the industrialised countries in what is now called the *North* exported manufactured goods in exchange for foodstuffs and raw materials produced by countries whose comparative advantage lay in the production of primary products — in modern parlance, the countries of the *South*.

Figure 20.4 North–North and North–South patterns of trade

However, in recent years, the pattern of world trade has become quite different from the North–South exchange of manufactured goods for primary products that characterised the nineteenth century. In a North–North pattern of trade, which is illustrated in Figure 20.4, the developed industrial economies now exchange goods and services mostly with each other. However, a growing fraction of their trade, particularly in the case of imports, is with **newly industrialising countries** (NICs) or **emerging markets**, particularly India, China and South Korea. A group of countries known as the **BRIC** countries (Brazil, Russia, India and China) are responsible for exporting large quantities of goods and services to the North. India, China and South Korea now export manufactured goods to countries in the North such as the UK and the USA, and import raw materials or commodities such as copper from developing countries such as Zambia. They also import a growing fraction of the crude oil produced by oil-exporting developing countries such as Saudi Arabia and Venezuela.

The shift of manufacturing to China and other NICs reflects changing competitive and comparative advantage and the **deindustrialisation** of Britain and North America. Only a relatively small proportion of the trade of North countries is with poorer countries in the non-oil-producing developing world.

EXTENSION MATERIAL

The Heckscher–Ohlin theory of international trade

In the 1930s two Swedish economists, Heckscher and Ohlin, explained the then dominant North–South exchange of manufactured goods for primary products in terms of factor endowments. The **Heckscher–Ohlin theory**, which is really an extension of the principle of comparative advantage, argues that a capital-rich country is likely to industrialise and export capital-intensive manufactured goods. However, if capital is scarce relative to labour, the country specialises in and exports labour-intensive primary products. The Heckscher–Ohlin theory was grasped by pro-free market economists because it appeared to give legitimacy to a pattern of trade in which rich counties exploited the poorer countries, over which they often exerted military and political control.

The UK's international trade

Table 20.1 shows that over the 56-year period from 1955 to 2011, the pattern of the UK's international trade changed from a 'North–South' to a 'North–North' pattern in terms of the global regions with which the UK trades. The UK now trades mainly with other developed countries in the North, and especially with other EU countries. In 1955, only 15% of UK exports and 12.6% of UK imports were with countries that eventually formed the EU. By contrast, 32.9% of UK exports and 31.4% of UK imports were with developing countries. By 2011, this situation was reversed: respectively 47.4% and 50.6% of UK exports and imports were with EU countries, while exports to 'other developing countries' had fallen to 25.1% of total exports, with imports marginally higher at 25.2% of total imports. However, 'other developing countries' include emerging-market 'giants' such as India and China, with the latter having become the world's largest exporter of manufactured goods to developed economies such as the UK. Indeed, while China's agricultural sector remains characteristic of a developing country, the same is not true for manufacturing and, increasingly, transport. The growing importance of emerging market countries, particularly China, in international trade explains why the share of their trade in UK imports and exports has been creeping upwards, compared for example to the 2002 figures in Table 20.1. By contrast, slippage in the percentages of UK trade with other EU countries has occurred, partly as a result of the depth of recession in many eurozone countries.

Table 20.1 The changing pattern of the UK's international trade with other world regions

UK trade with	1955 Exports (%)	1955 Imports (%)	2002 Exports (%)	2002 Imports (%)	2007 Exports (%)	2007 Imports (%)	2011 Exports (%)	2011 Imports (%)
EU	15.0	12.6	54.6	57.3	50.2	54.0	47.4	50.6
Other west European countries (EFTA)	13.9	13.1	3.8	4.4	4.3	5.7	4.3	7.2
North America	12.0	19.5	19.7	14.0	19.8	12.2	17.9	11.0
Other developed countries (OECD except 1955)	21.1	14.2	2.7	4.2	2.3	3.3	2.5	2.8
Oil-exporting developed countries	5.1	9.2	2.2	1.2	2.5	1.6	2.8	3.2
Other developing countries	32.9	31.4	17.0	18.9	20.9	22.2	25.1	25.2

Source: *Annual Abstract of Statistics, Monthly Review of External Trade Statistics*, 2012

In contrast to Table 20.1, which shows changes in the global pattern of UK trade, Table 20.2 focuses on changes in the commodities traded over a rather shorter time period — 2002–11. The table shows that, despite the impact of deindustrialisation, which has reduced manufacturing output to less than 15% of GDP, the UK's trade in goods is still dominated by the export and import of manufactured goods, though with the country importing significantly more than it exports. I shall take up this story again in the next chapter, when investigating the UK's balances of trade in goods and in services.

Table 20.2 Changes in selected items in UK trade in goods by type of commodity, 2002–11 (£m), (percentages of total trade in goods shown in brackets)

	2002 Exports	2002 Imports	2005 Exports	2005 Imports	2007 Exports	2007 Imports	2011 Exports	2011 Imports
Food, beverages and tobacco	10,010	19,389	10,673	23,713	11,753	26,708	18,085	35,990
	(5.4%)	(8.3%)	(5.0%)	(8.5%)	(5.3%)	(8.6%)	(6.0%)	(9.0%)
Raw materials	2,858	5,966	3,990	6,778	5,517	9,558	9,015	11,953
	(1.5%)	(2.6%)	(1.9%)	(2.4%)	(2.5%)	(3.1%)	(3.0%)	(3.0%)
Fuels and energy	16,031	10,288	21,613	26,002	24,393	32,307	42,762	61,926
	(8.6%)	(4.4%)	(10.2%)	(9.3%)	(11.1%)	(10.4%)	(14.3%)	(15.5%)
Manufactured goods	156,642	196,845	174,260	221,956	177,496	240,057	225,367	285,910
	(84.0)	(84.1%)	(82.3%)	(79.2%)	(80.5%)	(77.2%)	(75.4%)	(71.6%)
Total exports	**186,574**		**211,606**		**220,525**		**299,067**	
Total imports		**233,934**		**280,292**		**311,003**		**399,081**

Source: *Monthly Review of External Trade Statistics*, September 2012

Globalisation

Globalisation is the name given to the processes that integrate all or most of the world's economies, making countries increasingly dependent upon each other. Some economists argue that globalisation has occurred over centuries, going back at least as far as the creation of a system of relatively free worldwide trade in the nineteenth century. Perhaps it extends even further back to the Spanish and Portuguese occupation of much of South America.

KEY TERM

globalisation: the process of growing economic integration of the world's economies.

In the late nineteenth century and the period before 1914, communication and transport networks expanded throughout much of the world and international trade grew significantly. At the same time, older industrial countries, and particularly the UK, began to invest their surplus savings in capital projects located overseas rather than in their domestic economies.

However, these changes are better described as aspects of **internationalisation** rather than globalisation. Globalisation, which has come to mean rather more than mere internationalisation of economic relationships, began to feature in the economics literature of the mid-1980s. The use of the term has increased dramatically ever since.

Recent globalisation has been made possible by improvements in information and communication technology (ICT), as well as by developments in more traditional forms of technology. Examples of globalisation include service industries in the UK dealing with customers through call centres in India and fashion companies designing their products in Europe, making them in southeast Asia and finally selling most of them in North America.

The debate about globalisation

Free-market economists generally support globalisation and regard its growth as inevitable. They argue that the benefits of further global economic integration, which include the extension of political freedom and democracy as well as the economic benefits of more production and higher living standards, significantly exceed the disadvantages, such as the destruction of local cultures. However, opponents argue that globalisation is a respectable name for the growing exploitation of the poor, mostly in developing countries, by international capitalism and US economic and cultural imperialism.

For its critics, low-paid workers in sweatshops, farmers in the developing world being forced to grow genetically modified crops, the privatisation of state-owned industry to qualify for IMF and World Bank loans, and the growing dominance of US corporate culture and multinational companies symbolise what is wrong with globalisation. According to this view, globalisation has led to a 'McDonaldisation' or 'Coca-Colonisation' of significant parts of the world's economy, which involves the destruction of local and national products, identities and cultures by US world brands. What is needed is a counter-process of 'glocalisation', or local action that prevents or offsets the damage done by globalisation to vulnerable local cultures.

However, this view is not taken seriously by supporters of globalisation, who believe that people in the rest of the world demand US products because they consider them superior to traditional local produce.

Features of globalisation
Some of the main features of globalisation are:

- the growth of international trade and the reduction of trade barriers — a process encouraged by the World Trade Organization (WTO)
- greater international mobility of capital and to some extent of labour
- a significant increase in the power of international capitalism and multinational corporations (MNCs) or transnational companies
- the deindustrialisation of older industrial regions and countries, and the movement of manufacturing industries to newly industrialising countries (NICs)
- more recently, the movement of internationally mobile service industries, such as call centres and accounts offices, to NICs
- a decrease in governmental power to influence decisions made by MNCs to shift economic activity between countries

A Thai Coca-Cola advert

Figure 20.5 depicts some of these features of globalisation in the form of a 'mind map'.

Figure 20.5 Some of the main features of globalisation

Employment practices resulting from globalisation

Closely related to the 'world brand' process has been the alleged treatment of local labour by multinational corporations. This works in two ways. First, companies such as Nike are accused of selling trainers and footballs in developed countries such as the UK at prices far above the cost of raw materials and the low wages paid to workers in developing countries making the goods. In response, the multinationals argue that the 'low wages' they pay far exceed the local wages paid by firms indigenous to the countries in which they manufacture. They believe this encourages local wages to rise. MNCs also claim to improve health and safety and other labour market conditions in the poor countries in which they operate.

Second, by threatening to close down factories and to move production to poor countries, it is argued that MNCs reduce wages and living standards in developed countries. Whether this is true depends on the type of jobs that emerge in developed countries to replace those lost through deindustrialisation and globalisation. Are the new jobs created in the highly skilled service sector, or are they menial, low-paid, unskilled 'McJobs'?

Globalisation in the service sector

Until quite recently, it was said that manufacturing was much more internationally mobile than service sector employment. This is no longer true. Call centres became one of the fastest-growing sources of employment in the UK in the 1980s and 1990s. At that time, UK-based companies favoured locating call centres in regions of high unemployment (and relatively low wages) *within* the UK. To some extent this has now changed. Call centres and back office activities of firms in industries such as financial services are being moved to the Indian subcontinent. This results from the *death of distance*, which is a part of the globalisation process. The rapid development of electronic methods of communication means that many service activities can now be located anywhere in the world, with little or no effect on a company's ability to provide the service efficiently to its customers.

Four factors encouraging the overseas location of call centres are:
- relatively low wages
- highly reliable and cheap telecommunications
- 24-hour shift employment to overcome the problem of time zones
- workers fluent in English, which is now the world's business language

However, for call centres, a fifth factor is often lacking: many overseas workers are insufficiently familiar with UK culture and habits, which for call centres leads to a communication problem. This has recently led to some call centres being relocated back to the UK. This disadvantage is much less significant for back office employment: for example, employing people in India to administer a UK company's accounts.

Global labour and capital mobility

As the previous paragraphs indicate, globalisation involves moving capital to lower-cost labour much more than it involves allowing low-paid workers born in poor countries to enter rich countries in North America and Europe. However, since the late nineteenth century there has been a much greater movement of poor people into rich countries than ever before. To some extent, immigration controls introduced by countries such as the USA and Australia, which replaced an earlier completely free movement of labour, have slowed this process. But this has been offset by illegal immigration and by the fact that rich countries informally encourage migration to fill the relatively low-paid jobs that their own citizens do not wish to do.

Enlargement of the EU is increasing both labour and capital mobility on a regional basis. Western European firms have been moving eastward, but this is balanced by workers from countries such as Poland and Hungary migrating westward. Nonetheless, it is still much easier in a globalised world for a brain surgeon or a highly paid business executive to move between countries than it is for a Chinese or Indian peasant.

Globalisation and the power of national governments

In recent decades, globalisation has considerably reduced the power of national governments, certainly in smaller countries, to control multinational firms operating within their boundaries. National governments have also lost much of the freedom to undertake the economic policies of their choice with respect to managing domestic economies. Governments enjoy less freedom to introduce tariffs and other import controls. At the same time, capital flows into and out of currencies severely constrain a government's ability to implement an independent monetary policy, even when the country's exchange rate is freely floating.

The World Trade Organization's role in promoting globalisation

Economists and politicians who believe that the benefits of globalisation far exceed any disadvantages involved claim there has been *too little* rather than *too much* international integration of countries' economies. In their view, if countries get rid of *all* protectionist measures, then Adam Smith's 'invisible hand' of the market promotes international trade, which then benefits poor countries as well as rich ones. This view of the world lies behind the creation of the **World Trade Organization (WTO),** the international organisation established to remove trade barriers and liberalise world trade.

EXAM TIP

Along with the European Union, the WTO may figure in Unit 4 exam questions. By contrast, knowledge of the other main international economic institutions, the IMF and the World Bank, is useful but not essential.

To understand the WTO, it is necessary to go back to events occurring in the 1930s and 1940s. In the 1940s, during the Second World War, it was widely believed (especially in the UK and the USA) that the worldwide Depression and mass unemployment of the 1930s had been made worse, and was possibly caused, by a collapse of international trade. 'Beggar my neighbour' protectionist policies introduced by countries desperately trying to save local jobs were blamed. By 1945 the USA and the UK had decided to try to create a postwar world of free trade. Because this required international agreement, the **General Agreement on Tariffs and Trade (GATT)** was established as a multilateral organisation of member countries whose aim was trade liberalisation. To begin with, GATT was supposed to be a temporary organisation, to be replaced with a WTO as soon as member countries could agree. However, because member countries were unable to agree, the 'temporary' organisation lasted much longer than intended, from the 1940s until the mid-1990s, when the WTO at last replaced GATT.

GATT and later the WTO organised rounds of talks among member countries to reduce import controls. The rounds, which took place at roughly 5-year intervals, were often named after the city or country in which the talks were initiated: for example, the Tokyo round, the Uruguay round and, more recently, the Doha round. Out of respect, the Kennedy round in the mid-1960s was named after the then recently assassinated American president. Each round of talks ends with an agreement to reduce import controls. GATT, and latterly the WTO, have then tried to get member countries to implement the tariff cuts they have agreed.

GATT and WTO agreements have been successful in reducing import controls on manufactured goods. There has been much less success in securing agreement to reduce tariffs and quotas on trade in services and agricultural goods. Recently, the WTO has tried to get the developed countries of the EU and the USA to open their markets to cheap food imports from the developing world. However, the most recent rounds of talks organised by the WTO at Cancún (in Mexico) and Doha (in Qatar) were not successful. Economists and politicians in many developing countries claim that this lack of success provides further evidence of globalisation and international organisations serving the interests of rich countries at the expense of the poor.

The belief that globalisation benefits most countries, poor as well as rich, has been attacked by supporters of the **dependency theory** of trade and development. Dependency theorists argue that developing countries possess little capital because the system of world trade and payments has been organised by developed industrial economies to their own advantage. The **terms of trade** — the ratio of a country's export prices to its import prices — have as a general rule moved in favour of industrialised countries and against primary producers. This means that, by exporting the same amount of goods and services to the developing world, a developed economy can import a greater quantity of raw materials or foodstuffs in exchange. By the same token, the developing country must export more in order to buy the same quantity of capital goods or energy vital for development. Globally, the movement of the terms of trade in favour of developed nations has raised levels of income and standards of living in the richer countries at the expense of poorer developing countries. However, there have been some exceptions, namely NICs and the oil-producing non-industrial countries, which have benefited from substantial increases in the price of oil.

Economists of the dependency school argue that the transfer of wealth and resources to the richer countries is further promoted by profit flows and interest payments. On an international scale, dividends and profits flow to multinational corporations with headquarters in North America, western Europe and Japan from their subsidiaries in the developing world. Similarly, there is a flow of interest payments to western banks from loans originally made to finance development in developing countries. In most years, flows of dividends and interest payments from South to North exceed aid flows in the opposite direction.

EXAM TIP

The more or less continuous economic growth enjoyed by advanced industrialised countries in the 1990s and the first few years of the 2000s contributed to the globalisation process — and was also partially the result of globalisation. By contrast, the negative economic growth and recession that hit these (and other) countries in 2008 and 2009 has been blamed (in part) on globalisation, leading to renewed calls for protectionism and an end to globalisation processes. Despite some evidence of de-globalisation, globalisation still continues.

CASE STUDY 20.3

Has globalisation given way to de-globalisation?

Robert J Samuelson of Investors.com recently asked: 'What has happened to globalisation?'. He argued that for decades, growing volumes of cross-border trade and money flows have fuelled strong economic growth. But something remarkable is happening; trade and money flows are slowing and, in some cases, declining. Samuelson pondered whether this heralds prolonged economic stagnation and rising nationalism or, optimistically, whether it makes the world economy more stable and politically acceptable.

For workers employed or previously employed in US manufacturing industries, some aspects of de-globalisation are very attractive. Globalisation has sucked factory jobs out of North America. But now, the tide may be turning. Apple has announced a $100-million investment to return some Mac computer manufacturing back to the USA. Though small, the decision reflects a trend.

General Electric's sprawling Appliance Park in Kentucky once symbolised America's manufacturing prowess, with employment peaking at 23,000 in 1973. Since then, jobs have shifted abroad or succumbed to automation.

However, now GE is moving production of water heaters, refrigerators and other appliances back to Appliance Park from China and Mexico. Nor is GE alone. Otis is moving some elevator output from Mexico to South Carolina.

China's labour cost advantage has eroded. In 2000, Chinese factory wages averaged 52 cents an hour; but annual double-digit percentage increases will bring that to $6 an hour in high-skilled industries by 2015.

Although wages of US production workers average $19 an hour, other non-wage factors favour the USA. American workers are more productive; automation has cut labour costs, and cheap natural gas further lowers costs; finally, higher oil prices have raised freight rates for imports. By 2015, China's overall cost advantage will shrink to 7%.

As important for the USA is the likelihood that it will maintain significant cost advantages over other developed-country manufacturers: 15% over France and Germany; 21% over Japan; and 8% over Great Britain. The USA will be a more attractive production platform. In America, imports will weaken; exports will strengthen.

Follow-up questions
1 Has there been any evidence of manufacturing jobs being attracted back to the UK in recent years?
2 How might the slowing down of globalisation processes be linked to the recession which hit the global economy in 2008?

SUMMARY

- International trade widens a country's production possibilities and also its consumption possibilities.
- International trade enables countries to benefit from specialisation and the division of labour.
- Absolute advantage means that a country is technically more efficient in producing a good than other countries, being absolutely best at the activity.
- Comparative advantage is measured in terms of opportunity cost.
- Specialisation and trade in accordance with the principle of comparative advantage can lead to a net output gain.
- The net output resulting from trade gain can translate into a net welfare gain. In contrast, protectionism may lead to a net welfare loss.
- Import controls have been justified by strategic trade theory, the protection of infant industries and other arguments.
- The North–South pattern of world trade has largely given way to a North–North pattern.
- The older industrialised economies of western Europe and North America also import many of the manufactured goods they use from Asian NICs.
- Much of the UK's trade is with other European Union (EU) member states.
- Globalisation is the name given to the increasing integration of the world's economies.
- Trade liberalisation, international capital and labour mobility and the increased power of multinational corporations (MNCs) are important elements of globalisation.
- The World Trade Organization (WTO) promotes trade liberalisation, and some would say the interests of rich countries against the poor.
- Globalisation processes slowed down in the recent global recession but were not killed off. There has been some evidence of de-globalisation.

Exam-style questions

1 Explain the difference between absolute advantage and comparative advantage.   (15 marks)

2 Outline two arguments used to support import controls.   (15 marks)

3 Assess the view that the progress made towards free trade has brought significant economic benefits both to the global economy and to the UK.   (25 marks)

4 Do you agree that for a developed economy such as the UK, the advantages of globalisation exceed any disadvantages? Justify your answer.   (25 marks)

Extra resources to help you revise are available online at www.hodderplus.co.uk/philipallan

The balance of payments

Chapter 21

Many years ago, UK newspapers regularly featured headlines such as: 'Britain in the red — sterling crisis looms'. Then all went quiet for 30 or more years, not because the UK balance of payments current account deficit was necessarily small, but because fixed exchange rates had been replaced with floating exchange rates. Newspaper headlines were now more likely to be: 'Balance of payments problem? What problem?' By 2013, history has partly come full circle. Even though the pound's exchange rate still floats, the huge size of the UK's current account deficit is again viewed as an economic problem.

LEARNING OUTCOMES

This chapter will:
- remind you of the difference between the current account and capital flows in the balance of payments
- examine the structure of and recent changes in the UK balance of payments
- discuss the meaning of balance of payments equilibrium and disequilibrium
- question whether a current account deficit poses a problem
- compare expenditure-reducing and expenditure-switching policies aimed at reducing a current account deficit
- explain the J-curve effect
- discuss whether a current account surplus poses problems
- recap on how *AD/AS* diagrams can be used to illustrate the effect of changes in the current account

WHAT YOU SHOULD ALREADY KNOW

At AS, the Unit 2 specification on the national economy required candidates to understand the main items in the current account of the balance of payments, namely trade in goods, trade in services, investment income and transfers. An understanding of the meaning of current account deficits and surpluses was also required, together with the fact that achieving a satisfactory current account can be an important macroeconomic policy objective.

The meaning of the balance of payments

The **balance of payments** is the part of the national accounts that attempts to measure all the currency flows into and out of the country in a particular time period, for example a month, quarter or year. The balance of payments is only an estimate of currency flows. Activities such as smuggling, money laundering and late recording of data or sending inaccurate data to the government mean that there are always errors in the balance of payments.

KEY TERM

balance of payments: measures all the currency flows into and out of an economy in a given time period.

The structure of the UK balance of payments

Since the balance of payments is an official record collected by a government, the presentation of the currency flows depends on how the government decides to group and classify all the different items of payment. Until quite recently, the UK government divided the balance of payments into two main categories:

- the current account
- the capital account

But to fit in with the method of classification used by the **International Monetary Fund** (IMF), the format of the UK's balance of payments has been changed. Unfortunately, the new method of presentation, which is shown in slightly simplified form in Table 21.1, is confusing. Capital flows, which used to form the *capital account*, are now listed in the *financial account* of the balance of payments. Misleadingly, the capital account now comprises various transfers of income that were previously part of the current account before the new method of classification was adopted.

Table 21.1 Selected items from the UK balance of payments, 2012 (£m)

The current account (mostly trade flows)	
Balance of trade in goods	−107,893
Balance of trade in services	+73,992
Net income flows	−2,254
Net current transfers	−23,055
Balance of payments on the current account	**−59,210**
The capital account (*Transfers, which used to be in the current account*)	**+3,788**
The financial account (*Capital flows, which used to be in the capital account*)	
Net direct investment	−8,885
Net portfolio investment	−211,245
Other capital flows (*mostly short-term 'hot money' flows*)	+275,985
Drawings on reserves	−7,642
Financial account balance	**+48,213**
The balance (errors and omissions)	**+7,209**

Source: United Kingdom Quarterly Accounts, Quarter 1 2013

For this reason, this chapter presents a general survey of the current account and capital flows and tries to avoid unnecessary detail. The examination boards, including AQA, no longer require knowledge of official methods of presentation of balance of payments accounts.

EXAM TIP

The specification states that candidates are not expected to have a detailed knowledge of the structure of balance of payments accounts.

Recent changes in the UK current account

Figure 21.1 shows the changes that took place in the UK current account and in the main items in the current account between 1998 and 2012. 1997 was the last time that the UK current account more or less balanced, without a deficit or surplus. The graph clearly shows the massive deterioration that occurred in the UK's balance of trade in goods in the late 1990s and the early 2000s. Although the balance of trade in services generally showed a growing surplus, the services surplus was not sufficient to offset the trade in goods deficit. As a result, the overall current account deteriorated from its initial position of more or less balanced to the deficit at the end of 2012 of nearly £60 billion.

EXAM TIP

Exam candidates often confuse the balance of trade in goods with the whole of the current account. Likewise, the current account is confused with the balance of payments as a whole.

Recent statistics reflect the effect of the credit crunch and the decline in the overseas earnings of UK financial services industries.

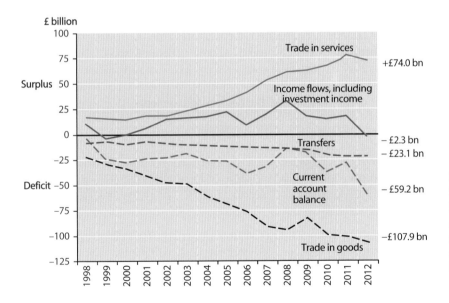

Figure 21.1 Changes in the UK current account and its main items, 1998–2012 (the 2012 totals are shown on the right)

Source: Office for National Statistics

The current account of the balance of payments

For the most part, the balance of payments on the current account measures the *flow* of expenditure on goods and services, broadly indicating the country's income gained and lost from trade. The **current account** is usually regarded as the most important part of the balance of payments because it reflects the economy's

KEY TERM

current account: the part of the balance of payments measuring income currency flows, especially payments for exports and imports.

international competitiveness and the extent to which the country may or may not be living within its means.

To measure the balance of payments on the current account, we first add together the **balance of trade in goods** and the **balance of trade in services**. (The balance of trade in goods can also be called the **balance of visible trade**, while the balance of trade in services comprises **invisible trade** items.) If receipts from exports of goods and services are less than payments for imports of goods and services, there is generally a **current account deficit**. Conversely, a **current account surplus** occurs when receipts from trade exceed payments for trade. However, because there are other items in the current account besides trade flows, this is not always true. The other items are **net income flows** and net current **transfers**.

KEY TERMS

transfers: payments flowing between countries in forms such as foreign aid, grants and gifts.

investment income: profit and interest income flowing into a country that is generated from assets the residents of the country own abroad.

Net income flows

Net income flows are made up mostly of **investment income** flows generated from profit and interest payments flowing between countries. In the chapter's next section, I explain how UK-based multinational companies (MNCs) invest in capital assets located in other countries. The profit income generated when an investment is complete flows back to the parent company and its UK shareholders. The investment itself is an *outward* capital flow, but the income it generates is *current* income, figuring in the current account of the balance of payments.

EXAM TIP

This book does not include tables or details of the balances of trade in goods and services for the UK. These are AS topics, which I explain in some detail in the *AQA AS Economics* textbook.

Profits also flow out of the UK to the overseas owners of assets located in the UK — for example, to Japanese or US multinational companies owning subsidiary companies in the UK. In Table 21.1, the item **net income flows** is largely determined by the difference between these inward and outward profit flows resulting from capital investment undertaken in the past. The fact that the UK's net income flows were around –£2.3 billion in 2012 indicates that in that year, UK companies owned less profitable assets in the rest of the world than overseas-based MNCs owned in the UK. In previous years, as Figure 21.1 shows, inward income flows had far exceeded outward flows. The collapse of foreign investment earnings in 2012 was the main factor contributing to the current account deficit rising to over £59 billion, up from over £22 billion in 2011. Finally, it is worth remembering that not all income flows are profit payments by multinational companies. Interest payments on loans within the international banking system contribute significantly to net income flows. By the time you read this book, further significant changes may have taken place in the UK current account. Make sure you keep up to date with these changes.

Capital flows

As the previous paragraph indicates, it is important to avoid confusing *capital flows* with *investment income*. As explained, *outward* capital flows generate *inward* investment income flows in subsequent years. The capital outflow enlarges the *stock* of capital assets located in other countries, owned by MNCs based in the country exporting the capital. **Net capital flows** are the difference between inward and outward capital movements. Positive net outward capital flows, over a period of years, mean that the country acquires capital assets located in other countries that are greater in value than the country's own assets bought by overseas companies.

Positive net investment income *flow* (in the current account), which occurred in years prior to 2012, suggests that, in these years, UK residents and MNCs invested in a larger and more profitable *stock* of capital assets in the rest of the world than that acquired by overseas residents and MNCs in the UK. Following the UK's abolition of virtually all foreign exchange controls in 1979, the UK became a large net exporter of capital, presumably because UK MNCs believed that investment abroad would be more profitable than investment within the UK. During the 1980s, the positive net capital outflow meant that the UK became a large owner of overseas capital assets. However, by 2010 the UK was becoming again a net debtor nation. The difference between foreign assets that domestic UK residents owned and domestic assets held by residents of other countries was $312,424 million. In 2010, the USA had the largest net debts ($2,470,989 million) whereas at the other extreme, Japan, China and Germany enjoyed net credits respectively of $3,087,704 million, $1,970,652 million and $1,386,254 million.

Long-term capital flows

In order to understand properly the importance of capital flows in the balance of payments, it is useful to distinguish between long-term and short-term capital flows. Long-term capital flows are dividable into direct investment and portfolio investment flows:

- **Direct overseas investment** involves acquisition of real productive assets, such as factories, oil refineries, offices and shopping malls, located in other countries. On the one hand, a UK-based MNC may decide to establish a new subsidiary company — for example, in the USA. On the other hand, direct investment can also involve acquisition, through merger or takeover, of an overseas-based company. These are examples of outward direct investment. Conversely, the decisions in the 1980s and 1990s by the Japanese vehicle manufacturers Nissan, Toyota and Honda to invest in automobile factories in the UK led to inward direct investment, or **foreign direct investment** (FDI).

KEY TERM

direct overseas investment: occurs when firms invest in or buy real productive assets located in foreign countries.

■ **Portfolio overseas investment** involves the purchase of financial assets (that is, pieces of paper laying claim to the ownership of real assets) rather than physical or directly productive assets. Typically, portfolio investment occurs when fund managers employed by financial institutions such as insurance

> **KEY TERM**
>
> **portfolio overseas investment:** occurs when financial services firms buy financial assets such as shares and government bonds issued in foreign countries.

companies and pension funds purchase shares issued by overseas companies, or securities issued by foreign governments. The globalisation of world security markets or capital markets and the abolition of exchange controls between virtually all developed countries have made it easy for UK residents to purchase shares or bonds that are listed on overseas capital markets. This has led to a massive increase in portfolio investment. UK residents can now buy shares and corporate bonds that were previously only available on the capital market of the company's country of origin. Securities issued by foreign governments, such as US Treasury bonds, can also be bought.

Nissan is one of the Japanese car companies with factories in the UK

The credit crunch, which began in America in 2007, and the so-called 'financial meltdown' that followed, had a significant adverse effect on portfolio investment both within and between countries. Many financial assets, particularly those bought and sold by banks, became known as 'toxic assets'. This term arose from the fact that a potential purchaser of a package of financial assets offered for sale by a bank could not know in advance whether assets in the package were of high risk and potentially little value or a sound investment (even the bank trying to make the sale might not know). In such conditions of imperfect information, trading in many types of financial asset collapsed.

Short-term capital flows

Long-term capital flows can partly be explained by comparative and competitive advantage. The flows are a response to people's decisions to invest in economic activities and industries located in countries that have a competitive advantage. Comparative advantage (which, as Chapter 20 explains, must not be confused with competitive advantage) may also rest in the same country. But since changes in competitive and/or comparative advantage usually take place quite slowly, long-term capital flows tend to be relatively stable and predictable.

This is not true of short-term capital flows. Short-term capital movements, which are also called 'hot money' flows, are largely speculative. The flows occur because the owners of funds, which include companies and banks as well as wealthy private individuals, believe that a quick speculative profit can be made by moving funds between currencies. Speculating that a currency's exchange rate is about to rise, owners of funds move money into that currency and out of other currencies whose exchange rates are expected to fall. 'Hot money' movements are also triggered by differences in interest rates. Funds flow into currencies with high interest rates and out of currencies with lower interest rates. International crises, such as the outbreak of a war in the Middle East, also cause funds to move into the currency of a safe-haven country, regarded as politically stable.

If the pool of hot money shifting between currencies was small, few problems would result. However, short-term capital flows have grown significantly over the last 50 or so years. A large-scale movement of funds from one currency to another creates an excess supply in the former currency and an excess demand for the second currency. To eliminate excess supply and demand, the exchange rates of the two currencies respectively fall and rise. As a result, the movement of funds between currencies produces the changes in exchange rates that speculators were expecting. More importantly, a large-scale hot money flow of funds between currencies destabilises exchange rates, the current accounts of balance of payments and, indeed, domestic economies. Such destabilisation occurred late in 2008 and early in 2009 when owners of hot money shifted their funds out of the pound on a massive scale.

Speculative capital flows between currencies such as the dollar, the pound and the euro, which occupy a central place in the finance of international trade, can destabilise the international monetary system. The most recent examples of destabilisation followed the credit crunch and the financial meltdown I referred to earlier. Banks and other financial institutions, and also governments, within a range of countries (which included the UK) lost their international credit ratings. To fight the recession that was hitting their economies, governments built up massive budget deficits, which they tried to finance by borrowing overseas.

The huge increase in overseas borrowing which accompanied burgeoning budget deficits put pressure on governments' international credit ratings. Before the recession, governments of industrialised countries typically enjoyed Triple A credit ratings. This meant they could borrow cheaply on

> **KEY TERM**
>
> **speculative capital flows:** occur when companies, banks and rich individuals buy a currency in order to earn higher interest rates on bank deposits held in that currency, or when they speculate that a rise in the currency's exchange rate will enable them to make a capital gain in the future.

international financial markets. But once a government loses its Triple A credit rating, international investors may charge higher rates of interest for loans to the government. The USA's credit rating was downgraded from AAA to AA-plus in August 2011, followed by a similar downgrading of the UK's rating in February 2013. A downgrade, or indeed fear of a downgrade, can cause international speculators to decide against holding financial assets denominated in the country's currency. (This is what happened to weaker eurozone countries such as Greece and Portugal, but at the time of writing in July 2013 it has not happened to the USA and the UK.)

CASE STUDY 21.1

America is a net debtor country, but does this matter?

If inward capital investment into a country exceeds outward capital investment, a country can become a net debtor country. By contrast, if outward investment exceeds inward investment, net creditor status may result.

In the early 1980s, after decades of almost continuous current account surpluses, the United States was a net creditor country, with a net stock of foreign assets worth about 10% of GDP. But persistent current account deficits turned the country into a net debtor in 1985, since when it has been getting deeper and deeper into the red. At the end of 2002, net external debt reached 25% of GDP. That is higher than the debt levels at which some Latin American countries hit financial disaster in the 1980s' debt crisis.

Can America afford this kind of indebtedness? That depends on the interest rate it must pay to overseas residents who have invested in US government securities. In the years ahead, America faces a sharply rising debt stock and, quite probably, higher interest rates, so net interest payments to foreigners could become very significant.

Source: news reports 2003

Follow-up question

What happened to the US government's international credit rating in 2011 and how may this be linked to the fact that the US is a net debtor country?

Balance of payments equilibrium

It is important to avoid confusing balance of payments *equilibrium* with the last item in Table 21.1, which ensures that the balance of payments *balances*. **Balance of payments equilibrium** (or external equilibrium) occurs when trade and capital flows into and out of the country are more or less equal over a

> **KEY TERM**
>
> **balance of payments equilibrium:** occurs when the current account more or less balances over a period of years.

number of years. Very often, balance of payments equilibrium is more narrowly defined, referring only to the current account. In this narrow sense, the balance of payments is in equilibrium when the current account more or less balances over a period of years. Defined in this way, balance of payments equilibrium is perfectly compatible with the occurrence of a short-term current account deficit or surplus. However, fundamental disequilibrium exists when there is a persistent tendency for payments for imports to be greater or less than payments for exports over a period of years.

EXTENSION MATERIAL

'Balance' in the balance of payments

The balance of payments is a balance sheet and, like all balance sheets, must balance in the sense that all items must sum to zero. In the UK balance of payments, this means that all items in the current account, the capital account and the financial account must sum to zero. In practice, this never happens because items are inaccurately measured and recorded — hence, the need for a **balancing item** to make the balance of payments sum to zero. The balancing item is a *mistakes* item equalling the number required to make the balance of payments sum to zero.

Government statisticians who construct the UK balance of payments use a *continuous revision* method of measurement. When the balance of payments statistics for a particular year are first published, soon after the end of the year in question, the balancing item may be quite large. In this situation, too much trust should not be placed in the figures. In subsequent months and years, the balancing item gradually decreases. In the light of new and previously unavailable information, the statisticians whittle away the balancing item, allocating elements of the item to one or more of the flows in real trade, investment income or capital.

Does a current account deficit pose a problem?

While a *short-run* deficit or surplus on the current account does not pose a problem, a persistent or *long-run* imbalance indicates a fundamental disequilibrium. However, the nature of any resulting problem depends upon the size and cause of the deficit or surplus, and also upon the nature of the exchange rate regime. The larger the deficit, the greater the problem is likely to be. The problem is also likely to be serious if the deficit is caused by the uncompetitiveness of the country's industries. In the short run, a deficit allows a country's residents to enjoy living standards boosted by imports, higher than would be possible from consumption of the country's output alone. But in the long run, the decline of the country's industries in the face of international competition may lower living standards.

A balance of payments deficit poses more problems when the exchange rate is fixed than when it floats freely. In both cases, the immediate cause of a deficit usually lies in the fact that exports are too expensive in overseas markets, while imports are too cheap at home. Obviously, there can be more deep-seated causes of over-priced exports and under-priced imports, relating, for example, to domestic wage costs being higher than in other countries. However, in a floating exchange rate regime, the exchange rate simply responds to market forces and falls, thereby restoring export competitiveness and curing or reducing balance of payments disequilibrium. I explain this in the next and final chapter of this book.

> **EXAM TIP**
>
> Exam candidates often assert that balance of payments deficits are bad and that surpluses are good. This does not necessarily follow.

By contrast, in a fixed exchange rate system, currencies may remain more or less permanently overvalued or undervalued. An overvalued fixed exchange rate leads to a large current account deficit, which then puts downward pressure on the exchange rate. However, in a fixed exchange rate system, the country's central bank takes action to prevent the exchange rate falling. In a process known as **exchange equalisation**, the central bank uses reserves of gold and hard currencies to purchase its own currency on the foreign exchange market.

Official reserves are limited, so a country cannot go on propping up a fixed exchange rate and financing a deficit for ever. In a fixed exchange rate system, eventually a country must take action to try to reduce or eliminate a persistent payments deficit.

Policies to cure or reduce a balance of payments deficit

A government (or its central bank) can use three different policies to try to cure a persistent deficit caused by an overvalued exchange rate. These are the '3 Ds' of **deflation**, **direct controls**, and **devaluation** or currency **depreciation**, which are shown in Figure 21.2.

Figure 21.2 The '3 Ds' of deflation, direct controls and devaluation

Deflation, which in this context refers to a reduction in the level of aggregate demand in the economy, reduces a current account deficit because it is mainly **expenditure reducing**. By contrast, import controls and devaluation are primarily **expenditure switching**.

> **EXAM TIP**
>
> Besides the '3 Ds' of deflation, direct controls and devaluation, you should also consider how **supply-side policies** may be needed to improve the long-term competitiveness of UK industries.

Deflationary policies

Deflationary policy involves using contractionary monetary and/or fiscal policy to reduce the demand for imports. For example, if the marginal propensity to import in the economy is 0.4, reducing aggregate demand by £10 billion should cause spending on imports to fall by £4 billion. This is an expenditure-reducing policy.

> **KEY TERM**
>
> **deflationary policy:** involves contractionary monetary or fiscal policy that shifts the *AD* curve to the left.

Although deflation is primarily an expenditure-reducing policy, it also has an expenditure-switching element. By reducing the rate of domestic price inflation relative to inflation rates in other countries, deflation increases the price competitiveness of exports and reduces that of imports.

However, in modern economies this is usually quite a small effect and the main effect of deflationary policies is to reduce aggregate demand and to depress economic activity in the domestic economy. Output and employment tend to fall rather than the price level. Unfortunately, as well as reducing the demand for imports, deflation affects the domestic economy. Falling demand for domestic output may force firms to seek export orders, so as to use spare production capacity. However, because exports are generally less profitable than domestic sales, a sound and expanding home market may be necessary for a successful export drive.

In summary, when deflating aggregate demand to achieve the external objectives of supporting the exchange rate and reducing a current account deficit, a government sacrifices the domestic economic objectives of full employment and economic growth. For this reason, governments may choose to use expenditure-switching policies of import controls and devaluation, in preference to expenditure-reducing deflation.

Direct controls

The direct controls used to reduce a payments deficit are import controls. **Embargoes** and **quotas** directly prevent or reduce expenditure on imports, while **import duties** or **tariffs** discourage expenditure by raising the price of imports. Import controls do not, however, cure the underlying cause of disequilibrium, namely the uncompetitiveness of a country's goods and services. Moreover, because a country essentially gains a 'beggar my neighbour' advantage at the expense of other countries, import controls tend to provoke retaliation.

Arguably, protectionism reduces specialisation and causes world trade, world output and economic welfare all to fall. Because of this, international organisations such as the EU and the World Trade Organization (WTO) have reduced the freedom of individual countries to impose import controls unilaterally to improve their current accounts. However, the EU uses its common external tariff to provide protection for all its members.

Devaluation

The word **devaluation** is used in a number of different ways. In a strictly narrow sense, a country devalues by reducing the value of a fixed exchange rate or an adjustable peg exchange rate. (Fixed exchange rates and adjustable peg exchange rates are explained in Chapter 22.) However, the term is also used in a looser way to describe a downward float or **depreciation** of a floating exchange rate. The word 'depreciation' can also confuse. Devaluation or a downward float causes an *external* depreciation of the currency; more units of the currency are needed to buy a unit of *another* currency. Don't confuse this with an *internal* depreciation of the currency, occurring when there is inflation *within* the economy.

> **KEY TERM**
>
> **devaluation:** a fall in a currency's exchange rate brought about either formally by a government and its central bank or informally through a downward float or depreciation of the exchange rate.

Unavailability of import controls means that a country must generally choose between *deflation* and *devaluation* if it wishes to reduce a current account deficit. As with import controls, devaluation has a mainly expenditure-switching effect. By increasing the price of imports relative to the price of exports, a successful devaluation switches domestic demand away from imports and towards home-produced goods. Similarly, overseas demand for the country's exports increases in response to the fall in export prices.

Price elasticity of demand and devaluation

The effectiveness of a devaluation in reducing a payment deficit depends to a significant extent upon the price elasticities of demand for exports and imports.

As Figure 21.3 shows, when the demands for exports and imports are both highly price elastic, a devaluation can reduce a current account deficit. Following a devaluation, the domestic price of imports rises from P_1 to P_2, while the overseas price of exports falls from P_3 to P_4. As a result, domestic residents spend less on imported goods following an increase in their relative prices. At the same time, residents of overseas countries spend more on the country's exports, whose relative prices have fallen

Figure 21.3 The effect of a devaluation (or downward float) of an exchange rate on the current account of the balance of payments

On the import side, area *b* in Figure 21.3 shows reduced expenditure on goods produced in other countries. Higher import prices mean that consumers switch to the now cheaper domestically produced substitutes. However, expenditure on the goods still being imported rises by area *a*. When demand for imports is price elastic — as in Figure 21.3 — total domestic expenditure on imports falls by area $(b - a)$.

In a similar way, expenditure on the country's exports increases by area $(d - c)$, providing overseas demand for the country's exports is price elastic. Area *d* shows increased expenditure on exports because prices of exports fall relative to prices of overseas produced substitutes. However, the foreign exchange earned by the goods exported before the devaluation falls by area *c*.

Overall, the current account improves by $(b - a) + (d - c)$, assuming the demand for imports and the demand for exports are both price elastic.

EXTENSION MATERIAL

The Marshall–Lerner condition

It is more difficult to see what may happen to the current account when, for example, the demand for exports is price inelastic but the demand for imports is price elastic. Fortunately, the **Marshall–Lerner condition** provides a simple rule to assess whether a change in the exchange rate can improve the current account. The condition states that when the *sum* of the export and import price elasticities is greater than unity (ignoring the minus sign), a fall in the exchange rate can reduce a deficit and a rise in the exchange rate can reduce a surplus. When, however, the export and import price elasticities of demand are both highly inelastic, summing to less than unity, a fall in the exchange rate can have the perverse effect of worsening a deficit (while a revaluation might increase a surplus).

The Marshall–Lerner condition is a *necessary* condition, but not a *sufficient* condition, for a fall in the exchange rate to reduce a payments deficit. For a devaluation or downward float to be successful, firms in the domestic economy must have spare capacity with which they can meet the surge in demand brought about by the fall in the exchange rate. This means that expenditure-reducing deflation and expenditure-switching devaluation should best be regarded as complementary policies rather than as substitute policies for reducing a current account deficit. Deflation *alone* may be unnecessarily costly in terms of lost domestic employment and output, yet may be necessary to provide the spare capacity and conditions in which a falling exchange rate can successfully cure a payments deficit.

The J-curve

Even if domestic demand for imports and overseas demand for exports are both price elastic and spare capacity exists in the economy, firms within the country may still be unable immediately to increase supply following a fall in the exchange rate. In the short run, the Marshall–Lerner condition (explained in the Extension material) may not hold because elasticities of demand are lower in the short run than in the long run. In these circumstances, the balance of payments may worsen before it improves. This is known as the **J-curve** effect, which is illustrated in Figure 21.4.

> **KEY TERM**
>
> **J-curve:** a curve, shaped like the letter 'J', that maps the possible time path of the state of the current account following a devaluation.

The initial worsening of the balance of payments that follows the fall in the exchange rate may reduce confidence in the idea that changing the exchange rate is the most appropriate method for reducing a payments imbalance. Falling confidence may, in turn, cause capital outflows that destabilise both the balance of payments and the exchange rate. The J-curve effect thus reduces the attractiveness of exchange rate adjustment as an instrument to correct payments disequilibrium. Even when the benefits of a falling exchange rate are realised, they may be short-lived. The increased price competitiveness produced by the devaluation is likely to be eroded as increased import prices raise the country's inflation rate.

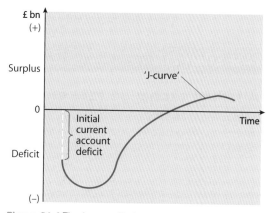

Figure 21.4 The J-curve effect

Nevertheless, if conditions are right, a devaluation can reduce a current account deficit. Despite occurring on so-called 'Black Wednesday', the pound's devaluation in September 1992 was extremely successful, at least for a number of years. There were two main reasons for this. First, expenditure reduction in the severe recession of the early 1990s created the spare capacity that enabled successful expenditure switching following the pound's devaluation. Second, the factories built in the UK by Japanese companies such as Honda and Toyota had just come on stream, producing goods of a quality that people wanted, in the UK and overseas.

Supply-side policies, export-led growth and the current account

Deflation, devaluation and direct controls (the '3 Ds') may be effective *short-term* policies for reducing current account deficits. However, it is now increasingly recognised that *long-term* improvement in trade flows requires appropriate and successful supply-side policies, which deliver **export-led growth**. The ability of the British economy to deliver sustained growth of exports and meet the challenge

> **KEY TERM**
>
> **export-led growth:** growth brought about by an increase in a country's exports, as distinct from consumption-led growth and investment-led growth which are caused by increases in other components of aggregate demand.

of imported goods and services depends on making UK exports quality competitive as well as price competitive. A low exchange rate, low interest rates at which British firms can borrow and low domestic inflation all contribute to increased export price competitiveness. However, price competitiveness on its own is not enough. Export-led growth requires UK goods and services to be quality competitive. This involves good design and well-made products. Improved quality competitiveness may only be achievable in the long run if helped by appropriate government supply-side policies together with supply-side reforms undertaken by the private sector. Greater investment in research and development and improved marketing strategies can have powerful long-term effects in improving quality competitiveness. Supply-side reforms, illustrated by an outward shift of the *LRAS* curve, provide the economy with increased capacity — enabling a reallocation of resources towards exporting.

CASE STUDY 21.2

A falling exchange rate and the UK's trade deficit

It is sometimes said that a significant fall in the exchange rate prices UK goods into international markets, which then in turn promotes export-led growth. But is this true? In the past, a 30% fall in the pound's exchange rate, such as the decline the government encouraged in 2008, would have boosted exports, limited imports and improved the country's trade figures. But this no longer seems to be the case. The UK's current account deficit in 2012 was higher than it had been in 2007, when the economy was

being fuelled by a consumer-spending spree financed by an expansion of personal debt.

Britain's poor record in exporting to emerging market countries, including the BRIC economies, has been said to be the reason for the weak trading performance. However, this interpretation is wrong. Exports to developing economies have been growing fast, up 65% for goods and 35% for services between 2006 and 2012. But it is trade with the EU that has been the problem, with exports of goods to European countries falling by 5% and services exports rising by 23% over the same 6-year period. It is worth noting that Britain runs a current account deficit of 4.5% with the EU and a surplus with the rest of the world.

Follow-up questions

1 Explain the difference between a trade deficit and a budget deficit (the so-called twin deficits).
2 What do you think is the best way to bring about long-term improvement in the UK's current account?

Does a current account surplus pose a problem?

While people readily agree that a persistent current account deficit can pose serious problems, fewer people realise that a balance of payments surplus on the current account can also lead to problems. Indeed, because a surplus is often seen as a sign of national economic virility and success, it is frequently argued that the bigger the surplus, the better the country's economic performance.

This is true to the extent to which the surplus measures the competitiveness of the country's exporting industries. There are, nevertheless, two reasons why a *large* payments surplus is undesirable, although a small surplus may be a justifiable policy objective.

One country's surplus is another country's deficit

Because the balance of payments must balance for the world as a whole, it is not possible for all countries to run surpluses simultaneously. Unless countries with persistently large surpluses agree to take action to reduce their surpluses, deficit countries cannot reduce their deficits. This means that deficit countries may be forced to impose import controls from which all countries, including surplus countries, eventually suffer. In an extreme scenario, a world recession may be triggered by a resulting collapse of world trade.

> **EXAM TIP**
>
> Possibly because the UK current account has been in deficit for many years, exam questions on current account surpluses have been rare. Nevertheless, the topic can always appear in future exams.

At various times since the 1970s, the current account surpluses of the oil-producing countries have led to this problem, as have the Japanese and latterly the Chinese payments surpluses, which have largely matched the US trade deficit. On several occasions, the US government has faced pressure from US manufacturing and labour interests to introduce import controls and other forms of protectionism. When introduced, US protectionism undoubtedly harms world trade.

Poorer non-oil-exporting developing countries also suffer chronic deficits, although these are different from the US trade deficit. The imbalance of trade between more developed and the least developed countries cannot be reduced without the industrialised countries of the North taking action to reduce surpluses that have been gained at the expense of the poorer economies of the South.

The current account surplus of oil-producing countries can lead to problems

A balance of payments surplus is inflationary

It is often forgotten that a balance of payments surplus can be an important cause of domestic inflation, particularly when the exchange rate is fixed. This is because a balance of payments surplus is an injection of aggregate demand into the circular flow of income, which, via a multiplier effect, increases the equilibrium level of nominal or money national income. If there are substantial unemployed resources in the economy, this has the beneficial effect of reflating real output and jobs. However, if the economy is initially close to full capacity, demand-pull inflation results. Note also that a balance of payments deficit has the opposite effect. The deficit is a leakage or withdrawal of demand from the economy, which deflates the equilibrium level of income.

Policies to cure or reduce a balance of payments surplus

The policies available to a government for reducing a balance of payments surplus are the opposite of the '3 Ds' of deflation, direct controls and devaluation appropriate for correcting a payments deficit. The policies are the '3 Rs' of **reflation, removal of import controls** and **revaluation**.

- Reflating demand, via expansionary monetary policy or fiscal policy, increases a country's demand for imports.
- Trade can also be liberalised by removing import controls.
- There have been calls on countries with large payments surpluses, such as Japan and China, to revalue in order to reduce global payments imbalances. But because there is much less pressure

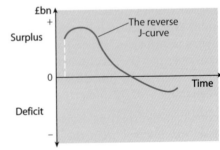

Figure 21.5 The reverse J-curve

on a surplus country to revalue than on a deficit country to devalue, such calls have not usually been successful. It is also worth noting that, for a revaluation to reduce a current account surplus, the Marshall–Lerner condition must be met. In addition, a reverse J-curve, illustrated in Figure 21.5, may operate, causing the payments surplus to get bigger immediately after the revaluation, before it eventually starts to get smaller.

Applying *AD/AS* analysis to the current account of the balance of payments

I shall now round off the chapter by reminding you about how *AD/AS* analysis can be used to explain the effect of a change in the current account on the balance of payments on the level of real output and the price level in the economy.

As I explained earlier in the chapter, the current account includes non-trade items (income and transfers) as well as exports and imports. However, for the sake of simplicity, I shall pretend that exports and imports are the only items in the current account. Given this assumption, there is a current account surplus when net exports are positive, i.e. $X > M$, and a deficit in the current account when net exports are negative, i.e. $X < M$.

As I also mentioned earlier, exports are an injection of spending into the circular flow of income, whereas imports are a leakage or withdrawal of spending from the flow.

Suppose that initially $X = M$, which means there is neither a surplus nor a deficit in the current account. Note also that in this situation, given my assumption that there are no non-trade flows in the current account, foreign trade injections into the circular flow of income exactly equal foreign trade withdrawals from the flow. To put it another way, when $X = M$, the current account has a *neutral* effect on the state of aggregate demand and on the circular flow of income.

However, suppose that at the next stage, overseas demand for British exports increases, but UK demand for imports remains unchanged. This means there is a net injection of spending into the circular flow of income. The current account moves into surplus, with $X > M$.

In the *AD/AS* diagram drawn in Figure 21.6, the increase in exports shifts the *AD* curve to the right. What happens next in the economy depends on the shape and slope of the *SRAS* curve around the initial point of macroeconomic equilibrium (point X in Figure 21.6).

Point X shows the economy in deep recession, suffering from deficient aggregate demand. In this situation, *any* event that

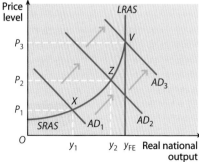

Figure 21.6 How an increase in exports can affect the national economy

increases aggregate demand increases the level of real output in the economy and causes demand-deficient unemployment to fall. An increase in exports is just such an event. In the diagram, increased exports shift the AD curve rightward from AD_1 to AD_2. This causes real output to rise from y_1 to y_2, though at the cost of inflation, since the price level rises from P_1 to P_2.

Following the shift to the right of the aggregate demand curve to AD_2, macroeconomic equilibrium is now shown at point Z. But as the $SRAS$ curve becomes steeper, moving up the curve, the diagram tells us that the main effect of a further shift of the AD curve from AD_2 to AD_3 falls on the price level rather than on output and jobs. Output increases, from y_2 to y_{FE}, but the price level also increases to P_3. As full employment approaches, export demand becomes *inflationary* rather than *reflationary*.

EXAM TIP

You must be able to use the *AD/AS* model and the circular flow of income to analyse how changes in exports and/or imports affect macroeconomic performance, i.e. growth, employment, inflation and international competitiveness.

Nevertheless, in this situation the growth in export demand eliminates the demand deficiency previously existent in the economy. The economy ends up on its long-run aggregate supply (*LRAS*) curve, with macroeconomic equilibrium at point V.

Once point V has been reached, what may happen next in the economy depends on assumptions made about the nature of short-run and long-run aggregate supply. According to Figure 21.6, when the economy produces on the vertical *LRAS* curve any further increase in the demand for exports leads only to the price level rising above P_3, without any increase in real output. However, there is another possibility. Foreign demand for a country's exports often creates favourable supply-side conditions in which the *LRAS* curve shifts to the right. This means the economy can produce and supply the goods needed to meet the increase in export demand without generating inflation. This is an example of **export-led growth** mentioned earlier in the chapter. The German and Japanese economies certainly enjoyed export-led growth from the 1960s to the 1980s and China has recently enjoyed similar benefits. However, the growth of demand for Chinese exports has also caused inflation in the Chinese economy.

A fall in export demand and/or an increase in domestic demand for imports triggers an opposite effect to the one just described. There is a net leakage of demand from the circular flow of income, the AD curve shifts to the left, and both real output and the price level fall (or, more realistically in the latter case, the rate of inflation slows down). Overall, the effect is *deflationary*.

EXAM TIP

You would illustrate the desired effect of supply-side policies aimed at increasing export competitiveness by shifting the vertical *LRAS* curve to the right. This could lead to a fall in the relative prices of exports. Quality and productivity improvements brought about by the supply-side policies could be depicted by the fall in the average price level.

- The balance of payments is the part of the national accounts that measures all the currency flows into and out of the country in a particular time period.
- The two main parts of the balance of payments are the current account and capital flows.
- The two main parts of the current account are the flows of spending on exports and imports.
- Net income from abroad, which is mostly net investment income, and current transfers are also items in the current account.
- Net investment income results from capital flows. For example, an outward capital flow generates an inward flow of investment income in future years.
- Capital flows divide into direct investment, portfolio investment, and speculative or 'hot money' flows.
- 'Hot money' flows can destabilise the exchange rate, the balance of payments, and indeed the whole economy.
- Balance of payments equilibrium occurs when the current account more or less balances over a number of years — as a simplification, when $X = M$. Disequilibrium is when there is a large and persistent current account deficit or surplus.
- A large deficit is not necessarily a problem, particularly if the exchange rate is floating, with capital flows financing the deficit.
- The expenditure-reducing policy of deflation and/or the expenditure-switching policies of import controls and devaluation can be used to reduce a current account deficit. Sometimes deflation and devaluation should be used in tandem.
- Likewise reflation, removal of import controls and revaluation can be used to reduce a surplus.
- Contrary to popular opinion, a large and persistent surplus may be undesirable.
- Current account deficits are themselves deflationary and surpluses may be inflationary.
- An increase in a current account deficit leads to a shift to the left of the *AD* curve in an *AD/AS* diagram. A decrease in a deficit or an increase in a surplus causes the *AD* curve to shift to the right.

Exam-style questions

1 Explain the difference between the concepts of balance of payments equilibrium and 'balance' in the balance of payments. **(15 marks)**

2 Explain the policies that may be used to reduce a payments deficit on current account. **(15 marks)**

3 Do you agree that successful supply-side reform is needed if the UK's current account is to improve in the long run? Justify your answer. **(25 marks)**

4 Evaluate the view that balance of payments surpluses on current account are always beneficial. **(25 marks)**

Extra resources to help you revise are available online at www.hodderplus.co.uk/philipallan

Chapter 22

Exchange rates, the pound, the dollar and the euro

Although domestic currencies are used to pay for internal trade within countries, imports are usually paid for in the currency of the country exporting the goods or services. An exchange rate measures how much of another currency a particular currency can buy; it is the external price of the currency quoted in terms of the other currency. Exchange rates can also be measured against gold, or against a weighted average of a sample or 'basket' of currencies. Currencies are bought and sold in the foreign exchange market, which is now an international 24/7 electronic market. On a global scale, the market never closes, and ICT-based buying and selling takes place throughout the day and night.

The chapter begins by describing different ways to measure a country's exchange rate, outlines the main types of exchange rate system, and explains and analyses how balance of payments disequilibrium is dealt with in floating and fixed exchange rate systems. Towards the end of the chapter, I shall explain the special features of and the relationships between a number of key world currencies. These are the UK pound, the US dollar and the euro.

LEARNING OUTCOMES

This chapter will:
- explain the meaning of an exchange rate and how an exchange rate is measured
- describe the different types of exchange rate system or regime
- analyse exchange rate and balance of payments equilibrium and disequilibrium in a freely floating exchange rate system
- assess the advantages and disadvantages of freely floating exchange rates
- examine how fixed and managed exchange rates operate
- survey the roles of the pound, the US dollar and the euro in world payments systems, historically and at the present day

WHAT YOU SHOULD ALREADY KNOW

At AS, you learnt about the link between monetary policy and the exchange rate; however, you did not learn fully how exchange rates are determined. You did learn how changes in exchange rates affect export and import prices, the balance of payments on current account and indeed the level of domestic economic activity in the national economy.

The meaning and measurement of an exchange rate

These days the **exchange rate** of a currency is simply the external price of the currency in terms of another currency, such as the US dollar. The convention of quoting exchange rates in terms of the US dollar is of fairly recent origin. Before 1914 most exchange rates were expressed in terms of gold and only after 1945 did the dollar become the near universally accepted standard by which the external values of other currencies were measured.

In recent years, in response to the changing pattern of UK trade, the pound's exchange rate is as often quoted against the euro as it is against the dollar. The **sterling exchange rate index (ERI)** is also used to measure the pound's exchange rate. The ERI does not measure the pound's external value against a particular currency. Rather it is a trade-weighted average of the pound's exchange rate against a number of leading trading currencies, calculated to reflect the importance of each currency in international trade with Britain.

At the close of market trading on 25 July 2013, the sterling index was 80.2 compared to its 2005 index of 100. This means that over the years since 2005, the ERI had depreciated or fallen in value by 19.8% when measured against the exchange rates of the UK's most important trading partners. As Figure 22.1 shows, much of the collapse of the pound's exchange rate occurred in 2007 and 2008. This amounted to a 30% devaluation. Since 2008 the exchange rate, depicted by all three measures shown in Figure 22.1, has steadied, not because the state of the UK economy improved, but because international speculators view the pound as a 'safe haven' currency, particularly in comparison to the euro.

The real exchange rate

The different exchange rates mentioned so far are all *nominal* exchange rates. These must not be confused with the *real* exchange rate, which measures the rate at which home-produced goods exchange for imports, rather than the rates at which currencies themselves are traded. The real exchange

> **KEY TERM**
>
> **exchange rate:** the external price of a currency, usually measured against another currency.

Figure 22.1 Three measures of the pound's exchange rate: the sterling exchange rate index, the dollar exchange rate and the euro exchange rate, Quarter 3 2007 to Quarter 4 2012

rate, which is a measure of competitiveness, is calculated by the following formula:

$$\text{pound's real exchange rate} = \text{sterling index} \times \frac{\text{domestic price level}}{\text{weighted foreign price level}}$$

The different types of exchange rate system

Figure 22.2 shows the main types of exchange rate system. The two extreme types are **freely floating exchange rates** (also known as **cleanly floating exchange rates**) and rigidly **fixed exchange rates**. A fixed exchange rate is the most extreme form of a **managed exchange rate**.

The managed exchange rates that lie between the extremes of freely floating and rigidly fixed exchange rates take two main forms: **adjustable peg** and **managed floating** (or **dirty floating**) exchange rates. Adjustable peg exchange rates resemble fixed exchange rates in many respects, but the rate at which the exchange rate is fixed may be changed from time to time. A formal devaluation reduces the fixed exchange rate, while revaluation increases the fixed rate.

Figure 22.2 The different types of exchange rate system

By contrast, as its name indicates, a **managed floating exchange rate** is closer to a freely floating exchange rate than to a fixed exchange rate. Market forces or supply and demand 'officially' determine the exchange rate, but the country's central bank intervenes 'unofficially' behind the scenes, buying or selling reserves and raising or lowering interest rates to move the exchange rate upward or downward.

Freely floating exchange rates

In a regime of freely floating ('cleanly' floating) exchange rates, the external value of a country's currency is determined on foreign exchange markets by the forces of demand and supply alone. Later in this chapter, I shall explain that in recent years capital flows and speculation have been extremely significant in influencing the supply of and demand for a currency, and hence its exchange rate. However, I shall first simplify by assuming that a currency is demanded on foreign exchanges solely for the payment of trade and that trade flows alone determine exchange rates. I shall assume, too, that any holdings of foreign currencies surplus to the immediate requirement of paying for trade are immediately sold on the foreign exchange market.

Explaining the slope of the demand and supply curves for pounds

When the exchange rate of the pound falls, UK exports become more competitive in overseas markets. The volume of UK exports increases, leading to greater overseas demand for pounds to finance the purchase of these exports. This explains the downward-sloping demand curve for pounds, which is illustrated in Figure 22.3.

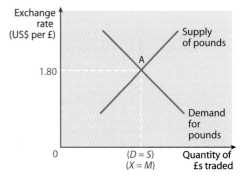

Figure 22.3 Exchange rate equilibrium in a freely floating exchange rate system

But just as UK exports generate a demand for pounds on foreign exchange markets, so imports into the UK generate a supply of pounds. The explanation lies in the fact that UK trading companies generally pay for imports in foreign currencies. Importers must sell sterling on the foreign exchange market in order to purchase the foreign currencies needed to pay for the goods they are buying. As the pound's exchange rate rises, fewer pounds are needed to buy a given quantity of foreign currency. This means that the sterling price of imports falls. UK consumers are likely to respond to the falling price of imports by increasing total spending on imports (which happens as long as the demand for imports is price elastic). A greater total quantity of sterling must be supplied on foreign exchange markets to pay for the imports — even though the sterling price of each unit of imports has fallen. The result is the upward-sloping supply curve of sterling depicted in Figure 22.3. This shows that at higher exchange rates, more sterling is supplied on the foreign exchange market.

EXAM TIP

It is useful but not essential to understand why the demand curve for a currency slopes downward and why the supply curve slopes upward. By contrast, it is essential to understand exchange rate equilibrium and disequilibrium and to be able to link both concepts to the balance of payments.

Exchange rate equilibrium in a freely floating exchange rate regime

Exchange rate equilibrium occurs at the market-clearing exchange rate at which the demand for pounds on foreign exchange markets equals the supply of pounds. In Figure 22.3, this is determined at point A. The equilibrium exchange rate is $1.80 to the pound.

At this exchange rate, the money value of exports (paid in sterling) equals the money value of imports (paid in foreign currencies). If I assume that exports and imports are the only items in the current account, the current account is also in equilibrium.

Because I am assuming away any complications introduced by capital flows, exchange rate equilibrium implies balance of payments equilibrium on current account and vice versa. The two equilibria are just different sides of the same coin: exchange rate equilibrium is price equilibrium, whereas balance of payments equilibrium (where $X = M$ in Figure 22.3) means that the quantity of the currency flowing into the country equals the quantity flowing out. Given the simplifying assumptions I have made, once the balance of payments is in equilibrium, there is no pressure for the exchange rate to rise or fall.

The adjustment process to a new equilibrium exchange rate

I shall now assume that some event or 'shock' disturbs the initial equilibrium, for example an improvement in the quality of foreign-produced goods causes UK residents to increase demand for imports, whatever the exchange rate. In Figure 22.4, the increase in demand for foreign exchange to pay for imports causes the supply curve of sterling to shift to the right from S_1 to S_2. (Remember, when more foreign currencies are demanded, more sterling must be supplied.) In the new situation, the current account of the balance of payments is in deficit by the amount $(X < M)$ in the diagram — as long as the exchange rate stays at $1.80. At the $1.80 exchange rate, UK residents supply or sell more sterling than before to pay for imports, but because overseas residents still demand the same quantity of UK goods (assuming that their view on the quality of UK goods relative to foreign goods has not changed), the overseas demand for sterling to pay for UK exports remains at its previous level.

Figure 22.4 How a current account deficit is eliminated in a freely floating exchange rate system

At the exchange rate of $1.80 to the pound, there is an excess supply of sterling on the foreign exchange market, equal to the distance B minus A. The market mechanism now swings into action to restore equilibrium — both for the exchange rate and for the balance of payments. When the excess holdings of sterling accumulated at the exchange rate of $1.80 are sold on the foreign exchange market, the pound's exchange rate falls. This increases the price competitiveness of UK exports while making imports less price competitive. The exchange rate falls until a new equilibrium exchange rate is reached at point C, where the exchange rate is $1.50 to the pound.

Note that the current account of the balance of payments is once again in equilibrium, but at $(X = M)_2$ rather than at $(X = M)_1$. This means that at the new equilibrium exchange rate, although they are again equal in size, the money values of exports and imports have both increased.

Conversely, if the initial equilibrium is disturbed by an improvement in the quality of UK goods or services, the demand curve for sterling shifts to the right. This moves the current account into surplus, causing the pound's exchange rate to rise or appreciate in order to relieve the excess demand for sterling. Providing UK residents don't change their views on the relative quality of imports, the exchange rate rises until the balance of payments and exchange equilibrium are once again restored.

> **EXAM TIP**
>
> You should practise drawing demand and supply graphs to show a floating exchange rate.

> **KEY TERM**
>
> **disequilibrium exchange rate:** the rate at which there is excess demand for, or excess supply of, the currency.

EXTENSION MATERIAL

The theory I have just outlined can be called the **traditional approach** to floating exchange rates. The traditional approach, which largely ignores capital flows, contrasts with the **monetary approach**, developed in the 1950s and 1970s by the monetarist economists Milton Friedman and Harry Johnson. The monetary approach argues that capital flows, brought about by conditions in global money and financial markets, are much more important than trade flows in determining changes in exchange rates.

The monetary approach to floating exchange rates provides better explanations of recent volatility in foreign exchange markets and wild swings of exchange rates than does the traditional approach, which side-steps the problems created by capital flows.

The advantages of floating exchange rates

Economists generally agree that providing there are no distorting capital flows, freely floating exchange rates have the following five advantages.

Balance of payments equilibrium

The exchange rate (which is the external price of the currency) should move up or down to correct a payments imbalance. Providing the adjustment mechanism operates smoothly, a currency should never be overvalued or undervalued for long. In the event of an overvalued exchange rate causing export uncompetitiveness and a payments deficit, market forces should quickly adjust towards an equilibrium exchange rate, which also achieves equilibrium in the balance of payments. Similarly, undervaluation should be quickly corrected by an upward movement of the exchange rate.

Resource allocation

If the world's resources are to be efficiently allocated between competing uses, exchange rates must be correctly valued. For efficient resource allocation in a constantly changing world, market prices must accurately reflect shifts in demand and changes in competitive and comparative advantage that result from technical progress and events such as discoveries of new mineral resources. In principle, a freely floating exchange rate should respond and adjust to these changes. By contrast, a fixed exchange rate may gradually become overvalued or undervalued, as demand or competitive and comparative advantage move against or in favour of a country's industries.

EXAM TIP

The advantages and disadvantages of floating exchange rates often figure in exam questions, including global context data-response questions.

Domestic policy objectives

It is sometimes argued that when the exchange rate is freely floating, balance of payments surpluses and deficits cease to be a policy problem for the government, as it is then free to pursue the domestic economic objectives of full employment and growth. Market forces look after the balance of payments while governments concentrate on domestic economic policy. If, in the pursuit of domestic objectives, the inflation rate rises out of line with other countries, in a freely floating world the exchange rate simply falls to restore competitiveness.

Inflation

In much the same way, a responsible country with a lower than average inflation rate should benefit from a floating exchange rate because the exchange rate insulates the country from 'importing inflation' from the rest of the world. If inflation rates are higher in the rest of the world, a fixed exchange rate causes a country to import inflation through the rising prices of goods imported from high-inflation countries. By contrast, a floating exchange rate floats upward, which lowers the prices of imports, insulating the economy against importing inflation.

Independent monetary policy

With a floating exchange rate, monetary policy can be used solely to achieve domestic policy objectives, such as the control of inflation. This is called an *independent* monetary policy. By contrast, with a fixed exchange rate, interest rates may be determined by events in the outside world (and in particular by capital flows out of and into currencies), rather than by the needs of the domestic economy. To maintain a fixed exchange rate, interest rates may have to be raised to prevent the exchange rate from falling. In this situation, monetary policy is no longer independent, in the sense that it can no longer be assigned to pursuing purely domestic policy objectives.

EXAM TIP

You must understand the links between exchange rates and monetary policy.

The disadvantages of floating exchange rates

Freely floating exchange rates nevertheless have some disadvantages, particularly relating to the fact that in the modern globalised world in which financial capital is internationally mobile, capital flows rather than exports and imports are the main determinants of floating exchange rates.

Speculation and capital flows

The argument that a freely floating exchange rate is never overvalued or undervalued for very long depends crucially upon the main assumption of the traditional theory of exchange rates, that currencies are bought and sold on foreign exchange markets only to finance trade. This assumption means that speculation and capital flows have no influence on exchange rates. But as the monetary theory of exchange rates argues, this is at odds with how the modern globalised economy works. These days, well over 90% of currency transactions taking place on foreign exchange markets stem from capital flows and from the decisions of individuals, business corporations, financial institutions and even governments to switch wealth portfolios between different currencies. In the short run, exchange rates are extremely vulnerable to **speculative capital** or **hot money** movements into or out of currencies. Just like a fixed exchange rate, a floating exchange rate can be overvalued or undervalued, which means it does not reflect the trading competitiveness of the country's goods and services.

EXAM TIP

Refer back to Chapter 21 and reread the section on hot money flows.

International trading uncertainty

It is sometimes argued that, whereas fixed exchange rates create conditions of certainty and stability in which international trade can prosper and grow, the volatility and instability caused by floating exchange rates slow the growth of, and even destroy, international trade. In fact, *hedging*, which involves the purchase or sale of a currency in the 'forward' market 3 months in advance of the actual delivery of the currency and payment for trade, considerably reduces the trading uncertainties associated with floating exchange rates. Indeed, fixed and managed exchange rates may also cause uncertainty, especially when a currency is overvalued and a devaluation is expected.

Cost-push inflation

Floating exchange rates sometimes contribute to cost-push inflation. Suppose a country has a higher rate of inflation than its trading partners. Trading competitiveness and the current account of the balance of payments both worsen, causing the exchange rate to fall in order to restore competitiveness. This may trigger a vicious cumulative downward spiral of faster inflation and exchange rate depreciation. The falling exchange rate increases import prices, which raise the rate of domestic cost-push inflation. Workers react by demanding pay rises to restore the real value of the eroded real wage. At the next stage, increased inflation erodes the export competitiveness initially won by the fall of the exchange rate, which in turn triggers a further fall in the exchange rate to recover the lost advantage, and so the process continues. The resulting downward spiral can eventually destabilise large parts of the domestic economy, causing unemployment and reducing economic growth.

EXAM TIP

It is important to understand the links between exchange rates and inflation.

Demand-pull inflation

Floating exchange rates can trigger demand-pull inflation as well as cost-push inflation. With a floating exchange rate, there is no need to deflate the domestic economy to deal with a balance of payments deficit on the current account. But suppose a large number of countries with floating exchange rates simultaneously increase aggregate demand. This can lead to excess demand on a worldwide scale, which fuels global inflation. This happened in the 1970s, when a worldwide expansion of demand created conditions in which oil and primary goods producers could raise prices and still sell in world markets. In countries such as the UK, the resulting inflation appeared to be import cost-push inflation, caused by the rising cost of imported energy and raw materials. However, the true cause lay in excess demand created by the simultaneous effects of demand expansion and floating exchange rates, when world supply could not increase, at least in the short run, to meet the surge in global demand. A similar situation occurred in 2007 and early 2008.

CASE STUDY 22.1

Is Britain going bust?

In September 1992, two currency speculators, George Soros and Jim Rogers, effectively 'broke' the Bank of England. They speculated against the pound on a massive scale and forced the UK chancellor and the governor of the Bank of England to withdraw the pound from the semi-fixed exchange rate regime known as the Exchange Rate Mechanism of the European Monetary System. The day on which this happened is known as 'Black Wednesday'.

Seventeen years later in January 2009, Jim Rogers famously again said that Britain is bust. Rogers advised young British people to 'Move to China; learn Chinese'. Below is an extract from an interview Jim Rogers gave to Sky News in January 2009 in which he described sterling as 'finished' and London's financial services as a disaster. He went on to say that the government had made a 'horrible mistake' in spending billions of pounds

to stop Britain's banks collapsing and added that Britain would soon have little to offer the world.

> After years of enjoying a strong currency and thriving financial sector, the winds of change blowing across the UK are fast turning into a storm.

> The fact is that the UK has had two things to sell to the world over the last 25 years, the North Sea oil and that's drying up — within a decade the UK is going to be importing oil — and the City of London. The UK's financial asset (the City) is a disaster and it's not going to revive.

> Sterling has got to go lower over the next decade or two because when the North Sea dries up I do not know what the UK is going to sell to the world.

> Source: Jim Rogers, 21 January 2009

Follow-up questions

1 Research what happened to the pound's exchange rate in September 1992 and assess whether this was good or bad for the UK economy.
2 In recent years the UK economy has often been said to be 'unbalanced'. What is meant by this and, if true, what have been the consequences?

EXTENSION MATERIAL

The purchasing power theory and long-term determinants of the exchange rate

Over three decades from the 1970s to the early 2000s, the pound's exchange rate generally fell against those of other currencies. Indeed, the downward trend occurred through most of the twentieth century and has continued right up to the present day. The **purchasing power parity** (PPP) theory provides the best explanation for such long-term changes in exchange rates.

Consider a situation in which a country's inflation rate is 10% higher than the inflation rates of its main competitors. The PPP theory predicts that, in this situation, the country's exchange rate falls by approximately 10% to offset the loss of trading competitiveness caused by the higher domestic inflation rate. As a result, the purchasing power of exports over imports returns to its earlier level: that is, the level existing before the domestic inflation rate moved out of line with inflation rates in the rest of the world.

Although the PPP theory provides a good explanation of long-term changes in exchange rates (taking place over many decades), it is less useful for explaining short-term changes. As I have indicated, short-term changes in exchange rates result mainly from speculative capital flows. Hot money flows cause exchange rates to overshoot, in which case the currency becomes overvalued, or to be undervalued. However, because speculative flows tend to even out over periods longer than a few years, hot money movements are less significant for explaining long-term changes in exchange rates.

Fixed exchange rates

With a freely floating exchange rate system, a currency's external value rises or falls to eliminate a balance of payments surplus or deficit on the current account. By contrast, with **fixed exchange rates**, a currency's external value remains unchanged, while the internal price level, or more usually the level of domestic economic activity and output, adjusts to eliminate balance of payments disequilibrium.

KEY TERM

fixed exchange rate: an exchange rate fixed at a certain level by the country's central bank and maintained by the central bank's intervention in the foreign exchange market.

Although most exchange rates now float freely, fixed exchange rates have been important for long periods in the last 100 or more years. In a rigidly fixed system, devaluation is ruled out as a means of reducing a current account deficit. This means that deflationary policies that decrease aggregate demand have to be used to improve the current account. As a result, deflation harms the domestic economy, which explains why modern governments generally reject a return to rigidly fixed exchange rates. Governments prefer to be able to devalue, or at least to be able to engineer a downward float of the currency.

EXAM TIP

A rigidly fixed exchange rate is the most extreme form of managed exchange rate.

The longest period of rigidly fixed exchange rates occurred in the nineteenth century and in the early years of the twentieth century. During this period, most major world currencies were fixed against gold in a system known as the **gold standard**. In addition, from 1999 until 2002, 12 currencies of the countries committed to adopting the euro were rigidly fixed against each other in preparation for their eventual disappearance when replaced by euro notes and coins in 2002. These countries, together with other counties such as Malta and Slovenia, which adopted the euro more recently, now form the eurozone. The eurozone will grow in size when the local currencies of other new EU member countries are eventually replaced by the euro.

EXAM TIP

Historical knowledge of the gold standard is useful, but by no means essential.

The advantages of fixed exchange rates

Because the advantages and disadvantages of fixed exchange rates are closely but oppositely related to those of floating rates, which I have already explained in some depth, I shall provide only a brief summary here.

The main advantages of fixed exchange rates are:

- certainty and stability
- the anti-inflationary discipline imposed on a country's domestic economic management and upon the behaviour of its workers and firms. I explain this in greater depth in the Extension material later in the chapter, which covers the relationship between fixed exchange rates and monetary policy

EXAM TIP

Make sure you can adapt my earlier coverage of the advantages and disadvantages of floating exchange rates so as to be able to explain the advantages and disadvantages of fixed exchange rates.

The disadvantages of fixed exchange rates

By contrast, the principal disadvantages of fixed exchange rates include:

- a possible increase in uncertainty if devaluation or revaluation is expected
- continued overvaluation or undervaluation of the currency
- severe deflationary costs of lost output and unemployment for a deficit country and the importing of inflation by a surplus country
- a possible balance of payments or currency crisis in a country whose currency is overvalued
- tying up of resources in official reserves, which could be used more productively elsewhere

Managed exchange rates

An exchange rate is managed when the country's central bank actively intervenes in foreign exchange markets, buying and selling reserves and its own currency to influence the movement of the exchange rate in a particular direction. By **managing the exchange rate**, a country's monetary authorities hope to achieve the stability and certainty associated with fixed exchange rates combined with a floating exchange rate's ability to avoid overvaluation and undervaluation by responding to market forces.

KEY TERM

managed exchange rate: similar to a fixed exchange rate (which itself is the extreme form of a managed exchange rate) in that the central bank intervenes in the foreign exchange market to determine its currency's exchange rate.

As well as by maintaining a rigidly fixed exchange rate, which is the extreme example of a managed exchange rate, exchange rates can be managed in two ways. These are through an adjustable peg (or fixed peg) system and by managed floating (or dirty floating).

Adjustable peg exchange rate systems

An **adjustable peg exchange rate** has a closer resemblance to a rigidly fixed exchange rate than to a freely floating exchange rate. Nevertheless, adjustable pegs are more flexible than rigidly fixed exchange rates. This is because the exchange rate is adjusted upward or downward from time to time by the country's central bank. An upward *revaluation*

KEY TERM

adjustable peg exchange rate: a managed exchange rate similar to a rigidly fixed exchange rate except that the central bank may alter the exchange rate's central peg by devaluing or revaluing.

corrects an undervalued exchange rate, whereas a downward adjustment or *devaluation* is used to correct overvaluation.

Figure 22.5 illustrates devaluation of the pound in an adjustable peg exchange rate system. The exchange rate is initially fixed at a *central peg* of $1.50. Supply and demand then determine the day-to-day exchange rate. Providing the exchange stays between a ceiling and a floor set at the time that the central peg was fixed, the exchange rate is correctly valued for trade. There is no need for central bank intervention. However, the graph shows the exchange rate falling to the floor of $1.48, possibly because of a speculative capital flow against the currency. At this point the central bank intervenes, raising domestic interest rates to attract capital flows into the currency and using reserves to support the fixed exchange rate. By selling reserves and buying its own currency, the central bank creates an artificial demand for its own currency. A policy of buying and selling currencies to support an exchange rate is known as **exchange equalisation**.

As Figure 22.6 shows, maintaining the exchange somewhere between the ceiling and the floor is almost identical to the way a buffer stock agency buys or sells stocks of an agricultural good or a metal to stabilise the price of the primary product.

If you refer back to the middle panel of Figure 22.1, you will see that the pound's exchange rate against the dollar was around the $2.00 dollar mark in the first half of 2008. However, from August onwards, a hot money flow out of the pound and into the dollar led to a collapse of the exchange rate, with the pound's value falling in the latter months of 2008 by about 30%

Figure 22.5 A devaluation of an adjustable peg exchange rate

KEY TERM

exchange equalisation: takes place when a central bank buys or sells its own currency to maintain its exchange rate at a particular level.

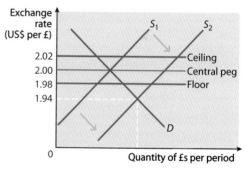

Figure 22.6 How managing the exchange rate resembles buffer stock intervention

against the dollar. At the time, the pound's exchange rate was floating, as it still is, but consider what would probably have happened had the pound's value been fixed against the dollar, say at $2.00 to the pound. In its early days, the outflow of speculative funds would have shifted the supply curve of pounds to the right, say to S_2 in Figure 22.6. In a floating system, the capital outflow would have taken the exchange rate down to $1.94 (at least to start with). However, with a managed exchange rate, support-buying by the Bank of England would be triggered at $1.98 to prevent the pound diving below the floor. If buying up its own currency was successful, the Bank of England would have succeeded in maintaining the fixed exchange rate. However, given the massive size of the speculative flow out of the pound, it is much more likely that the $2.00 peg would be abandoned, either by devaluing to a lower central peg, or by waving goodbye to the managed exchange rate.

Persistent support for a currency means that its exchange rate is overvalued, condemning the country to over-priced exports, under-priced imports and a current account deficit. In a rigidly fixed exchange rate system (which can be illustrated by the left-hand part of Figure 22.5), this is the end of the story. The country's government has to deflate the domestic economy and/or impose import controls, since devaluation and revaluation are not permitted in a rigidly fixed system.

However, Figure 22.5 goes on to show the authorities devaluing the exchange rate to a new central peg of $1.00 so as to correct the imbalance. This illustrates the difference between adjustable peg and rigidly fixed exchange rate systems.

CASE STUDY 22.2

Benign neglect and the exchange rate

Since 2008, in attempts to 'kick-start' the British economy into economic recovery, successive governments and the Bank of England have followed a policy of 'benign neglect' with regard to the pound's exchange rate. Benign neglect is a policy of not intervening in the foreign exchange market to influence the external value of the pound. In a sense, it is a form of 'anti-policy', leaving everything to free-market forces. However, since it also involves the authorities 'talking down' the value of the pound, benign neglect goes one stage further.

In February 2013, Ashraf Laidi, City Index's chief global strategist, stated that sterling's recent weakness has been due to the 'benign neglect' charted by the Bank of England and the UK Treasury. 'The latest pronouncements from Bank of England governor Mervyn King and his future successor Mark Carney appear to be a contest over who could deliver the most dovish measures in terms of further quantitative easing.' But King said that there are limits to what can be achieved using quantitative easing and low interest rates in stimulating the economy. He urged the government to 'find ways of boosting overseas demand for our products' and push through 'supply-side reforms'. In King's view, monetary stimulus and benign neglect have not been enough.

Follow-up questions

1 Members of the Bank of England's Monetary Policy Committee (MPC) are often divided into 'doves' and 'hawks'. What does this mean?

2 Research what has happened to the pound's exchange rate since 2013.

Managed or dirty floating

Fixed and adjustable peg exchange rate systems have now been abandoned throughout most of the world. Virtually all exchange rates now float, though there is a difference between 'clean' and **dirty floating**. Clean floating is the same as free floating and pure floating, i.e. there is

KEY TERM

dirty floating: a managed exchange rate system in which the central bank intervenes in the foreign exchange market when the exchange rate is still floating.

absolutely no central bank intervention to prop up the exchange rate or to manipulate its value. In earlier sections of this chapter I have explained clean or pure floating.

By contrast, 'dirty' or 'managed' floating occurs when the exchange rate is *officially* floating, in the sense that a country's monetary authorities announce that market forces are determining the exchange rate, but in fact they intervene *unofficially* behind the scenes to buy or sell their own currency to influence the exchange rate.

At one extreme, dirty or managed floating is simply a *smoothing operation* for a clean or freely floating exchange rate. However, at the other extreme, currency intervention may try to secure and then maintain an unofficial exchange rate target. China regularly intervenes in foreign exchange markets to keep its currency, the renminbi (rnb), low against the dollar. The authorities in some of the smaller EU countries that have not as yet adopted the euro have also tried to maintain the exchange rates of their currencies against the euro. (Their currencies have been 'shadowing' the euro with the intention eventually of replacing the national currency with the euro.)

The pound, the dollar and reserve currency roles

The US dollar is the world's **reserve currency**. A reserve currency is a currency that governments and central banks outside the country that issues the currency wish to hold.

KEY TERM

reserve currency: a currency widely held in the foreign currency reserves of other countries and used by them to pay for trade.

The US dollar is the world's reserve currency

To take on a world reserve role, a currency must be transmitted into overseas ownership. In the second half of the nineteenth century, the pound became the world's reserve currency, alongside gold. At the time, the pound was on the gold standard, which meant that the Bank of England fixed the pound's exchange rate against gold and guaranteed to exchange pounds for gold on demand at this fixed rate.

EXAM TIP

It is useful but not essential to know about reserve currencies.

This brings me to the two rather paradoxical circumstances that enable a currency to become a reserve currency. On the one hand the currency must be 'hard', i.e. one which people and banks in other countries wish to hold. However, on the other hand, there must be a mechanism that transmits ownership of the currency on a large scale to people and banks in other countries. The transmission mechanism is the country's balance of payments deficit.

Normally when a country runs up a huge balance of payments deficit, its currency's exchange rate falls or 'softens' because of its excess supply on foreign exchange markets. In the case of a reserve currency, this is generally not so. People and banks in the rest of the world are only too happy to get their hands on and then to keep the currency without feeling the need to sell it. In this way, large holdings of the currency are transmitted into ownership outside the currency's country of origin.

In the late nineteenth century and up to 1914, Britain benefited from its *hegemonic* position in the world economy. Because of the UK's military, political and economic power in the nineteenth century, residents of other countries wanted to hold the pound. The accumulation of pounds owned outside the UK led to the currency taking on a world reserve role.

After 1918, the UK's economy weakened and this led to a quick decline in the pound's reserve role. The role was finally finished by the Second World War. After the war, the pound was not freely convertible into other currencies and therefore was undesirable to hold. By this time, the US dollar had become the world reserve currency, reflecting the hegemonic power that the USA now enjoyed. The dollar continues to be the world's main reserve currency. As was the case with the pound over 100 years ago, the USA's huge balance of payments deficit on the current account has provided the main transmission mechanism, along with the willingness of governments and people worldwide to hold the dollar. The recent and current eurozone crisis has largely prevented the euro from becoming a desired reserve currency.

Vast overseas ownership of the dollar renders the currency vulnerable to a mass-selling panic as was threatened in late 2013 when China feared that the US government would default on its debts. At other times, when pursuing a policy of benign neglect the US government has encouraged the dollar's fall, hoping that, by making US goods more competitive in world markets, the problem of a growing US payments deficit would diminish.

However, two factors temper mass selling of dollars. First, a large-scale sale of dollars inevitably involves mass purchase of other currencies, such as the euro. For this to occur, dollar holders' confidence in the euro and in the economies of eurozone countries must exceed their doubts about the dollar and the US economy. The sheer size and hegemonic role of the US economy means that the dollar is still generally regarded as a better bet than other currencies. Second, the USA's huge current account deficit means that other countries, particularly China, have surpluses, which means that their currencies are in short supply on foreign exchange markets. This in turn means a lack of a transmission mechanism to convey the currencies into widespread overseas ownership and into a world reserve role equalling the past role of the dollar

Indeed, the reserve currency status of the dollar also means that individuals and companies worldwide, for example in South America and Africa, hold the dollar as a wealth asset in preference to their national currencies. The UK pound still performs a minor reserve currency role. China's renminbi could develop into a reserve currency but, as mentioned, lacks the transmission mechanism of a balance of payments deficit to bring this about.

EXTENSION MATERIAL

Fixed exchange rates and monetary policy

At various times in recent decades, though not currently, UK governments used a high exchange rate as a policy instrument with which to control inflation. A high exchange rate reduces inflation in three different ways. First, it causes the prices of imported food and consumer goods to fall. The second effect operates through falling prices of imported raw materials and energy. These reduce costs of production, which in turn reduce cost-push inflationary pressure within the domestic economy. The third effect is more subtle, since it operates through changes in human behaviour. If the exchange rate remains high, firms that raise prices by more than their international competitors suffer falling profits and even bankruptcy. At the same time, workers who push for higher wage increases than those on offer in competitor countries face the risk of unemployment. Realising it is against self-interest to behave in an inflationary way, firms and workers choose to moderate price rises and wage claims. The economist Sir Alan Budd argues that the pound's membership of the ERM at a high exchange rate had precisely this effect, 'bleeding' the economy of inflationary expectations between 1990 and 1992.

A high exchange rate thus disciplines or constrains domestic inflationary pressures. However, if devaluation is expected, the counter-inflationary discipline provided by the high exchange rate quickly disappears. If the government's commitment to a high exchange rate is questioned, the credibility of counter-inflation policy may vanish. In this situation, inflationary pressures are unleashed, which reduces international competitiveness and causes the current account to deteriorate. An overvalued exchange rate leads to a hot money outflow, which puts downward pressure on the exchange rate. To prevent the exchange rate from falling, the country's central bank may have to increase domestic interest rates. Higher interest rates contract or deflate aggregate demand in an economy already suffering a loss of export competitiveness brought about by the high exchange rate.

Using a high exchange rate in this way to reduce domestic inflation means that monetary policy in general, and interest rates in particular, are not available to stimulate or reflate aggregate demand within the economy. Indeed, the deflationary effects of a high exchange rate and high interest rates mean that the domestic policy objectives of full employment and economic growth have to be sacrificed to the external objective of supporting the exchange rate.

The euro

For most people, the European Union's single currency, the **euro**, came into existence on 1 January 2002 when euro notes and coins entered circulation. However, economists usually date 1 January 1999 as marking the euro's introduction, as this was the date on which the exchange rates of the 12 countries that became the first members of the **eurozone** or euro area were irrevocably fixed against each other. (The eurozone and the euro area are the names used for the group of EU countries that have replaced their national currencies with the euro.)

> **KEY TERMS**
>
> **euro:** the single currency used in some, but not all, European Union member states.
>
> **eurozone:** contains the EU countries in which the euro has replaced national currencies, also known as the euro area.

Currently, the UK is *inside* the EU but *outside* the eurozone, retaining the pound as the national currency and implementing a strictly national UK monetary policy. By contrast, eurozone member countries are subject to the monetary policy implemented in Frankfurt by the **European Central Bank (ECB)**. The pound's exchange rate floats against the euro, but as I have indicated, some of the other non-eurozone EU currencies are more or less fixed against the euro.

> **KEY TERM**
>
> **European Central Bank (ECB):** the central bank for eurozone countries.

The European Central Bank in Frankfurt

At the time of writing in July 2013, in addition to the 12 original members of the eurozone, a further five EU countries have adopted the euro, taking eurozone membership to 17 countries. The most recent is Estonia, which joined in 2011. In addition a further six countries, including the Vatican City, officially use the euro but are not EU member states.

European monetary union (EMU) and the euro

The euro was created to facilitate greater economic integration among EU member states. Indeed, the euro is a stepping stone to full **monetary union** between EU states and, possibly in the future, to a much fuller **economic union (EMU)**.

> **KEY TERM**
>
> **economic and monetary union (EMU):** involves common monetary arrangements among EU countries to create a common currency and then to achieve fuller economic union among EU member states.

At this point it is worth noting that EMU means two different things. The official EU meaning is *economic* and monetary union. Defined in this way, EMU suggests that common monetary arrangements adopted by EU member countries are part of a grander scheme to integrate the national economies of member states. More narrowly defined, the acronym means *European monetary union*, which involves a common monetary policy applied to all EU member states adopting the euro. In the latter meaning, EMU can be interpreted simply as a step towards making the EU's single market work better and more efficiently.

The process of creating the euro and EMU began in the early 1990s, around the time the exchange rate mechanism disintegrated. The first step in the process centred on the publication of a timetable for introducing the single currency. The timetable required a European Central Bank to be established prior to the euro's introduction.

The impact of the euro upon eurozone economies

When the eurozone first came into existence, it was claimed that member countries would benefit in the following ways: **reduced transaction costs**, **elimination of currency risk**, **greater transparency** and possibly **greater competition because prices are easier to compare**. According to Paul Krugman: 'The creation of the euro was supposed to be another triumphant step in the European project, in which economic integration has been used to foster political integration and peace; a common currency, so the thinking went, would bind the continent even more closely together.' But Krugman then stated: 'What has happened instead is a nightmare: the euro has become an economic trap, and Europe a nest of squabbling nations. Even the continent's democratic achievements seem under threat, as dire economic conditions create a favourable environment for political extremism. Who could have seen such a thing coming?'

The eurozone is *not* an optimal currency area

But Krugman and many other economists did foresee chaos in some of the countries which use the euro because they realise that the eurozone is not an **optimal currency area**. The USA and the UK, which are optimal currency areas, use a single currency (the dollar and the pound), enjoy complete internal free trade, and have a fiscal policy as well as a monetary policy covering the whole of the union. The USA, in particular, also enjoys a very high mobility of labour which enables workers who lose their jobs in the poorer parts of the country to find jobs in richer states such as Colorado.

Mobility of labour and a common fiscal policy are essential if a common currency area is to work. Without outward labour mobility from poorer parts of the union the only way to regain lost jobs, caused by lack of competitiveness, is through a large fall in relative wages to make the region more competitive. This could be achieved within the EU if a poorer country has its own currency to devalue. But given that this is impossible, a high mobility of labour can deal with the unemployment problem. Emigration can shrink the labour force to the jobs available.

A common fiscal policy is particularly important, since it allows wealth to be transferred by centralised fiscal authority from the richer to the poorer parts of the union. Transfers of wealth, via taxation and public spending, are essential to counter the fact that a common currency means that poorer parts of the union cannot achieve competitive advantage by devaluing their national currencies.

A common currency thus requires coordination in fiscal policy as well as in monetary policy. The European Central Bank (ECB) achieves monetary policy coordination, but there is no supranational authority in the eurozone similar to the ECB to coordinate fiscal policies.

The lack of fiscal policy coordination has led to some eurozone countries having high levels of government debt. Debt also built up in the so-called 'club-med' countries in the southern eurozone, such as Greece and Portugal, because governments in the poorer countries of the South believed they would always be bailed out painlessly by the richer governments of countries such as Germany and the Netherlands.

The single market means that in theory there is complete mobility of both labour and capital within the EU. In practice, labour mobility is limited, particularly in comparison with the USA where workers move in large numbers from state to state. With regard to capital, after the creation of the euro, there was massive capital movement from Europe's core — mainly Germany — to its periphery, leading to an economic boom in the periphery and significantly higher inflation rates in Spain, Greece and so on than in Germany. But when private capital flows from the core to the periphery came to a sudden stop in 2008, the 'club-med' countries were left with prices and unit labour costs well out of line with those in the core. Suddenly the eurozone faced a major adjustment problem it has yet to deal with. Indeed, without a common fiscal policy, it may be impossible to deal with.

SUMMARY

- An exchange rate is the external price of the currency in terms of another currency.
- There are three types of exchange rate: freely floating, fixed and managed.
- A freely floating (clean floating) exchange rate is determined by supply and demand.
- Provided there are no capital flows, a freely floating exchange rate should automatically eliminate a current account deficit or surplus.
- Free floating enables a country to pursue an independent monetary policy.
- There are, however, disadvantages with a freely floating exchange rate system: for example, exchange rate instability or volatility.
- Speculative or hot money capital flows also destabilise floating exchange rates, sometimes leading to severe overvaluation or undervaluation.
- In a rigidly fixed exchange rate system, the exchange rate cannot rise or fall to eliminate or reduce a payments surplus or deficit.
- The advantages of a fixed exchange rate relate closely to the disadvantages of a floating rate, while the disadvantages relate to a floating system's advantages.
- Adjustable peg and 'dirty' floating are types of managed exchange rates.
- In an adjustable peg system, the exchange rate can be revalued or devalued to try to correct a payments imbalance.
- The pound and the US dollar have both been reserve currencies. The dollar continues to have this status and the euro is developing a world reserve role.
- The euro has replaced national currencies for the EU member states in the eurozone, but not in the UK.
- In recent years there has been a eurozone crisis, partly caused by the fact that the eurozone is not an optimal currency area.

Exam-style questions

1 Using a demand and supply diagram, explain how a current account deficit is eliminated in a freely floating exchange rate system. (15 marks)

2 Explain the advantages and disadvantages of a floating exchange rate. (15 marks)

3 Do you agree that the UK economy should be *within* the European Union but *outside* the eurozone? Justify your answer. (25 marks)

4 Evaluate possible effects on the British economy if the UK were to adopt the euro. (25 marks)

Extra resources to help you revise are available online at www.hodderplus.co.uk/philipallan

Unit 4 key terms

absolute advantage: occurs when a country is absolutely best (or more technically efficient) than other countries in a particular industry.

adaptive expectations: describe how economic agents adapt their expectations of what is likely to happen in the future on the basis of what has happened in the recent past.

adjustable peg exchange rate: a managed exchange rate similar to a rigidly fixed exchange rate except that the central bank may alter the exchange rate's central peg by devaluing or revaluing.

aggregate demand: total planned spending on the goods and services produced within the economy in a particular time period.

automatic stabiliser: a factor that changes in such a way as to automatically stabilise aggregate demand and the economic cycle. Examples are progressive taxation and unemployment benefits.

balance of payments: measures all the currency flows into and out of an economy in a given time period.

balance of payments equilibrium: occurs when the current account more or less balances over a period of years.

balanced budget: total government spending equals total government revenue in a particular time period.

bank: an institution that accepts deposits and creates deposits when lending to customers who wish to borrow.

borrowing requirement: the amount the government or public sector must borrow to finance a budget deficit.

budget deficit: total government spending exceeds total government revenue in a particular time period.

budget surplus: total government spending is less than total government revenue in a particular time period.

central bank: the bank that implements monetary policy and also issues and controls fiat money or cash.

claimant count: measures the number of people claiming unemployment-related benefits.

classical or real-wage unemployment: a form of disequilibrium unemployment that occurs when the aggregate labour market fails to clear. This is caused by real wage rates being too high.

closed economy: an economy that undertakes no trade with the rest of the world.

comparative advantage: this is measured in terms of opportunity cost. The country with the least opportunity cost when producing a good possesses a comparative advantage in that good.

consumer prices index (CPI): the UK price index most central to UK monetary policy.

contractionary fiscal policy: uses fiscal policy to decrease aggregate demand and to shift the *AD* curve to the left.

cost-push inflation: caused by rising business costs of production.

crowding out: a process through which private sector spending and output is displaced by the growth of public sector spending and output.

current account: the part of the balance of payments measuring income currency flows, especially payments for exports and imports.

deflation: a continuous and persistent fall in the price level and increase in the value of money.

deflationary policy: involves contractionary monetary or fiscal policy that shifts the *AD* curve to the left.

demand-deficient unemployment: also known as **cyclical** and **Keynesian unemployment,** this is umemployment caused by deficient aggregate demand in the economy.

demand-pull inflation: caused by excess aggregate demand for output.

devaluation: a fall in a currency's exchange rate brought about either formally by a government and its central bank or informally through a downward float or depreciation of the exchange rate.

direct overseas investment: occurs when firms invest in or buy real productive assets located in foreign countries.

dirty floating: a managed exchange rate system in which the central bank intervenes in the foreign exchange market when the exchange rate is still floating.

disequilibrium exchange rate: the rate at which there is excess demand for, or excess supply of, the currency.

economic and monetary union (EMU): involves common monetary arrangements among EU countries to create a common currency and then to achieve fuller economic union among EU member states.

economic cycle: a period of between about 4 and 10 years in which actual output fluctuates above and below trend output.

economic growth: an increase in the potential output an economy can produce.

equilibrium unemployment: the level of unemployment when the economy's aggregate labour market is in equilibrium.

euro: the single currency used in some, but not all, European Union member states.

European Central Bank (ECB): the central bank for eurozone countries.

eurozone: contains the EU countries in which the euro has replaced national currencies, also known as the euro area.

exchange equalisation: takes place when a central bank buys or sells its own currency to maintain its exchange rate at a particular level.

exchange rate: the external price of a currency, usually measured against another currency.

expansionary fiscal policy: uses fiscal policy to increase aggregate demand and to shift the *AD* curve to the right.

export-led growth: growth brought about by an increase in a country's exports, as distinct from consumption-led growth and investment-led growth which are caused by increases in other components of aggregate demand.

fiscal policy: the use of government spending, taxation and the government's budgetary position to achieve the government's policy objectives.

fixed exchange rate: an exchange rate fixed at a certain level by the country's central bank and maintained by the central bank's intervention in the foreign exchange market.

freely floating exchange rate: determined solely by demand and supply, i.e. by market forces.

frictional unemployment: unemployment that occurs while people are between jobs.

full employment: according to the Beveridge definition, occurs when 3% of the labour force are unemployed.

globalisation: the process of growing economic integration of the world's economies.

government budget: total government spending minus total government revenue in a particular time period, e.g. a year.

government spending multiplier: measures the relationship between a change in government spending and the resulting change in the equilibrium level of national income.

import controls: include tariffs or import duties, quotas, export subsidies and informal controls.

inflation: a continuous and persistent rise in the price level and fall in the value of money.

international division of labour: describes different countries specialising in producing different goods.

investment income: profit and interest income flowing into a country that is generated from assets the residents of the country own abroad.

J-curve: a curve, shaped like the letter 'J', that maps the possible time path of the state of the current account following a devaluation.

Keynesian fiscal policy: policy used to manage aggregate demand, named after John Maynard Keynes.

Labour Force Survey: estimates unemployment by surveying 60,000 households to see if people are looking for work.

Laffer curve: shows tax revenue first rising and then falling as tax rates increase.

long-run aggregate supply: the real output that can be supplied when the economy is on its production possibility frontier and producing at full potential.

long-run economic growth: shown by an outward movement of the economy's production possibility frontier, which increases the potential output the economy can produce.

long-run Phillips curve: a vertical Phillips curve along which trade-offs between reducing inflation and reducing unemployment are not possible.

macroeconomic equilibrium: occurs when $AD = AS$ and when injections into the circular flow of income equal leakages from the flow.

managed exchange rate: similar to a fixed exchange rate (which itself is the extreme form of a managed exchange rate) in that the central bank intervenes in the foreign exchange market to determine its currency's exchange rate.

monetary policy: the part of macroeconomic policy that uses monetary instruments, e.g. interest rates, to achieve policy objectives, e.g. the control of inflation.

money: a medium of exchange and a store of value.

national income multiplier: measures the relationship between a change in any of the components of aggregate demand and the resulting change in the equilibrium level of national income.

natural level of output: the long-run equilibrium level of potential output.

natural rate of unemployment (NRU): the rate of unemployment when the aggregate labour market is in equilibrium. It is located where the long-run Phillips curve intersects the unemployment axis on a Phillips curve diagram.

negative output gap: the difference between actual output and trend output when actual output is below trend output.

open economy: an economy completely open to trade with the rest of the world.

output gap: the difference between actual output and trend output.

Phillips curve: based on evidence from the economy, showing the relationship between the rate of inflation and the level of unemployment.

portfolio overseas investment: occurs when financial services firms buy financial assets such as shares and government bonds issued in foreign countries.

positive output gap: the difference between actual output and the trend output when actual output is above trend output.

price index: an index number that measures the average price level.

principle (or **canon**) **of taxation:** criterion for judging whether a tax is a good tax or a bad tax.

productivity: output per unit of input, e.g. labour productivity is output per worker.

progressive tax: a tax for which the proportion of a person's income paid in tax rises as income increases.

proportionate tax or **flat tax:** a tax for which the proportion of a person's income paid in tax stays the same as income increases.

quantitative easing: the introduction of new money into the money supply by a central bank such as the Bank of England. The opposite policy of quantitative tightening (which might be used in the future) involves 'clawing back' new money previously released into the money supply.

quantity theory of money: the theory that assumes inflation is caused by a prior increase in the money supply.

rational expectations: explain how economic agents form expectations of what is likely to happen in the future on the basis of the most up-to-date and relevant information that is available.

reflation: an increase in real output and employment following an increase in aggregate demand.

regressive tax: a tax for which the proportion of a person's income paid in tax falls as income increases.

reserve currency: a currency widely held in the foreign currency reserves of other countries and used by them to pay for trade.

seasonal unemployment: results from seasonal fluctuations in the demand for labour.

short-run aggregate supply: shows the quantities of real output businesses plan to produce and sell at different price levels, assuming there is spare capacity in the economy.

short-run economic growth: an increase in the output that results from making use of spare capacity and unemployed labour. Also known as economic recovery.

short-run Phillips curve: a downward-sloping Phillips curve showing a trade-off between reducing inflation and reducing unemployment.

speculative capital flows: occur when companies, banks and rich individuals buy a currency in order to earn higher interest rates on bank deposits held in that currency, or when they speculate that a rise in the currency's exchange rate will enable them to make a capital gain in the future.

Stability and Growth Pact: an agreement by EU countries to limit budget deficits in order to promote economic convergence among the member states of the European Union.

structural unemployment: results from the structural decline of industries and the inability or difficulty of workers switching to new industries.

supply-side fiscal policy: policy used to increase personal incentives, favoured by free-market economists.

supply-side policies: aim to make markets more competitive and efficient, increase production potential, and shift the *LRAS* curve to the right. Supply-side fiscal policy is arguably the most important type of supply-side policy.

taxation: compulsory levies charged by the government to raise revenue, primarily to finance government spending.

transfers: payments flowing between countries in forms such as foreign aid, grants and gifts.

Index